Art & Soul

Howard Priestley

NEW HAVEN PUBLISHING LTD

Published 2023
New Haven Publishing
www.newhavenpublishingltd.com
newhavenpublishing@gmail.com

All Rights Reserved
The rights of Howard Priestley, as the author of this work, have been asserted in accordance with the Copyrights, Designs and Patents Act 1988.
No part of this book may be re-printed or reproduced or utilized in any form or by any electronic, mechanical or other means, now unknown or hereafter invented, including photocopying, and recording, or in any information storage or retrieval system, without the written permission of the Author and Publisher.

Cover art ©Howard Priestley
Cover design ©Pete Cunliffe

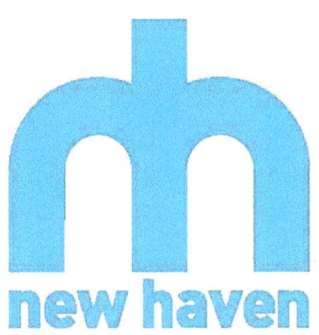

Copyright © 2023 Howard Priestley
All rights reserved
ISBN: 978-1-912587-89-6

Content

Page 5   The Beginning
Page 10   Funk Is Its Own Reward
Page 22   Funk
Page 24   Mothership Connections
Page 26   Prince
Page 28   What Is Soul?
Page 30   What The F#&k Is Going On
Page 36   Ray Charles
Page 38   Swamp Dogg
Page 40   Detroit
Page 42   Berry Gordy Jr
Page 44   Detroit musicians
Page 46   David Ruffin
Page 48   Four Tops
Page 50   The Supremes
Page 52   Laura Lee
Page 54   Holland Dozier Holland
Page 56   General Johnson
Page 58   Little Willie John
Page 60   Marvin Gaye
Page 62   Tammi Terrell
Page 64   Stevie Wonder
Page 66   Chicago
Page 68   Chicago musicians
Page 70   Chicago Soul
Page 72   The Impressions
Page 74   Curtis Mayfield
Page 76   Donny Hathaway

Page 78   Etta James
Page 80   Fontella Bass
Page 82   Jackie Wilson
Page 84   Jerry Butler
Page 86   Minnie Riperton
Page 88   Sam Cooke
Page 90   The Dells
Page 92   New York
Page 94   Aretha Franklin
Page 96   Betty Davis
Page 98   Cissy Houston
Page 100   The Isley Brothers
Page 102   King Curtis
Page 104   Linda Jones
Page 106   Millie Jackson
Page 108   The Parliaments
Page 110   The Drifters
Page 112   Sylvia Robinson
Page 114   Roberta Flack
Page 116   Esther Phillips
Page 118   Melba Moore
Page 120   Philadelphia
Page 122   Gamble & Huff
Page 124   Thom Bell
Page 126   Barbara Mason
Page 128   Billy Paul
Page 130   The Jones Girls

Page 132 Phyliss Hyman
Page 134 The O'Jays
Page 136 Patti Labelle
Page 138 Teddy Pendegrass
Page 140 The Delfonics
Page 142 Three Degrees
Page 144 Van McCoy
Page 146 Memphis
Page 148 Al Green
Page 150 Ann Peebles
Page 152 Booker T. & The MGs
Page 154 Carla Thomas
Page 156 James Carr
Page 158 Johnnie Taylor
Page 160 Otis Redding
Page 162 Otis Redding & The Bar Kays
Page 164 Sam & Dave
Page 166 Shirley Brown
Page 168 William Bell
Page 170 Willie Mitchell
Page 172 Florida
Page 174 Betty Wright
Page 176 Casey & Finch
Page 178 Clarence Reid
Page 180 Cornelius Brothers & Sister Rose
Page 182 George McCrae
Page 184 Gwen McCrae
Page 186 Henry Stone
Page 188 Jimmy 'Bo' Horne
Page 190 King Sporty

Page 192 Latimore
Page 194 Little Beaver
Page 196 Timmy Thomas
Page 198 New Orleans
Page 200 Allen Toussaint
Page 202 Betty Harris
Page 204 Dr John
Page 206 Ernie K-Doe
Page 208 Irma Thomas
Page 210 King Floyd
Page 212 The Meters
Page 214 Jean Knight
Page 216 Lee Dorsey
Page 218 Neville Brothers
Page 220 Willie Tee
Page 222 Wardell Quezergue
Page 224 California
Page 226 Barry White
Page 228 Bill Withers
Page 230 Deniece Williams
Page 232 Ike & Tina Turner
Page 234 Sly Stone
Page 236 Larry Graham
Page 238 Lenny Williams
Page 240 Natalie Cole
Page 242 O.C. Smith
Page 244 Stevie Wonder
Page 246 The Coasters
Page 248 For the Record
Page 250 About the Author

The Beginning

When I started buying 'pop' records, my brother Ian and I would buy 45 rpm singles together but gradually he went down the 'rocky road' and I chose Soul. From 14 I began to read everything I could, not only Soul as a musical form but also about African Americans, which set me aside from my fellow learners. It was hard to imagine how a white Yorkshire lad could become a victim of racism but somehow, I managed it. My school nickname at the time was Tads and I remember having a parcel of Angling magazines sent as a practical joke from a school 'friend'. What wasn't so funny was that the parcel was addressed to H.T. Blackman. I told Mum that it must have gone to the wrong address and the parcel was returned. Humour is a funny thing, sometimes.

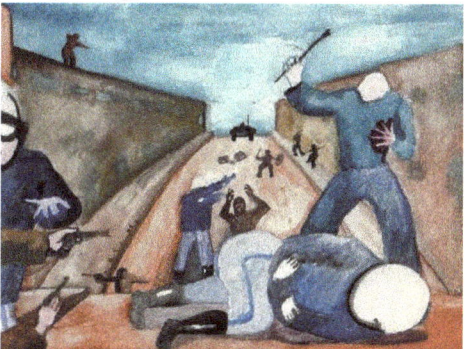 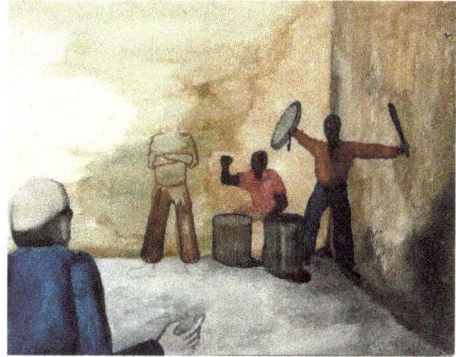

The stories I was reading started to be sketched, also from 1972 who needed drugs when you could draw like this.

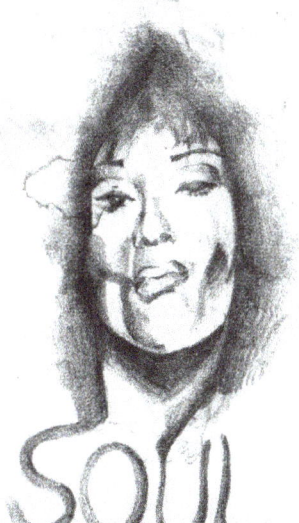 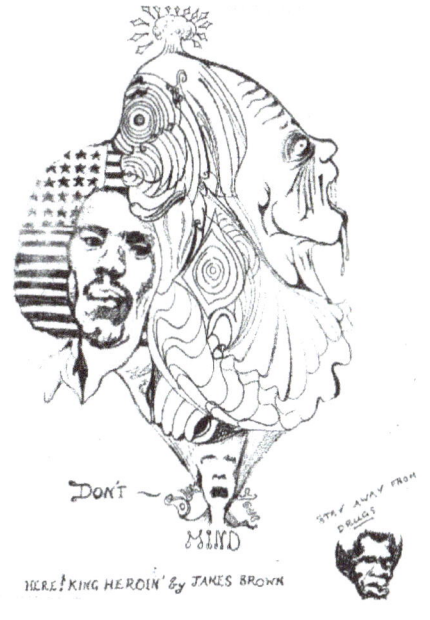

That same year I couldn't get a Superfly film poster so I made one as I prepared for the next stage which would be to do an Art Foundation course at the Percival Whitley College in Halifax.

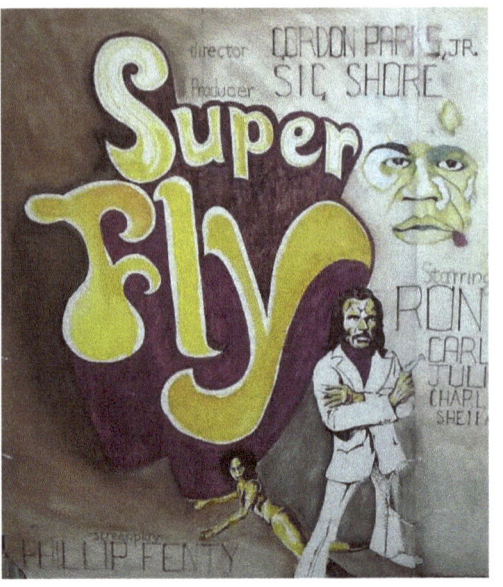

The intention was to go for a career in advertising, but my work was too messy or slightly off kilter to see me going down the Ad Agency path.

In 1974 using mixed media from a paper mâché face mask to collage, I created a Funk self-portrait, my first Funk related artwork probably inspired by my interest in comics and my newly found fascination in the Funkadelic album covers of Pedro Bell.

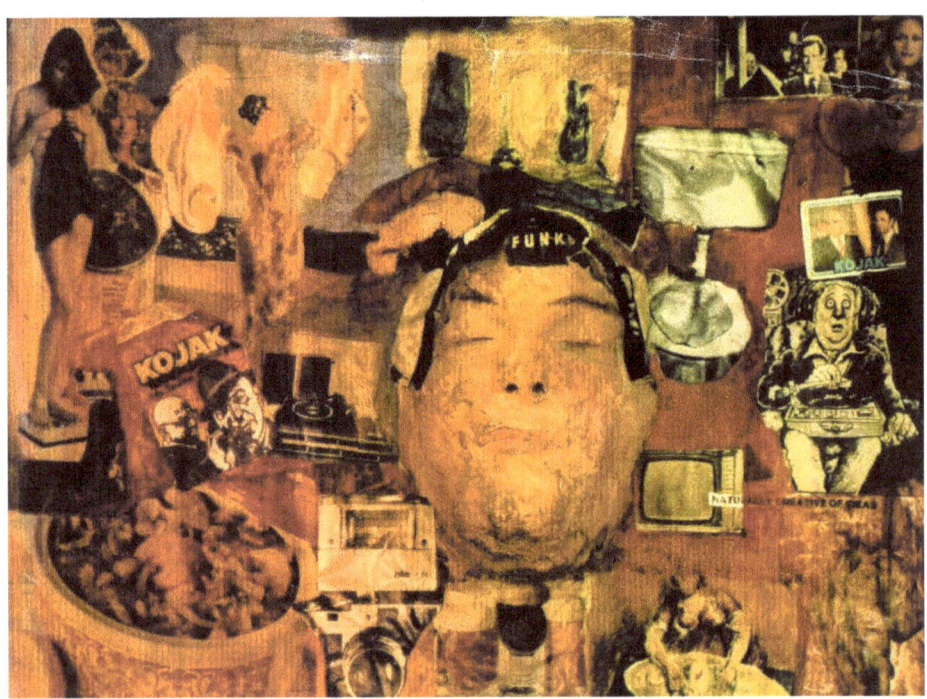

In 1989, when I was still collecting Blues & Soul magazine, I spotted a request in their classified ads for cartoons for a new magazine based in Germany called The New Funk Times. I sent a sketch of Prince and George

Clinton as Clinton had just signed to Prince's Paisley Park Label and got a favourable response.

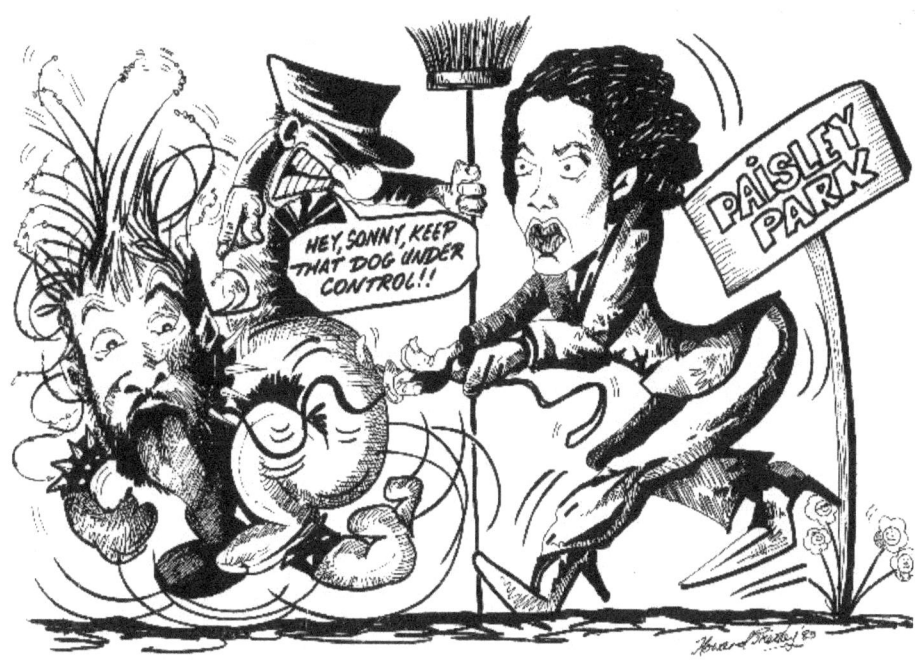

I was asked to create a new regular strip "Dog Tales". The strip was later reprinted in P-Views, another P-Funk fanzine from Germany for whom I designed the logo and then I became a regular writer and illustrator for a variety of music publications from Germany, Finland and England, including 'Blues & Soul'. Because it was being read by the P-Funk guys it came to the attention of Pedro Bell who even stated, "Who is this Presley guy over in England?" "Dog Tales" explored the world of P-Funk mainly through George Clinton's Atomic Dog character as well as Bootsy Collins. Interestingly and more importantly though, Aris Wilson, possibly the biggest P-Funk fan from over in Long Beach, California wrote to me and started to feed me information as to who in the P-Funk world were in the studio and suggested that I send them samples of my art. This led me to develop designs for Bootsy Collins, Rick Gardner of the Horny Horns, Tika Nelson (Prince's sister), Frank 'Cash' Waddy (former James Brown drummer and P-funkster) and other members of Bootsy's Rubber Band.

Art & Soul

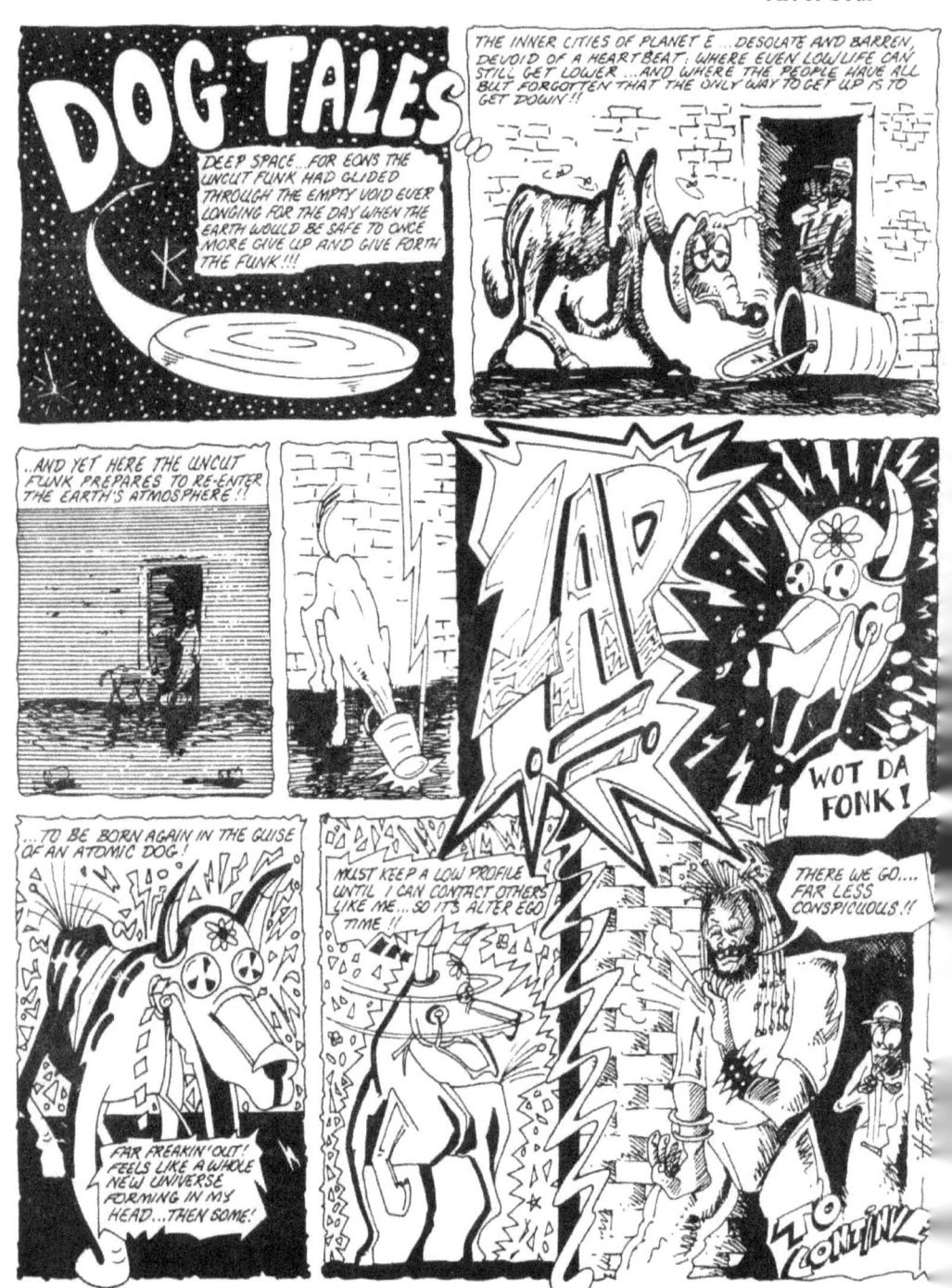

I continued to design CD covers and art for Mallia Franklin, George Clinton, Ruth Copeland featuring Parliament but above all for Jerome Brailey, master drummer for The Five Stairsteps, Chamber Brothers, Funkadelic/Parliament and his own group Mutiny.

As you look through this book these designs will be revealed but here are some of the sketches produced back then.

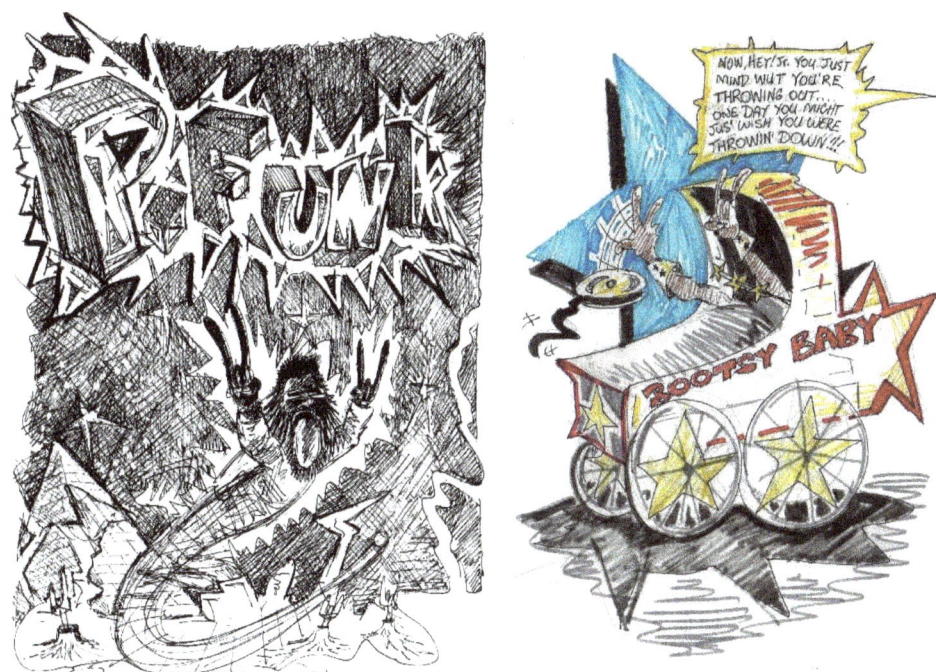

I even got given my own P-Funk 'tag' and so I knew that my journey had well and truly begun. I can't say that it's been an easy journey, but it led me to go from being a fan to becoming a collaborator who met and worked with people I have admired from afar and who I can now call friends.

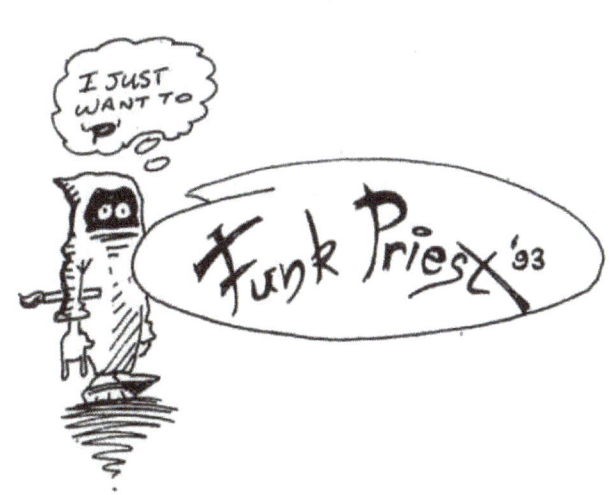

Funk is its Own Reward

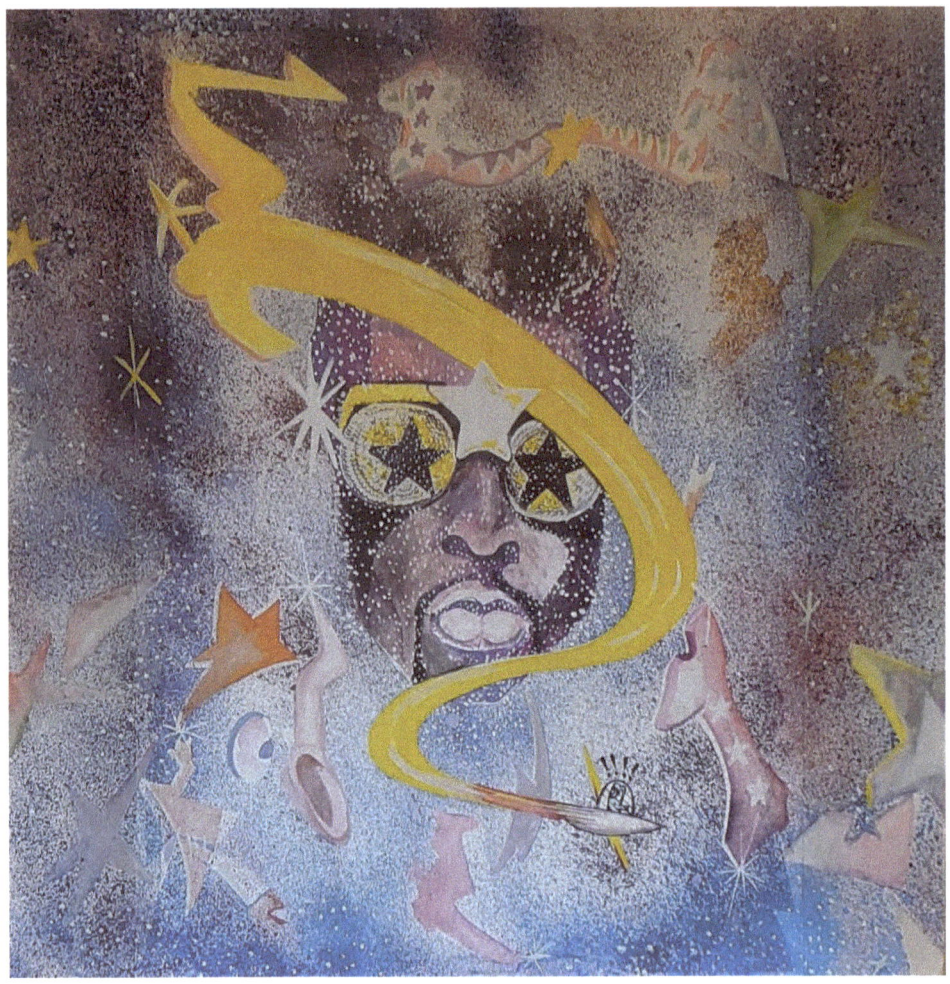

One night my phone rang, I answered it and the voice said, "Priestley?" which sounded abrupt so I just said, "Yeah?" This was followed by

"Bootsy Collins here, how you doin' man?"

Having melted into a quivering mass of human jelly, I composed myself and had a conversation with the man. He loved the painting I'd sent and although the label chose not to use it, I was told that it was hanging in his studio, which was okay by me.

Art & Soul

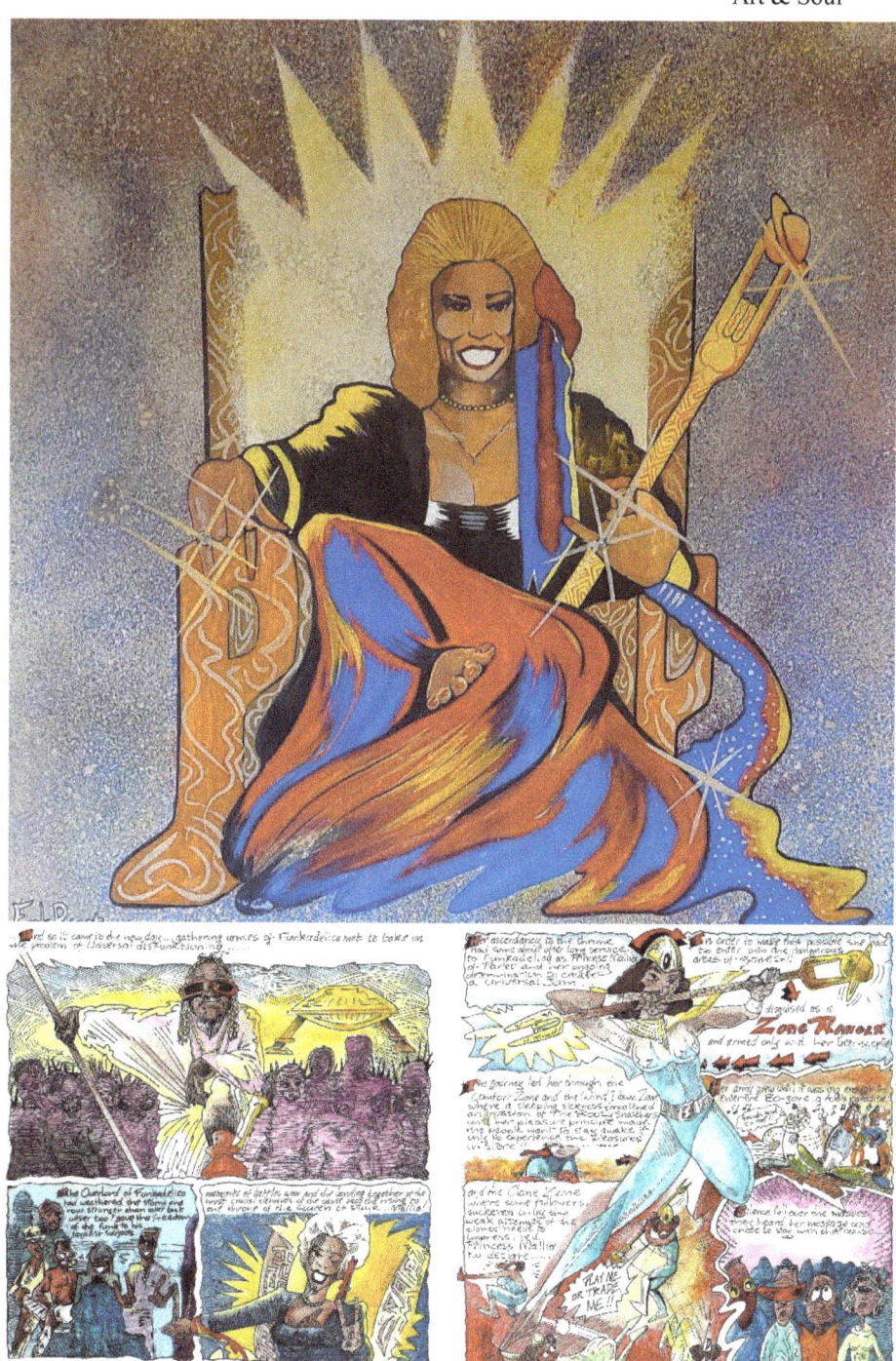

Mallia Franklin's 'Funk Intersceptre' artwork.

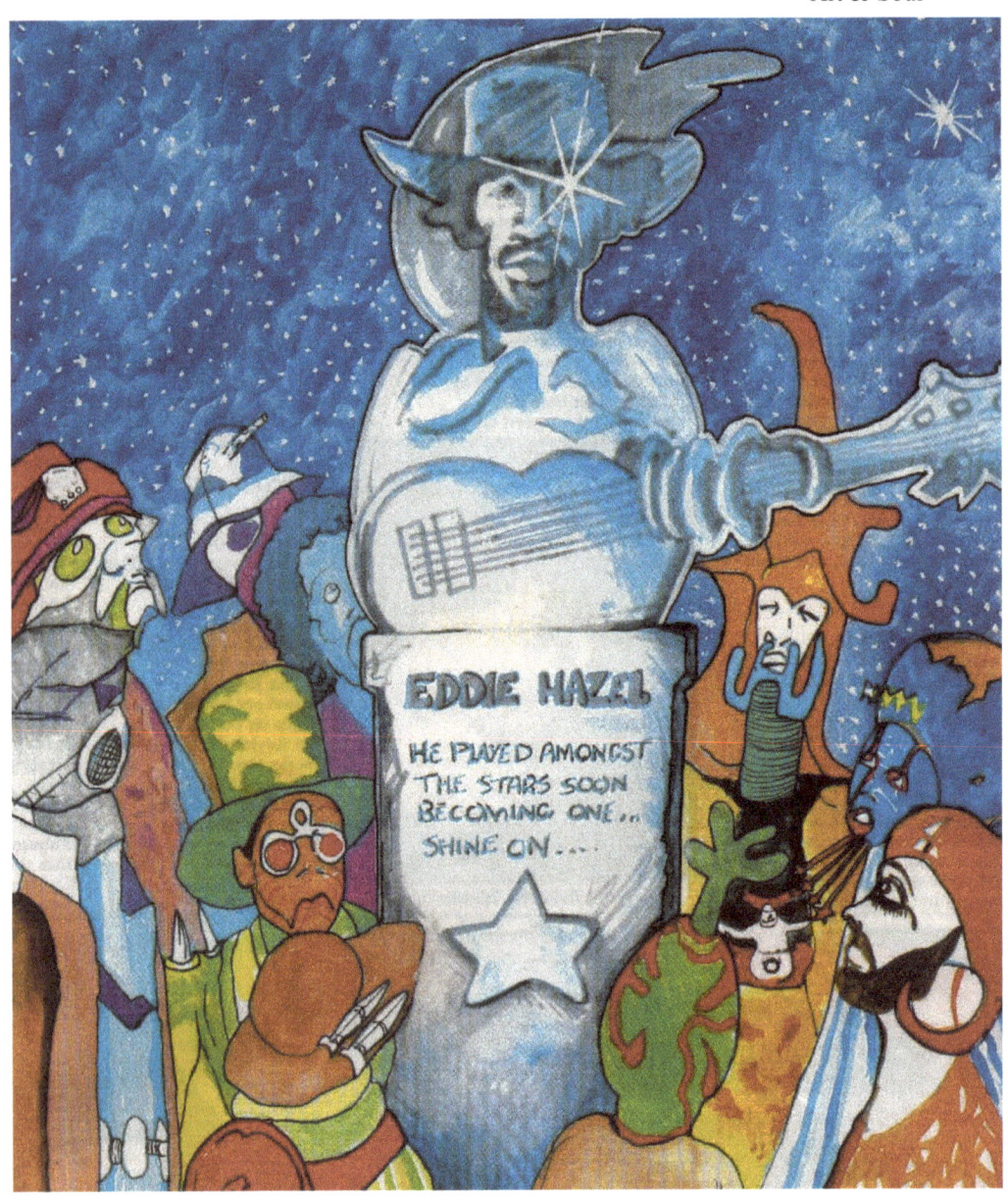

When Eddie Hazel flew away, I dedicated a painting to Blues & Soul magazine I chose to do it in the style of Funkadelic's great cover artist Pedro Bell and later came close to having a P-Funk Graphic novel agreed by Marvel

Art & Soul

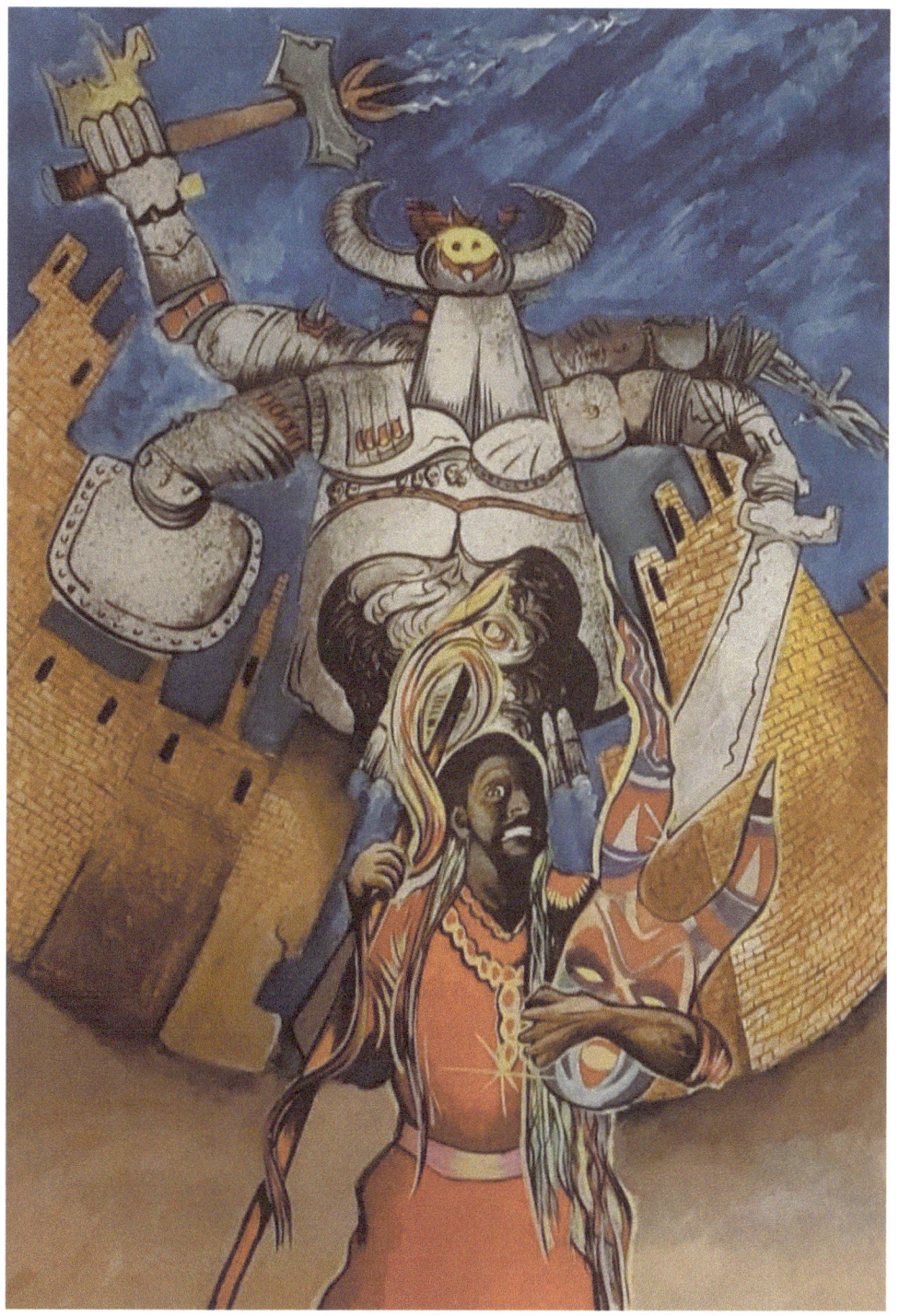

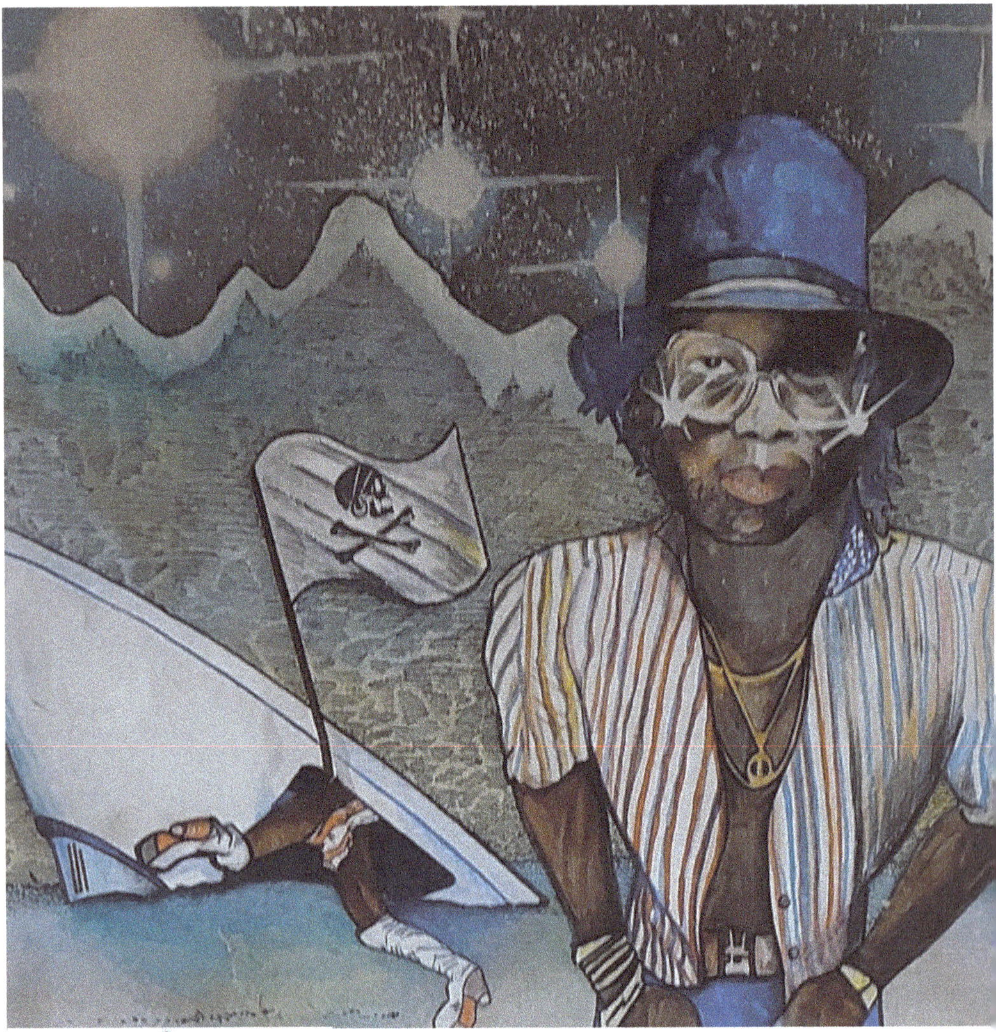

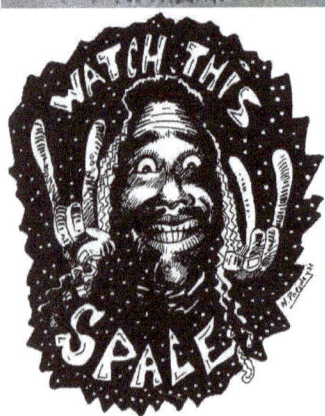

The first person to 'leave P-Funk was drummer Jerome Brailey. Unsurprisingly his group was called Mutiny. The painting above was designed as part of a CD compilation which I was able to persuade Castle Communications to issue. Over the years I have worked with Jerome on several projects. The most successful was for "Aftershock 2000" produced by Bill Laswell. The caricature of George Clinton (left) was included on the CD release of his 'Computer Games' album.

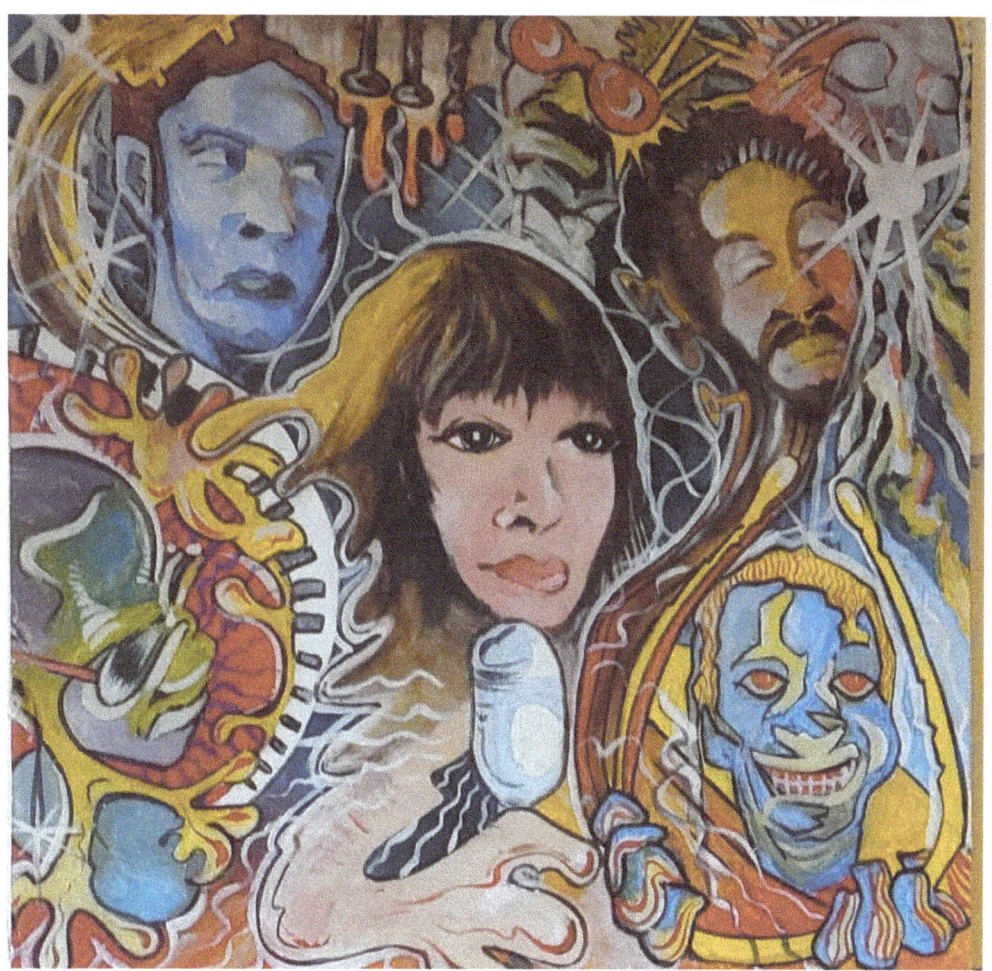

Within George Clinton's band of brothers and sisters there appeared another outsider, an English folk singer from Durham, Ruth Copeland. Copeland's own albums "I Am What I Am" and "Self Portrait" were well balanced mixes of commercial Rock, Soul, Folk and Blues relying heavily on input from George Clinton and the embryonic Funkadelic who supplied some incredible instrumentation to both sets. Acoustic clarity one minute, giving way to raucous rock the next. How Ruth Copeland arrived in Detroit remains a mystery equalled only by where she went to after Invictus folded. I was instrumental in getting the material released on CD for the first time and managed to sneak in the cover as another homage to that master of Funkadelic fame, Pedro Bell.

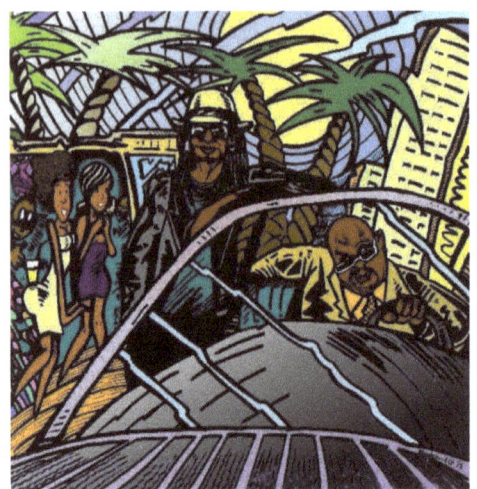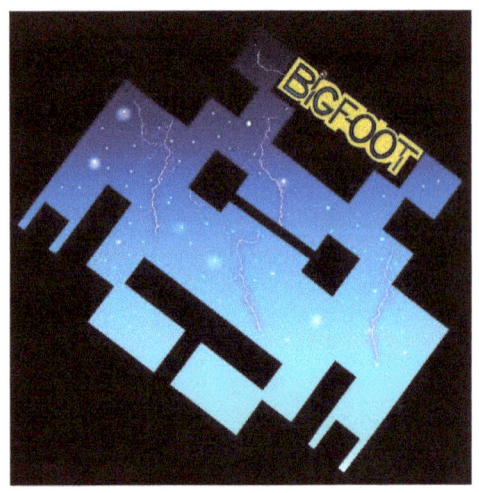

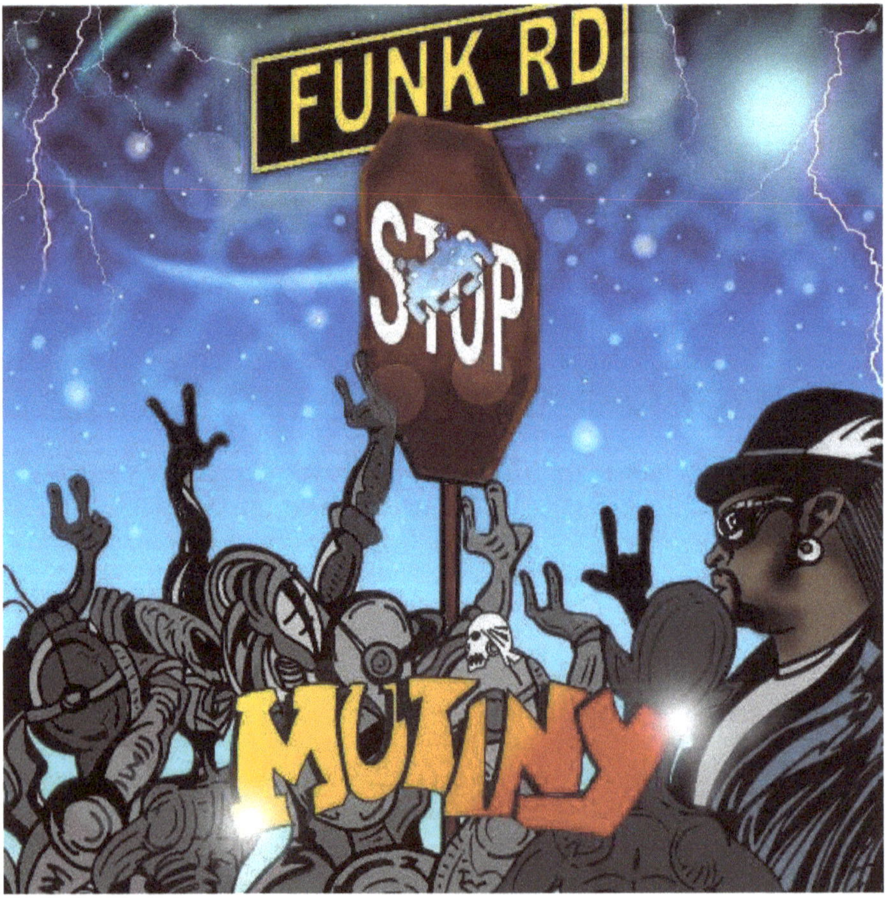

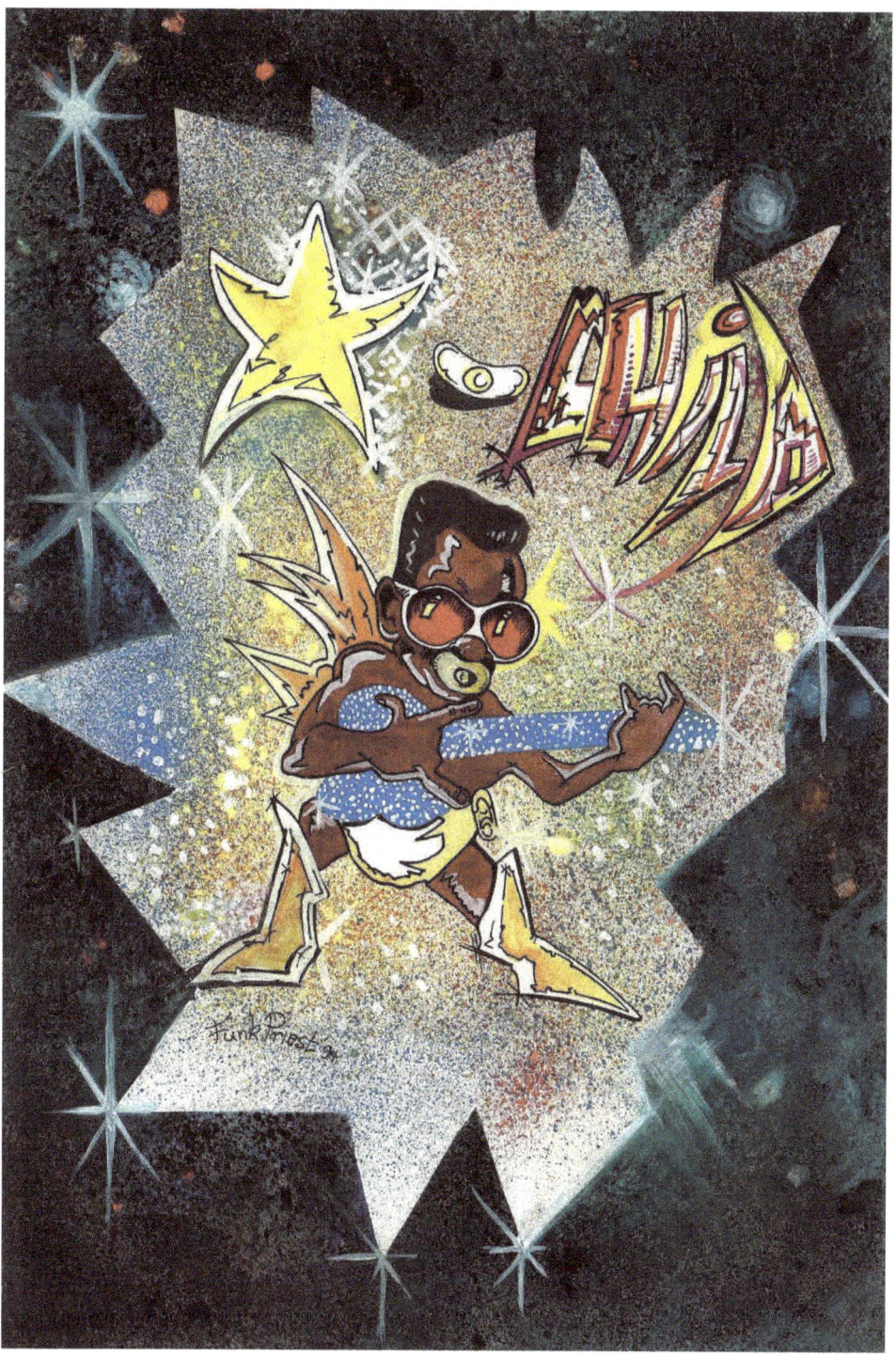

Art & Soul

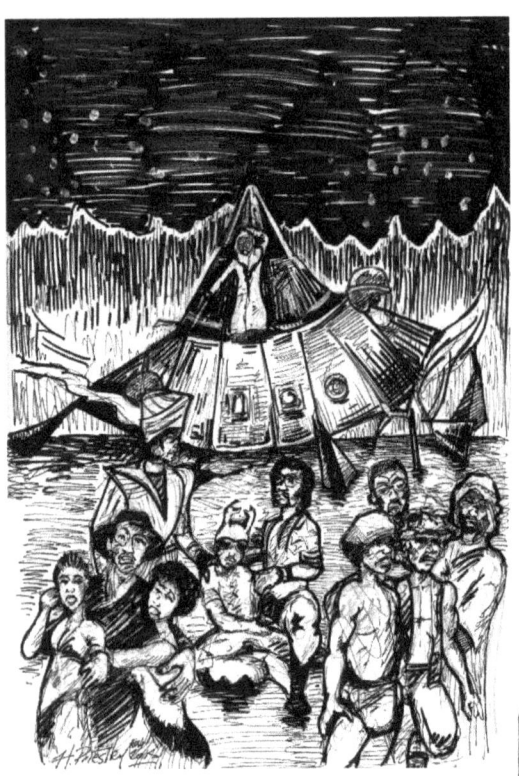

In 2015 Jerome contacted me to see if I'd be interested in creating a poster for a new documentary which was going to be premiered at the Sundance Film Festival. The festival has been going since 1985 and this documentary and "Tear the Roof Off – The untold story of Funkadelic and Parliament" was being directed by award-winning documentarian Bobby J. Brown. Jerome was Parliament's drummer and had co-written "Tear The Roof Off The Sucker" in 1975 for Parliament as part of their groundbreaking album "Mothership Connection".

By now it was industry-wide knowledge about how George Clinton, whilst undeniably being the mastermind behind the group, had a tendency to dabble in cocktails of assorted drugs which led to a less than organised way in which to pay the group members, unless of course you were happy to snort payment through the nose. Hard to explain that to a banker. Eventually the group, or groups imploded with many members escaping with their sanity whilst others sadly did not.

After all the work was done and a contract signed, Brown decided to go with a photograph of the band leading to another coulda-shoulda moment.

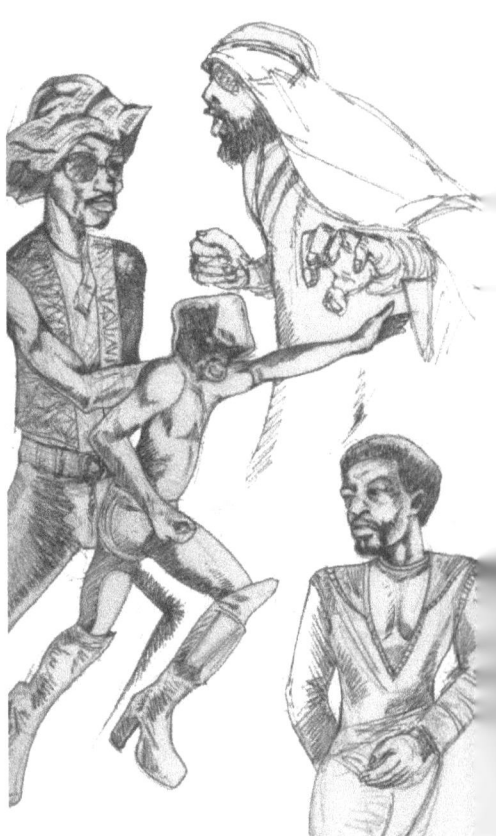

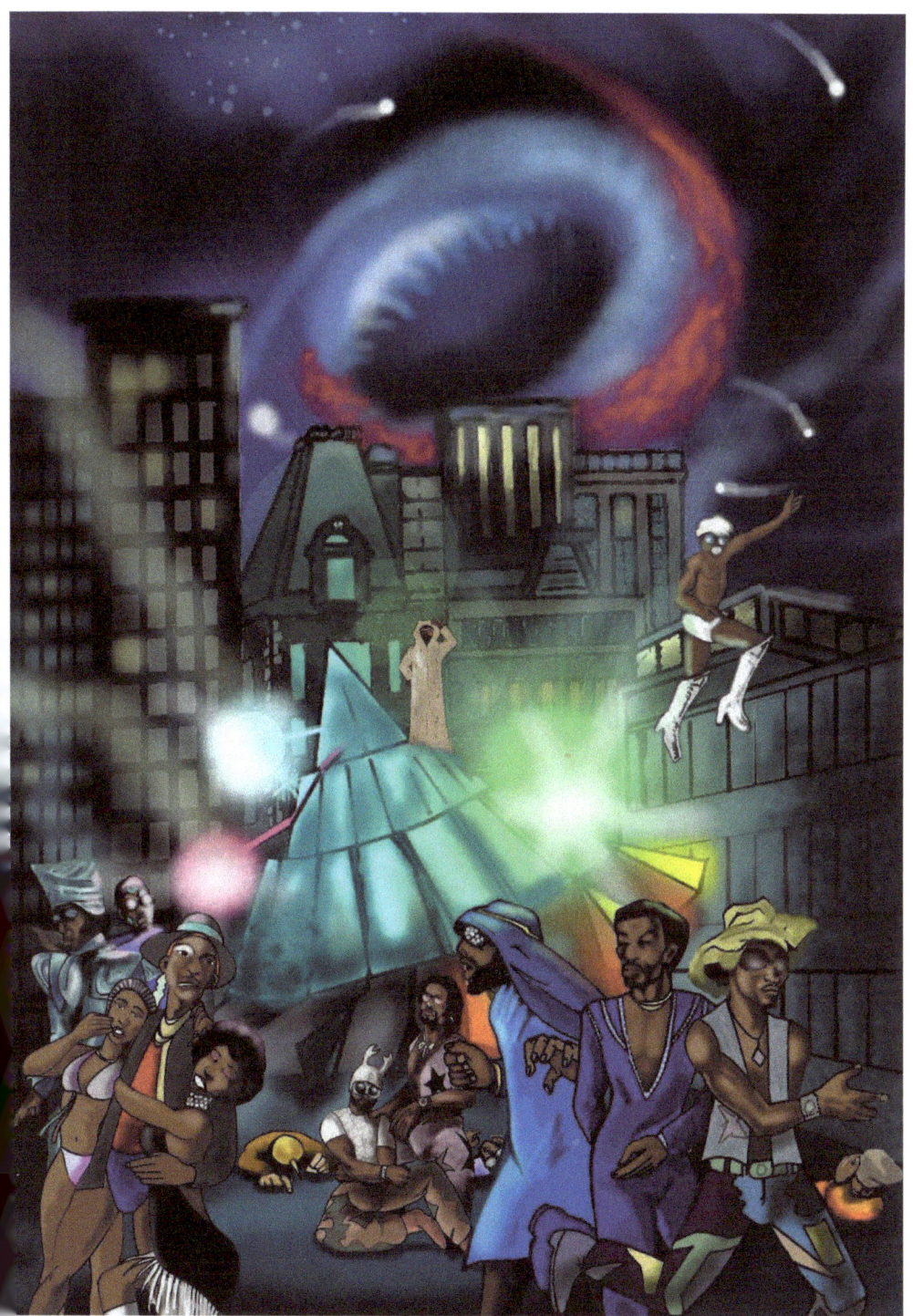

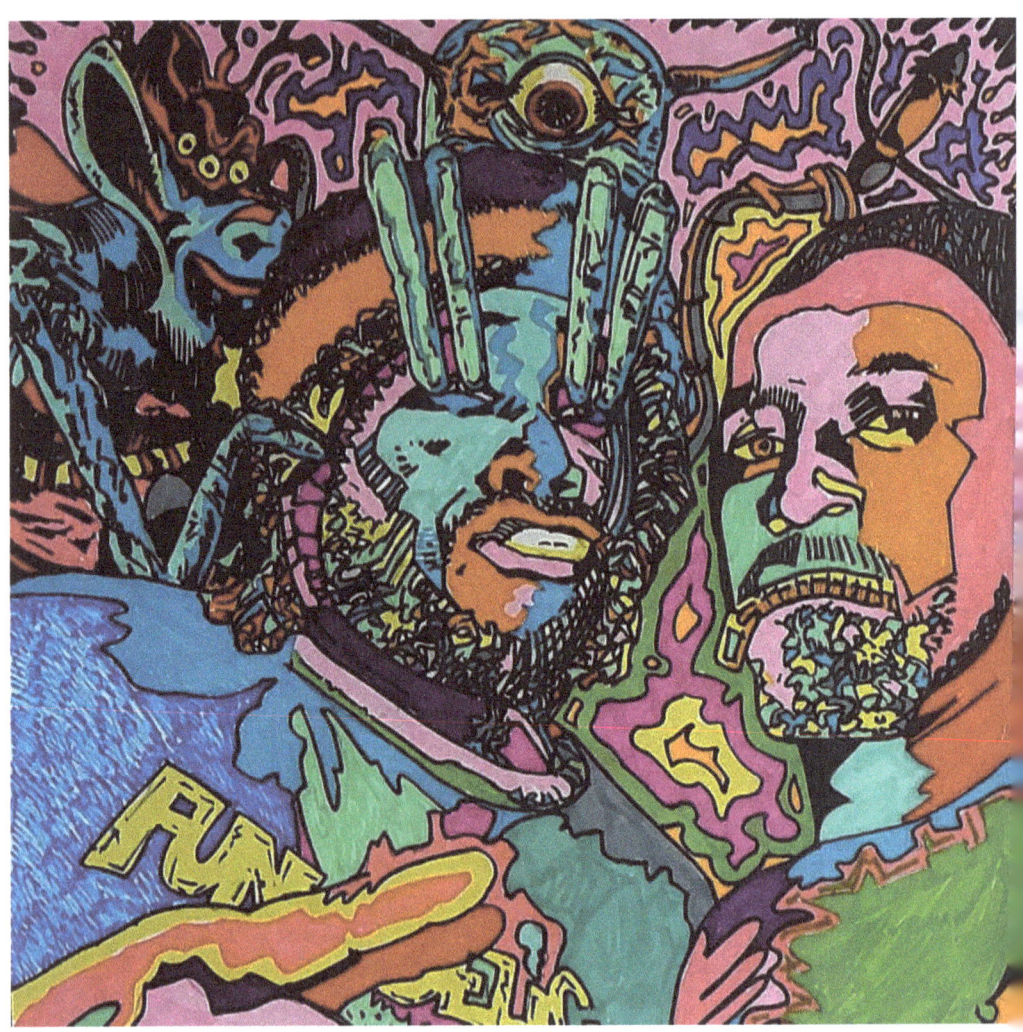

Over the last thirty years Aris Wilson has kept in touch from California. In 2022 he called to discuss a new project with Trey Lewd or Tracey Lewis, son of George Clinton and Pat Lewis. Trey's career has included unissued material under the name Trey Lewd's Flastic Brain Flam which finally surfaced on George Clinton's Family series. Great tracks included "I Can't Stand It", "Michelle" (loosely based on The Beatles original) and "Clone Ranger". He did have one album released on Reprise in 1991, "Drop The Line" and also appeared on George Clinton's 2005 album "How Late DO U Have 2BB4UR Absent" on the track "Su, Su, Su" by the P-Funk All-Stars.

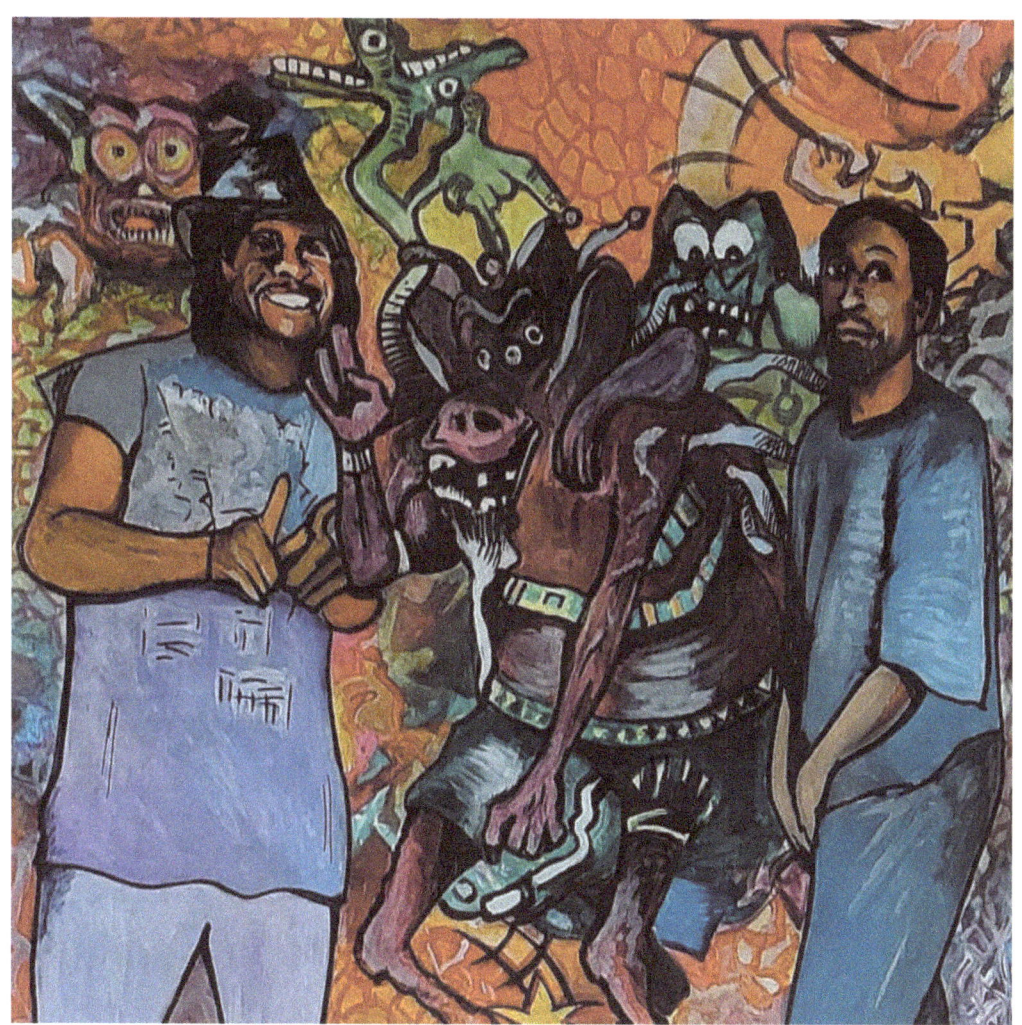

In 2020 Trey released "a 6 Pack Of P" available on Bandcamp. Here is Trey and Aris for the back cover of "Ignant Bystanders".

Funk

There have been questions asked as to where Funk started. Just like people used to ask me "What Is Soul?" maybe the same question should be asked of Funk". You know, it's hard to pinpoint something beginning; some things sneak up on you and before you know it, it just seems like it was always there. Like a new love. I fell in love with Funk back in 1970 when I was fourteen years old. Don't ask me why; here I was in the North of England, and yet something pulled me into the music. I'd arrived through the more traditional door opened by Motown and Stax, but it was buying Parliament's "Silent Boatman" single on Invictus followed by their album "Osmium" that started me searching for this other world. Mojo Records in London were busy releasing obscure funk that, at the time, included one Kool & The Gang. I was really hooked. A Nation of Black heroes and role models had already ignited the 1960s politically and creatively and it would also be the decade that saw the birth of the first African American President, Barack Obama, born 4th August, 1961. Making him, in my mind, the Funky President as foretold by George Clinton and James Brown and not the Hip Hop President as some would have us believe. Funk cruised through the troubled '60s when free love came face to face with a price to pay in the streets of Los Angeles, Chicago and Detroit as a country at war in Vietnam fought its own war at home. It was no coincidence that Black music was about to take a more aggressive direction. If we look at the historical changes from 1965 to 1970 there are factors arising that would have left the prominent and popular Soul music ostracised by the Black record buyers if it hadn't changed and with the likes of Curtis Mayfield showing himself to be the most astute commentator on the '60s, others were bound to follow. Funk was therefore a hybrid of the times, like Soul before, it had been born from many seeds. It drew heavily upon African and Latin American rhythms coming through from both the new Black consciousness as well as other ethnic groups whose art and culture were readily embraced in the 'melting pot' of America. Referring back to its slave origins you could also argue that it was music of liberation and at the time it appeared, as a force that could only be seen as such. At its lowest level the word was simply used as a replacement for the 'f' word as in "Get The Funk Out Ma Face" or "If It Moves Funk It" and at its highest level as a cult on a par with other quasi-religions of the time. When it worked both its lowest and highest levels merged; the relentless rhythm sending the listener into a frenzied yet calming state that can be attained either through sexual or religious fulfilment. When it failed it was simply tedious.

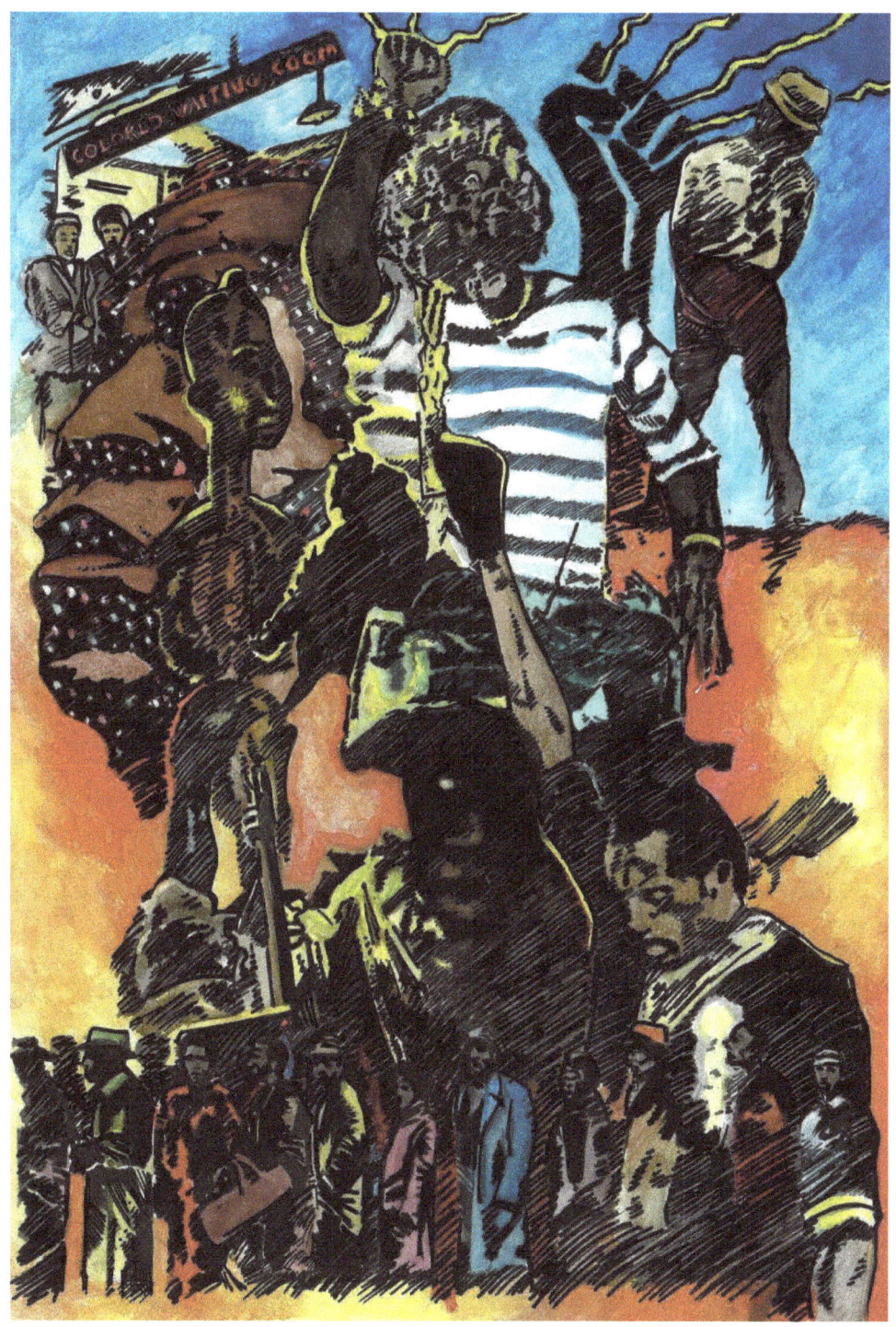

Mothership Connections and Disconnections

It's hard to believe that an album I bought when I was a student and played to death at the College Discos is now placed in the Library of Congress as a recording of historical significance, but The Mothership Connection has proved to be one of the most influential recordings on a generation of African American artists. In 1955 George Clinton was aged 14 and living in Newark, New Jersey, where he practiced with his group, The Parliaments, at night. The Civil Rights Movement was fresh on the lips of every black man and woman in America and sour on almost as many whites. A black astronaut had conquered space and questioned prejudice in the trouble pages of EC Comics in the story "Judgement Day". Just over a decade later, in 1968, just as The Parliaments were about to go through a major change with new personnel and a less than healthy interest in recreational drugs, Clinton was a sci-fi fan and in 1961 a new TV series, The Outer Limits, had proved ground-breaking in its own way and would find its way into the equally ground-breaking opening track of Mothership Connection some 14 years later. Despite its success P-Funk, or Pure Funk, was soon to implode into a black hole of its own making with arguments over monies owed within the organisation and also with record labels squabbling over the fact that Clinton was signing his group of renegade funkateers to as many labels as you could find, Warner Brothers, Casablanca, Arista, Elektra, Westbound and Atlantic were all sharing part of the P-Funk pie! Sadly, the gold became tarnished as Clinton's failure to pay his team the money they expected slowly chipped away at the once unbreachable Empire. Clinton had always said that behind P-Funk's apparently banal lyrics and concepts, serious issues were discussed and yet a debate raged in America as to whether Clinton actually took the wrong turn with funk. Jimi Hendrix was planning to collaborate with Miles Davis in a move now seen as the way the music could have developed. Did Clinton trivialise what African Americans viewed as an important time in political and artistic development? Whatever, the sound of P-Funk and its unique set of creative musicians continued to influence the sound of Funk into the 1980s. In 1997 Parliament and Funkadelic were inducted into the Rock and Roll Hall Of Fame. In 2002 Mothership Connection was included in Vibe Magazine's "Essential Black Rock Recordings" and 2003 saw the television network VH1 name Mothership Connection the 55th greatest album of all time. The same year the album was ranked number 274 on Rolling Stone magazine's list of the 500 greatest albums of all time and also got included in the book "1001 Albums You Must Hear Before You Die".

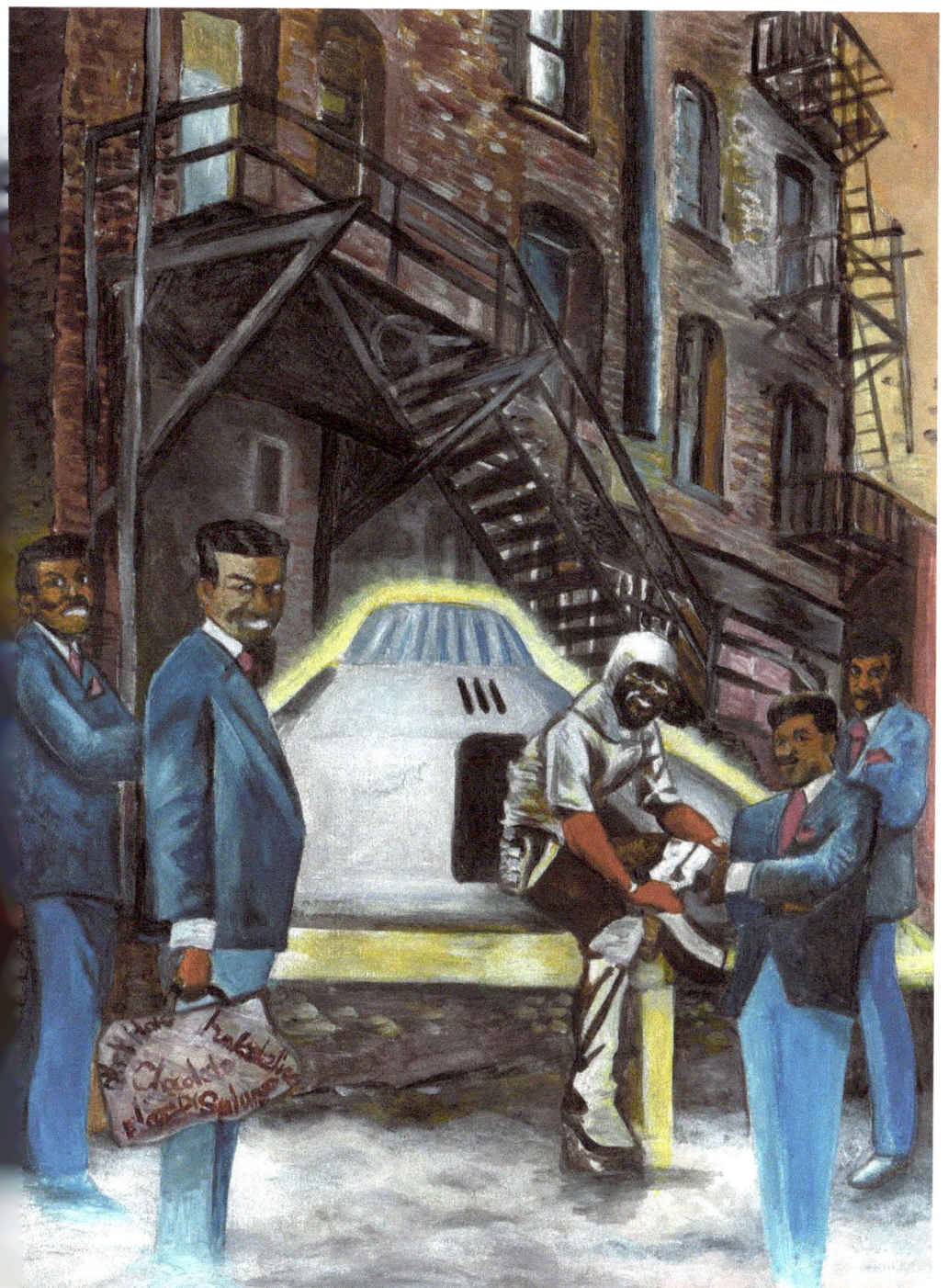

Prince

Prince Rogers Nelson was born on June 7th, 1958, in Minneapolis, Minnesota. He attended Minneapolis's Central High School and in 1976 created a demo tape eventually leading to a contract with Warner Bros. His debut album "For You" was released in 1978, Prince produced, arranged, composed and played all 27 instruments. In October 1979, Prince released a self-titled album, then a year later "Dirty Mind" the first to be recorded in his own studio. In October 1981 the album turned to gold and was quickly followed by "Controversy". Everything was going well he was billed as the opening act for The Rolling Stones and towards the end of 1982 released one of his finest albums "1999". He followed this with a dip into the movies with 1984s "Purple Rain" which stayed at the top of the Billboard Chart for 24 consecutive weeks and won him the Oscar for best original song. As per usual something stops the party, in this case it was a mother, Tipper Gore. She had heard her 12-year-old daughter listening to the track "Darling Nikki" and successfully pushed for a Parental Advisory Explicit Lyrics label to be added to record and CD covers. 1985 saw Chaka Khan scoring with her version of Prince's "I Feel For You" and in 1986 his song "Manic Monday" was recorded by The Bangles. Prince abolished his group The Revolution and started working on "Sign O' The Times" released in 1987 and despite critical praise his album sales began to decline. After "Lovesexy" he returned to films, scoring the soundtrack for Tim Burton's "Batman" and again in 1990 he finished production on a new film, Graffiti Bridge, but the film flopped. It was during negotiations with Warner Brothers over his next album "The Gold Experience" and legal wrangling over artistic and financial control that Prince appeared in public with the word 'slave' written on his cheek. He then dropped his own name and was known either as 'The Artist Formerly Known As Prince' or The Love Symbol. He began moving product from one label to another but was still receiving awards and accolades. Prince released his album "20ten" in July 2010 as a free giveaway on a newspaper. He refused access to the album to digital download services and also closed his official website, LotusFlow3r.com. claiming that the Internet was completely over and turning his back on the computer age as far as distributing his music. Prince was inducted in the Grammy Hall of Fame on December 7, 2010 and sold over 100 million records worldwide in his career also giving other artists their own moment of fame. He died at the age of 57 in 2016 after an accidental fentanyl overdose. To paraphrase, nothing compared to Prince.

Art & Soul

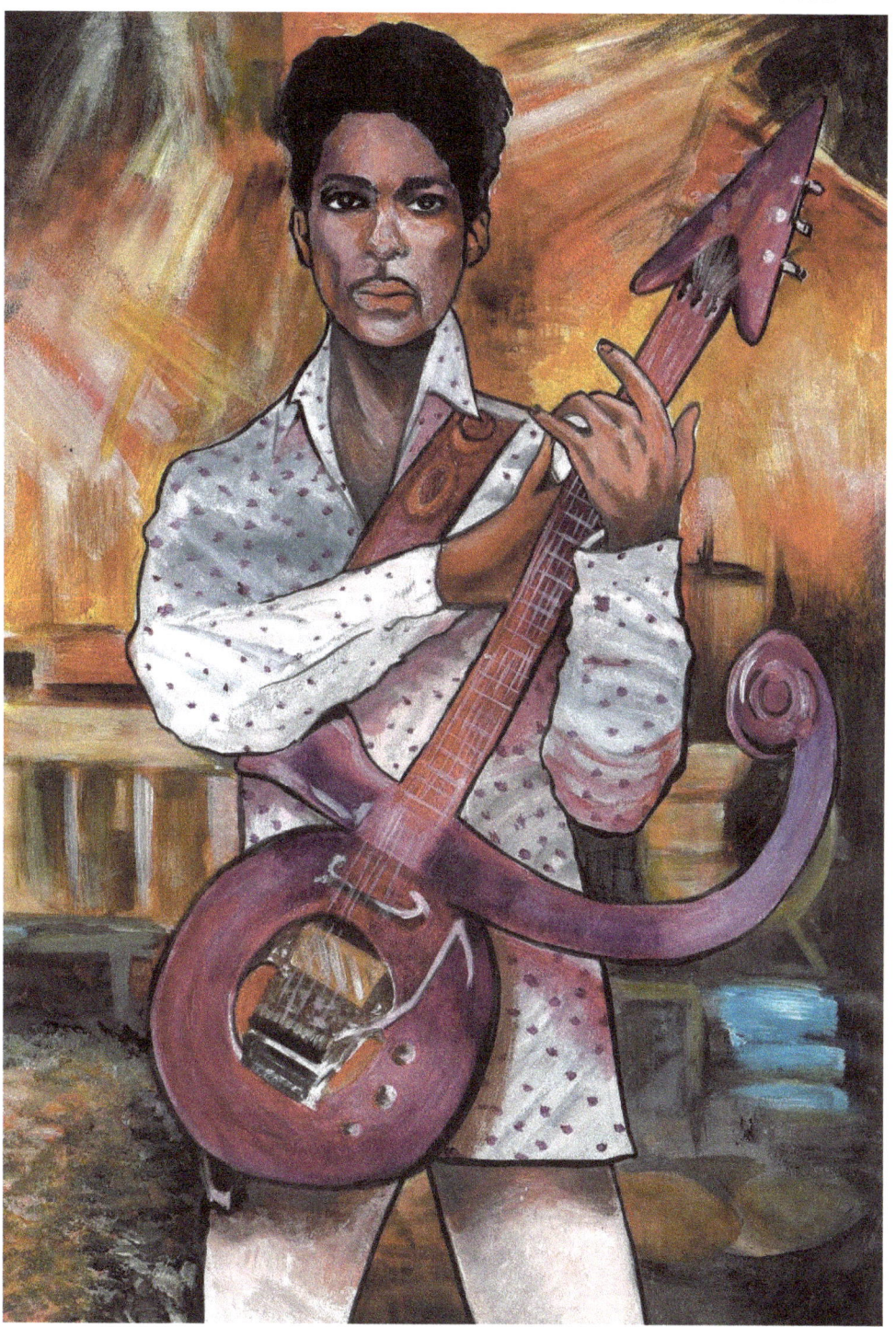

What Is Soul?

When you look through this book, you'll see that what I may consider a tough path to travel was nothing more than a gentle stroll compared to what others had to go through.

Soul is love, the joy felt by two people sharing their thoughts, their hopes.

Then again it is the loss of love, the hurt felt by two people who could no longer share the same thoughts, for whom hope had died and who had now reached their point of no return, for it's so hard to say goodbye to yesterday.

Soul is a struggle for acceptance and the memory of the consequences brought about by others short-sightedness and the hate that their lack of understanding brings - but it is also faith -the hope of better things to come based on a strong church foundation. Knowledge that whatever was thrown at them there was always something greater than themselves who would look after their interests come judgement day.

Soul is defiance. Anger at being suppressed, confusion amidst the frustration of being born with the wrong colour skin.

Undefinable and yet all embracing. Spiritual and yet physical. Music born from the love and the loss, the pain and the suffering, the search for peace through God and the threat of achievement through revolution.

Soul music was born around the same time as the American Civil Rights movement and in many ways travelled the same routes around America. This new music was created by unique musicians, innovative producers, and writers as well as unequalled singers. Along the way Soul also found inspiration in local culture and traditions giving every city its own identity. In 1966 Ben E. King released "What Is Soul?" on ATCO and defined it as a burning feeling inside, made from love and loss but then in 1970 Funkadelic redefined it, telling us that Soul was a ham hock in your cornflakes or the ring around your bathtub which showed just how deep Soul could be and how it wasn't that easy to define. African Americans contributed to the recording industry, pushing creators' rights, developing record labels, supporting communities and local economy but also showing what was possible to achieve when black and white Americans worked in harmony.

THIS IS SOUL.

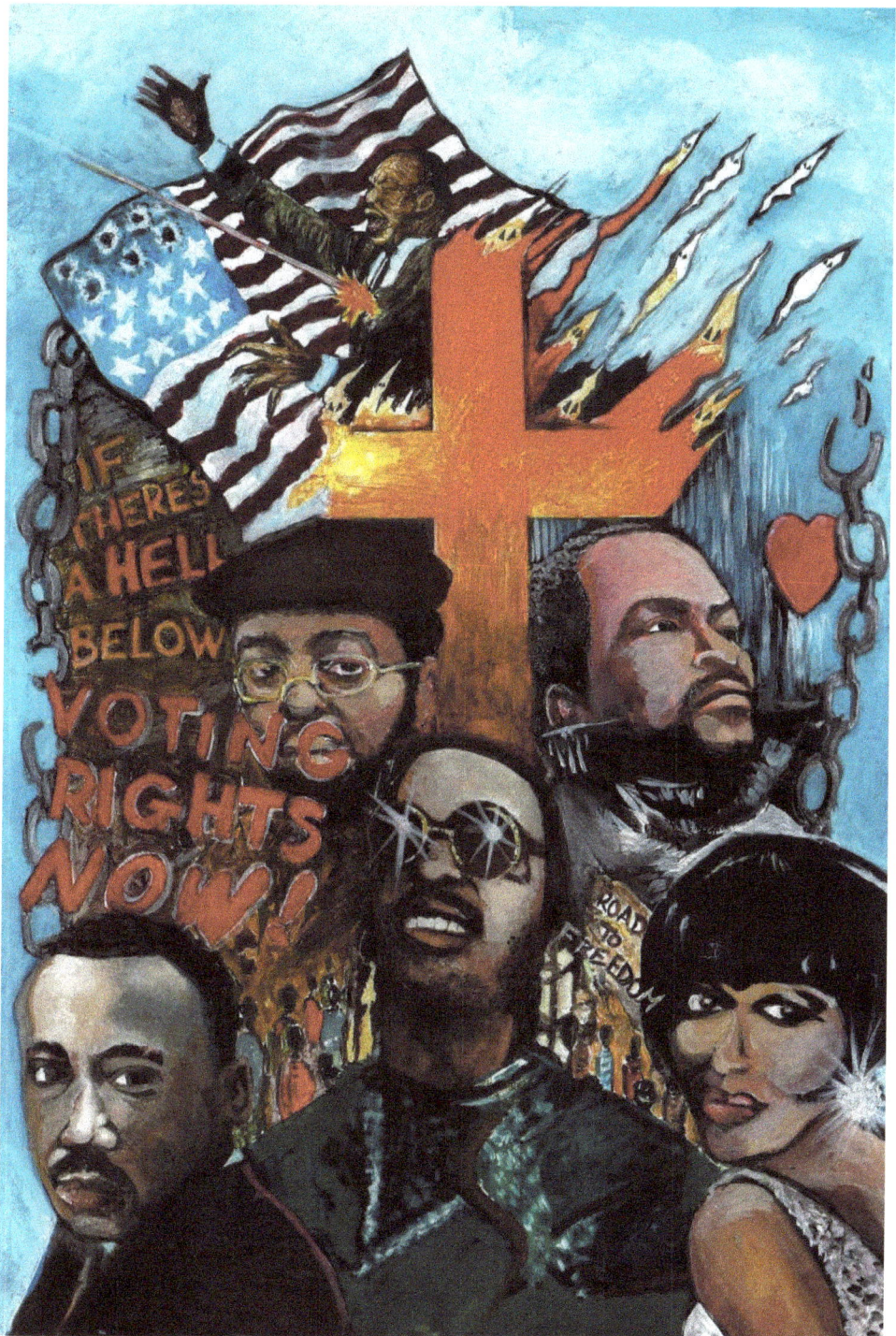

What The F#&k Is Going On

Let's move to when I was fifteen and to what was arguably the most inspiring and thought-provoking year for me. I've never seen myself as political and yet the music I chose led me to learn about the American political scene as well as the social injustice being meted out to African Americans. This led to arguments both at school and home. People always criticised Soul music as being love songs, performed by people who could only sing and dance, other people played the music and wrote their songs. Again, this fired me up and I hope that throughout this book we can see how many people behind the music not only swam against the tide but contributed some of the most thought-provoking songs as well as being inspirational in many of their other achievements.

The year of 1971 really established my commitment to Soul music. I had started to buy records and collect copies of Blues & Soul Magazine, whenever I could find them in 1970 but it was really the music released in 1971 that was my baptism. The year had started with the release of "Melting Pot" by Booker T & The MGs, Donald Trump became President of the Trump Organization that year. If only he'd remained President there because his contemporary behaviour has set America back sixty years and Booker T's melting pot would have been preferrable to the pot of racism that had been simmering since the American Civil War ended in 1865 when someone lifted the lid, gave it a stir and had people talking about the possibility of a second Civil War. It is significant but sad that the messages in some of the songs we are going to refer to weren't taken more seriously because 50 years on, we are where we are.

What is shocking is the catalogue of events that took place in 1971 and how they resonate with what is happening now. January turned to February and we saw the posthumous album "The Baby Huey Story" by Baby Huey And The Babysitters released on Curtom. During the late-1960s, the band were inspired by Sly & The Family Stone becoming a psychedelic soul act but by 1970 Ramey had developed an addiction to heroin and his weight had increased to over 400 pounds. James Ramey died of a heart attack on October 28, 1970, at the age of 26. To me the standout track from the album was "Hard Times". February was also the month that Rufus Thomas released "Do The Push And Pull" on Stax Records, which no doubt inspired the dancing of Donald Trump during his campaigning, something I won't miss.

March brought us "Ungena Za Ulimengu" by The Temptations on Gordy, Swahili for "Unite The World" whilst over in Chicago "Give More Power To The People" by The Chi-Lites on Brunswick cast them in a Norman Whitfield/Temptations mould with a track that could now be considered incendiary. The month had already started with a bomb exploding at the U.S. Capitol. It had been placed there by the Weatherman group, now calling themselves the Underground Weather organization, a group of white males who had formed in 1969 out of anti-Vietnam protests. Home grown terrorists. A week later, on March 8, 1971, anti-Vietnam War activists broke into an FBI office in Philadelphia and stole documents that proved the kind of subversive behaviour the Bureau had conducted under J. Edgar Hoover.

In an attempt to answer, or at least question, the things that were dividing the country Marvin Gaye released "What's Going On" on Tamla. Famously ignored at the time by Berry Gordy, the track would eventually become Gaye's most significant song. The album that followed in May was voted the Number 1 album of all time by Rolling Stone Magazine in 2020 hopefully because of the merit and not because of the moment, as the world woke up to Black Lives Matter after the police killing of George Floyd and others. It's ironic that the title track was written after Renaldo Benson of the Four Tops had watched the Police actions at the Berkley Riots of 1969 and written the lyrics. The pardoning spree of Trump was nothing new either. Towards the end of March, Lieutenant William Calley was found guilty of 22 murders in what became known as the My Lai Massacre in Vietnam and sentenced to life in prison. That was until President Nixon quashed the sentence, setting him free 3 years later.

In April "Do Yourself A Favour" by Stevie Wonder appeared on his "Where I'm Coming From" album, it foretold of things to come from the Wonder and was a far more political album than the 1972 'coming of age' set, "Music Of My Mind"; On April 24th, 500,000 people marched against the Vietnam War in Washington with a further 125,000 doing the same in San Francisco. May 3rd saw further protests in Washington when Anti-war activists attempted to disrupt government business; the police and military units arrested up to 12,000 people. Meanwhile, Frankie Beverly had been busy developing a harder sound with a new collective called Raw Soul who would form the nucleus of what would eventually become Maze. The extremely rare "Open Up Your Heart" was their first release on Eldorado, co-written and produced by Charles Earland. From 1971 Frankie Beverly's Raw Soul started making noise with "Color Blind" released on Gregar in May. That same month The Isley Brothers were joined by a younger strain of Isleys, Ernie and Marvin with cousin, Chris Jasper on keyboards. As a trio they had been playing together since 1969 and in 1971 they cut their cover of Stephen Stills' "Love the One You're With" taking the title from a remark often said by Billy Preston. The Vietnam war was still raging and in June Bobby Powell released one of the best protest songs of the year with "Peace Begins Within" on the Whit label out of Shreveport, Louisiana. On

Gordy, Edwin Starr released the Norman Whitfield produced album "Involved" that included both "War" from the previous year and its 1971 follow up "Stop The War Now". "Pieces of a Man" was the first studio album by Gil Scott-Heron, recorded in April 1971 and released later that year by Flying Dutchman Records, it charted in June. The album contained "The Revolution Will Not Be Televised" and his original version of "Home Is Where the Hatred Is", later a hit for Esther Phillips on Kudu. On the 13th of June, The New York Times began publishing The Pentagon Papers, a series of leaked articles condemning the Government's actions in the Vietnam War. The 2017 Steven Spielberg directed movie "The Post" starring Meryl Streep and Tom Hanks told the story superbly. This was a turning point in the War. July saw the release of the single "Smiling Faces Sometimes" by The Undisputed Truth, originally a social commentary laden track that had originally appeared back in April on The Temptations "Sky's The Limit" set and that, here, was a slow-burning piece of Soul superbly sung by Joe Harris in his finest Jerry Butler tone.

In 1865, a phrase had entered the American language, "40 Acres and a Mule", a term used for the compensation that was awarded to freed slaves straight after the American Civil War. By June of that year around 40,000 freed slaves were settled on 400,000 acres in Georgia and South Carolina but soon afterwards the President, Andrew Johnson went back on the deal and the land was given back to its former white landowners. A century after the American Civil War had ended the less than conclusive results were still being questioned and was beginning to be expressed in the music of such groups as Sound Experience, a group formed at Baltimore's Morgan State College in 1970 moving up to Philadelphia to record with producer Stan Watson. "40 Acres And A Mule" by Sound Experience came out on Soulville in September of '71. October introduced me to Curtis Mayfield through his second solo album, "Roots". The lead single was "We Gotta Have Peace". There were other thought-provoking songs on view, though, like "Underground" and "Keep on Keeping On". Incidentally, NF Porter released a different song but with the same title on Lizard the same month and in New York, the Knapp Commission began public hearings on Police corruption.

Isaac Hayes' career was to take yet another incredible turn when he 'scored' his biggest success with the release of "Shaft", the music for the Gordon Parks film of the same name. Hayes won an Academy Award for Best Score the first African American composer to receive such an honour. The single "Theme from Shaft,'" reached Number One on November 20th with the Bar Kays guitarist Michael Toles delivering one of the most recognisable guitar riffs in the history of Popular music. It also won two Grammys, a Golden Globe award and the NAACP Image Award. Billy

Preston lined up alongside George Harrison, Ringo (not Edwin) Starr, Leon Russell and Eric Clapton in an all-star band for the Concert for Bangla Desh but away from these successful collaborations his recording label, Apple, was turning into a disaster and Preston needed to move. He signed to A&M based in Los Angeles where he enjoyed his most prolific, commercial period. Here he wrote and produced the album "I Wrote a Simple Song" featuring George Harrison on lead guitar and arranged by Quincy Jones. The title track was issued as a single but the funky instrumental B-side was receiving more attention on the radios and so it was flipped. "Outa-Space" went to No 2 on the US charts and won the 1972 Grammy for Best Pop Instrumental. Along with Stevie Wonder his stunning electronic keyboard sounds paved the way for others to follow, the Commodores similar sounding "Machine Gun" was 2 years in the future. There had been a two and a half year gap before Sly Stone reappeared with the album, "There's A Riot Goin' On", at the end of November 1971. The long delay had partly been due to the erratic behaviour brought on by drugs; at this point the whole group was into drugs and guns, a volatile cocktail. By now the band had virtually become second string to Stone's stoned confusion and the family was breaking up but despite the inner struggles, the new album showed the continued popularity of the group. The album entered the Soul Chart at Number 6 and reached the top in just one move. Within 3 days of its American release the album had turned Gold. The first single from the set, "Family Affair", followed the leader to the top of the charts but whatever took place during this period left a scar on the members of the Family. So, we reached the end of a fascinating year and December brought us another piece of social consciousness, wrapped up in a Christmas song. That song was *"Hey America*" recorded by *James Brown*. It had actually appeared on his Christmas album of 1970 and was released as a single that failed to chart in the United States. A year later it reached number 47 on the UK Singles Chart. Finally, George Lucas launched Lucasfilm Ltd on the 10th of December, so at least we had some more escapism to look forward to, although 1972 would prove just as explosive but then 2016 would 'trump' it all.

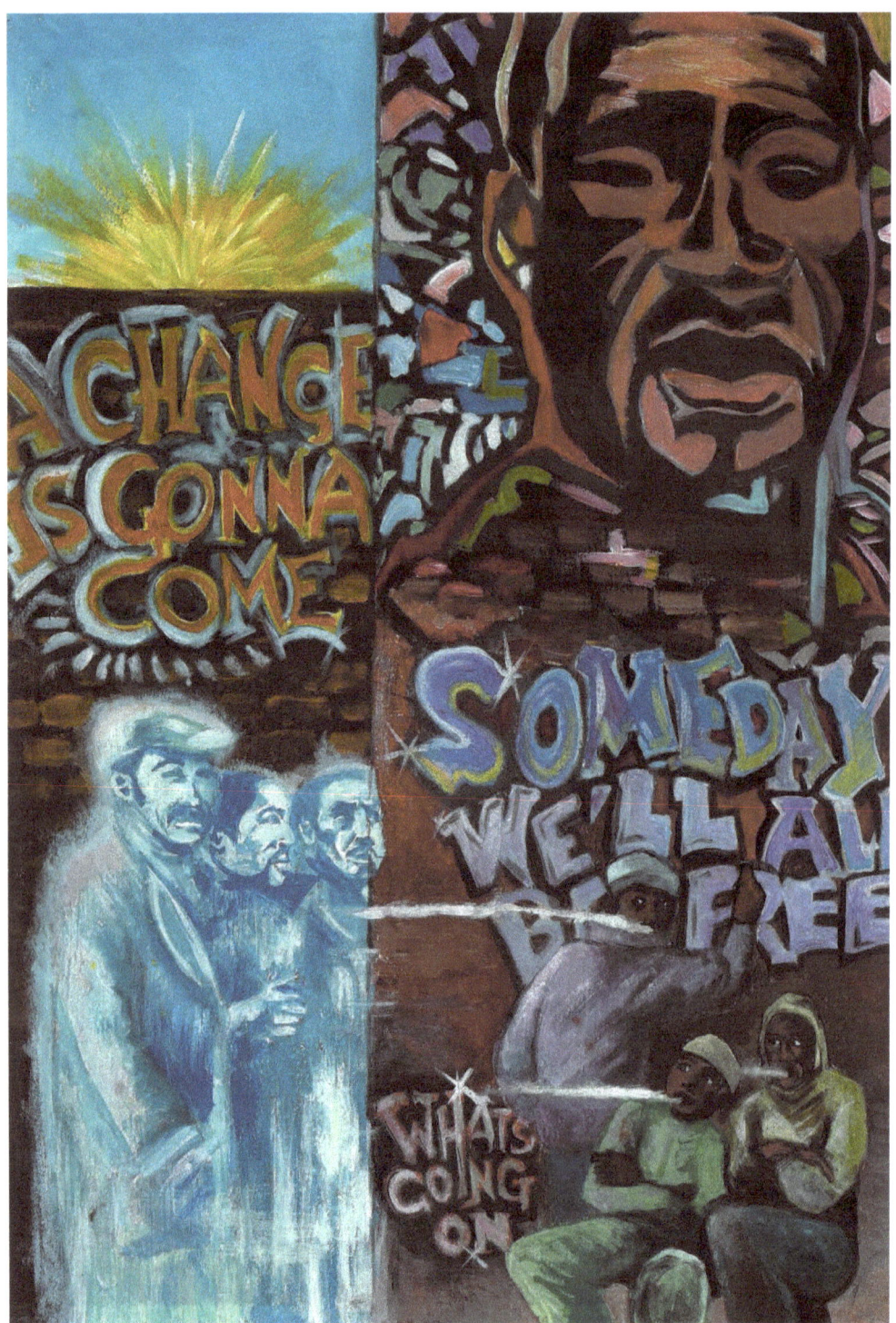

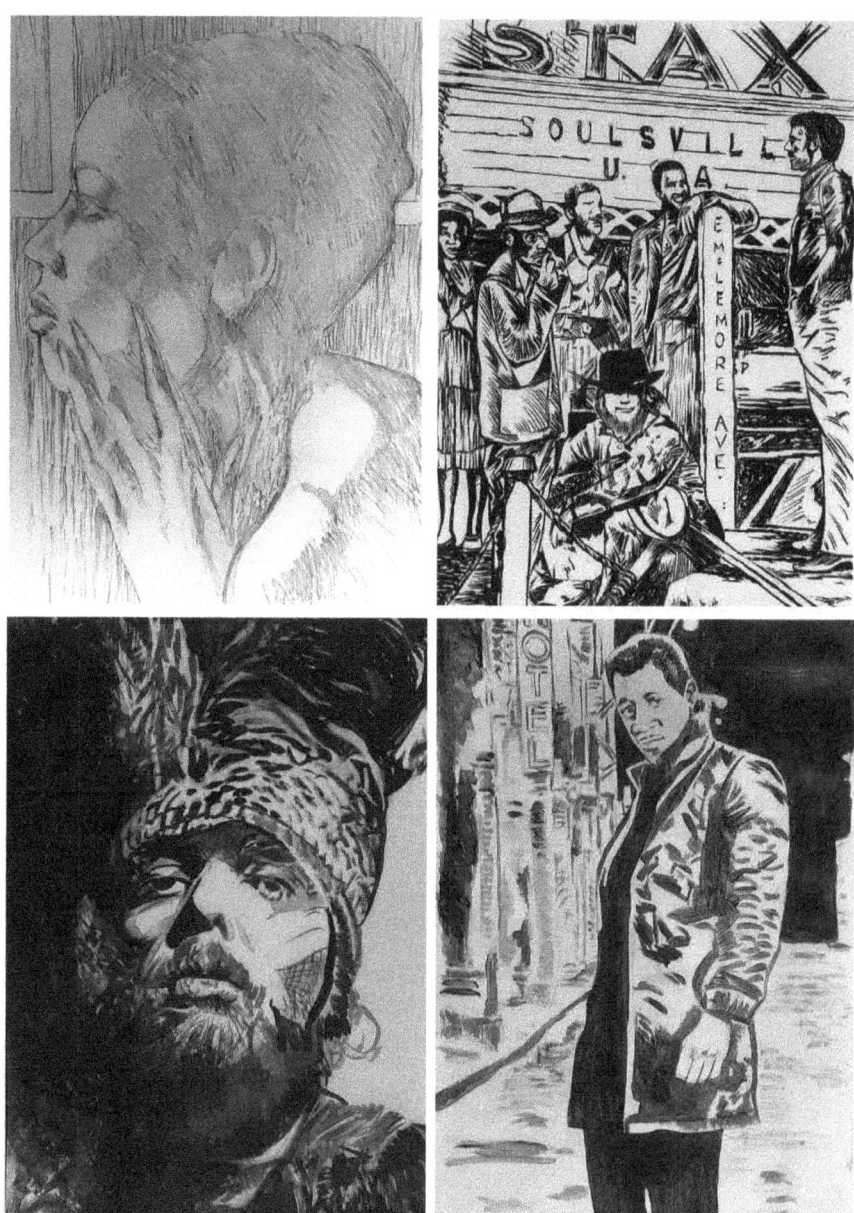

Ray Charles

Here's a question. When Kevin Spacey played Bobby Darin in "Beyond The Sea" critics praised the portrayal but when Jamie Foxx played Ray Charles in "Ray", one critic called it an impersonation. Why? Actors act, isn't that what they do, be it a fictional or non-fictional character. It just makes me wonder. Here's another one, how can you break the rules if they haven't been made yet? Ray Charles was born on September the 23rd in Albany, Georgia and was a singer, composer, multi-instrumentalist, bandleader and record label owner. After a move to Greenville, Florida he started playing piano in a local café; he was five years old. Ray was raised by both parents and a brother, George but then everything changed. He witnessed his brother George's drowning in his mother's laundry tub, began to lose his sight when he was six and by seven was blind, then his father died when Ray was still only ten. He had already started his musical studies at the Florida School for the Deaf and Blind where he had to study classical music but his mother died from cancer when he was fifteen. He decided he had to leave school to become a professional pianist. What else was there for him to lose? His early work centred around the style of Nat 'King' Cole before he branched out into a Rhythm & Blues direction with tracks like "Mess Around" from 1953 and the same year he arranged Guitar Slim's "The Things That I Used to Do" which became a Blues million seller. By 1954 Ray Charles had begun to embrace Blues, Rhythm & Blues, Jazz and Gospel and signed a contract with Atlantic Records. Here the indescribable style of Ray Charles bloomed. "I've Got a Woman" and "I Love You So" both released in 1957 were hits whilst "What'd I Say" released in 1959 was considered the birth of Soul and also gave him his own first million-seller. In 1960 another of his best was released, the country tinged "Georgia On My Mind" which was followed in '61 by "Hit The Road Jack". From 1962 came the million selling album "Modern Sounds In Country and Western Music" which gave us the single "I Can't Stop Loving You". This was a prolific time for Ray as he formed his own Tangerine record label that year most famously releasing material on his backing singers The Raelettes. A decade later he formed another label, Crossover and in 1980 starred with John Belushi and Dan Aykroyd in "The Blues Brothers". In his life Ray Charles received 13 Grammy Awards and was inducted into the Rock and Roll Hall of Fame in 1986. He passed away on June the 10th, 2004. Maybe we should think of it this way, if you're the father of a child sometimes you don't have a name in mind and sometimes others suggest a name for you, like for instance Soul.

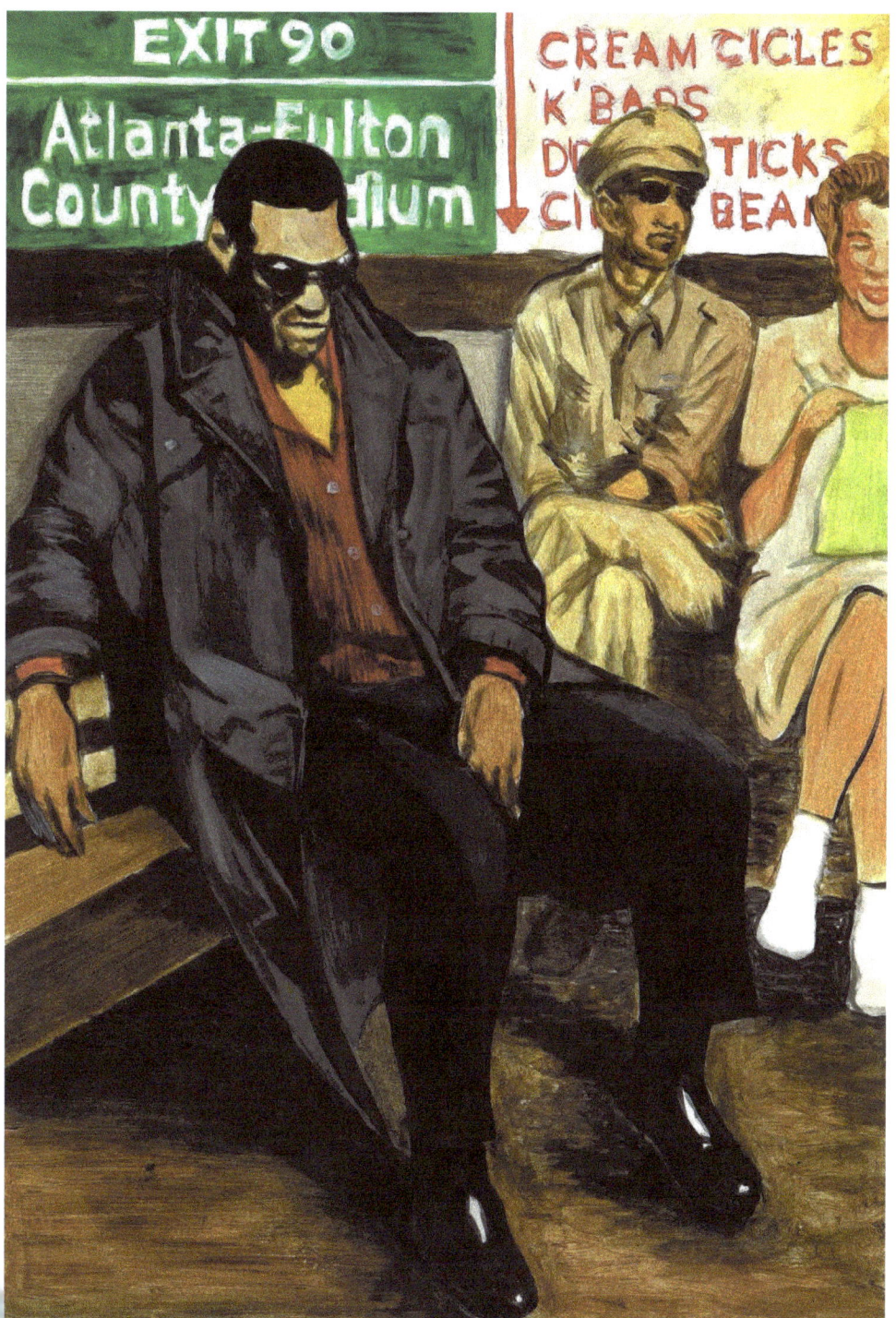

Swamp Dogg

Within the confines of any creative form there is the restless spirit always willing to expand that form: some may wish to call it progress. In the case of Swamp Dogg, the progression would take the form of that liberalism allowed only to those who offer no real threat. He was never destined to be a superstar and thus be placed upon a pedestal of power. Therefore no one would raise an eyebrow when Jerry Williams Jr. teamed up with Jane Fonda in 1971 for an anti-US involvement in a Vietnam tour. Jerry Williams Jr. was born in Portsmouth, Virginia on July 12th, 1942. Twenty-eight years later, he in turn would give birth to Swamp Dogg. In between times Williams would struggle on as an unsuccessful and frustrated singer and songwriter following a move to New York where he would work for Musicor/Dynamo Records, and where he would become acquainted with two other natives of Virginia, Charlie Whitehead and Gary US Bonds. Eventually Williams, Bond and Whitehead would create a unique team of songwriters but from 1965 until the end of the decade, Williams would precariously balance his career making minor ripples as a singer. In 1970 and with an ailing career Jerry Williams was approached by Wally Roker Jr who was forming his own label, Canyon. He persuaded Williams to sign for him and, acting more as an analyst than a record label owner, told him to write about the subjects that occupied his mind. Dangerous considering what would later explode from that mind. Thus, Williams became Roker's chief writer/producer and in so doing conceived his alter ego. At Canyon Williams would start to receive artistic if not commercial recognition through two albums. First his own debut "Total Destruction to Your Mind" and secondly, "I'm a Loser" by Doris Duke.

On the Dogg's own album the theme became his own with "Mama's Baby, Daddy's Maybe", whilst "The Baby's Mine" was sung by a divorced man wanting to see his baby even though he felt uneasy about entering the home of his ex-wife and her new husband to do it. Marital issues would take up the whole of William's output where lady singers were concerned; whereas the Dogg's own output would vary from marital to global issues alongside some sharp observations on human successes and failings.

As with Ray Charles, Williams was very close to the country side of things and in 1971 had Freddie North's single "She's all I get" released. Again, the first time I heard it was on AFN and was quick to grab it when it got issued in the UK. This would also have the unique honour of becoming both a soul number one and a country number one covered by Johnny Paycheck.

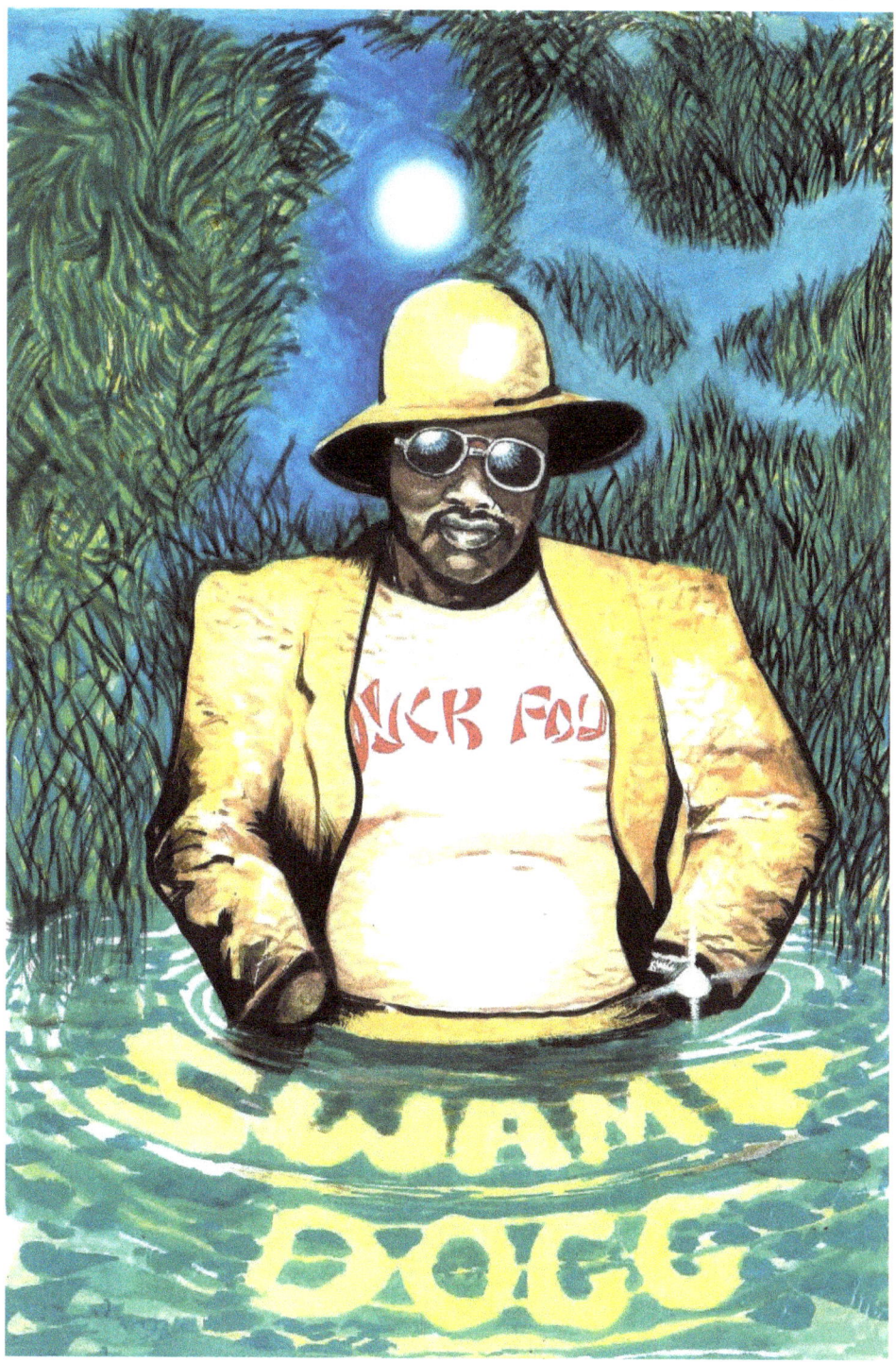

Art & Soul

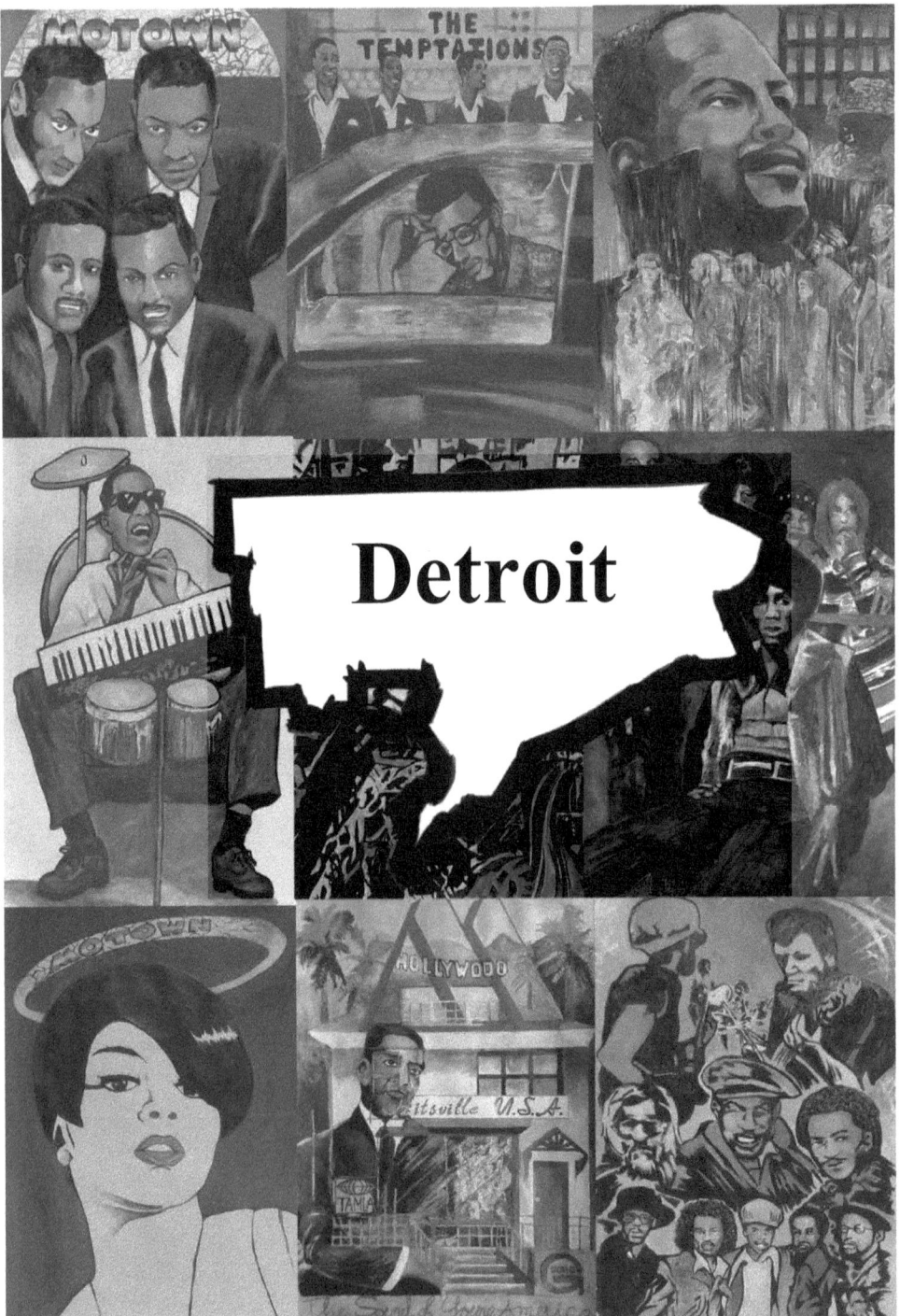

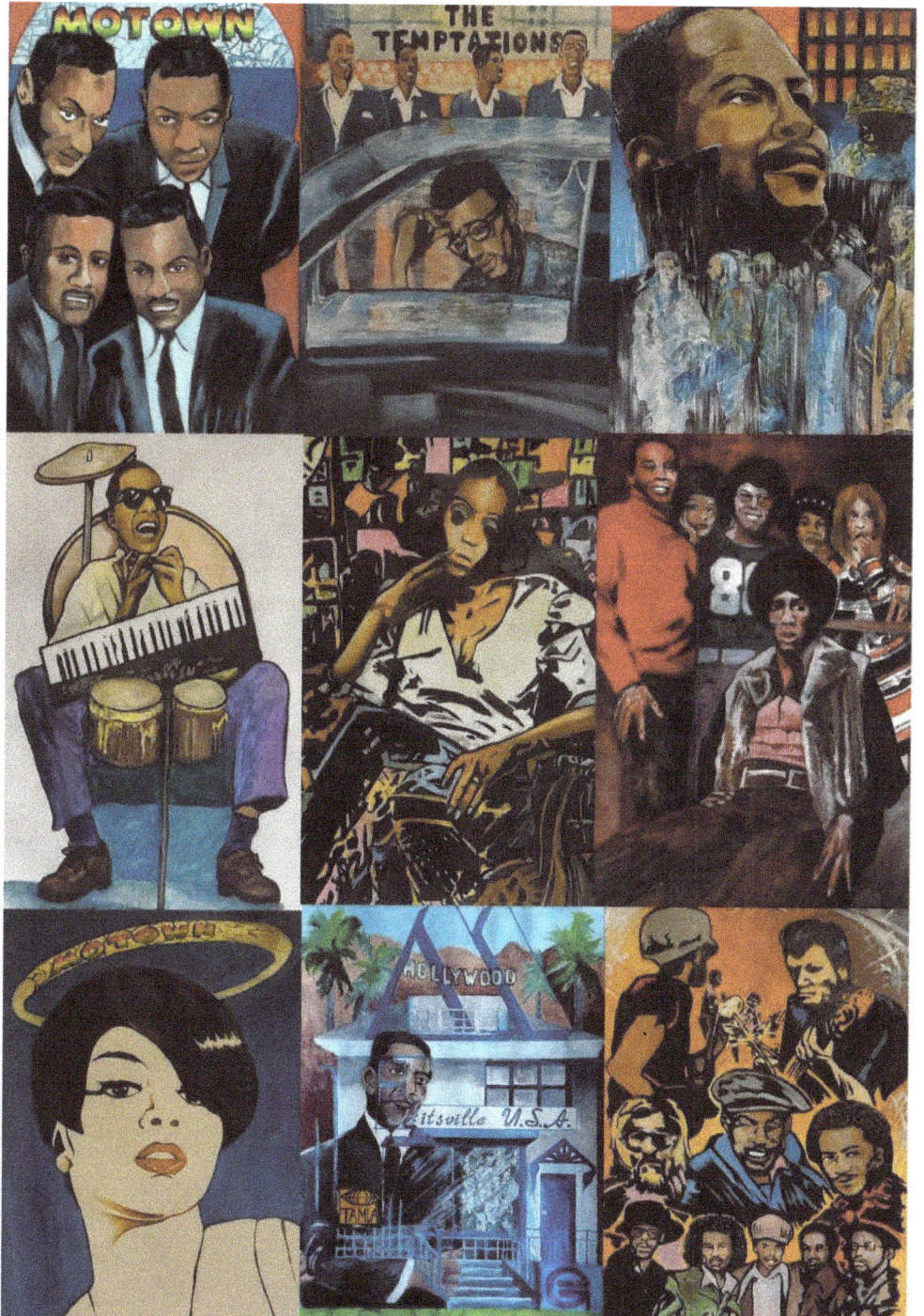

Berry Gordy Jr

When Berry Gordy Jr created Motown back in 1959, he gave the American Dream to a portion of black America who grew and grew as Motown itself did. Some fell from the dizzy heights but, in general, many would stay at the top for a long, long time. No mean feat in itself, in an industry often built on sand. Motown was destined to become the world's most successful independent record company: a black owned corporation in a white led industry. Now, although many critics condemned Gordy for selling out or 'whitening' black music with his clever mix of rhythm & blues and popular white musical trends, the fact remained that Gordy also benefited the local black community by giving opportunities, albeit as an opportunist himself, to many people who otherwise may have been destined to live a life in the Projects, inner city housing developments. Nobody was in the business to lose money and to be commercially viable, it was necessary for Gordy to take up certain popular musical themes and blend them with his own ideas and traditions. Berry Gordy Jr stood as a black man who grabbed for the American Dream and made it a reality, much like Sam Cooke, opening the way for others to follow. A tradition still felt strongly today when new creators look at Motown as an organisation to emulate. Time showed though that not all the creative talent gathered by Gordy had the same eye for business. By now Gordy had gained a partner and later second wife, Raynoma Liles who he had met in 1959.

During Motown's formative years Raynoma Liles found 2648 West Grand Boulevard, in Detroit that would become recognised as the first home of Motown. It was from here that the label's earliest recordings were made. Motown may have begun to dominate the commercial Soul market but, on nearly every street corner, for every artist signed to the label there were plenty more out there trying their hardest to be heard and if Berry Gordy Jr wasn't going to listen to them then another label owner just might. Many rival label owners had a deep hatred for Gordy's empire, an unscratchable itch that would fester and even lead to their ultimate demise as in the case of Mike Hanks, owner of D-Town records. Some, though, like Ed Wingate enjoyed the challenge and came close to toppling Gordy's Motown empire, first with the Golden World label and then with the Northern Soul favourite Ric-Tic that would continue to be thorns in the side of Berry Gordy Jr.

Something else was also about to hit Detroit. Motown was changing as was the city itself and Gordy was so totally out of touch that he failed to even notice. In July, the city came to the boil and in three days a riot split Detroit wide open, so devastating that it would never truly heal.

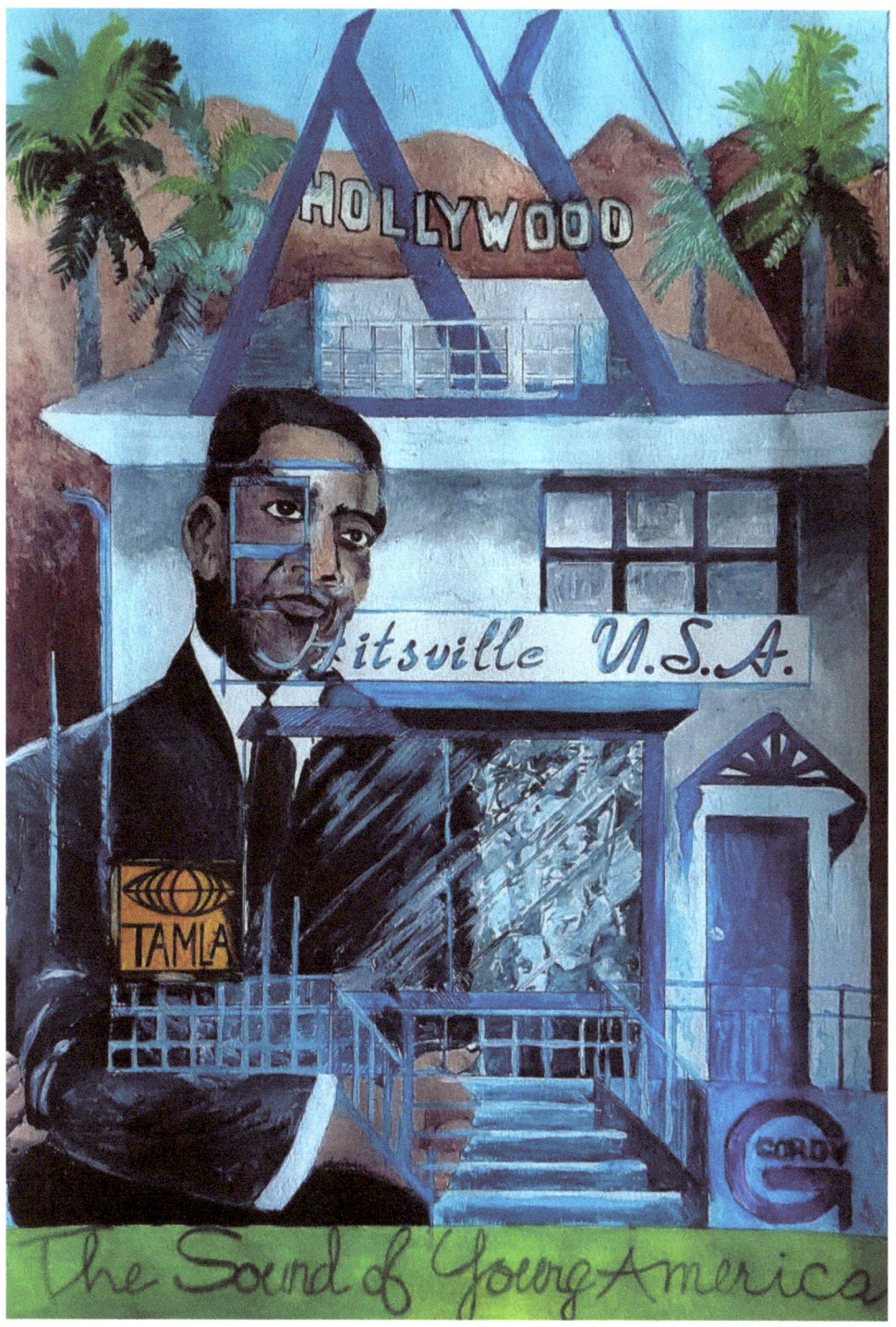

Detroit Musicians

In Detroit, Michigan, Berry Gordy Jr was making history with the black owned Motown label but we have to remember that the music supplying the hits wasn't a Motown sound, it was a Detroit sound being laid down by a group of jazz oriented individuals who were predominantly black but as the 60s progressed, the music began to be laid down by a multi-racial rhythm section including white guitarists Joe Messina, Dennis Coffey and Ray Monette, who had been raised in Detroit's R&B scene and bass player Bob Babbit, house bass player for the Golden World company alongside guitarist Coffey. Coffey had performed his guitar tricks on most of the Ric Tic material, featuring heavily on the instrumentals, notably Al Kent's Northern Soul stomper "You Gotta Pay the Price" as well as The Parliaments breakthrough "I Wanna Testify". Dennis Coffey was also responsible for bringing the wah-wah guitar to Motown, most notably on Norman Whitfield's psychedelic Temptations era beginning with 1968's "Cloud Nine". He later branched out to become a recording artist in his own right for Sussex Records with the epic "Scorpio" with the Detroit Guitar Band which included the stunning bass solo by Bob Babbit. However, when Motown wasn't paying enough, these guys would do the rounds of other smaller labels which added to the whole Detroit sound.

Having left Motown in 1968 the post-Motown sound of Holland-Dozier-Holland, through their own Invictus/Hot Wax set up was tight, percussive and funky as supplied by the finest of the established Detroit session men and new, eager young musicians proud to sit alongside the guys who had laid down the Detroit groove up until then. These newcomers included another Caucasian guitarist, Ron Bykowski who was part of the 100 Proof Aged In Soul unit before joining the ranks of Funkadelic.

After working for Holland-Dozier-Holland, Ray Monette progressed, literally, to Motown's premier Rock band, Rare Earth. Rare Earth, though, held on to their black indulgences becoming the first White band to play the legendary Apollo Theatre in Harlem as well as benefiting from the production wizardry of Norman Whitfield.

It's interesting that we refer to the musical side of Soul and Funk because it reminds me of an article I once read in an old copy of Blues & Soul Magazine, when the author questioned the 'Soul' of a Northern Soul Instrumental, it may have been "Festival Time" by the San Remo Strings. From memory he suggested that the musicians could be Chinese, so what makes it Soul? Good question. If it's the way it is sung, then there's not many can argue when they hear Soul coming through the vocal delivery; but how do you judge the Soul in a musical instrument?

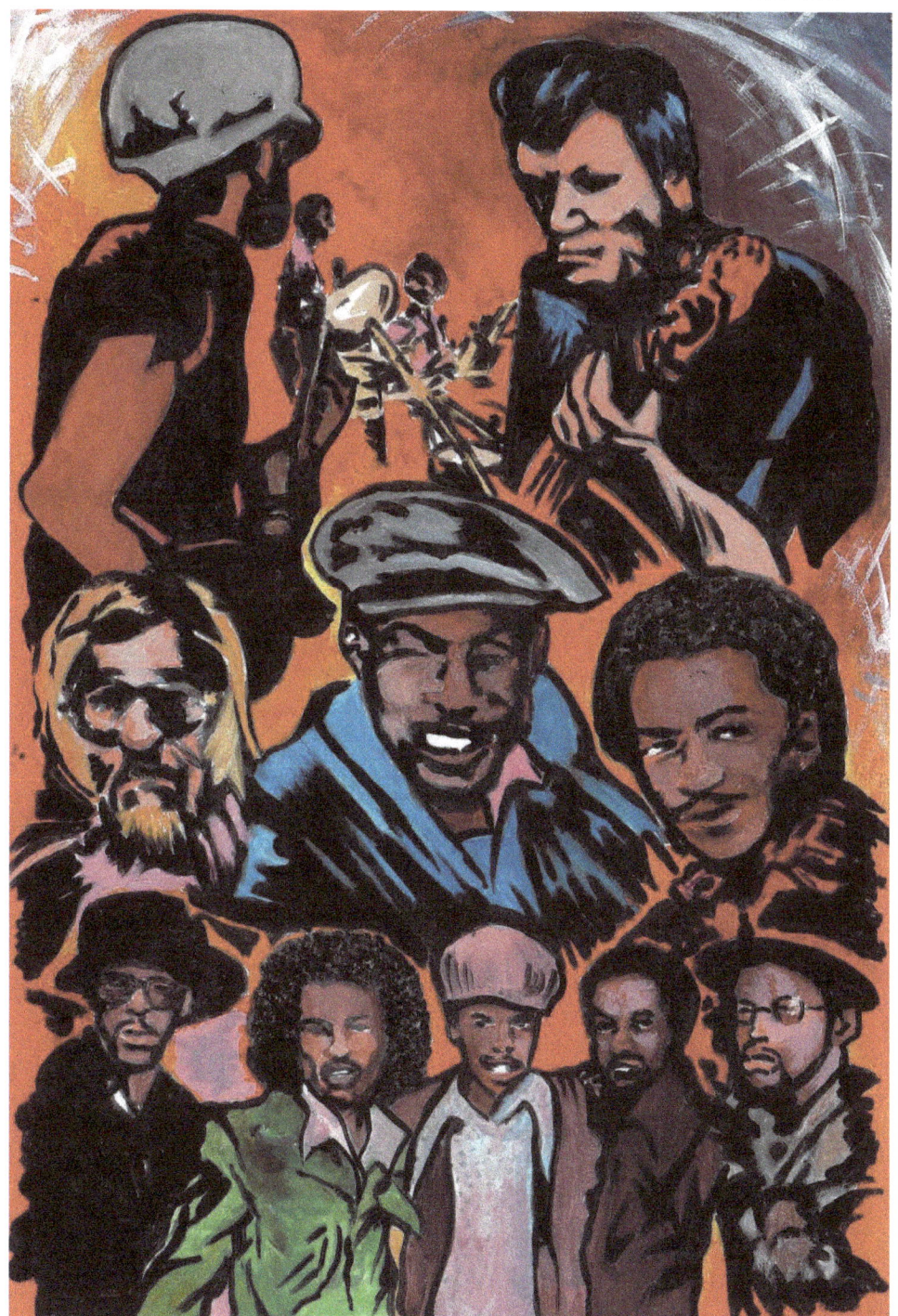

David Ruffin

David Eli Ruffin was born on the 18th of January 1941 in Mississippi and has to be one of the most recognisable voices to ever come out of Motown. His eldest brother was Jimmy Ruffin and he was also the cousin of Melvin Franklin, The Temptations bass vocalist. Ruffin's singing started with the Dixie Nightingales before he moved to Detroit where he played drums and sang with the Voice Masters before signing to the Anna label, Anna being Anna Gordy. Other material was issued on Checkmate in 1961 but his break came in January of 1964 after brother Jimmy's hopes of joining The Temptations were dashed and David was asked to replace the outgoing tenor, Eldridge Bryant. The original plan was for Ruffin to be background to Eddie Kendricks' falsetto lead but by 1965 Ruffin was sharing the lead along with Kendricks. "My Girl", "Wish It Would Rain", "I'm Losing You" and "Ain't Too Proud to Beg" were just four Temptations songs which benefitted from his unique delivery. The success and accolades he was receiving triggered a negative side and he began making demands which would eventually lead to his dismissal. As The Supremes had changed to Diana Ross & The Supremes, he wanted their name to become David Ruffin & The Temptations. That wasn't going to happen and in 1968 he left. He did stay at Motown though and embarked on a solo career beginning in 1969 under the production of Harvey Fuqua and Johnny Bristol. "My Whole World Ended" was a top ten hit and the album of the same name showed promise but "Feelin' Good", his second album didn't feel good to Ruffin and his material gradually failed in the sales despite some great material and an album that he cut in 1970 with his brother Jimmy, "I Am My Brother's Keeper". This all changed in 1975 when he recorded "Who I Am" in New York with producer Van McCoy. The first single, "Walk Away from Love" reached Number five on the Billboard Pop chart and Number one on the R&B Chart. 1976 brought further success with "Everything's Coming Up Love" and the next year "In My Stride" hit the shops and included a Marv Johnson song, "Rode By The House Where We Used To Stay" which, despite its sad theme, became a popular floor filler on the British Northern Soul scene. In 1979, he moved to Warner Brothers. "So Soon We Change" was followed in 1980 by "Gentleman Ruffin" but commercial success eluded him and he was also imprisoned for tax evasion. In 1982 he was welcomed back to The Temptations for their "Reunion" album. He reconnected with Eddie Kendricks and recorded "Ruffin and Kendricks" for RCA in 1987. The two joined forces for live performances with Hall and Oates and more ironically, they then teamed up with Dennis Edwards who had replaced him in The Temptations. A few weeks later he was dead from a crack cocaine overdose.

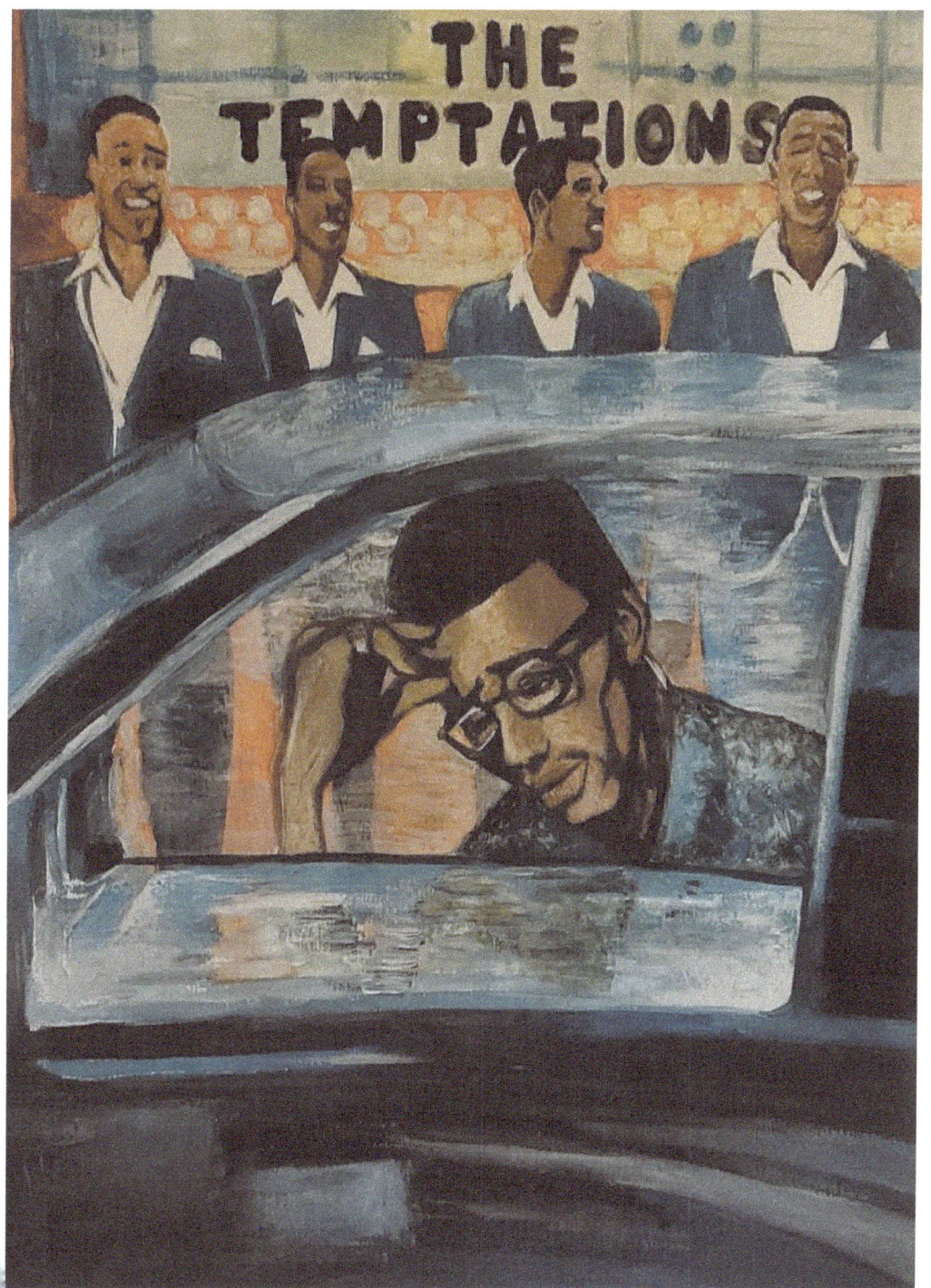

Four Tops

The Four Tops had been together since 1954 and until the death of Laurence Payton on 20th of June 1997 had held the enviable record within the recording industry of remaining unchanged for some 43 years. In 1956 the Four Tops were still trying to find that elusive hit and tried again with "Could It Be You" for Chess Records but with no success and so moved on to the Red Top label then Riverside who released "Pennies from Heaven" in 1962. Again, this met with no success and so Berry Gordy, having pursued the Four Tops in previous years, finally signed them up to Motown's Jazz Workshop label that same year. He gave the four friends $400 with a promise of hits but their "Breakin' Through" album was shelved prior to release. The Tops remained calm, waiting for their moment. Then one night, while watching The Temptations at a local club Brian Holland approached the four friends and asked them if they would go down to the Motown studios after the show because there was a tune the trio had that might just be the answer to the Four Tops' prayers. The song had been laying around for nearly 2 years, with the instrumental track already to go. "Baby I Need Your Loving" was dusted off for Levi Stubbs to work wonders with. In July of 1964 "Baby, I Need Your Loving" heralded the arrival of the Four Tops commercially and gave them a Number 11 pop hit and by the time the first Four Tops album was rushed out to cash in on the success of the single, the group was established. When you flipped the cover over what you saw was part of Holland-Dozier-Holland's future as the Four Tops sat mimicking the statue at whose feet they sat, Auguste Rodin's 'Thinker', the image that HDH would use as the design for their Invictus label in 1968 after they had left Motown. Unfortunately, this wasn't to be the Four Tops future. With the exception of 1965's "Ask the Lonely" and "Loving You Is Sweeter Than Ever" in 1966, Holland-Dozier-Holland were responsible for the producing and, again with two 1968 exceptions, the writing of fourteen hits including two number ones for the Four Tops.

When Holland-Dozier-Holland left, the Tops stayed but struggled to emulate the success they had become used to. Within their ranks they had a hidden gem though in Renaldo Benson. I have always considered 1970s "Still Waters Run Deep" co-written by Smokey Robinson and Frank Wilson, a fore runner to Marvin Gaye's 1971 "What's Going On" which Benson wrote after witnessing police brutality. Amazingly the Four Tops refused it because it was seen as a protest song. Joan Baez rejected it so Marvin Gaye was third time lucky.

Art & Soul

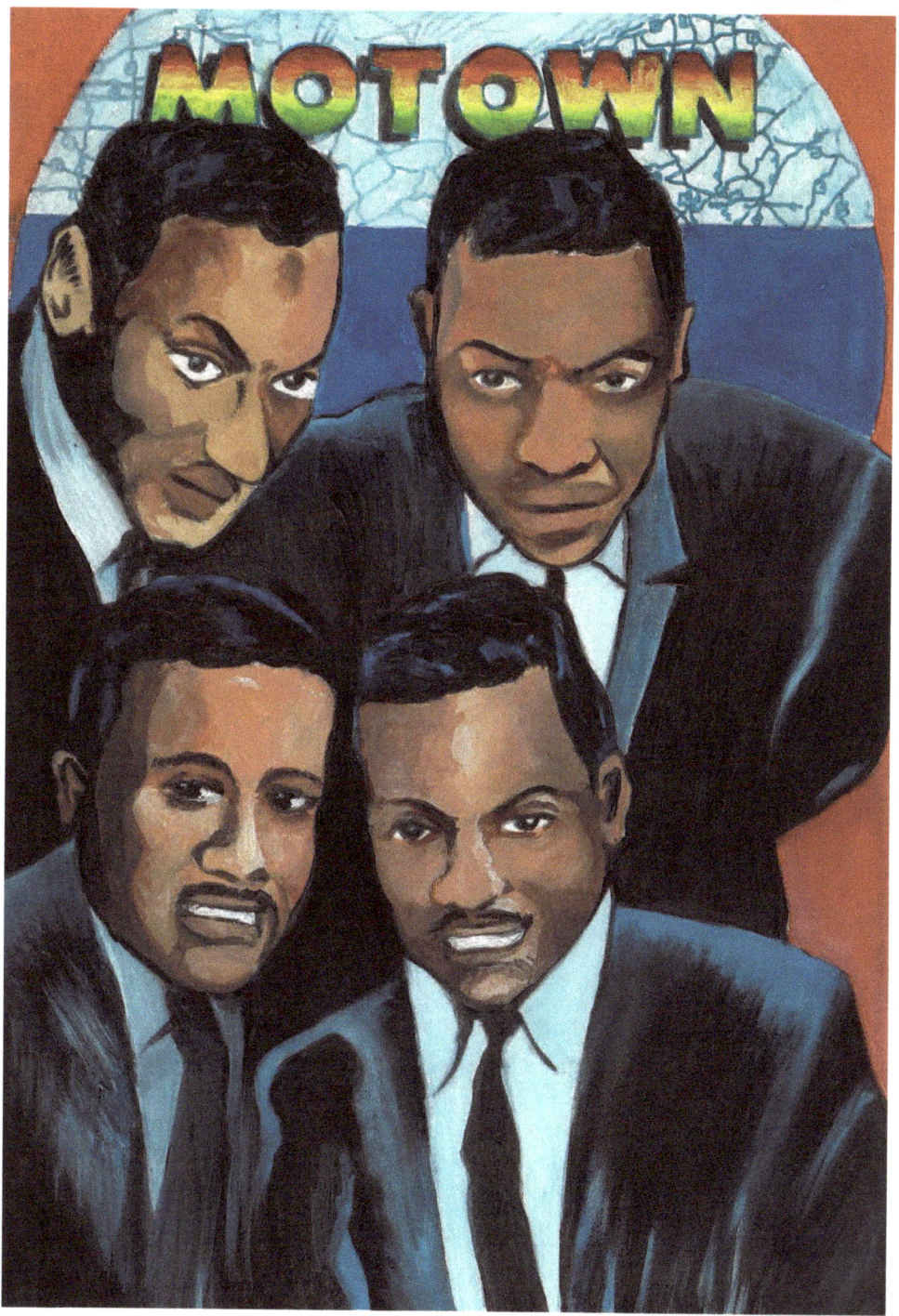

The Supremes

The Primettes, (who had started out as sister group to The Primes, a male quartet that included Eddie Kendricks and Paul Williams who would later form part of The Temptations), were attempting to push open the door of Motown. Robert Bateman had been responsible for inviting the girls to Motown to audition for the fledgling label but after the audition with Smokey Robinson the group was turned down and so signed to another local label, Lupine. However, group leader Florence Ballard was determined to work at Motown and so day in day out the group would hang around the Motown building doing background singing or handclaps until their determination was rewarded and they signed to the label in 1960. Florence Ballard changed the name of The Primettes to The Supremes and they debuted in 1961 with "I Want a Guy" recorded on the 9th of March, written by Freddie Gorman of The Voice Masters but the song failed to make any impact and they would remain in the shadows of the label's already established girl group, The Marvelettes for quite some time.

Gordy offered Robert Bateman the opportunity to manage The Supremes, he turned it down saying that "no one wanted to get involved with that skinny kid who sang through her nose". Having tasted success with The Marvelettes he seemed reluctant to take a chance with the new untried kids on the block. Under the guidance of Smokey Robinson, the 'no-hit Supremes', as they were cruelly nicknamed, kept up their track record with "Who's Loving You" in 1962. 1963 through to early '64 continued to be a lean period for The Supremes who could only look on with envy at the company's premiere girl group The Marvelettes who had grown from strength to strength from 1961 with their first number one "Please Mr. Postman" to become Motown's most consistent chart group. The Supremes fortunes changed because of one factor: the founder of the company seemed determined to make a star out of Diana Ross. A role Diana appeared to relish and a situation visibly evident within the structure of the group. Smokey Robinson had tried to work the same magic that he had conjured up for Mary Wells and The Miracles, this time though the spell was miscast and so another writer/production team had to be brought in, Holland-Dozier-Holland. "When the Love Light Starts Shining Thru His Eyes" reached Number 23 on the Pop Chart. This signalled a liaison that would remain until Holland-Dozier-Holland left Motown in 1968, giving The Supremes ten Number Ones starting with their second release by them, "Where Did Our Love Go", also in 1964.

Art & Soul

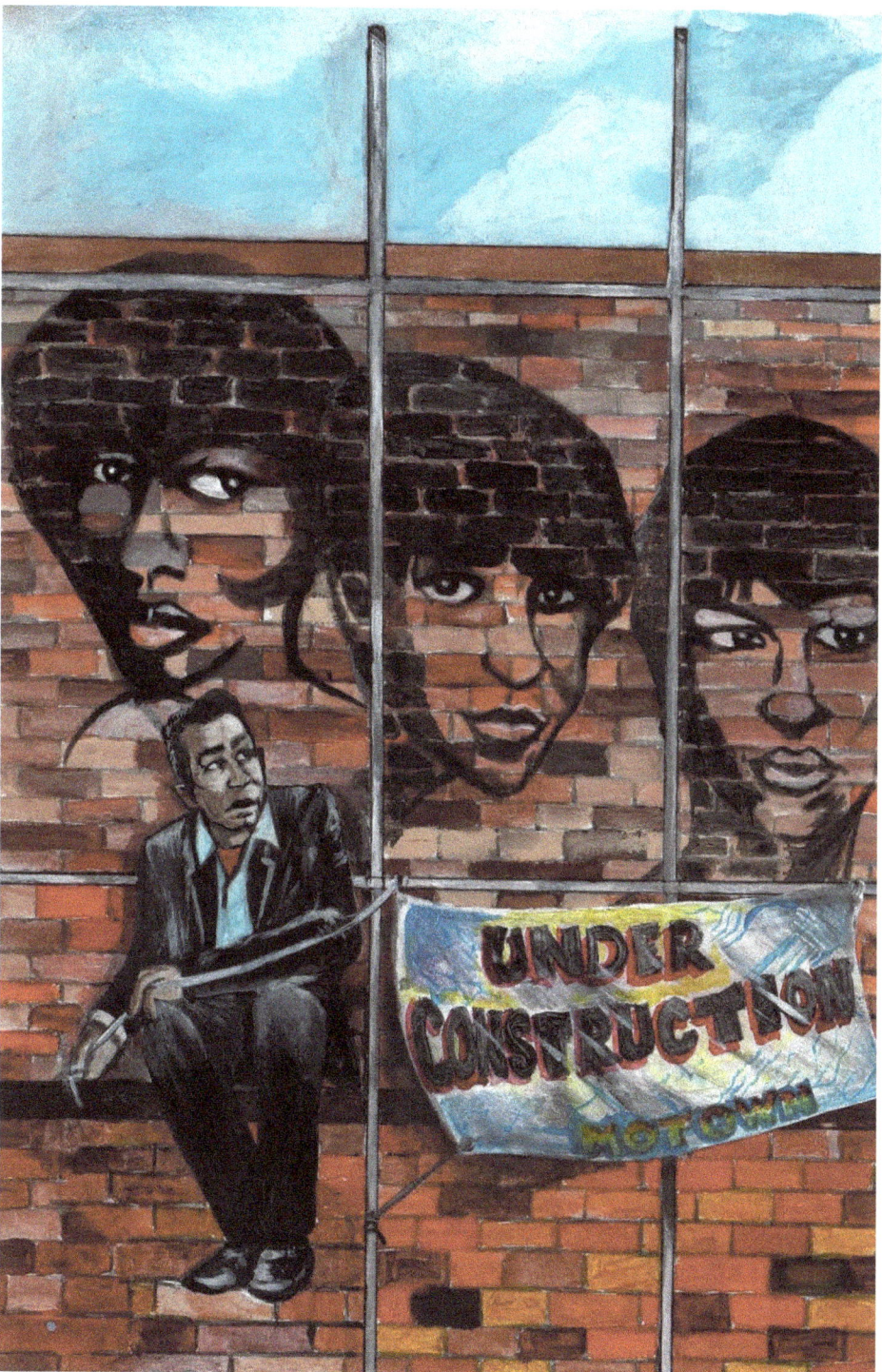

Laura Lee

Laura Lee was born in Chicago on March 9th, 1945 before moving after adoption to Detroit where she was raised by the Reverend E.A. Rundless. Her musical education began in Gospel, in Laura's case with The Meditation Singers, her adopted mother Mrs Ernestine Rundless' group. In an attempt to move across from Gospel into secular black music, Laura Lee removed the Rundless part of her name and in 1966 cut the Northern Soul Ric-Tic classic "To Win Your Heart". Because the situation at Ric-Tic was becoming increasingly rocky Chess took up Laura Lee's contract in 1967. A string of rocking dance and ballad tracks overseen by Rick Hall at his Fame studios in Muscle Shoals, Alabama followed. "Dirty Man" established her firmly in the non-Gospel arena and established her as a singer not to be overlooked. In April, 1968 "As Long As I Got You" was followed by her reading of Curtis Mayfield's "Need To Belong" and "Hang It Up". In 1969 Laura left Chess and remained without a contact until the following year when she was signed up to Hot Wax records, Holland-Dozier-Holland's post-Motown label. Her new career was launched with "Wedlock is a Padlock" but it was the follow-up, "Women's Love Rights" that really heralded her arrival back on the scene. The stunning debut album by Laura Lee entered the Soul chart at number 42 finally rising to number 3. "Love And Liberty" was doing the business for her in the singles market and Lee remained in denial about the liberation path she seemed to be treading. What she was doing, however, was clearing the way for artists like Millie Jackson to make a far more commercial living out of this formula. Laura Lee's emotive handling of the standard "Since I Fell for You" was a change of pace for Hot Wax's leading lady and Laura responded magnificently launching a successful attack on the singles chart reaching the Soul Top Ten. The album version lasting some ten minutes as Lee told us about the day she met 'him' and the relationship that blossomed only to die. When she led in with her singing, the grip on your emotions was so tight that you could almost scream along with her, a moment only equalled by and comparable to the feeling you got from Linda Jones' handling of "Your Precious Love". She left the company around 1974 and returned to church. The Reverend Al Green, benefited from Laura Lee's mighty lungs on their rendition of Curtis Mayfield's "People Get Ready" in 1983 and released "Jesus is the Light of My Life" on Myrrh Records. Laura Lee preferred to remain within the Church and in 1985 released "All Power" on Circle City Records. If you're listening to Laura Lee, you will experience not only women's love rights but also those love wrongs.

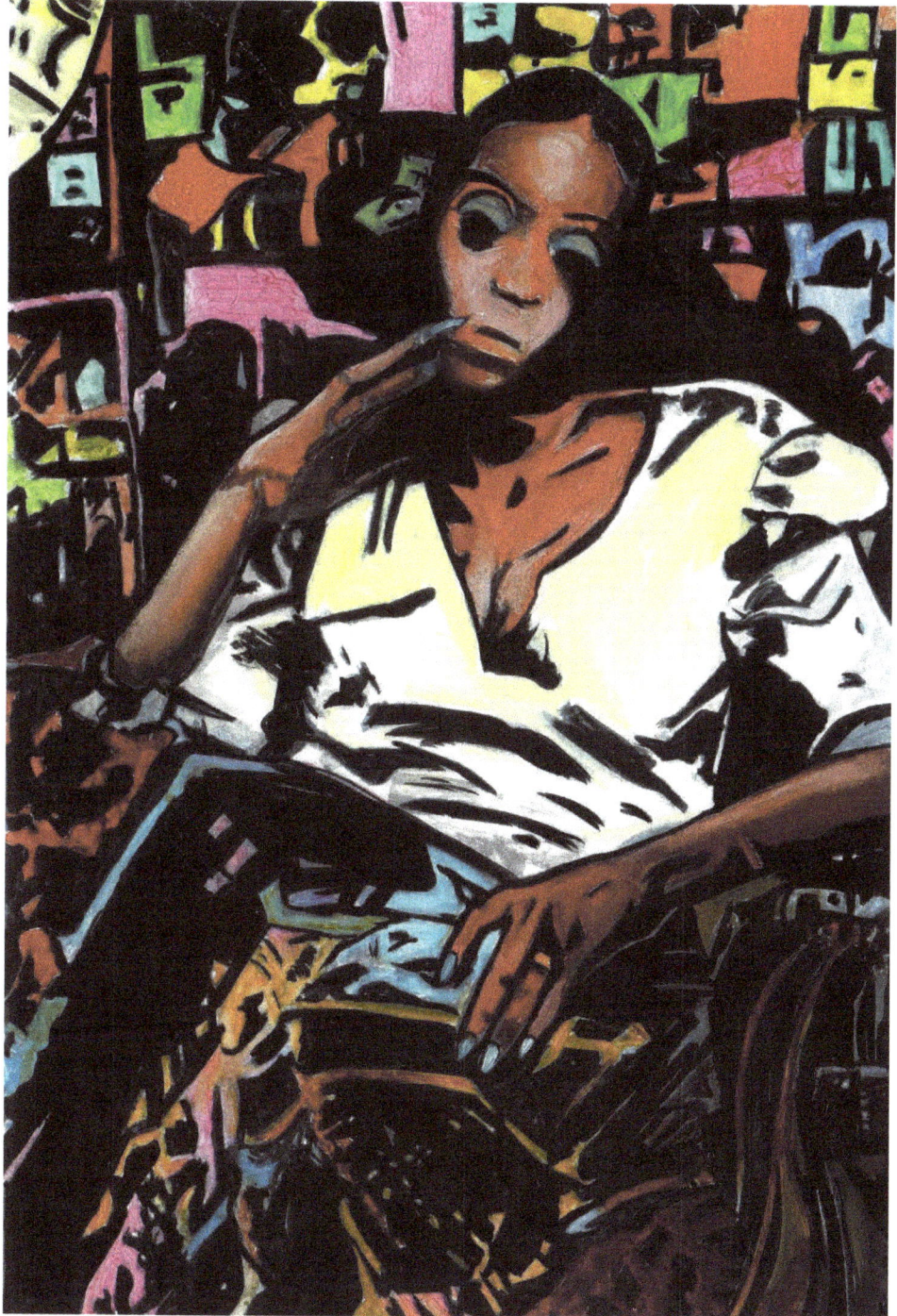

Holland Dozier Holland

The Motown sound was honed to perfection by three young hopefuls: Brian Holland, Lamont Dozier and Eddie Holland. This music making machine started to make major irreversible changes in Detroit's new commercial enterprise whilst working for the biggest of them all, Motown. As Gordy's Empire grew so too did Dozier's song writing activities, even though he was still ambitious to become a singer. In 1957 Brian Holland came to be the lead singer with The Satintones, a Rhythm & Blues vocal group and also had an early Berry Gordy release, in 1958, "(Where's The Joy?) In Nature Boy". Eddie Holland joined The Quailtones for a brief period before bringing along his brother Brian to form part of the Fidelitones. In the same year, Eddie Holland had had an unsuccessful solo baptism into the music business when Berry Gordy released "You" on Mercury by Holland. A struggling songwriter Gordy, a cousin of Jackie Wilson, chanced upon Wilson's manager who was searching for material for him. Gordy was able to get Wilson to record "Lonely Teardrops" and "Reet Petite". Gordy had met Eddie Holland at the Graystone Ballroom in Detroit when Holland, aged 16 and having a vocal range not dissimilar to Jackie Wilson vocally, became the featured session singer on demos for Wilson and continued working with him until 1959 prior to his fulltime involvement in Motown.

Now Gordy was hiring studio time and musicians as well as developing a team of songwriters that included Lamont Dozier, grooming a sound engineer called Brian Holland and staying true to a sometime singer, Eddie Holland. By 1963 the newly formed team's success began with the first official Holland-Dozier-Holland release "Come and Get These Memories" by Martha & The Vandellas which gave everybody involved their first major hit, after its release reached Number 29 on the National Pop Chart. With "Come and Get These Memories" not only did Holland Dozier Holland begin to make noises at Motown and throughout the country but globally. Their unique writing was a golden age for Motown and brought to international attention not only Martha & The Vandellas but the Four Tops, The Supremes and Marvin Gaye. After the Holland-Dozier-Holland team had approached Gordy about money without satisfaction they had gone on a 'go-slow'. Gordy would call Brian Holland's office then Eddie Holland's to find neither of them around. After checking up he discovered a two-month period of inactivity. The war was about to start, Motown firing the first shot in the Wayne County Circuit court on the 29th of August 1968, asking Holland-Dozier-Holland to pay damages of $4 million and further asking the court to restrain them from doing work for any other record company.

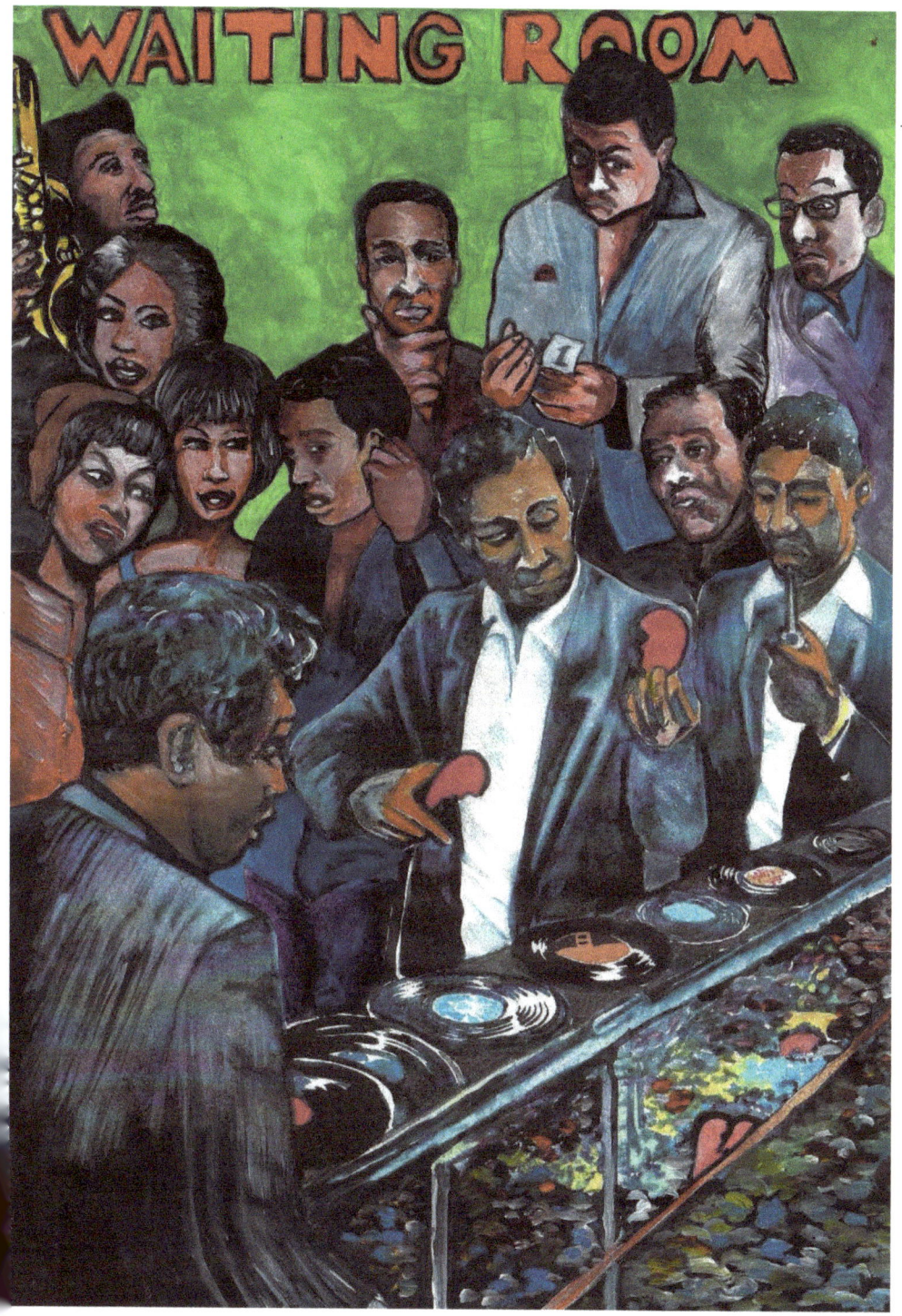

General Johnson

After hearing "It Will Stand" by The Showmen, Brian Holland was determined to get the band's charismatic singer General Norman Johnson signed to their Invictus label. The Chairmen of The Board were an attempt to fill the gap left by The Four Tops for Holland, Dozier and Holland. As well as fronting the Chairmen, Johnson was one of Invictus' most prolific writers and producers working alongside Greg Perry. Prior to becoming a Board member Johnson had fronted The Showmen from Norfolk, Virginia for ten years. The first time the Chairmen met each other was in 1969. There had been various prospective Chairmen and two years had passed during which time Johnson had been locked away, living in Lamont Dozier's Detroit home writing material for the group and their self-titled album established his unique style with both their debut single "Give Me Just a Little More Time" and follow-up, "You've Got Me Dangling On a String". Johnson had begged for one of his new co-compositions on the album, "Patches", to be the follow up to their first single but HDH insisted that they had a better choice and "Patches" became a hit for Clarence Carter instead. "Somebody's Been Sleeping In My Bed" by 100 Proof Aged In Soul was written by Johnson with Greg Perry and lyricist Angelo Bond and after a series of their own minor hits, their latest, a potential Number 1 just around the corner, "Elmore James. This country-tinged song trod the path of "Patches". The new sets from Honey Cone and 100 Proof had Johnson's stamp on them and by the time the third Chairman album appeared Johnson and Perry were the most fruitful partnership HDH could boast. Johnson's solo career had not been the anticipated success with his first and second singles bombing but in 1972 he was honoured as R&B Songwriter of the Year by BMI and at the beginning of 1973 a new album by Johnson was announced but like before it was commercially unsuccessful. Shortly after Johnson left the company and left Detroit simply because he had needed a complete break from the turmoil he had found there and three years later released a self-titled album on Arista cut in New York, but the association was again a less than happy one. The music scene was changing to disco and Johnson felt that artists like Smokey Robinson, for example, were struggling to come to terms with this new style, so he moved to North Carolina to get away from everything for a while. The freedom he had previously been denied suddenly became his, once he found his way to the beach! For in Beach music, Johnson discovered a virtually untapped gold vein that he was able to prospect.

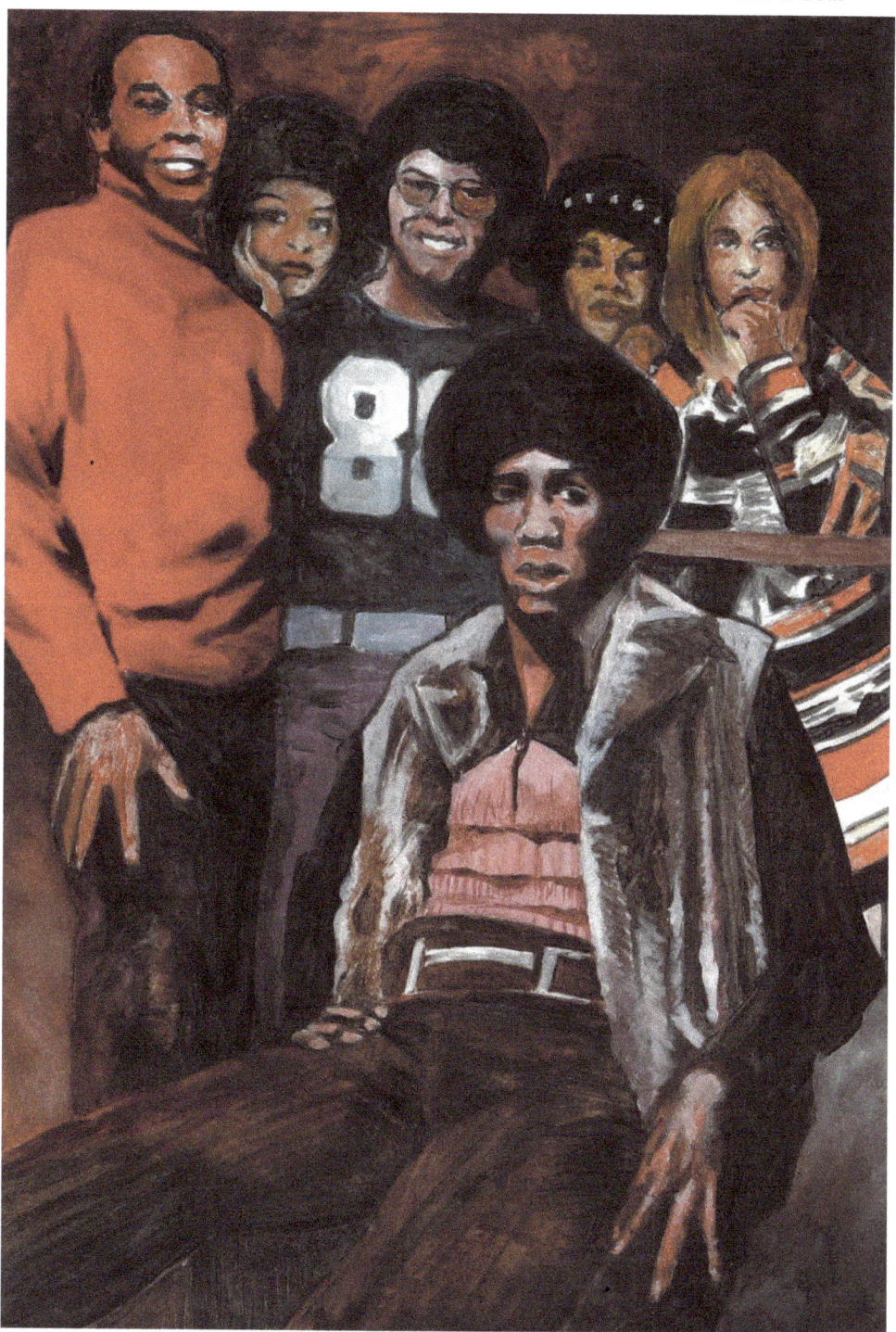

Little Willie John

I was first made aware of Little Willie John because of my brother's Fleetwood Mac collection. During Peter Green's tenure with them he sang "Need Your Love So Bad" which started my journey into finding out more about the person who not only sang it but wrote it. Although William Edward John was born in Cullendale, Arkansas on November the 15th 1937, his family moved to Detroit when he was four so his father could find work in the city's factories. By the end of the forties the elder children formed a Gospel group whilst Willie went on his own performing in local talent shows. He caught the attention of Johnny Otis who tried to recruit him but he was too young. However, Henry Glover who was himself a musician as well as an arranger and writer got him signed to King Records in 1955. He had immediate success with his cover of Titus Turner's "All Around the World" reaching Number 5 on the Billboard R&B chart. This was followed by the original version of "Need Your Love So Bad" that he wrote with his older brother Mertis. In 1956 he recorded "Fever" before Peggy Lee re-invented it two years later. John's version went gold and gave him an R&B number one and a pop success with a number 24 position. 1958 saw another gold award for "Talk To Me", also another national pop hit. Throughout his career Little Willie John, so called because of his height, had fourteen pop hits. Also, that year he performed alongside Ray Charles and Sam Cooke at the Cavalcade of Jazz concert in Los Angeles. Remember that like those two he was one of the pioneers of what would become Soul but in 1958 it hadn't yet been labelled. In 1964 he performed at a benefit concert for the NAACP (National Association for the Advancement of Coloured People) supporting the Civil Rights Movement which warranted his reputation as a caring and giving person but there was another side to his nature. He was known for his alcohol abuse and was arrested several times for grand larceny, swindling and drugs but worst of all was his short temper which sealed his fate. In 1963 King Records dropped him because of his behaviour and the slowing down of interest in his music; then in 1965 he was convicted of manslaughter for the stabbing of Kendal Row in Seattle, 1964.

He was incarcerated at Washington State Penitentiary where he was later admitted into the hospital for pneumonia and where he was rumoured to have been strangled on May the 26th, 1968. The death certificate read heart attack. In December, King Records released James Brown's album "Thinking About Little Willie John and a Few Nice Things". Brown who had opened shows for Little Willie John had always stated that he was the greatest singer he'd ever heard. He was posthumously inducted into the Rock and Roll Hall of Fame in 1996 and to paraphrase, his music continues to mesmerise people 'all around the world'.

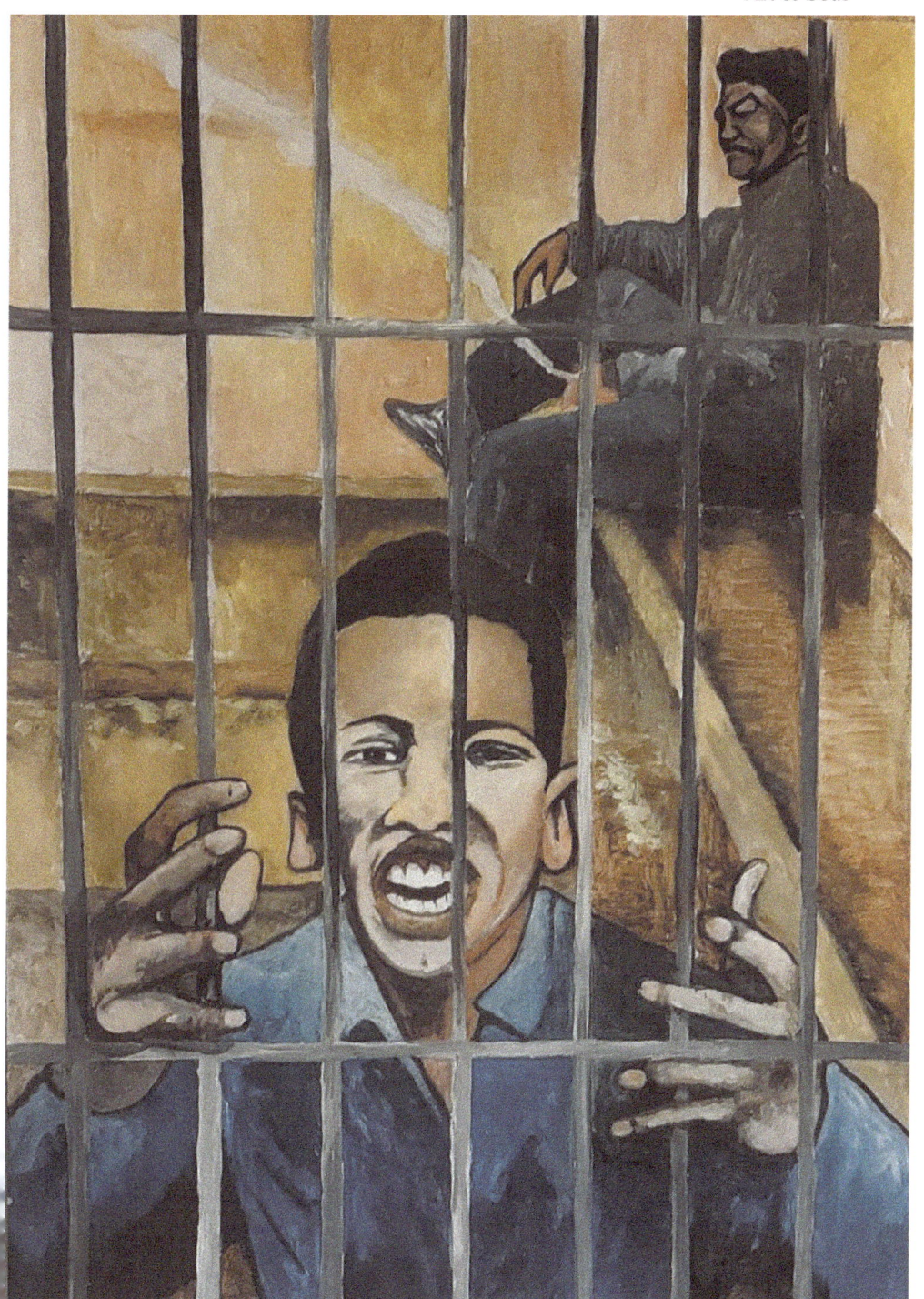

Marvin Gaye

In 1971 I had just gone 15 and remember requesting this album for my birthday and being allowed to play it a day early, I just couldn't wait to hear it and was disappointed. However, I wasn't alone in this feeling. Without any consultation with the man, I later found that my opinion was shared by Berry Gordy Jr. as well as many music critics of the time. Perhaps the impatience of youth was to be my punishment, maybe I wasn't meant to appreciate the album before it was time to. When Marvin Gaye cut this album, he had just come out of self-exile after mourning the death of his stage and recording partner Tammi Terrell that had shifted him into a state of depression and drug dependency. Locked in the studio and stalking Motown like a ghost, Marvin Gaye finally resurfaced with the single, "What's Going On". The Motown sound had begun to disappear: Marvin Gaye had belonged to that earlier empire and his previous product remained steeped in that Motown mould. Nobody was prepared for this release and that is possibly why it received lukewarm reviews; very often this is the way with anything new and untried. The simple fact is that this is a damned fine album and is why it has been elevated to the top of many critics lists of greatest albums of all time. Marvin must have known that had struck gold and could feel a sense of achievement in going against the establishment that was Motown, an ongoing exercise that he had throughout his turbulent career. That said, this is an essential, if not THE essential Soul album to own. It departs from love songs, although the message of hope could be deemed a message of love. It is more a collection of questions from "What's Going On" through to the final "Inner City Blues". The structure itself departed from the norm and predates Stevie Wonder's production technique of commencing a track before the previous one had ended, fairly innovative for Soul music. The saddest part is that the message remains as pertinent today as it did the day it was recorded. The tracks question the state of the world, soldiers returning from Vietnam, drug abuse, fears for the children, God, ecological issues and inner-city conditions by a master who was aided by fine David Van DePitte arrangements and the Motown instrumentalists known as the Funk Brothers being given freedom to explore their undoubted skills. "Inner City Blues" stops and a lone piano introduces Marvin repeating lines from "What's Going On" before fading away into musical history. It isn't the longest album but is testimony to the fact that quality counts above quantity. In 1971 there were many changes in Soul music and the truth is that 52 years later, you should listen to this album as it might just help you to understand what's going on.^

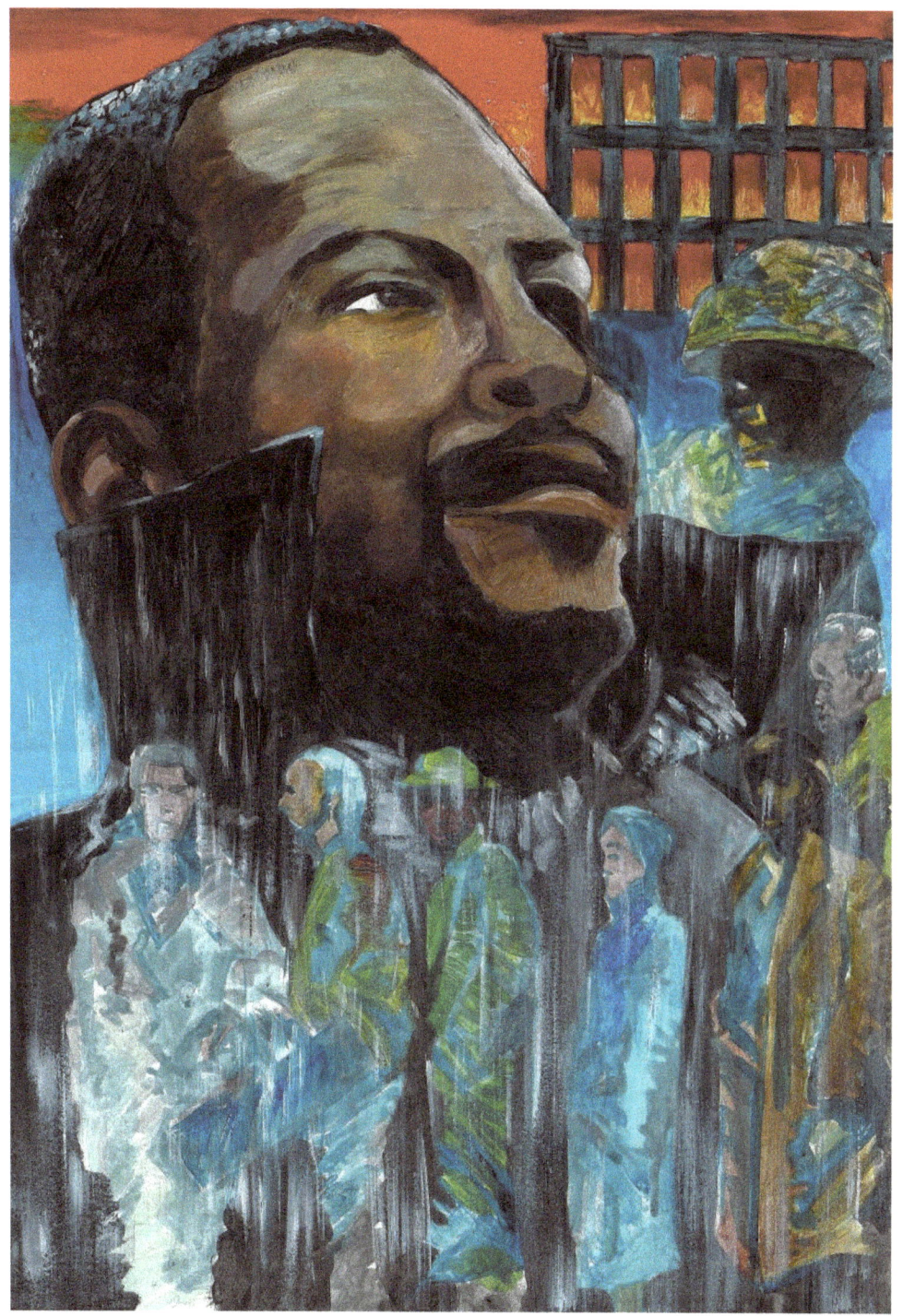

Tammi Terrell

Tammi Terrell was born Thomasina Winifred Montgomery in Philadelphia to Jennie and Thomas Montgomery on April the 29th, 1945. At the age of eleven she was raped by three boys and shortly after started to suffer from migraines. Her musical career began as a teenager, recording "If You See Bill" for Scepter Records in 1960 under the name of Tammy Montgomery. She also cut demos for The Shirelles before spending nearly nine months as a member of James Brown's Revue and recording "I Cried" for his Try Me label. In 1962 and still only seventeen she became involved in a relationship with Brown. A year later and after Brown assaulted her for not watching his full show, she walked out but later walked into another abusive relationship, this time at Motown the label she signed to in 1965 after a brief stint at the Checker label where she cut "If I Would Marry You", a duet with Jimmy Radcliffe, which she co-wrote. After working alongside Jerry Butler, she performed at Detroit's Twenty Grand Club where Berry Gordy saw her and signed her up to Motown. In 1966 she joined the Motortown Revue and started a relationship with David Ruffin. That same year he proposed to her but after announcing the engagement on stage she found out that he was married with three children and another girlfriend in Detroit. Ruffin's addiction to drugs led to violent arguments which often led to her getting headaches. In 1967 it ended between them after Ruffin hit her over the head with his motorcycle helmet. As a solo artist her music career was going nowhere but in that same year her first album with Marvin started a positive high point which should have helped her away from the negativity that seemed to surround her as far as relationships went. "United" included "Ain't No Mountain High Enough" which was nominated for Best Rhythm & Blues Performance at the 10th Annual Grammy awards in 1968 but was later inducted into the Grammy Hall of Fame in 1999. On October 17th while performing at Hampden-Sydney College, Tammi collapsed into Marvin Gaye's arms and was later diagnosed as having a brain tumour. Despite this news "You're All I Need to Get By" was released the next year with the title track released as a single alongside "Ain't Nothing Like the Real Thing". As well as this her solo album, "Irresistible" was also issued and in 1969 a third album by the two was released, "Easy" which was far from the truth. Singles included "The Onion Song" written by Valerie Simpson and Nick Ashford and because of Tammi's failing health, Valerie Simpson sang most of her parts. By 1970 Tammi Terrell was in a wheelchair, experiencing blindness and hair loss and after her eighth operation she died on March 24th at the age of 24. Her funeral took place at Janes Methodist Church in Philadelphia and Marvin Gaye gave a final eulogy. He was all she needed to get by.

Art & Soul

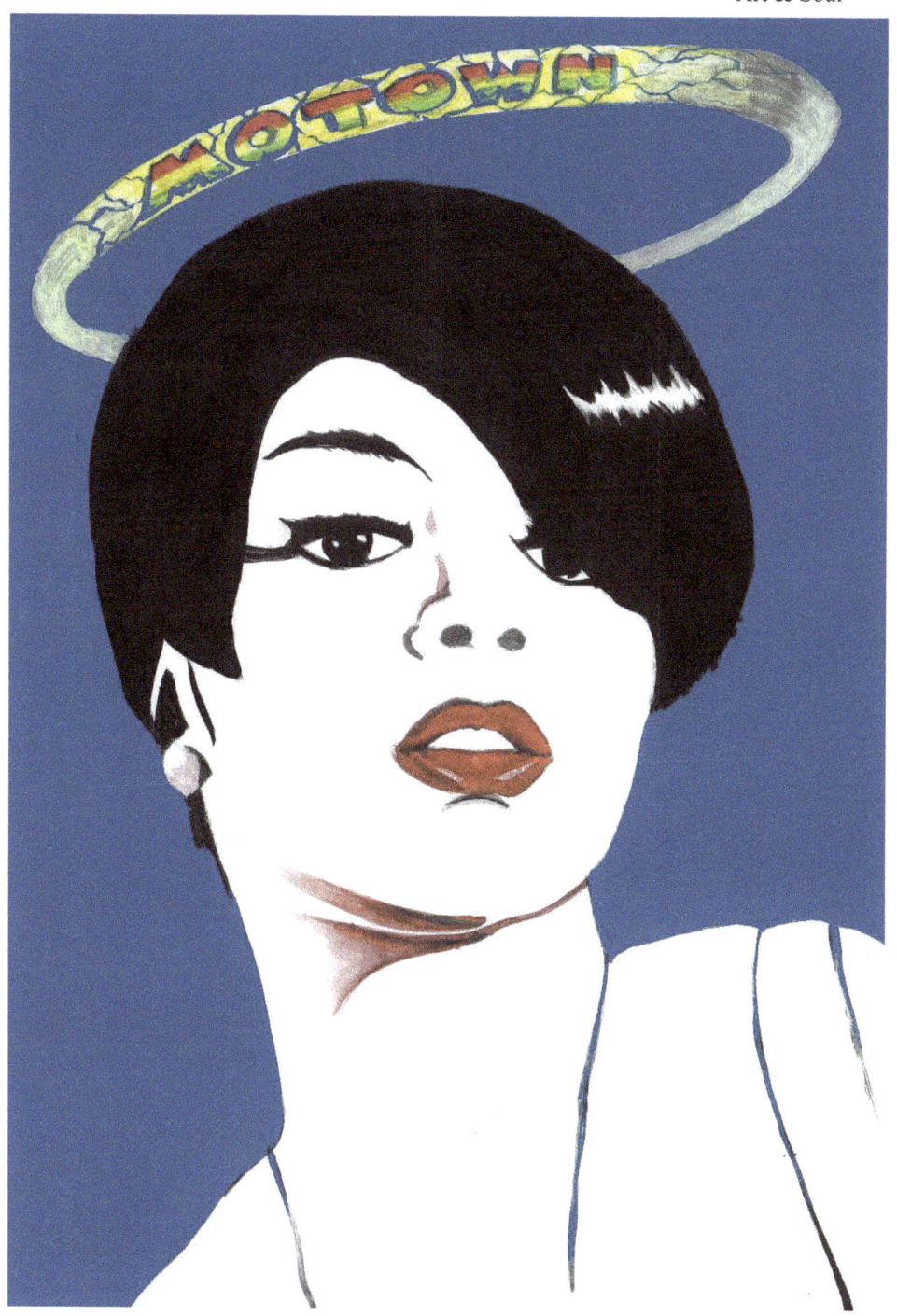

Stevie Wonder

Stevland Hardaway Judkins was born blind due to oxygen starvation on May 13th, 1950. Normally I would use the term visually impaired, but an impairment suggests a disability. As Stevie Wonder he is a multi-instrumentalist, songwriter, record producer and a civil rights activist so argue away. We the 'enabled' can very quickly create disabilities in others. At the age of 11 he sang his own song, "Lonely Boy" to Ronnie White of The Miracles who then arranged for Stevie and his mother to go for an audition at Motown records. He was signed to the Tamla imprint where Clarence Paul dubbed him 'Little Stevie Wonder'. Their first two albums working together were "Tribute to Uncle Ray" where Wonder paid tribute to his musical hero Ray Charles and "The Jazz Soul of Little Stevie". Already Stevie was including his own compositions on these sets. It was felt that Wonder was ready to hit the singles market and although he had a song "Mother Thank You" planned, the debut belonged to Berry Gordy with "I Call It Pretty Music but The Old People Call It the Blues". For now, the planned success failed but by the end of 1962, when he was still only 12, he was added to the Motortown Revue and at the Regal Theatre in Chicago a 20 minute live set was recorded. A year later the latest album "Recorded Live: The 12 Year' Old Genius" was a game changer. From it came "Fingertips". This had him highlighting his harmonica and bongo skills and the track hit the top spot on the R&B Chart. By 1964 the lack of success led Berry Gordy to consider cancelling his contract but writer Sylvia Moy asked him to give Wonder another go. Gordy agreed and success came in 1966 with "Uptight" and from there everything was alright, outta sight! That spurred Wonder to write for other Motown acts and in 1966 he supplied The Contours with "Just a Little Misunderstanding" followed a year later "Tears Of a Clown" for Smokey Robinson & The Miracles. His own hits continued with "For Once In My Life", "I Was Made To Love Her" and "My Cherie Amour", amongst many. When he was 20 in 1970, he married Rita Wright who was making inroads into the company. The marriage didn't last as long as their musical legacy but their artistic collaboration continued after their divorce. They talked about their commitment to making their lyrics far more meaningful and reflective to the world's social problems which became more relevant to Wonder in later years. At this time songs composed by Wonder and Wright together included Wonder's "If You Really Love Me" "Signed, Sealed, Delivered I'm Yours", Wonder's first production and The Spinners' "It's A Shame". In 1971 Wonder released the album "Where I'm Coming From" which really heralded where he was going to.

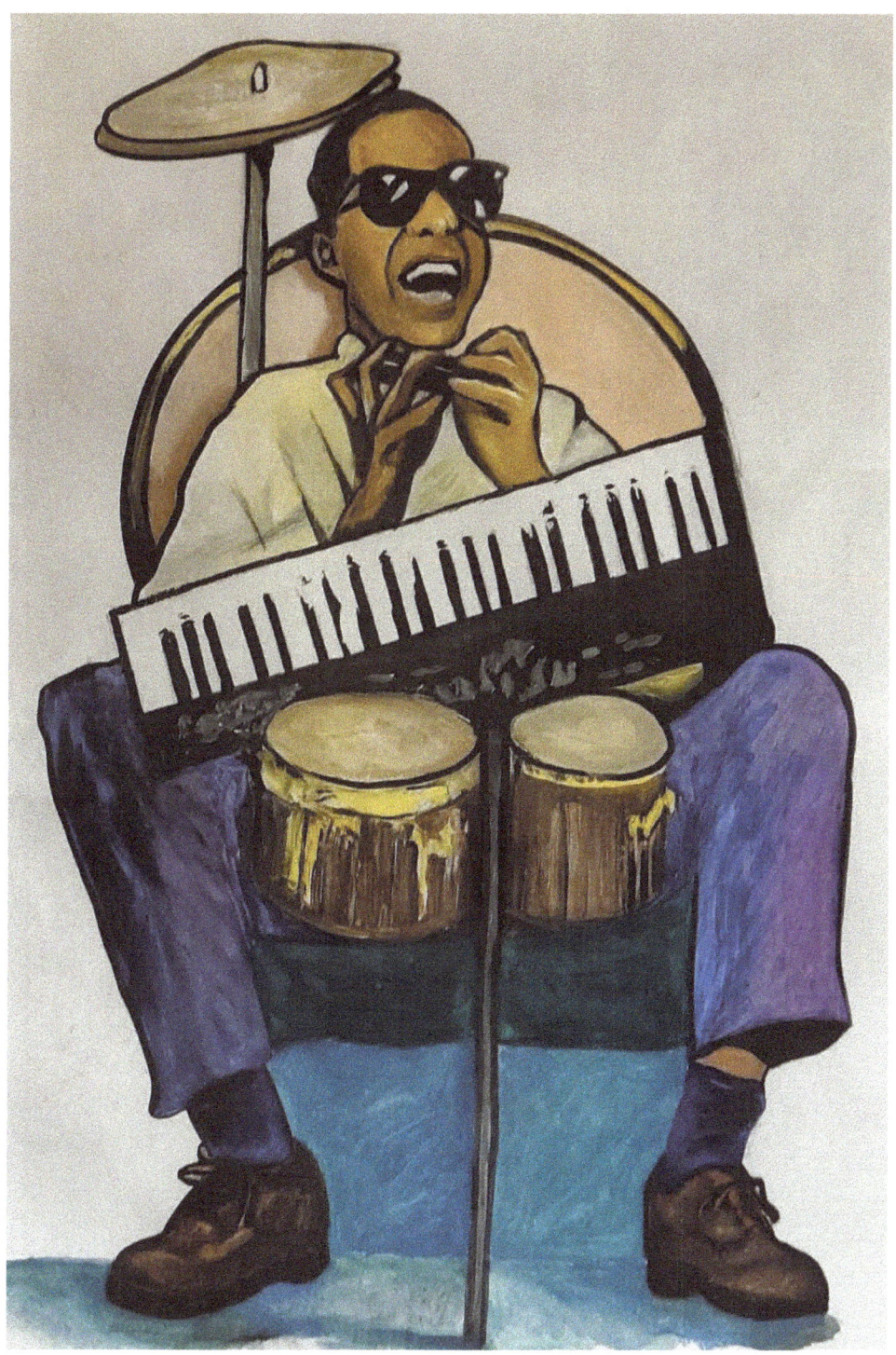

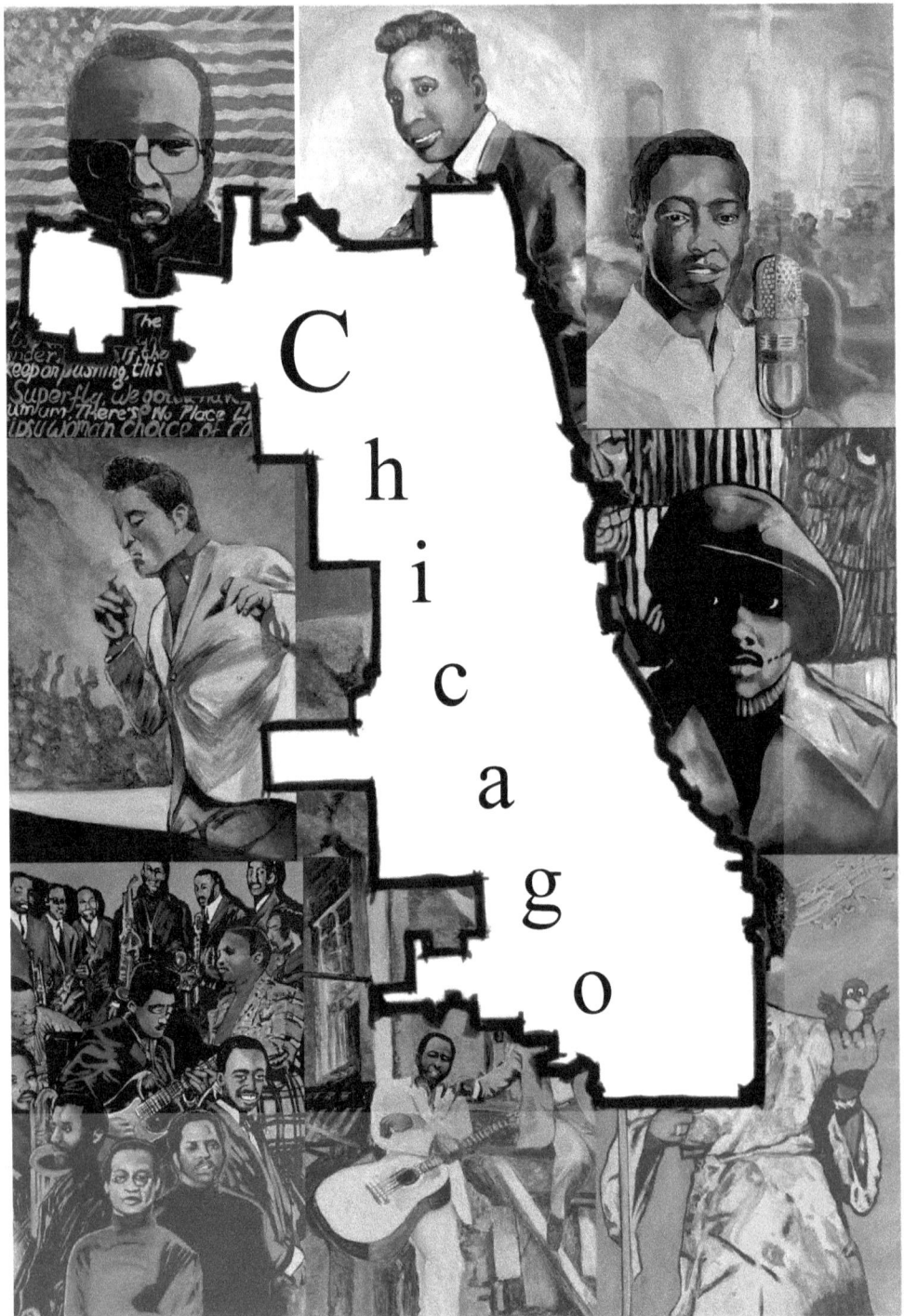

Art & Soul

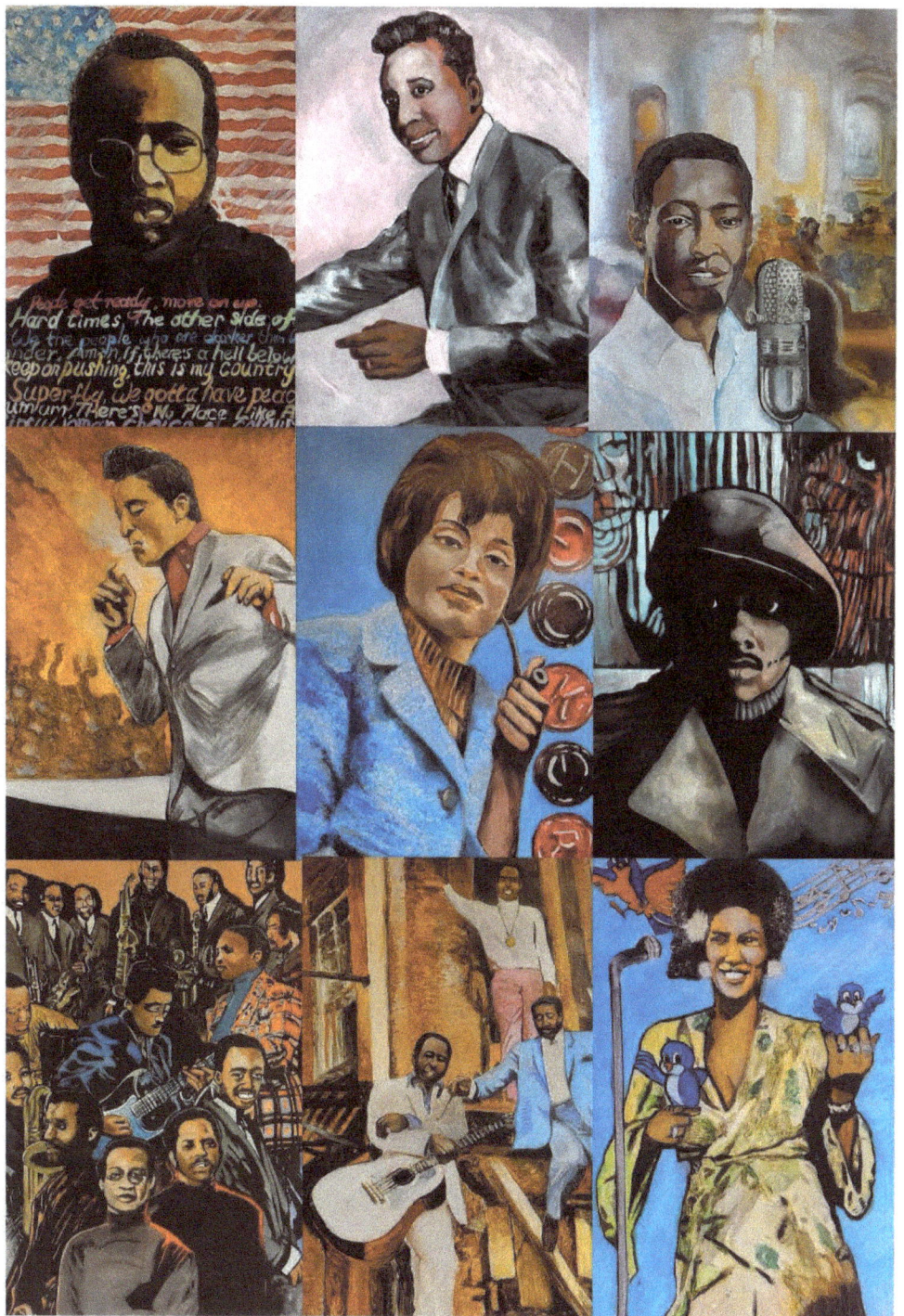

Chicago Musicians

As far as musicians laying down tracks for other artists, at Chess there was Donny Hathaway who played keyboard along with former Motown funk brother Johnny Griffith. Charles Stepney played organ and vibraphone as well as being a songwriter/producer and arranger working alongside Maurice White of Earth, Wind & Fire. Stepney was often assisted by renowned guitarist Phil Upchurch. Throughout their histories artists and producers who crossed the state line to create individual yet related sounds in the Windy City seemed to be more disjointed than in Detroit. Generally, Soul coming out of Chicago belonged to a few self-contained units or session musicians brought in to add their virtuosity to the musical needs of the times as dictated by individual artists. Hathaway's initial set was entitled "Everything Is Everything". The album included contributions from Phil Upchurch who co-wrote the title track as well as Henry Gibson on congas, a musician who became a prominent fixture on Curtis Mayfield's material and Willie Henderson on baritone saxophone. As a child, Henderson had moved with his family to Chicago where he started to play the saxophone. While in his twenties some of his earliest work was with Alvin Cash and by 1968 he had started to work for Brunswick Records as studio bandleader where he produced a slew of top Chicago soul artists alongside Carl Davis. Henderson also released several singles in 1970 on Brunswick as Willie Henderson and the Soul Explosions and in 1974 "Dance Master", "Break Your Back" and "Gangster Boogie Bump" were released by Henderson after leaving Dakar and moving to Playboy Records. Pianist, arranger and producer Thomas Clay Washington, also known as Tom Tom, was Chicago born and bred, being raised in the Ida B. Wells projects on Chicago's South Side. He first played drums before taking up keyboards and then becoming an arranger. When Motown relocated to Los Angeles in 1972 and on advice given by Quincy Jones about signing for a smaller company, former Motown drummer and bandleader Hamilton Bohannon, having made the decision to stay local signed to Chicago's Dakar label. Between 1973 and 1975 another Chicago's Southside Movement arrived on the scene, originally signed to the Wand label after being the band behind Simtec & Wylie who were signed to Gene Chandler's Mr Chand label and who had a hit with 1971's "Gotta Get Over the Hump". The group was made up from guitarist Bobby Pointer, keyboardist Morris Beeks, bassist Ronald Simmons, drummer Willie Hayes, alto saxophonist Milton Johnson, trumpeter Stephen Hawkins and trombonist Bill McFarland.

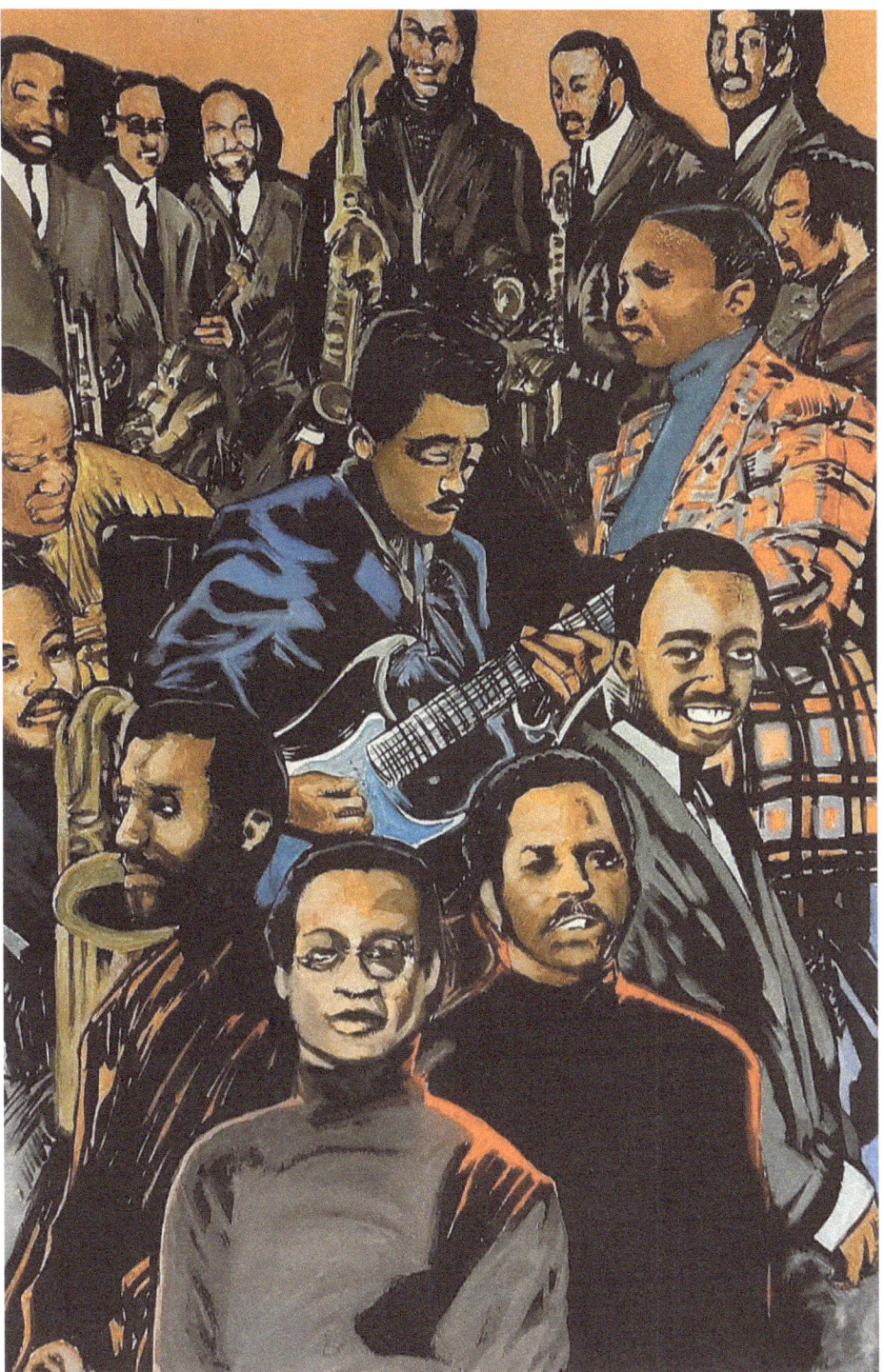

Chicago Soul

At the beginning of Soul music everyone was in the running to be top dog. As time would tell, it was neighbouring Detroit that would overshadow the Soul scene in Chicago despite the fact that the recording industry of Chicago was in full bloom long before Berry Gordy created his Empire in Detroit. Without the Chicago connection Motown could have been a different proposition. As well as being the adopted home of the acknowledged Father of Soul, Sam Cooke, the Chess Label of Chicago would be responsible for early distribution of Motown productions by amongst others, The Miracles whilst native Detroiter, Jackie Wilson more recognised as a product of Chicago Soul would give Gordy early success as a writer with "Reet Petite" and "Lonely Teardrops. Throughout their histories artists and producers have crossed the state line to create individual yet related sounds: a fourteen-year-old Detroiter named Aretha Franklin would record early tracks for Chess in 1956 and The Four Tops would sign for the Chess Brothers prior to signing for Motown. Whilst Etta James, one of the stalwarts of Chess Records through original cuts like "I'd Rather Go Blind " had reached Number One in 1960 with "All I Could Do Was Cry ", written by Berry Gordy along with his sister Gwen and Billy Davis. Along with Chess Records, Vee Jay would be fundamental in forming the ever-growing Chicago Soul scene for along with The Dells, the label was home to The Impressions who boasted Curtis Mayfield and Jerry Butler amongst its members. Like VeeJay before it Okeh was not simply a Soul label but was responsible for many classic sides. Behind the success of Okeh was the man who may have been without the muscle of Berry Gordy but who would remain from the earliest stages in Chicago Soul's development until the curtain came down on its sound, Carl Davis. Carl Davis was offered an A&R job at Columbia Records and here he took over the creative handling of its subsidiary, Okeh one of the recording industry's oldest labels; a dormant label previously regarded as a 'Race music' label but soon to reach legendary status - ignoring the fact that Davis failed to sign The Jackson Five, Kenny Gamble (who would later team up with Leon Huff to conceive The Philly Sound) and the team of Isaac Hayes and David Porter (who would find fame at Stax). Davis planned to create a Chicago sound on par with Motown: he intended to develop a Curtis Mayfield, Johnny Pate (noted arranger) Carl Davis Sound. Unfortunately, Okeh's allegiance was shifted within The Columbia corporation and Davis's new team leader didn't share the vision.

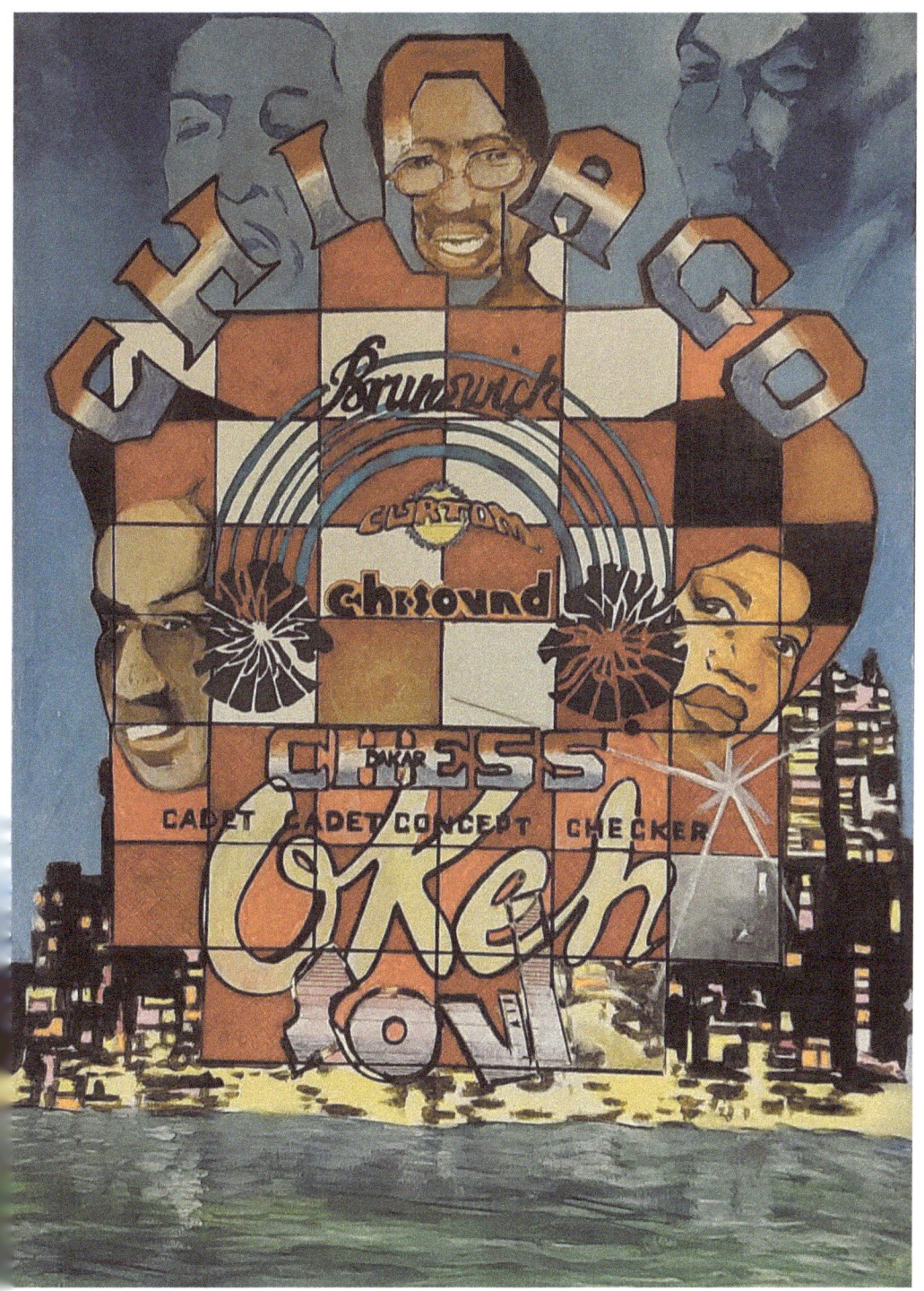

The Impressions

In Chicago the Veejay label was home to The Impressions who boasted Curtis Mayfield and who would serve the city well as an artist/writer/producer and label owner. Curtis was born in Chicago and was a member of his Grandmother's choir the Travelling Soul Spiritualistic, where he became friends with a fellow traveller Jerry Butler. Curtis was also making inroads into the secular side of music as leader of his own group The Alphatones. Butler persuaded Mayfield to join him and brothers Arthur and Richard Brooks with Sam Gooden to form firstly The Roosters followed by a quick name change to The Impressions. In 1958 the group signed to VeeJay and had a breakthrough with "For Your Precious Love". The rise of black consciousness was beginning to show through Mayfield's ever developing lyrics. Threads wove through these compositions, "Keep On Pushing" and "Amen" both from 1964, "People Get Ready" a year later and "Meeting Over Yonder" in 1966 reflected the Civil Rights struggle and the faith attached to it. In 1968 the Curtom label co-owned by Curtis and Eddie Thomas was formed and Mayfield's lyrical direction changed quite radically. New influences within both general Pop music and more directly with the Sly Stone approach to black music began to give compositions a harder edge both musically and lyrically. Black politics had started to change too. The mounting black deaths, riots and the recently assassinated Dr Martin Luther King led many African Americans to seek other solutions. Mayfield, while appearing apolitical used his music to express to a community his fears and hopes for the future. In 1968, The Impressions released "We're a Winner" it was considered too political for white radio stations and subsequently ignored. This was the group's final outing for ABC before switching to Curtom and whether it was an intentional act of defiance or not Curtis took the 'we're a winner' and added it to the label's logo design. The group's first release on Curtom, "Fool for You" was followed by another Mayfield political statement, "This Is My Country".

More of the same followed with "Choice of Colours", "Mighty, Mighty, Spade and Whitey" and albums like "Check Out Your Mind" released in 1969, making further socially relevant points known. The lyrical content of the material began to outweigh the musical contribution and it seemed only a matter of time before the group would have to go through yet another change. The Impressions needed to retain an identity at the same time as the name of Curtis Mayfield was sounding louder as a voice to be listened to. In 1970 the decision to separate was made.

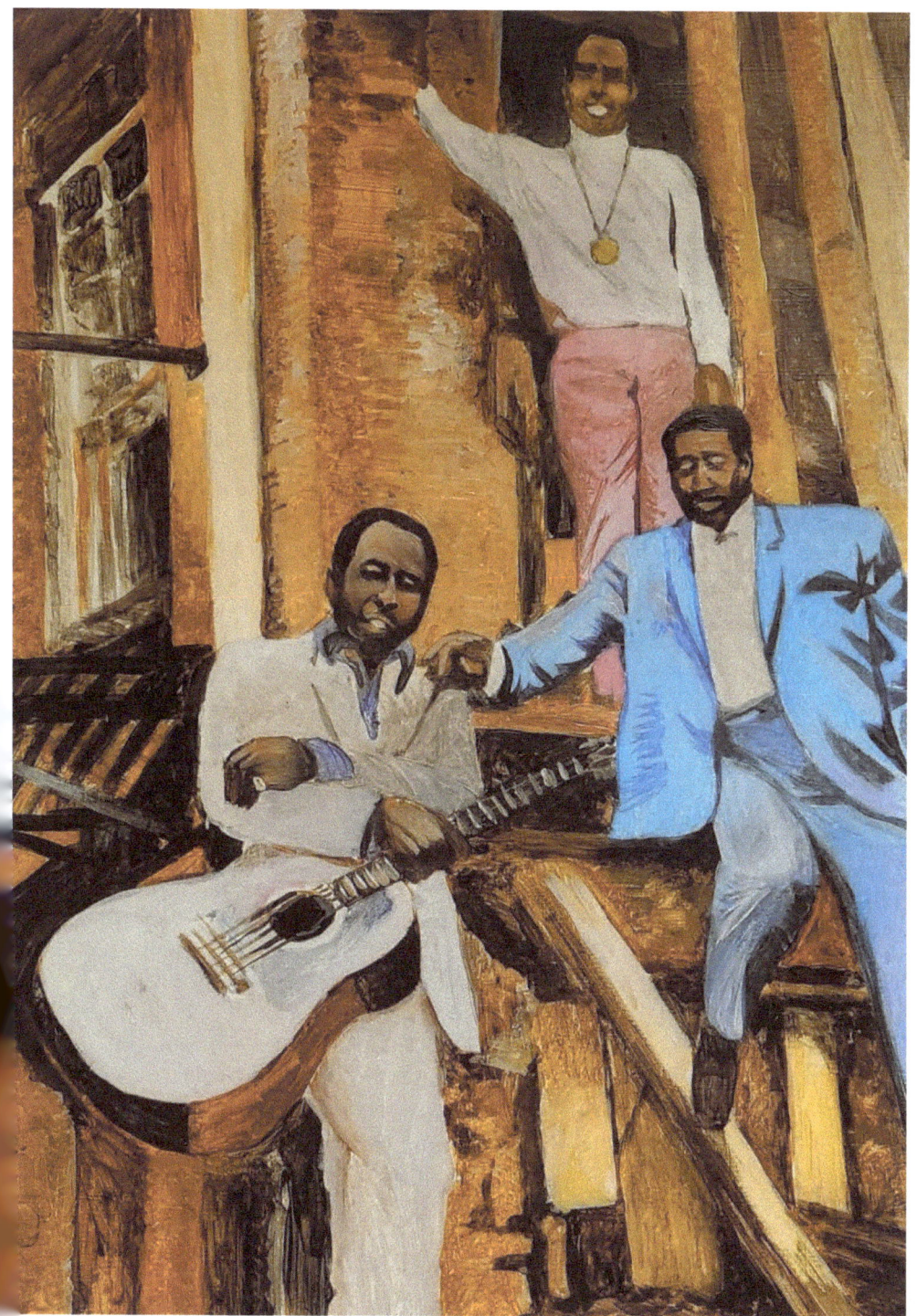

Curtis Mayfield

In 1970 Mayfield chose a solo career away from The Impressions and his million selling "Curtis" set spawned such classics as "Move On Up" and "If There's a Hell Below"; he further progressed with "Roots" in 1972 that included the single "We've Got To Have Peace". Curtis was at the height of his creative powers when he took yet another turn in his career, the movies. Hollywood had started to show commercial interest in Black filmmaking even if the results are now sometimes considered a less than positive view of African Americans. "Superfly" in 1972 was Curtis's entry into soundtracks. The runaway success of the "Superfly" soundtrack meant guaranteed interest in any follow up album and high-quality product was met with high sales for "Back to the World" issued in 1973. From 1972 to 1976 Curtis continued to involve himself with other soundtrack work that meant supplying material for Gladys Knight & The Pips, The Staple Singers and Aretha Franklin. Sales of Mayfield's other albums began to dwindle even though much of the product remained of a high standard, most notably the hard hitting "There's No Place Like America Today" in 1975 but as with many performers of quality, the ever-growing threat of Disco meant that those who once set trends were having to now follow new trends and thus sacrifice certain values in order to survive. He continued to write and produce for groups outside of the Curtom stable re-uniting with Mavis Staples and the rest of her family on two separate projects. During the '80s Mayfield seemed destined to become a memory but for the exposure given him by British pop musicians: Paul Weller of The Jam and later The Style Council who recorded a version of "Move On Up". Renewed interest in Mayfield and collaborations began to give Curtis Mayfield a new audience.

In September 1990, Curtis Mayfield prepared to do live dates in England not as some has-been or re-run but as an acknowledged master of his craft; then tragedy struck. On August the 13th while performing in high winds at an outdoor concert in Brooklyn a dislodged lighting rig fell on his neck, paralysing him from the neck down. When that lighting rig fell, Curtis was doing what he did best which made the tragedy more telling; but still, he continued through his strength of spirit to be an influential figure on all forms of music proving that there is more to a man or woman than the physical shell in which we spend all our conscious hours. The subconscious is a different matter altogether. Before he died in 1999, he left us with a nigh impossible new album "New World Order" in 1996, given his physical capabilities but physical strength can never compose like Curtis did; the mind holds the key to that ability.

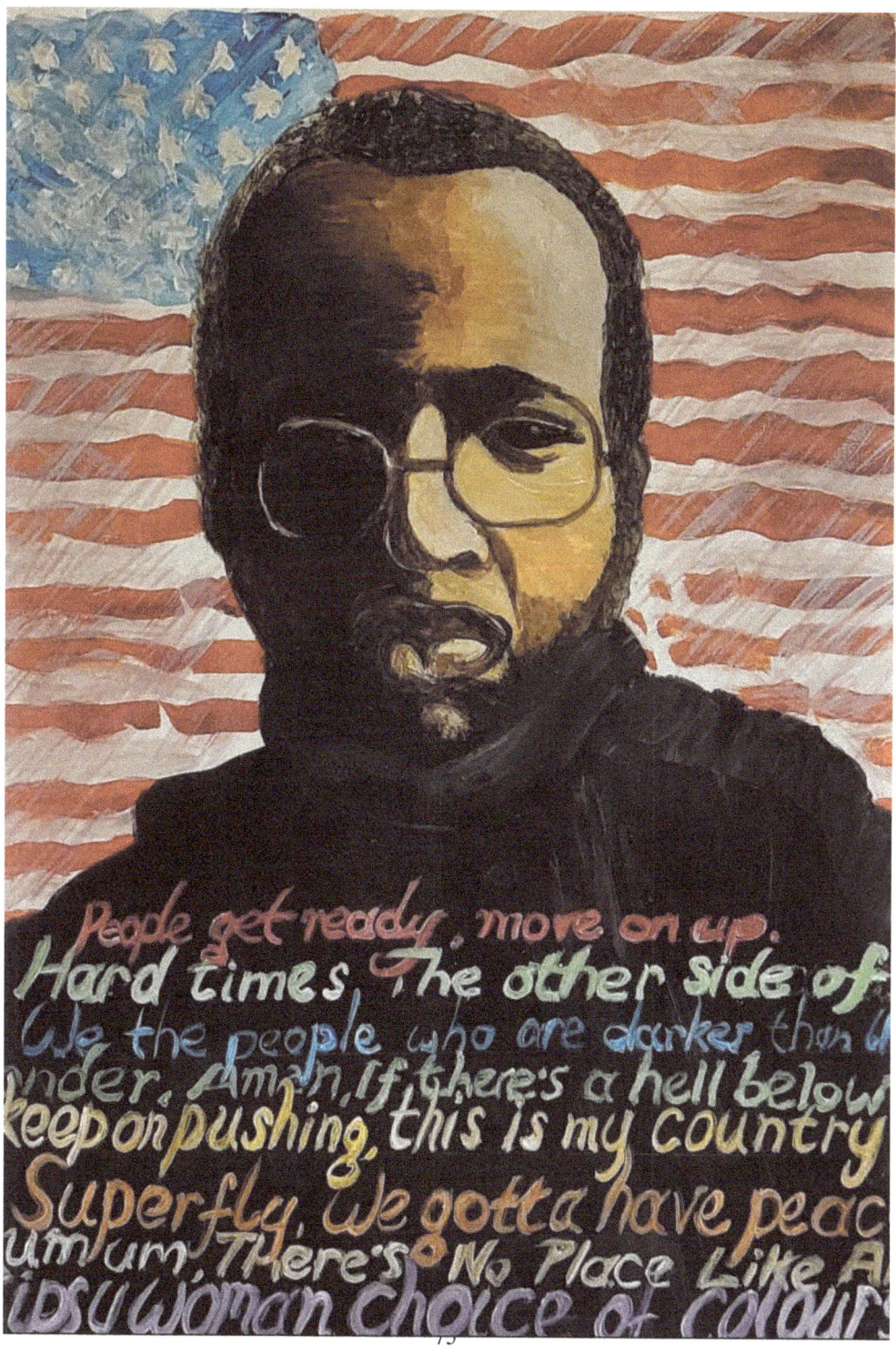

Donny Hathaway

When I wasn't listening to Luxembourg I was listening to AFN (American Forces Network out of Germany) where a serviceman, Milt Kemp had a half hour Soul Show every Monday and Friday night at 7.30. I would switch on my reel-to-reel tape recorder and push the microphone up to the radio to discover Donny Hathaway. In 1964 he was impressive enough to win a fine arts scholarship to Howard University to study music but left without a degree due to growing demands from the record industry. Hathaway first worked behind the scenes as a producer, arranger, songwriter and session pianist/keyboardist and supported Aretha Franklin, Jerry Butler and the Staple Singers, among many others. The Impressions cut his composition "Gone Away" for their album "This Is My Country. 1969 saw the first collaboration between Hathaway and former Howard University classmate, Roberta Flack who recorded his song," Our Ages or Our Hearts" on her debut album "First Take". He also signed to Atlantic Records where he released his debut single, "The Ghetto" toward the end of 1971. This set the stage for his acclaimed debut LP, "Everything Is Everything", which was released in early 1970. His second LP, the self-titled "Donny Hathaway" released in 1971 included the definitive version of Leon Russell's "A Song for You" and Van McCoy's "Giving Up". "Giving Up" included a spine-chilling sax solo by King Curtis. In 1972 Hathaway released a live album which has been called one of the best ever recorded. In 1971, he recorded a full album of duets with Roberta, released in 1972. The ballad "Where Is the Love?" won a Grammy whilst the album went gold. However, in the midst of his blossoming success he was also battling severe bouts of depression and paranoid schizophrenia and was known to take strong medication daily to try to control the illness but was non-compliant which occasionally required him to be hospitalized. His mood swings also affected his partnership with Flack, which began to crumble in 1973. His final studio album, the ambitious "Extension of a Man" came out that year and then he retreated from the spotlight. On January 13th, 1979, Hathaway began a recording session and although his voice sounded good, he began behaving irrationally, seeming to be paranoid and delusional. Given Hathaway's behavior the recording session could not continue. Hours later, Hathaway was found dead on the sidewalk below the window of his 15th-floor room in New York's Essex House hotel. He had jumped from his balcony. The glass had been neatly removed from the window and there were no signs of struggle, leading investigators to rule Hathaway's death a suicide. Ironically the full title of "Everything Is Everything" included "I Hear Voices".

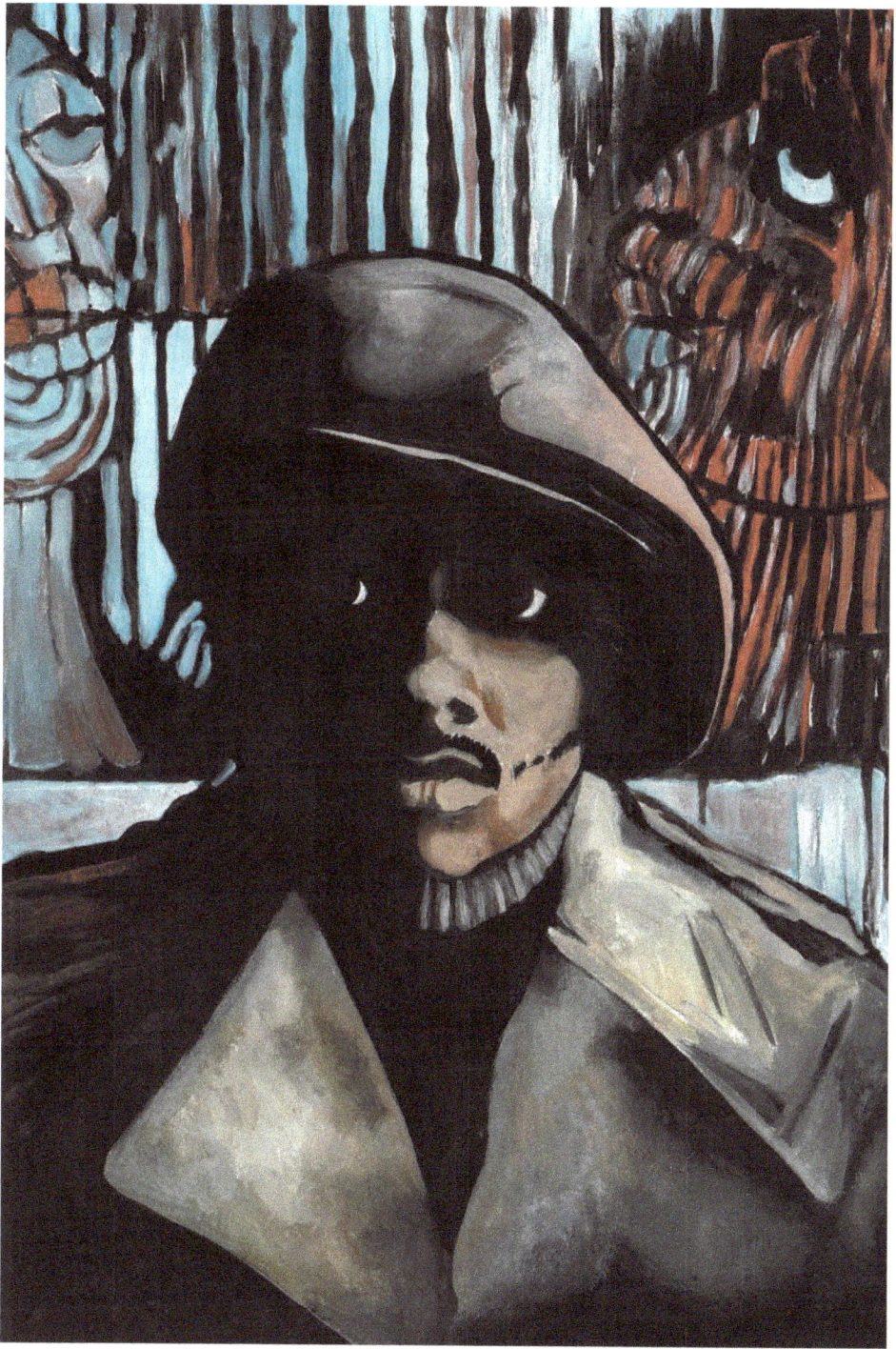

Etta James

Jamesetta Hawkins was born on January the 25th, 1938, in Los Angeles, the daughter of Dorothy Hawkins. She was a 14-year-old black girl who hung around that city's jazz scene and was discovered at the age of 15, when she would sing on street corners in the Northern California city of San Francisco by bandleader Johnny Otis. James forged her mother's signature in order to go with Otis for a recording session, and after her 1955 debut, she toured with Otis' revue. She soon scored her first hit when she was just a teenager with the suggestive "Roll with Me, Henry", which had to be changed to "The Wallflower" in order to get airplay. On her first album, recorded for Chicago's Argo label in 1960 Etta performed several duets with her then boyfriend, Harvey Fuqua of The Moonglows. Leonard Chess, owner of Chess that Argo was part of, believed that Etta could do well in the pop market. He was correct and yet her translation of 1941's "At Last" has become an Etta James original despite its Glenn Miller origins. On the flip side was "I Just Want to Make Love to You" a 1954 Willie Dixon Blues song but try to convince anyone that this wasn't another Etta James original. "Stop The Wedding" was released on Argo in 1962 and a year later Motown's Kim Weston added to that plea with "It Should Have Been Me". As well as duetting with Harvey Fuqua, Etta also cut sides with another Chess artist and another of Johnny Otis' discoveries Sugar Pie DeSanto most famously on "In the Basement". In the late summer of 1967 James went to Muscle Shoals, Alabama's FAME Studios for an album produced by the studio's owner Rick Hall. The album, "Tell Mama", produced one of her best songs, "I'd Rather Go Blind.". In the 1970s her ongoing drug problem led her to rehab but she re-established herself with live performances. In 1988 after another stint in rehab, this time at the Betty Ford Clinic, she made a comeback album, "Seven Year Itch," on the Island label. Throughout her career, James suffered through drug addictions but managed to return to the stage each time. James' accolades included an induction into the Rock Hall of Fame in 1993 as well as a Grammy award in 1994. "Love's Been Rough on Me" was released in 1997. Etta James was still performing and recording almost to the end. She had been suffering from dementia, kidney problems and diabetes, and in December 2011, her physician announced that her leukaemia was terminal. That year she had still managed to release what would prove to be her final album, "The Dreamer" and slipped away but hardly unnoticed, on January the 20th 2012.

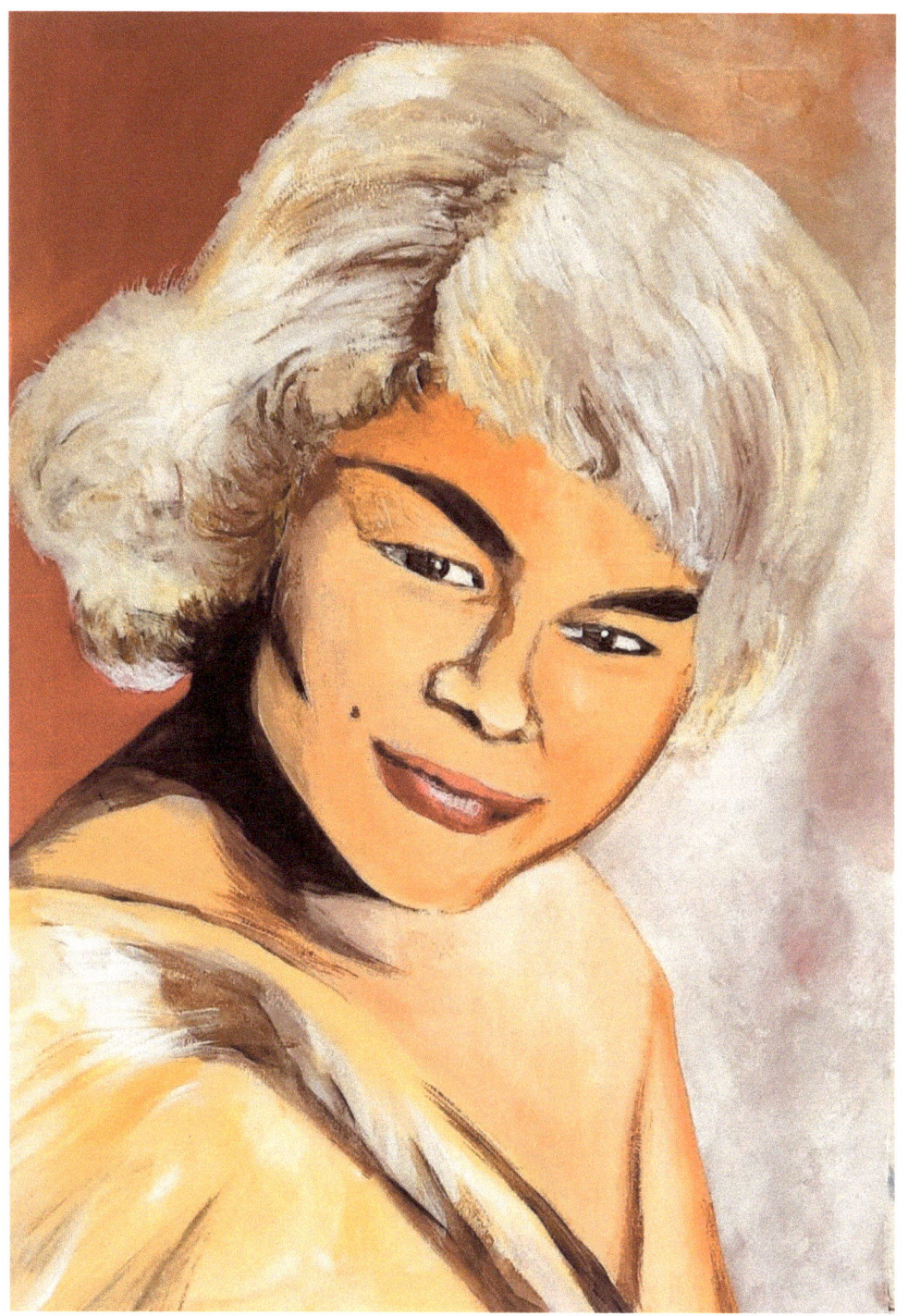

Fontella Bass

Fontella Bass was born on the 3rd of July 1940 in St Louis, Missouri, the daughter of Gospel singer Martha Bass who was a member of the great Clara Ward Singers. Her younger brother, David Peaston, was also a Soul singer. By the age of five Fontella accompanied her grandmother's singing, by six she was in the church choir and by nine out on the road accompanying her mother. This continued until Bass was sixteen when secular music began to attract her. She attended Soldan High School from where she graduated in 1958 but she had already entered local contests singing R&B. By the time she was seventeen she was working professionally at the Showboat Club near Chain of Rocks, Missouri then in 1961 she was heard by Little Milton and Oliver Sain who was his bandleader. Sain hired Fontella to back Little Milton on piano, both on stage and in recording sessions. One night, Little Milton was late to a gig so Sain asked Bass to do a vocal spot. Little Milton was to part company with Sain and Fontella Bass stepped up. After falling out with Oliver Sain she moved to Chicago, auditioned for Chess Records and was snapped up straight away joining the Checker label's roster. In 1965 her Chess career started with a duet, "Don't Mess Up a Good Thing" performed with Bobby McClure who she had previously toured with. This reached number five on the R&B chart and a healthy Number 33 on the pop one. A follow-up "You're Gonna Miss Me" was released during the summer but didn't reach the same heights and Bass took to touring before returning to the studio. When she did, history was to be made. Up to this point Chess were still steeped in Blues, R&B and Jazz but had been watching how Motown was capturing the commercial Soul market so they decided to go for it with the studio band made up of Maurice White on drums, Louis Satterfield who would play one of the most famous bass riffs ever put on plastic, saxophonist Gene Barge and Minnie Riperton on backing vocals.

    A million selling gold record was on its way, as Fontella Bass stepped up to the microphone and pronounced "Rescue Me". For a month it was top of the R&B chart reaching Number 4 on the pop chart but after two years she left the label disillusioned and disgruntled after her name was excluded from the label as a co-writer. Bass wanted more artistic control and a better royalty rate; what she got was a reputation as a troublemaker. She toured Europe with her brother David Peaston before illness took hold of them. Peaston was diagnosed with diabetes and in 2004 both his legs were amputated. The following year Fontella Bass survived a series of strokes and breast cancer. In 2012 Peaston was dead at 54 due to the diabetes and the same year Fontella Bass joined him after a heart attack at 72.

Art & Soul

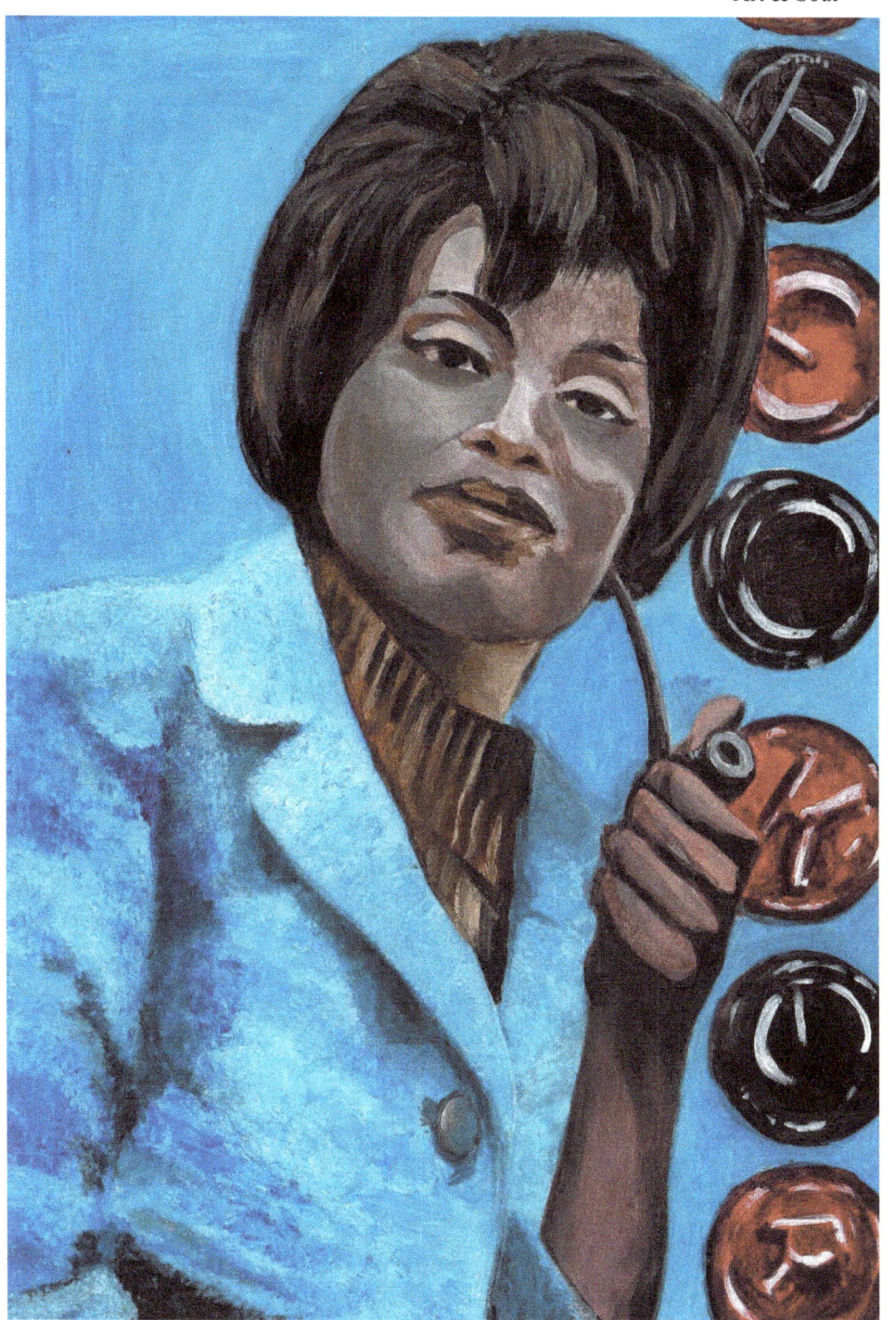

Jackie Wilson

Jackie Wilson was recognised as a product of Chicago Soul but was born in Detroit on June the 9th 1934. If Detroit had Goliaths like Berry Gordy, Chicago had its David's who would become giants themselves, sometimes at staggering costs. "Mr Excitement" as he was known had started out singing Gospel and in his teens was a boxer. His mother asked him to stop boxing though and so he changed direction veering toward the music industry where he replaced Clyde McPhatter as lead vocalist for Billy Ward & The Dominoes. It just so happened that Wilson's cousin was Berry Gordy Jr who, himself was trying to make it in the industry. Gordy had chanced upon Wilson's manager who was searching for material for him so in 1957 and now signed to the Brunswick label, Wilson scored with Gordy's composition "Reet Petite" followed by two more Gordy songs "To Be Loved" and in December of '58 his first number 1 R&B hit "Lonely Teardrops" which also became a National top ten Pop hit. In 1961 Wilson was living in Manhattan where he was shot outside his apartment by one of his girlfriends, Juanta Jones after Wilson showed up with another woman, Harlean Harris, who he would later marry. He lost a kidney because of it and a bullet was too close to his spine to be removed. Wilson was always a womaniser as well as a drinker, not a healthy cocktail. Both Gordy and Wilson would make musical history although Wilson's was a less favourable one. Gordy owned Motown but Brunswick owned Wilson.

Chicago was known for more than music and the mob had a big part to play in the recording industry. Wilson's manager, Nat Tarnopol had connections and New Jersey based Gaetano Vastola, who belonged to the DeCavalcante family had terminated Tarnopol's contract with Wilson but left him contracted to record for the Brunswick label. Added to this conundrum, by now Tarnopol owned Brunswick so either way Wilson was screwed. He owed Brunswick money as well as the Internal Revenue for back taxes that he thought Nat Tarnopol had filed and paid. His final hit was "Higher and Higher" in 1967. Eight years on, Wilson was still out there performing but on September the 29th 1975 he suffered a heart attack while on stage which left him in a coma from which he never recovered. By 1977 he was ironically living in a retirement community in New Jersey and on January the 21st 1984 he passed away, he was only 49 years old. The funeral took place at Russell Street Baptist Church in Chicago where Wilson went as a teenager and the attendees included all Four Tops (Levi Stubbs like Berry Gordy being a cousin), The Spinners and Esther Gordy representing Motown. Reverend Anthony Campbell made the point that there were four escape routes from the ghetto, crime, politics, sport and entertainment. Jackie Wilson seemed to be embroiled in all four but without an escape.

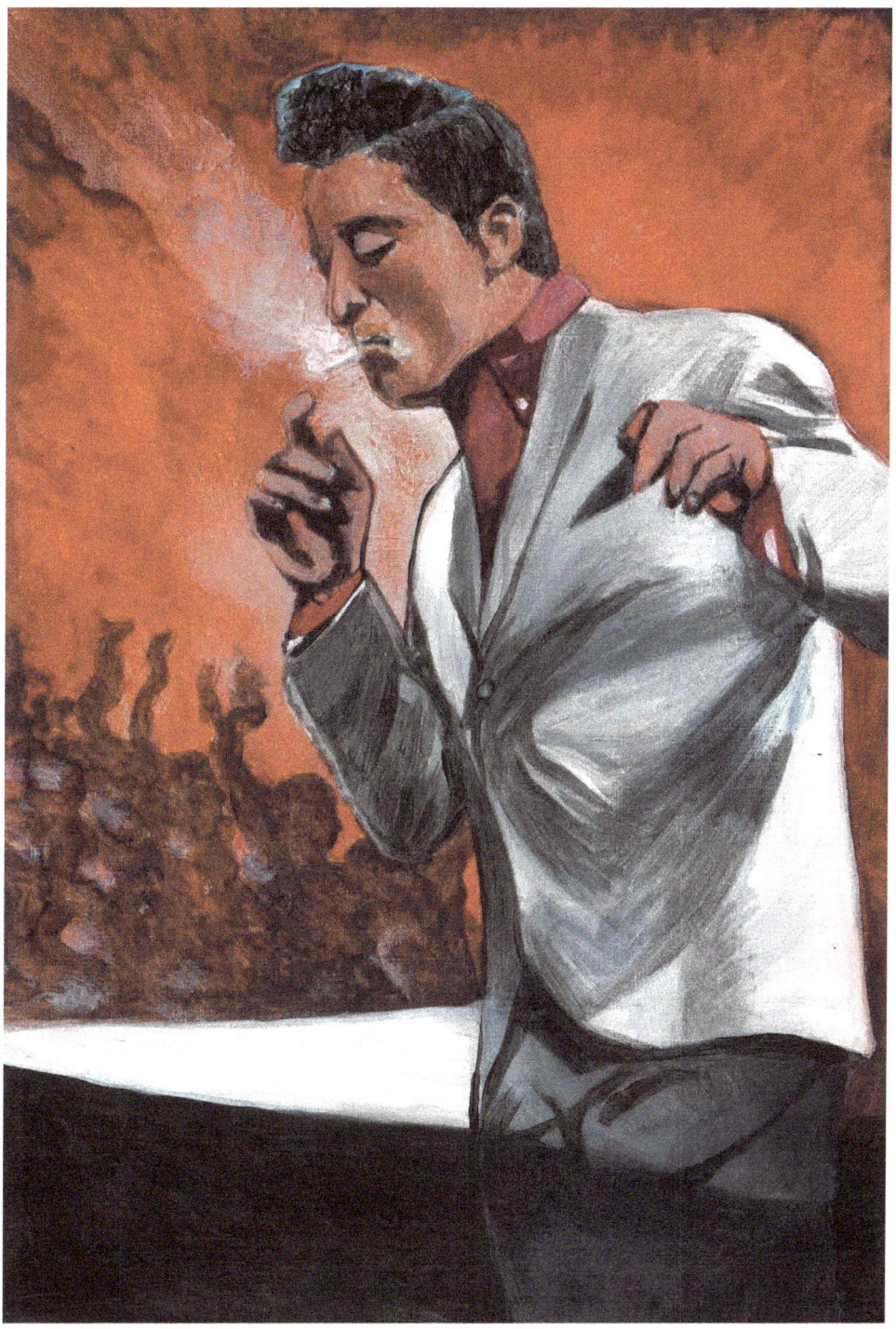

Jerry Butler

When I was 18, I discovered Jerry Butler in a junkshop. Now I wasn't in Chicago and Jerry wasn't there in person. No, this was that magical time of discovery when records could be unearthed from dusty boxes in dingy second-hand shops for loose change huddled in the corners of your pockets. "Got to See if I Can't Get Mommy to Come Back Home " cost pennies but soon became priceless to me. Perhaps one of the coolest vocalists Soul music has ever produced that left little doubt as to why Jerry Butler was dubbed 'The Ice Man' by Philadelphia Disc Jockey, Georgie Woods from Station WDAS. That and Woods knowledge of Butler's work in the field of ice sculptures. During his Gospel apprenticeship Butler met up with Curtis Mayfield when both appeared with The Travelling Soul Spiritualistic Church and then, in 1957, they both began to pursue a career in popular music. Butler moved away from the church to more secular/commercial pastures joining The Quails and then became reunited with Curtis Mayfield in his group The Impressions. "For Your Precious Love" found its way to the VeeJay label in 1958. This was the start of Butler's solo career but Mayfield kept the group together playing a dual role continuing as guitarist and writer, penning amongst others the classic "He Will Break Your Heart" while Butler, along with brother Billy was also contributing such soul classics as "I Stand Accused". Mayfield's role in Butler's aspiring career is also significant at this stage for the insight shown by the two young men in making moves to secure creators' rights as far back as 1961. In 1965 he co-wrote "I've Been Loving You Too Long" with Otis Redding, often considered one of Redding's finest moments. Butler's name wasn't credited on the single but did return on Ike & Tina Turner's cover released in 1969. Butler signed to Mercury where in 1967, after a chance meeting with Kenny Gamble and Leon Huff of Philadelphia fame, he departed from Chicago for a vintage two years' period in the City of Brotherly Love and the establishing of the cool Butler style with two self-explanatory albums entitled, "The Ice Man Cometh" and "Ice on Ice". It was a vintage period but the Philadelphia International organisation was developing too fast for Gamble and Huff to be able to concentrate on outside productions that included Jerry Butler, and so in 1970 he returned to Chicago where he would contribute immensely to the growth of the music industry through the Butler Workshop which helped to bring on Terry Callier and the team of Chuck Jackson and Marvin Yancy who would later help Natalie Cole's career. As well as this he became the owner of the Chicago distributors for Carling Black Label and Guinness. After several journeys, including one to Motown, he reunited with Gamble & Huff in 1978.

Art & Soul

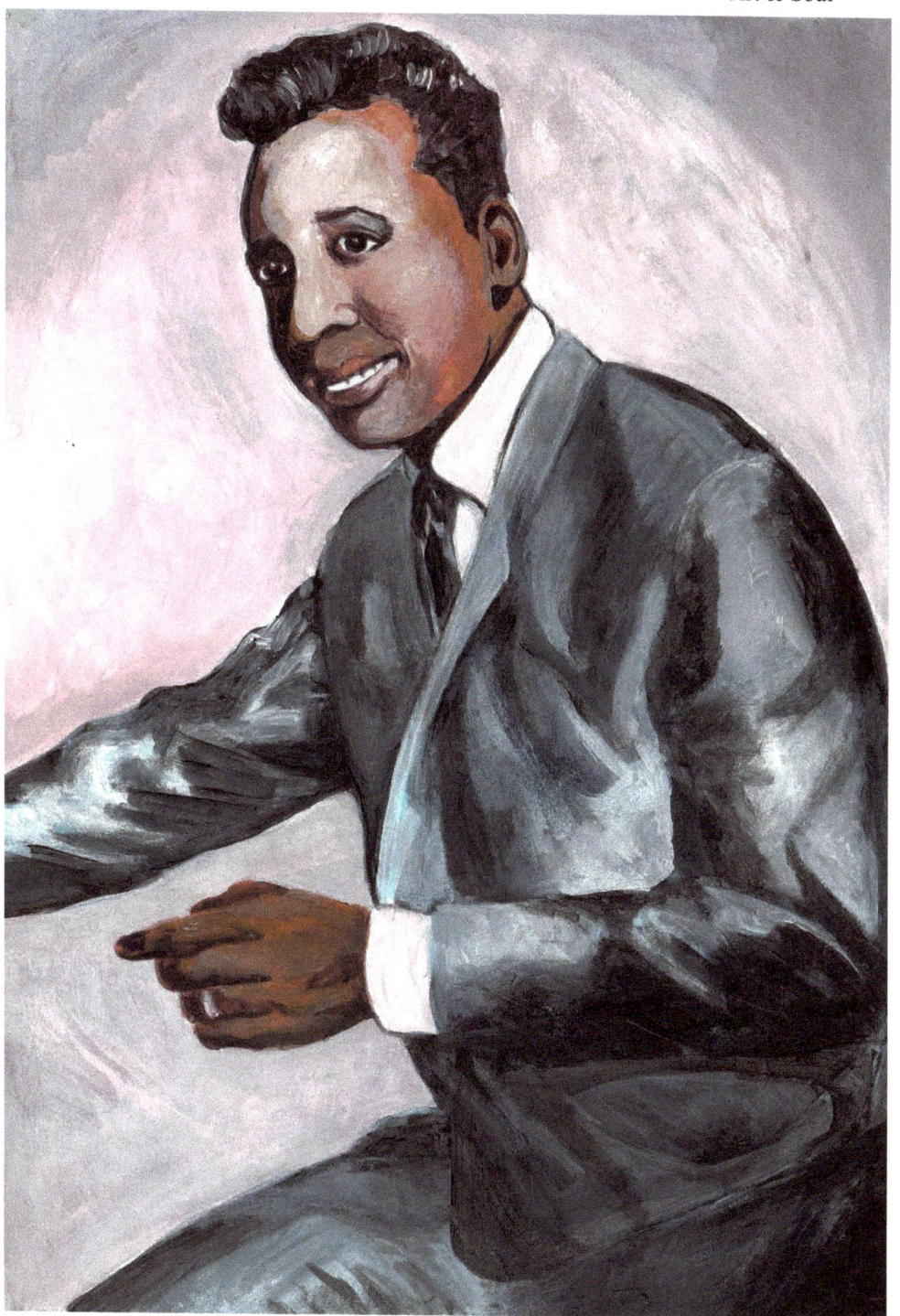

Minnie Riperton

Minnie Julia Riperton was born in Chicago on November the 8th 1947. From an early age her parents could see her vocal ability and musical talent so she was coached in operatic skills by Marion Jeffery who encouraged her to use her phenomenal range, hoping that she would become an opera star but Minnie was more interested in Soul, R&B and Rock. Her first recordings were in the group The Gems when she was fifteen. The Gems changed their name to Studio Three and provided backing on Fontella Bass' "Rescue Me". In Studio Three she found a mentor in Billy Davis and honoured him by releasing two singles under the name of Andrea Davis. In 1966 she joined the progressive Soul and Rock group Rotary Connection on Chess Records before branching out as a solo artist with "Come to My Garden" produced by former Rotarian Charles Stepney who wrote some of the songs with Richard Rudolph who would marry Minnie in August 1970.

The album was artistically recognised but failed commercially and so Minnie semi-retired to Florida to raise her two children but in 1973 a college intern at Epic records came across a demo of hers. He was able to get the tape listened to and Minnie signed to the label which meant another move, this time to Los Angeles where she began working on her second album "Perfect Angel". Minnie had already worked with Stevie Wonder on his album "Fulfillingness First Finale" in 1974 and he offered to co-produce her album and the song "Take a Little Trip" which was released as the second single. Three singles hadn't worked so the company was ready to work on the next album, but Rudolph persuaded them to have one more try.

In April 1975 "Lovin' You" not only reached number one in The States but in 24 other countries. The song turned gold as did the album. In 1975 the next album "Adventures in Paradise" was started and in 1976 she appeared on Stevie's "Song in the Key of Life album". In the same year she told everyone that she had had a mastectomy and that the diagnosis had revealed that the cancer had spread to her lymphatic system and she was given six months to live. She continued recording and in 1977 the album "Stay in Love" featured a collaboration with Stevie Wonder, "Stick Together", something they seemed destined to do. Minnie became the national spokesperson for the American Cancer Society's 1978-79 campaign and in April 1979 she released her final album "Minnie". Her cancer's progression caused her horrendous pain and immobilised her right arm, yet she was still out there performing but the arm was in a fixed position. By the middle of June, she was taken to Cedars-Sinai Medical Centre, Los Angeles where, on July the 10th, she passed away in her husband's arms. On her memorial stone are the opening lines from her most famous song, "Lovin' you is easy 'cause you're beautiful".

Art & Soul

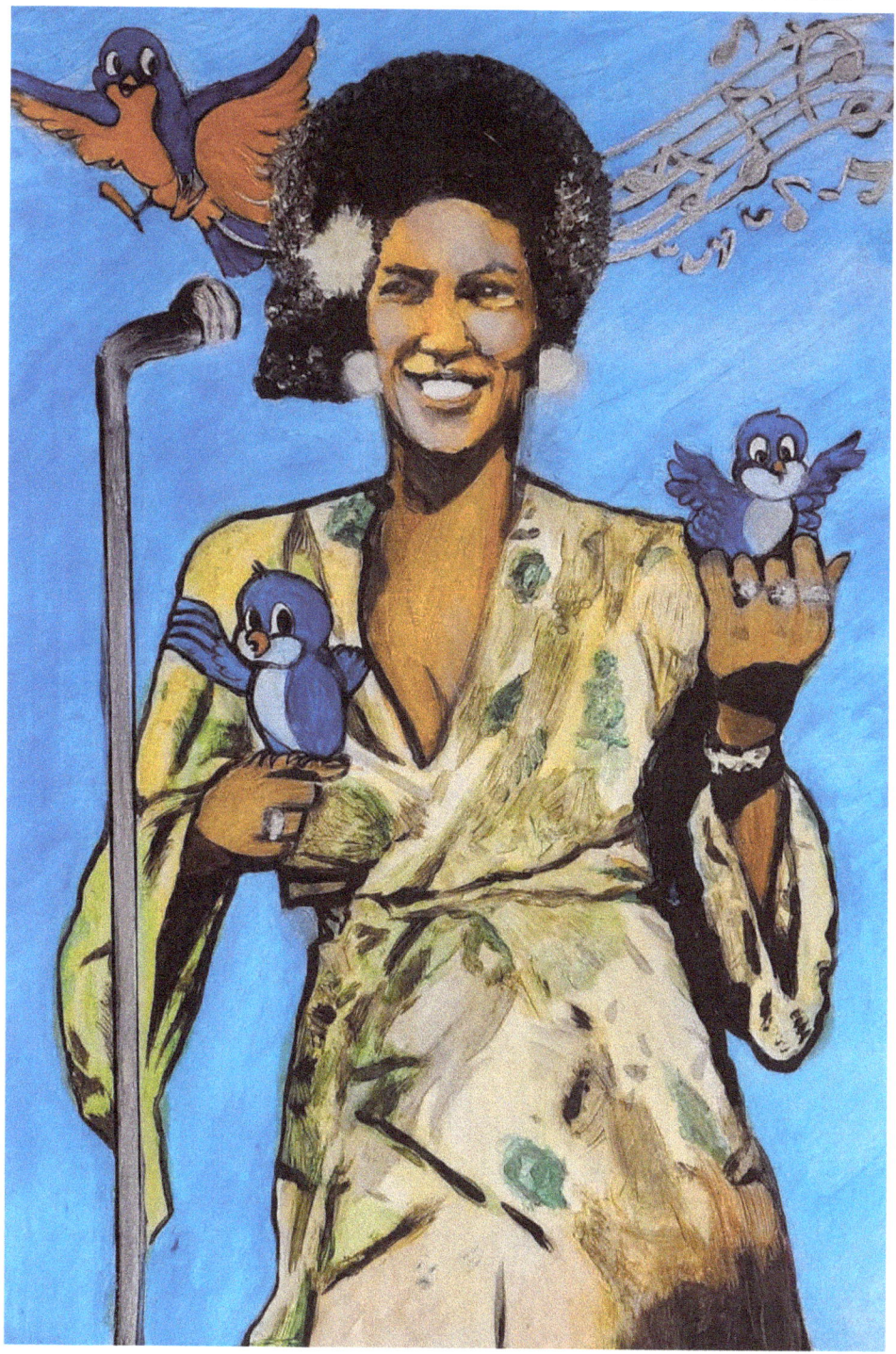

Sam Cooke

Samuel "Sam" Cook was born in Clarksdale, Mississippi on January 22, 1931. The family moved to Chicago in 1933 and Cooke began his career singing Gospel with his siblings in a group called The Singing Children. He first became known as lead singer with the Highway QC's as a teenager. In 1950, Cooke replaced gospel tenor R.H. Harris as lead singer of the landmark gospel group The Soul Stirrers and under Cooke's leadership, the group signed with Specialty Records and recorded the hits "Peace in the Valley", "How Far Am I From Canaan?", "Jesus Paid the Debt", "One More River" and "That's Heaven to Me".

Cooke had twenty-nine Top 40 hits in the U.S. between 1957 and 1964 and was also among the first modern African American performers and composers to attend to the business side of his musical career. He founded both a record label and a publishing company as an extension of his careers as a singer and composer and took an active part in the Civil Rights movement. His first pop single, "Lovable" in 1956 was released under the alias "Dale Cooke" in order not to alienate his gospel fan base. At this point there was a considerable stigma against gospel singers performing secular music. Cooke signed with Keen Records. His first release being "You Send Me". In 1961 Cooke started his own record label, SAR Records with J.W. Alexander and his manager, Roy Crain. The label was intended to be a place where Sam Cooke could expand his artistic abilities as a writer/producer and to give other struggling African American artists a venue to record during the racially charged 1960s. Cooke then created a publishing imprint and management firm before signing to RCA Victor. One of his first RCA singles was the hit "Chain Gang" that reached Number 2 on the Billboard pop chart and was followed by more hits, "Bring It on Home to Me" that featured the vocal of Lou Rawls, "Another Saturday Night" and "Twisting the Night Away".

Cooke died on December the 11th, 1964 at the Hacienda Motel in Los Angeles. Bertha Franklin, manager of the motel, told police that she shot and killed Cooke in self-defense because he had threatened her. Police found Cooke's body in Franklin's office, wearing only a sports jacket and shoes, but no shirt, pants or underwear. The reasoning appeared to be that he had been entertaining a prostitute who robbed him and escaped through the window, Sam ran into the lobby in pursuit of the woman where he was attacked by Franklin. The shooting was ultimately ruled justifiable homicide. Sam Cooke was 33 years old. "A Change is Gonna Come" was released after his death and deemed a new direction that Cooke wasn't allowed to take.

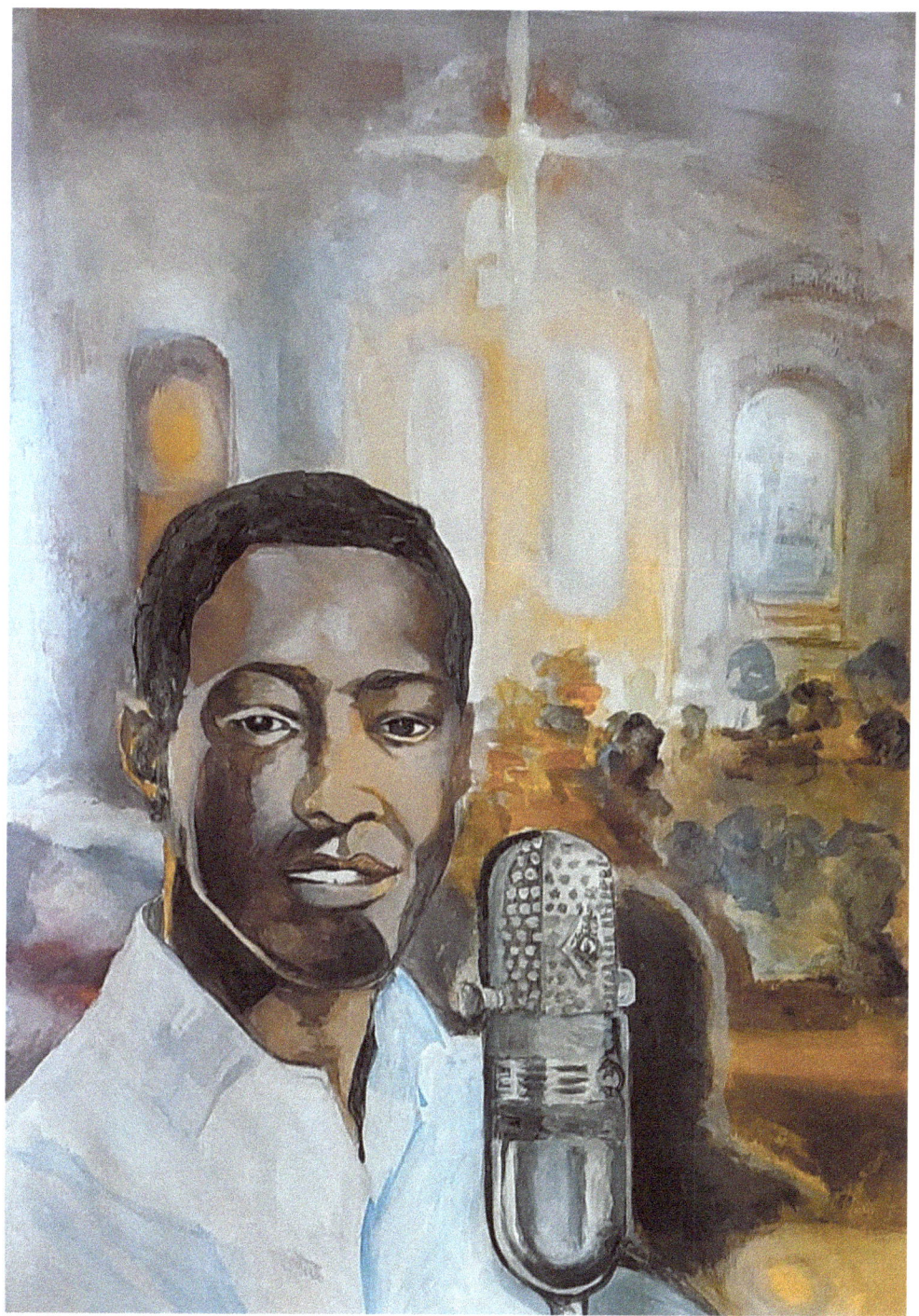

The Dells

Testimony to a city that is associated more with the Blues was the choice of Robert Townsend, Director of the films " Hollywood Shuffle " and " I'm Gonna Git You Sucka" to base his film, "The Five Heartbeats", on the story of The Dells, one of Chicago's most enduring harmony groups. The Dells pre-dated pop music stretching back to 1952 and starting life as a street corner acapella outfit, they cut their first single, "Christine", in 1953 under the name, The El Rays for the Checker Label, a subsidiary of Chess Records. After "Christine" Leonard Chess took Marvin to one side and told him that he was never going to make it as a lead singer and to go to school and get a good education. Most voices coming out of Rhythm & Blues into Soul were predominantly beautiful, light falsetto, tenor voices, a far cry from his. However, when they re-signed, Leonard Chess tried to get him on an individual contract but he refused. To Marvin Junior when you'd been unit, you had that unity. Subsequent releases were by The Dells but before further Chess releases, they signed with another local label, VeeJay. In 1956 they first recorded one of their evergreen ballads, "Oh What a Night" They had been working Friday and Saturday nights at a small venue earning two dollars a night and a hamburger. One night a group of girls came by and invited them to their house the next day. So, on that Sunday they went to their house and had everything they needed. Plenty of food and drinks. On the Monday, during rehearsal they were saying, "What a Night" which Johnny extended to "Oh What a Night" with Marvin adding "To love you dear", a song was born. It was 1971 when I started listening to them with the beautiful million seller "The Love We Had Stays on my Mind".

Listening to this stunning ballad, it's the whole sound of The Dells that touches your heart. As the predominant voice of the Dells there are those times in there where Marvin Junior's voice just tears it up, then there's other things like on a 1991's "Oh My Love", there's a softness, a smoothness in the voice that just lays across the track in a completely different way. The 60s and 70s saw The Dells continuing as a staple part of Soul but it was in 1991 when they signed to the Philadelphia International label for the album "I Salute You" and when Robert Townsend created the movie, "Five Heartbeats", the soundtrack produced yet another masterpiece, "A Heart is a House for Love". Kanye West, 50 Cent and Ghostface Killah began sampling The Dells presenting them to a new audience, but I wonder who we'll be listening to more in the years ahead?

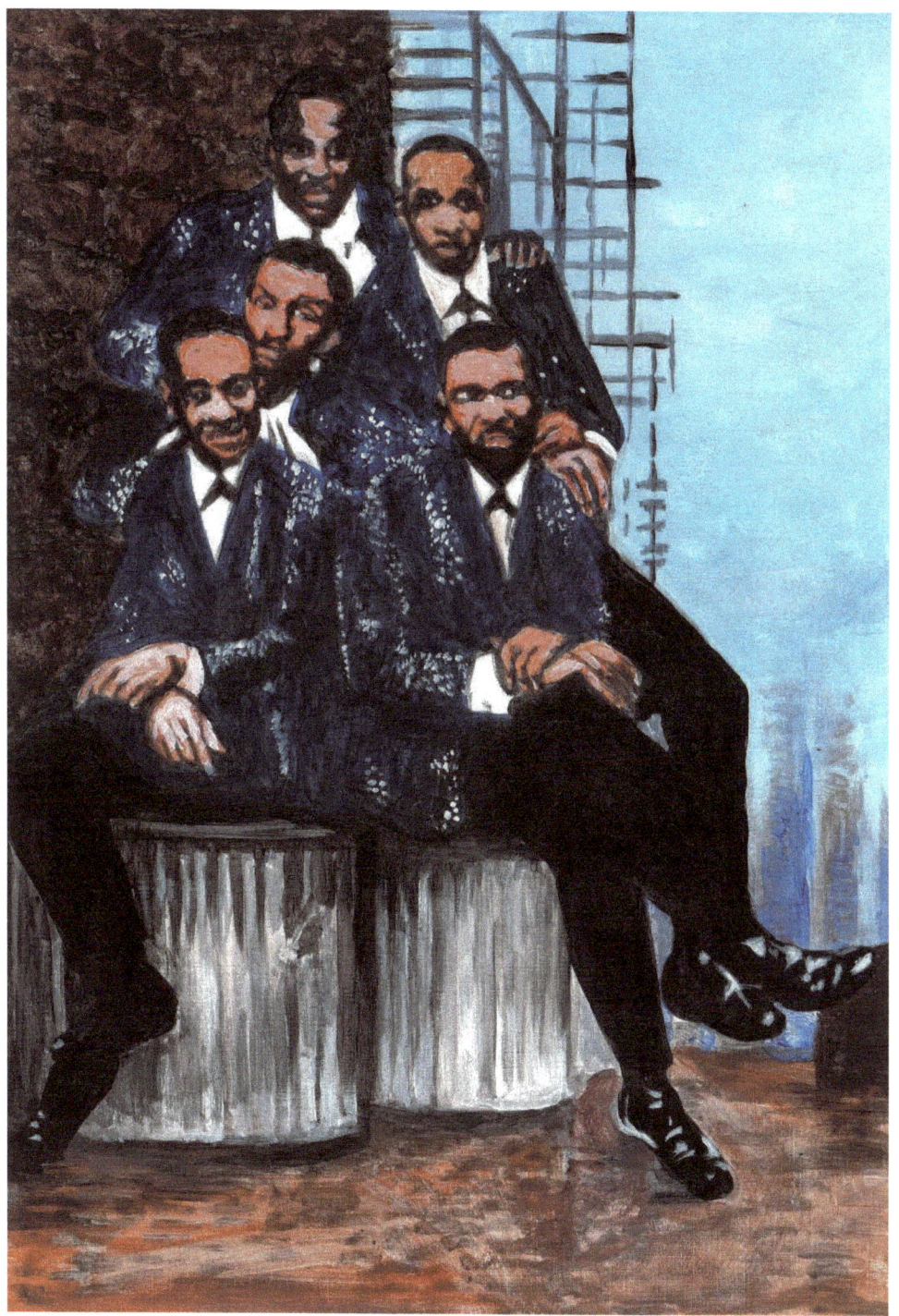

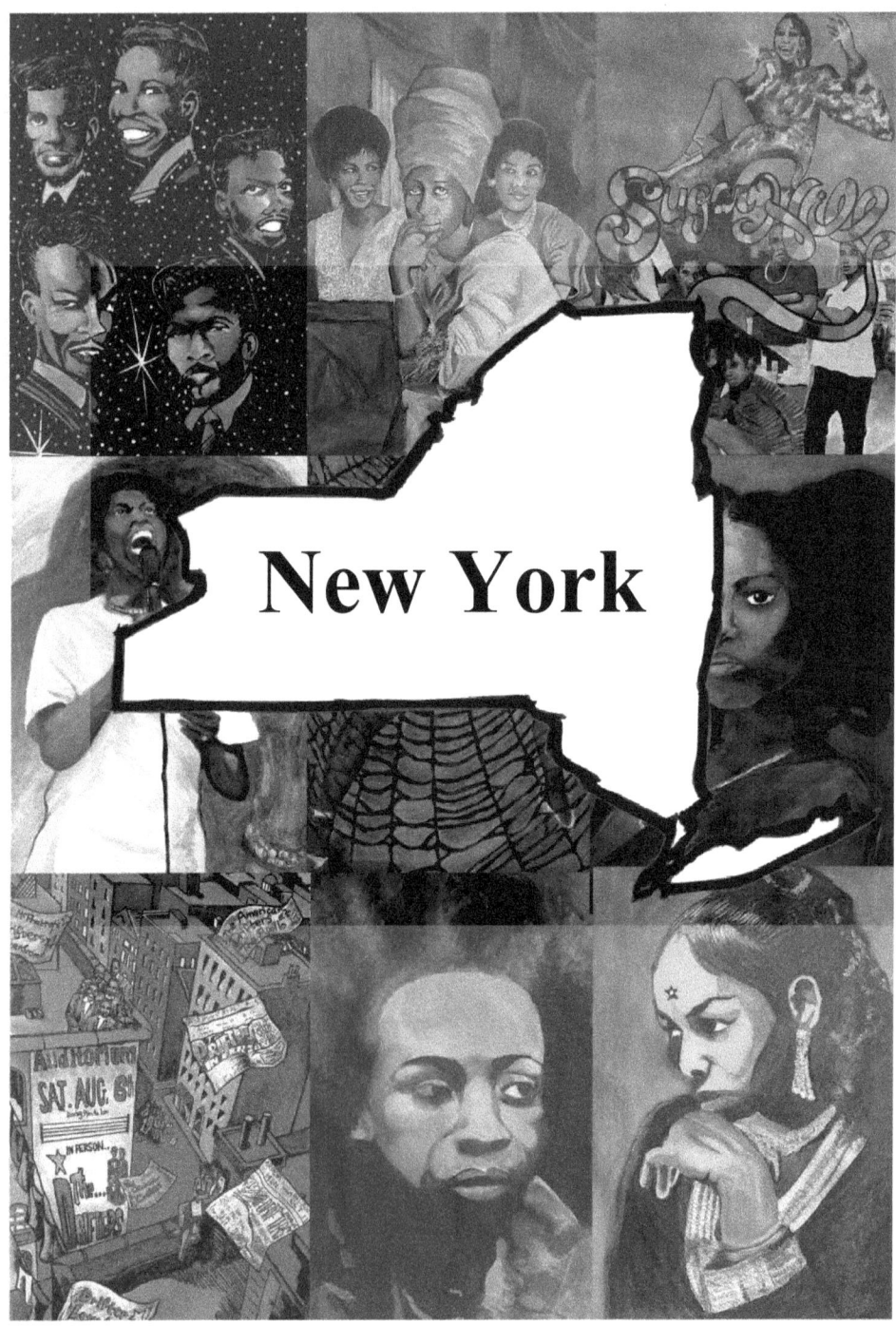

Art & Soul

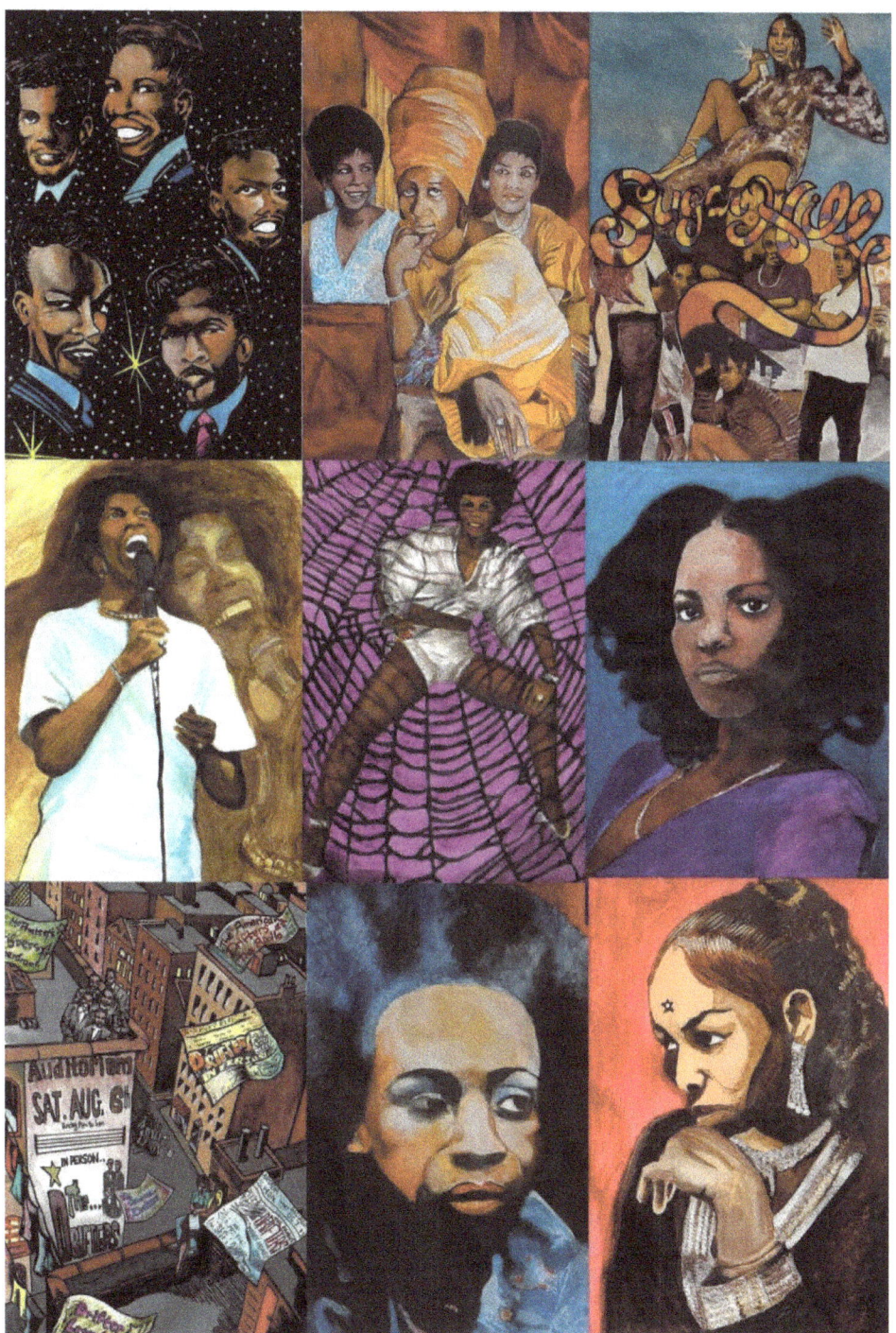

Aretha Franklin

Aretha Franklin was born in Memphis, Tennessee on the 25th of March 1942. Her father was a Baptist preacher, and her mother was a gospel singer. In her career Aretha won 18 Grammy Awards but it took a long journey to get those. When she was 5 years old, her family relocated to Detroit where her father founded the New Bethel Baptist Church. He recognized her talent and started to manage her from the time she was 14, trying to get her a deal with a record company. In 1956, her first album came out under J. V. B. Records label, 'Songs of Faith'. She signed to Columbia Records in 1961 but in January 1967, Jerry Wexler signed her to Atlantic having spent too long, for too little reward at Columbia. In the Deep South, integration was still bedding in and not favoured by many and yet music was breaking down the barriers. These recording studios were a sanctuary for sense and a snub to segregation. No more so than at Muscle Shoals, where Rick Hall employed an all-white rhythm section. The first song Aretha was to record was "I Never Loved a Man (The Way I Love You)" but the session took time to warm up. Aretha was in an unfamiliar studio surrounded by white musicians when she was anticipating black ones. However, once Spooner Oldham struck gold on his electric keyboard the die was cast, and musical alchemy was created. More hits followed, including her version of Carole King's "A Natural Woman", "Do Right Woman, Do Right Man" and Otis Redding's "Respect". In 1968, she released her albums: 'Lady Soul' and 'Aretha Now' and that year also saw the release of another one of Aretha's signature tunes, "Think", co-written by Aretha. In 1970, as well as cutting covers such as B. B. King's "The Thrill Is Gone" and Elton John's "Border Song" she continued to cut her own compositions such as the moving "Call Me" and redefined two Ben E. King classics in 1970 and 1971 respectively, "Don't Play That Song" and "Spanish Harlem". In 1972 she released her first Atlantic Gospel album titled 'Amazing Grace' which included a version of Marvin Gaye's "Wholly Holy". Also, in 1972 "Day Dreaming", another Aretha composition, showed off her versatility; being, as it was, the complete opposite to '71s "Rock Steady". In the following years she recorded her first live album 'Aretha Live at Fillmore West' and released more successful singles such as "Until You Come Back to Me", a Stevie Wonder co-composition, "Angel", co-written by her sister Carolyn and "I'm in Love" written by Bobby Womack. In 1976 Aretha worked with Curtis Mayfield on the soundtrack to the movie "Sparkle" from whence came the track "Giving Him Something He Can Feel", later cut by En Vogue in 1992.

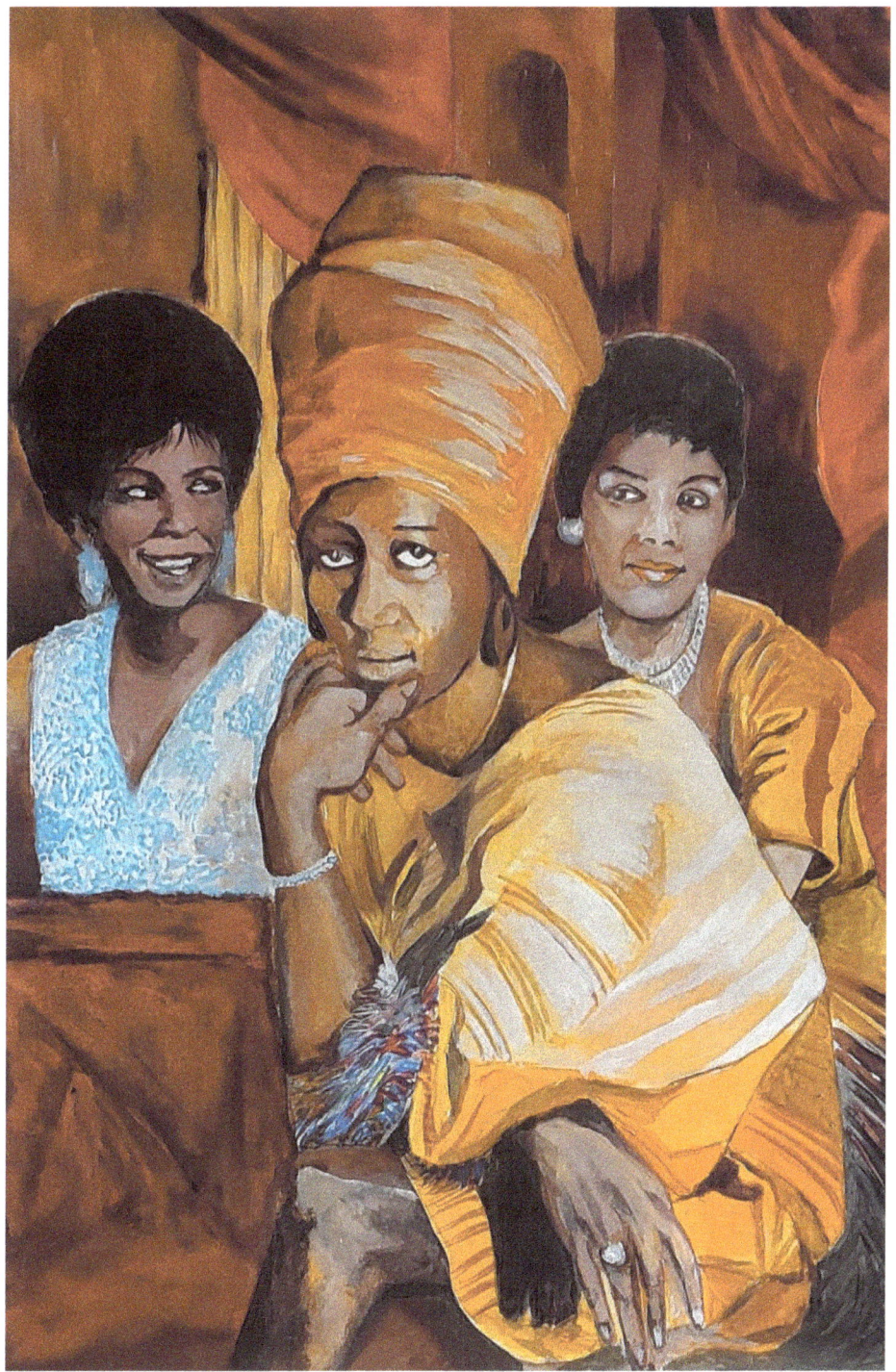

Betty Davis

Betty Mabry was born on July 26th, 1944 in Durham, just outside Pittsboro and composed her first song, "I'm Going to Bake You a Cake Of Love" at the age of 12. By 16 she moved to New York, enrolling in the Fashion Institute of Technology and being drawn to the anti-establishment Greenwich Village cultural scene. Around 1963 she got her first chance to record, courtesy of Lou Courtney who produced the track "The Cellar", in honour of the club she would frequent. In 1964, she released her composition "Get Ready For Betty" backed by "I'm Gonna Get My Baby Back" on the DCP International label, all stepping-stones, as she continued to pursue a modelling career where she was meeting such musical royalty as Jimi Hendrix and Sly Stone and very soon South African trumpeter Hugh Masekela. However, it was in 1967 when her breakthrough as a songwriter came with the track "Uptown (to Harlem)" cut by the Chamber Brothers, a track that found its way onto the "Summer of Soul" Soundtrack. Betty Mabry continued with her modelling aspirations but was aware that this direction would only last as long as her looks did. Then in 1968 she began recording for Columbia Records. Two tracks were released as a single, "It's My Life", an upbeat number, backed by the ballad "Live, Love, Learn"; soon after she began seeing Miles Davis. In September of 1968 they married and Betty was now Betty Davis. She was 23 and within one year she had introduced him to a whole new group of musical influences including Hendrix and Stone. Miles tried to get her an album but neither Columbia nor Atlantic showed interest. However, she was ready to establish herself on her own terms but even if she was ready, the general public wasn't. She recorded the "Betty Davis" album in San Francisco in 1973 for the Just Sunshine label and although it wasn't a commercial success it helped Davis to create a hat trick of ground-breaking Funk albums that continued with 1974's "They Say I'm Different" and 1975's "Nasty Gal". If her albums weren't lighting up the charts, singles barely made a flicker. On stage she strutted and crouched in thigh high boots and lingerie but away from the stage she was strictly business, preferring mineral water and rice cakes to drugs. Betty was deemed too controversial with both her sexually charged lyrics and equally promiscuous stage act. She was banned from television, had some of her shows boycotted and her songs weren't played on the radio due to pressure from certain religious groups and the NAACP. Arguably she was the Princess of Funk before Prince came on the scene and even before Rick James cornered the sexual revolution in the genre. Then she turned away from the music industry and moved back to Pittsburgh to become a recluse.

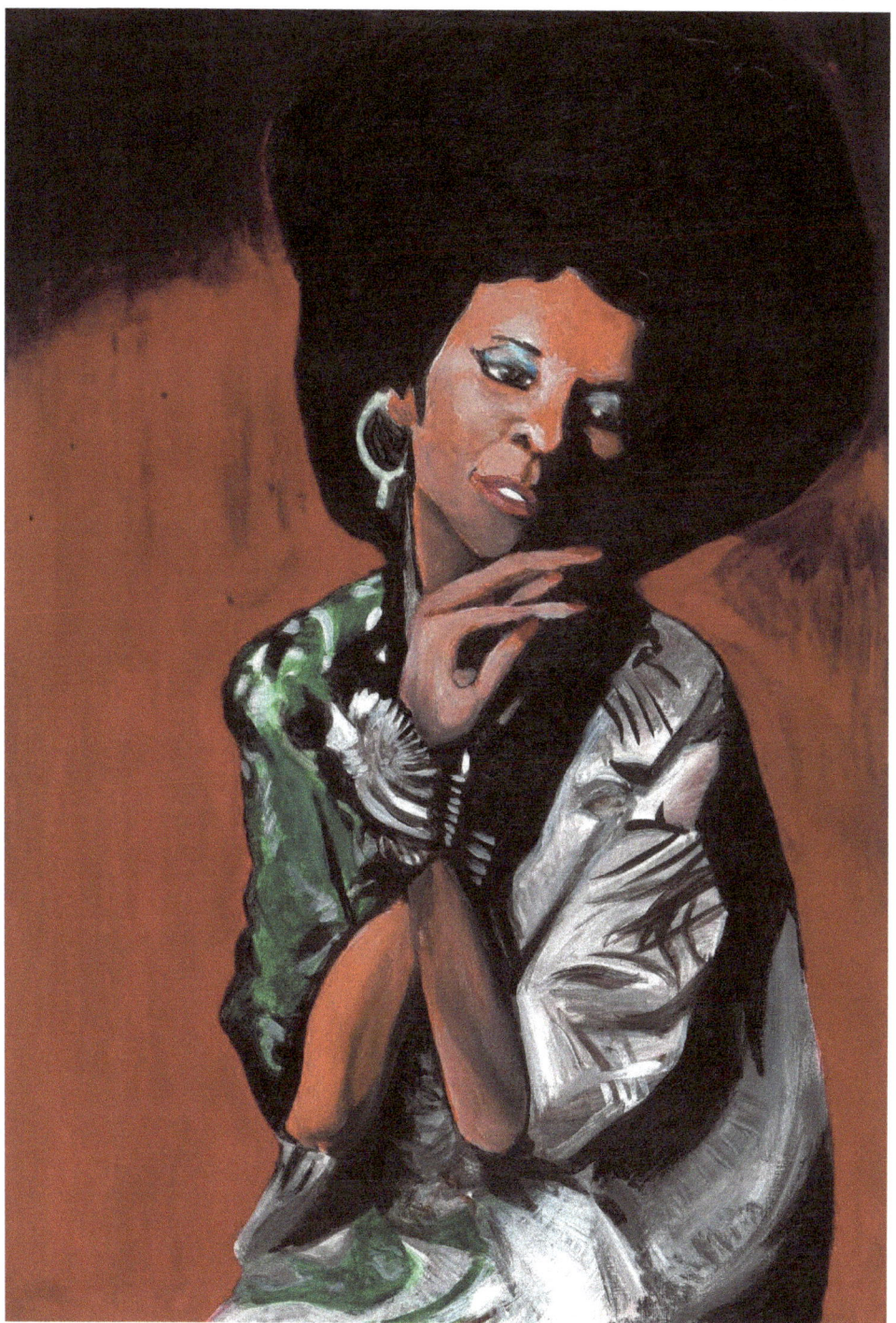

Cissy Houston

Cissy Houston was born Emily Drinkard on September the 30th 1933 in Newark, New Jersey. The Drinkard family had a decent amount of farmland in Georgia at a time when African Americans weren't known to own land. As this dwindled, they found their way to New Jersey during what became known as the Great Migration. This had started in 1916 when there was a need for more industrial output which eventually saw six million black Americans migrate to the North seeking better social conditions and employment. In 1938 she joined the family Gospel group The Drinkards but the same year her mother suffered a stroke. Eight-year-old Cissy lost her mother in 1941 from a cerebral haemorrhage and in 1952 her father passed away from stomach cancer. She moved in with her older sister and her husband, the Warricks who had a son and two daughters, Dionne and Delia, better known as Dee. With the Drinkards Cissy's taste of recording came with the first Gospel act to release an album "A Joyful Noise" on a major label, RCA in 1958. In 1963 Cissy Houston was due to give birth to Whitney but took time to form The Sweet Inspirations. As their career blossomed, the group became one of the most sought-after backing groups giving support to Otis Redding, Wilson Pickett, Lou Rawls, The Drifters, Aretha Franklin and Cissy's niece Dionne Warwick who had changed her surname slightly. By 1967 they were given the opportunity to have their own material released on Atlantic and famously appeared on Van Morrison's single "Brown Eyed Girl" as well as on Jimi Hendrix' "Burning of the Midnight Lamp" in 1968. A year later they backed Elvis Presley and Cissy went solo. As her children were growing up, she chose to stop touring and concentrate on her recording career. She already had a taste of this as far back as 1963 under the name of Cecily Blair but in 1969 she signed to the Commonwealth United Record label and "Presenting Cissy Houston" was released in 1970. Back up singing continued with Paul Simon's "Mother and Child Reunion" in 1972, the same year she cut the original of "Midnight Train to Georgia". As well as her recording career Cissy was still drawn to Gospel and was choirmaster at the New Hope Baptist Church in Newark. Cissy continued her multi-faceted career but her daughter was the one whose name was being talked about now. In 1987 they duetted on "I Know Him So Well" but then Cissy took on a role she would not have wished for, that of a grieving parent. On the 11th of February 2012 Whitney Houston was found submerged in a bathtub and pronounced dead. Her death was caused by drowning and the effects of atherosclerotic heart disease and cocaine which she appeared to have taken prior to her death. Cissy performed "Bridge over Troubled Water" at the tribute for her daughter at the BET Music Awards.

Art & Soul

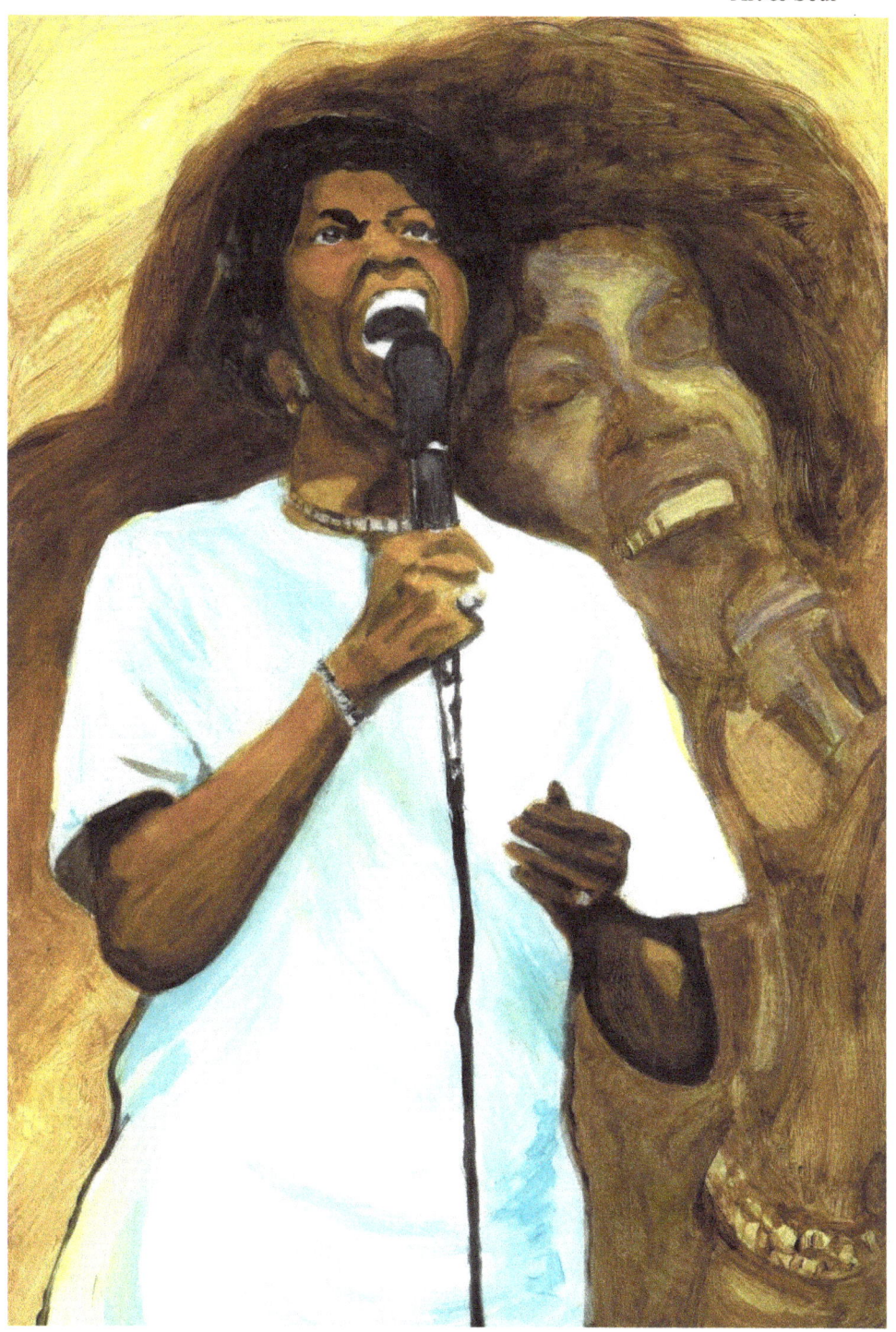

The Isley Brothers

When you look at The Isleys' history and the songs we know through others' covers I felt for once a group was justified in taking something back. The Isley Brothers had been around as long as Soul, having left Cincinnati for New York where they released their first single, "Angels Cried" for the Teenage label. They came to prominence in 1958 with the original version of "Shout". After this they moved to Atlantic and Wand where their version of The Top Notes "Twist and Shout" reached Number 17 on the National Chart in 1964. Prior to their signing to Motown, they had begun to develop their own T-Neck operation. T-Neck had been named after their new hometown of Teaneck, New Jersey but the Atlantic distributed label failed to do anything for them as the opening release in 1964, "Testify" saw no chart action. The track is probably more famous for including a searing guitar solo by their resident guitarist, 'Spider', known to the world as Jimi Hendrix. Likewise, the next three T-Neck productions released on the Atlantic label failed to chart. So, by the time the brothers joined Motown they were already an established act and therefore a little away from the other Motown acts who had come through the Motown groom. The Brothers didn't seem to fit into, or rather were unprepared to be moulded into being just another Motown act. On departing the label, they formed their own label, T Neck scoring first time around with "It's Your Thing", aimed at Berry Gordy Jr. The original three Brothers were later joined by a younger strain of Isleys - Ernie and Marvin with cousin Chris Jasper on keyboards. As a trio they had been playing together since 1969 but with T Neck going to CBS for distribution, they prepared the "3 + 3" album in 1973 in conjunction with 'That Lady" the most successful single they had put out despite an already impressive track record. "That Lady'" had first seen light of day back in 1964 and now with Ernie Isley's stunning electric guitar many punters cried out that he was the natural successor to Jimi Hendrix. "Summer Breeze" drove us to the Coast with its evocation of all things hot and for once the argument over watered down versions being cut from originals is turned around and as The Isley Brothers showed they too could make a song their own and far more effectively than when the role was often reversed. The crossover was so successful that most people still relate the song to The Isleys rather than its originators Seals & Crofts. If this wasn't enough, we still 'The Highways of My Life'. If they had only the three pop successes of "That Lady", "Summer Breeze" and 'The Highways of My Life' they'd have left their legacy but theirs had already been established and continued way after the three became six.

Art & Soul

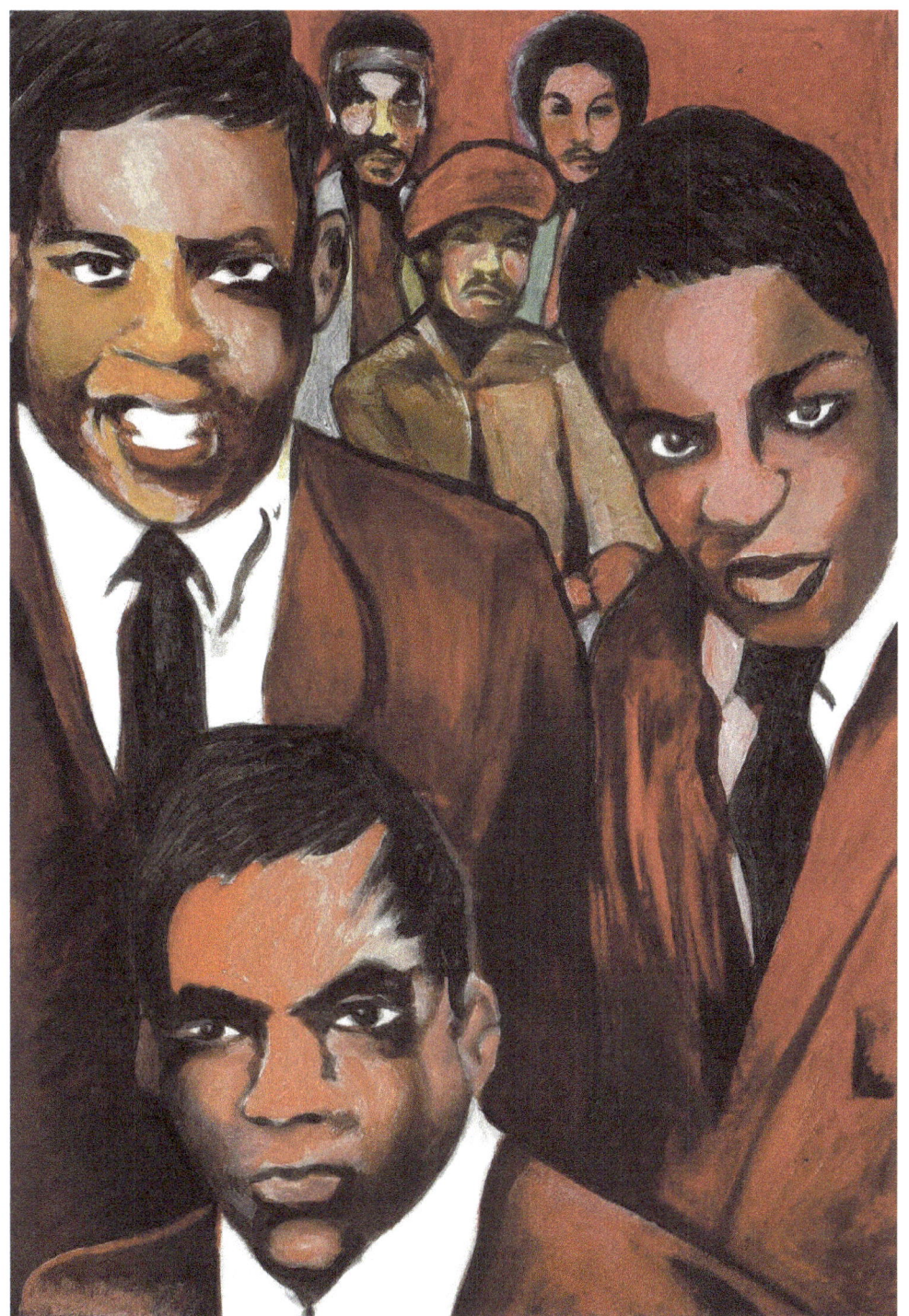

King Curtis

Curtis Ousley was born Curtis Montgomery in Fort Worth, Texas on the 7th of February 1934 but both he and his sister were adopted by Josie and William Ousley hence the name change. King Curtis had started playing at the age of twelve and at I.M Terrell High School in Fort Worth, he studied and also performed with Ornette Coleman, no slouch himself on the sax and turned down college scholarships so that he could join Lionel Hampton's band. In 1952 Curtis moved to New York and became an in-demand session musician for several labels and by 1958 was often called the fifth Coaster starting with "Yakety Yak". The Coasters material would have been completely different had his saxophone solos not have been there to jolly along the humour filled storylines. 1958 also saw him recording with Laverne Baker, most notably on "I Cried A Tear". Curtis also put his own group, The Kingpins, together consisting of Richard Tee, Cornell Dupree, Jerry Jermott and Bernard Purdie. A Supergroup of sidemen who would impress on such tracks as "Soul Twist" in 1962 which reached Number One on the R&B chart and Number Seventeen on the Billboard Pop chart, the haunting "Soul Serenade" cut in 1964 and most famously after moving to Atlantic Records in 1965, "Memphis Soul Stew" released in 1967. Prior to that the Kingpins had opened for The Beatles in 1965 at the Shea Stadium on their debut tour of the States and in 1966 he cut three unissued tracks with Jimi Hendrix. As well as these skills Curtis was also a musical director and record producer then in March 1971 Curtis and his Kingpins backed Aretha Franklin at Fillmore which became a Live Album and July saw him appearing on John Lennon's "Imagine" album. The same year he recorded the theme for Don Cornelius' television show "Soul Train" called "Hot Potatoes". Never one to be boxed in he returned to his Jazz roots performing at the Montreux Jazz Festival on June the 17th alongside Champion Jack Dupree. Then two months later King Curtis was stabbed and killed after an argument with two drug dealers who refused to move off his steps. That was the year I first heard "Giving Up" performed by Donny Hathaway which also introduced me to King Curtis because of his outstanding saxophone solo while the slow steady drumbeat was supplied by Al Jackson of Booker T. & The MGs. Atlantic closed its offices on the day of his funeral and Reverend Jesse Jackson conducted the service. The Kingpins played "Soul Serenade", Aretha sang the Spiritual "Never Grow Old" and Stevie Wonder performed "Abraham, Martin and John" and included King Curtis. In 1975 Al Jackson was shot by an intruder in his home. Donny Hathaway committed suicide in 1979 and by the end of 1980 John Lennon was shot in the street. Maybe somewhere there's an angelic jam going on with these lost artists. Imagine.

Art & Soul

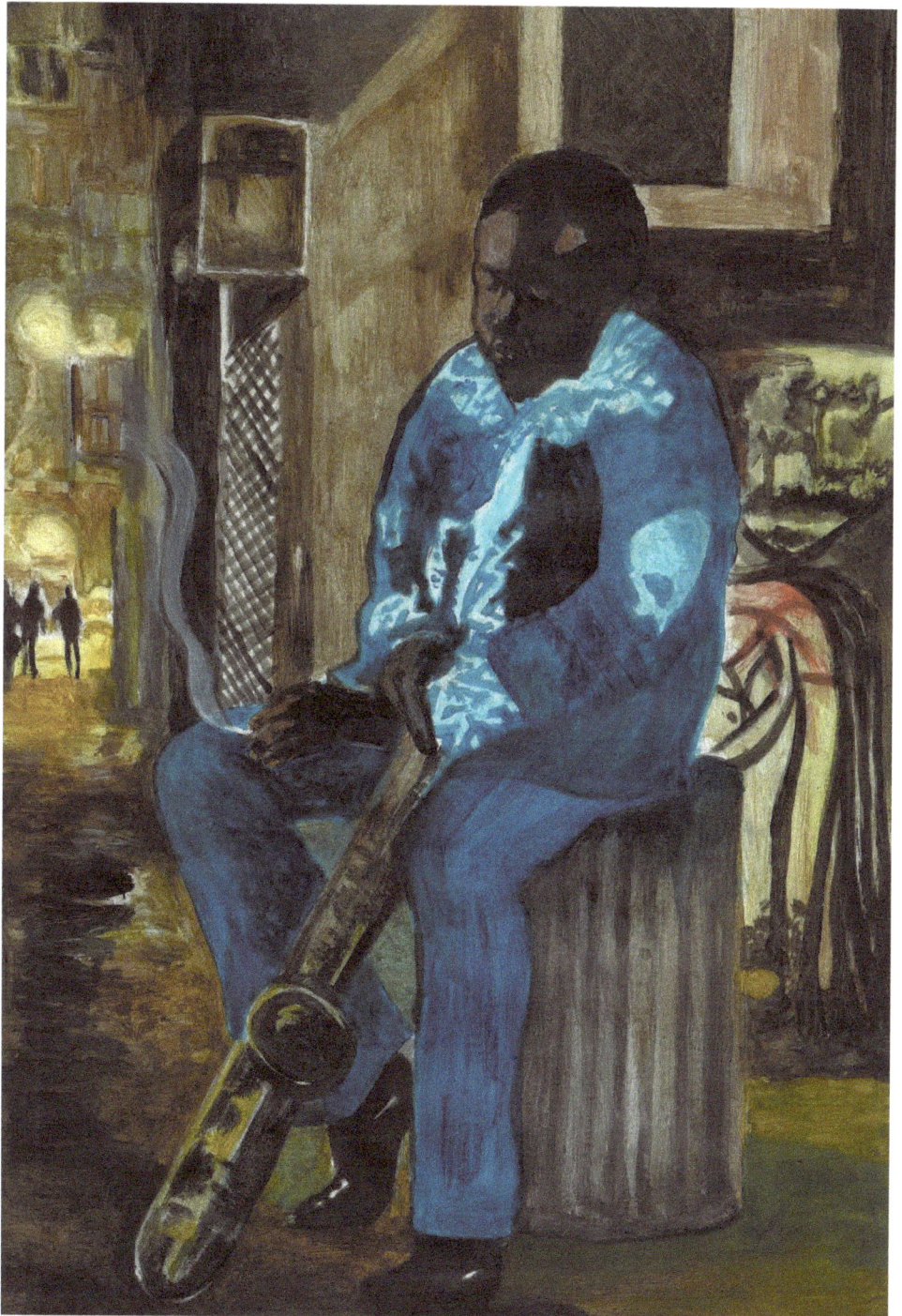

Linda Jones

At Art College I always tried to share my music with my friends and one night I played "For Your Precious Love" by Linda Jones. This is the only time I have ever seen somebody 'floored' by her voice. He may have been taking his non-prescribed 'medicine' but it was a sight to behold. Ninety miles from Philly and just across the river from the Big Apple lay New Jersey. Linda Jones was born in Newark, New Jersey on the 14th December 1944 and started singing in her family's gospel group the Jones Singers at the age of six. Under the name of Linda Lane, she cut her first record "Lonely Teardrops" for the Cub label in 1963 then after being noticed by songwriter Jerry Harris was introduced to George Kerr, a renowned producer from Motown through to Philly who hit the New Jersey scene and she then recorded for the ATCO label in 1964 and Blue Cat the following year. From there Kerr took her to the Warner Brothers label where she signed to their Loma label in 1967. Her first release "Hypnotised" fell short of making the U.S. Top 20 but did reach number four on the Billboard R&B chart. This was the label's bestselling single and was followed by "What've I Done?" as well as her first album then after Loma closed in late 1968, Jones had a final single on the main Warner label. After a very brief period with Contique records, Kerr managed to get her a deal with Gamble and Huff's Neptune label, but the collapse of Neptune cut her career short until she signed to Stang/All Platinum in 1971 where she was reunited with Kerr for releases on the Turbo label. It finally seemed that her career was beginning to take off. To some listeners Linda Jones had the potential to be as big a star as Aretha Franklin but a heavy performing schedule was to prove too much for her. Linda had been involved in a national promotional tour and was performing at Harlem's famous Apollo Theatre as part of a two weeks' engagement. Sadly, her health was already poor, something she tried to deny right to the end. Linda Jones was diabetic and although she was feeling the warning signs of a diabetic attack she went on stage. While resting between the matinee and evening shows she went to her mother's home to rest and slipped into a coma. Linda Jones died on the 14th of March 1972. She was 27 years old. On June the 3rd 2021 the Grammy Museum in Newark honoured Linda by placing some of her artifacts in the New Jersey Legends exhibit and on December the 14th, the same year the city honoured her further by renaming the Sherman Avenue where she lived Linda Jones Way. Linda Jones was able to take a classic like "For Your Precious Love" on Turbo, deeper than any ocean.

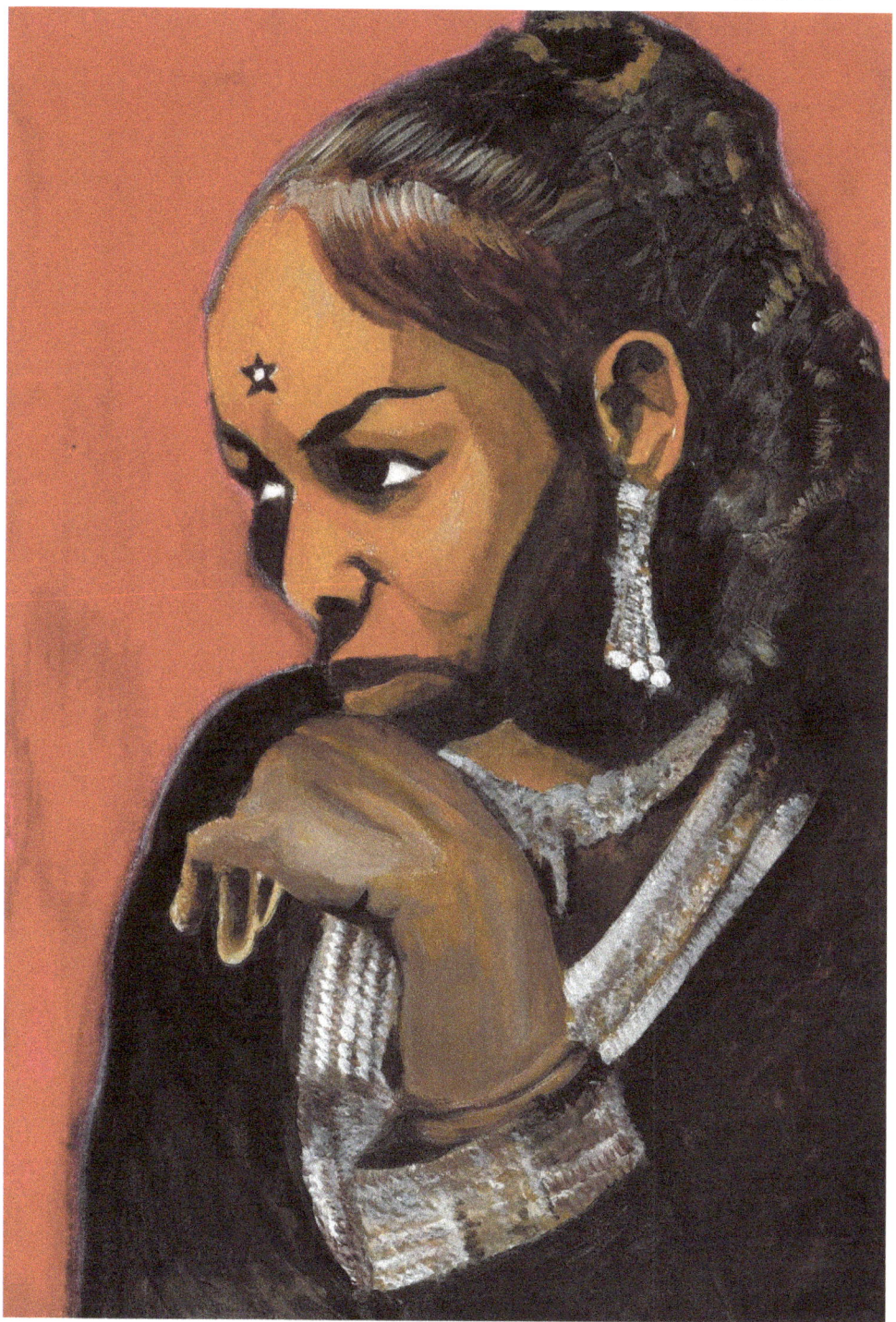

Millie Jackson

I've never been a fan of stand-up comedy, so when I saw Millie Jackson live at the Birmingham Odeon in 1977, I can't say it was the best gig I ever witnessed, and it may be considered vandalism but I've recently been transferring my vinyl onto mp3s and having chosen to make a Millie Jackson collection I removed all her comedic dialogue. I can listen to the same music all day long but once you've heard a joke that's it for me. Mildred Virginia Jackson was born on July the 15th 1944 in Thomson, Georgia: her father was a sharecropper and her mother passed away when Millie was a child, so Jubilee Jackson moved with his daughter to Newark, New Jersey. By her mid-teens she moved into the main city to live with her aunt in Brooklyn and found some modelling along the way to her musical career which started in 1964 with a series of one-nighters at Harlem's Smalls Paradise, allegedly after winning a bet to perform. After a brief spell at MGM in 1970 she signed to Spring Records and in 1971 brought out the thought-provoking "A Child of God (It's Hard to Believe") which she co-wrote. The song opens with a spoken intro which was brief, to the point and acceptable to my ears. The rest of the track was a condemnation of hypocrisy by religious followers, referencing the Ku Klux Klan and infidelity amongst other topics. I personally would have liked to hear more like this from Millie, still, it reached Number 22 on the R&B chart but more importantly announced her arrival. 1972 gave her a top ten R&B hit success with "Ask Me What You Want", another co-composition, as was its follow-up "My Man, a Sweet Man". This track proved popular in the UK on the Northern Soul scene as did 1976's "House For Sale". Back though to 1974 and the album that decided her future direction had been a well-trodden path in both Soul and Country but "Caught Up" gave a musical slant to that tangled web we weave. Jackson chose a change of personnel and recorded the album in Muscle Shoals. The album's concept was Millie's even if most of the material wasn't. Luther Ingram's "If Loving You is Wrong" opened the proceedings and Bobby Goldsboro's "Summer the First Time" closed them. Overall, an exceptional album that like any good story deserved a sequel. Hence 1975's "Still Caught Up" which followed the same pattern and went gold as did its predecessor. In 1977 her next album was a continuation of the last two, "Feelin' Bitchy". A great blend of Country and Soul classics, the highlight being "If You're Not Back in Love by Monday" originally a hit for Merl Haggard. Millie's ballad "Hurts So Good" originally released in 1973 was also included in the "Cleopatra Jones" soundtrack the same year. Millie Jackson continued to tap into the same lucrative vein until her retirement.

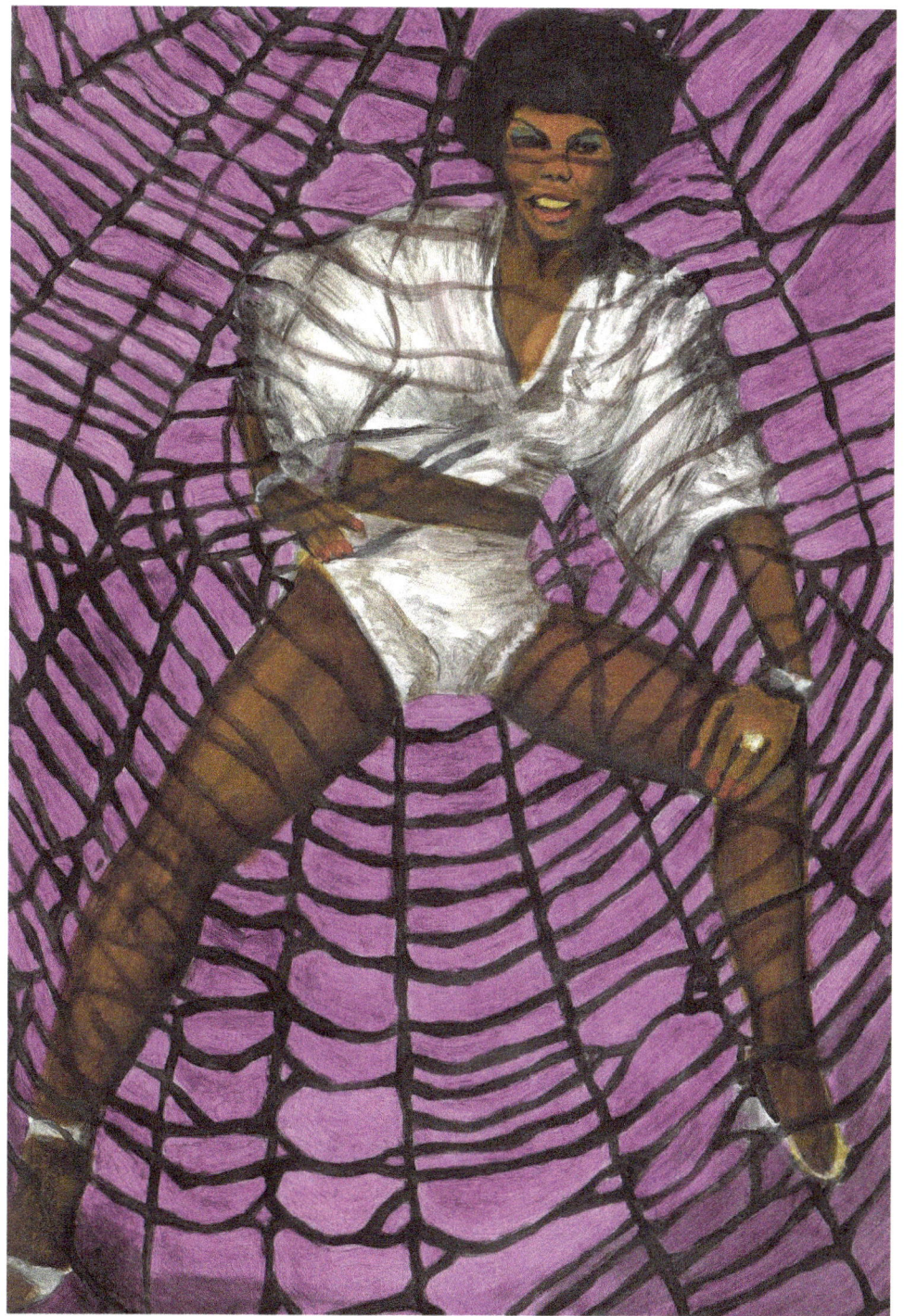

The Parliaments

The Parliaments were originally named after a brand of cigarettes and had formed in New Jersey in 1955. The members were all working in barbershops in Plainfield, New Jersey at the time and in 1957 released "Poor Willy" on ABC Records which did nothing. Their second release, "Lonely Island" issued on the local New Records also failed to make an impression and it would not be long before they realised that they would have to set their sights further than New Jersey and so set their compass to point towards Detroit. A desire to be a part of the Motown dream had seen The Parliaments move to the Motor City to work and try and get a deal and at one point were contractually tied to the label through Jobete Music in New York City in 1962 but there was some friction between that office and Headquarters in Detroit. After five frustrating years it was obvious that Motown were simply using them as a way of getting the Temptations to work harder. Their group leader, George Clinton, did work as a songwriter for Motown but after their contract expired, they signed to the rival Golden World company at a time when the label was in its final few months and released the double header "That Was My Girl" and "Heart Trouble". During his time at Golden World, he joined forces with Mike Terry and Sidney Barnes to form Geo-Si-Mik Productions. Clinton and Barnes were well acquainted by the time they arrived in Detroit as they had been introduced to each other by George Kerr in New York. Sidney moved on to Sue Records, then Red Bird Records, as a songwriter and artist. Having released themselves from their Motown contract, The Parliaments couldn't believe their misfortune when the label they had escaped from was about to buy the company they'd moved to and so they fled to LeBaron Taylor's Revilot label where they finally succeeded with "I Wanna Testify" the following year. Before that, for the Solid Hit label Clinton produced and wrote "Headache in My Heart" and "Loving You Takes all of my Time" for The Debonairs as well as producing "Day Tripper" for J.J. Barnes on Ric Tic, both in 1966. On Wednesday July 26th 1967 The Parliaments took part in the Swinging Time Revue at The Fox Theatre, on Woodward Avenue which coincided with the start of the Detroit riots. Luckily, they weren't caught up in it unlike other groups but misfortune struck once more when the Revilot label went out of business in 1969 selling all its masters to Atco. The group had to wait another year until the contract on them expired. Atco bought their masters but due to complications they could not take up individual artists contracts which meant that as The Parliaments the group became inactive. When The Parliaments finally escaped from the chains of Atco, they dropped ''The' and 's' and became plain Parliament. Although plain is perhaps the wrong word.

Art & Soul

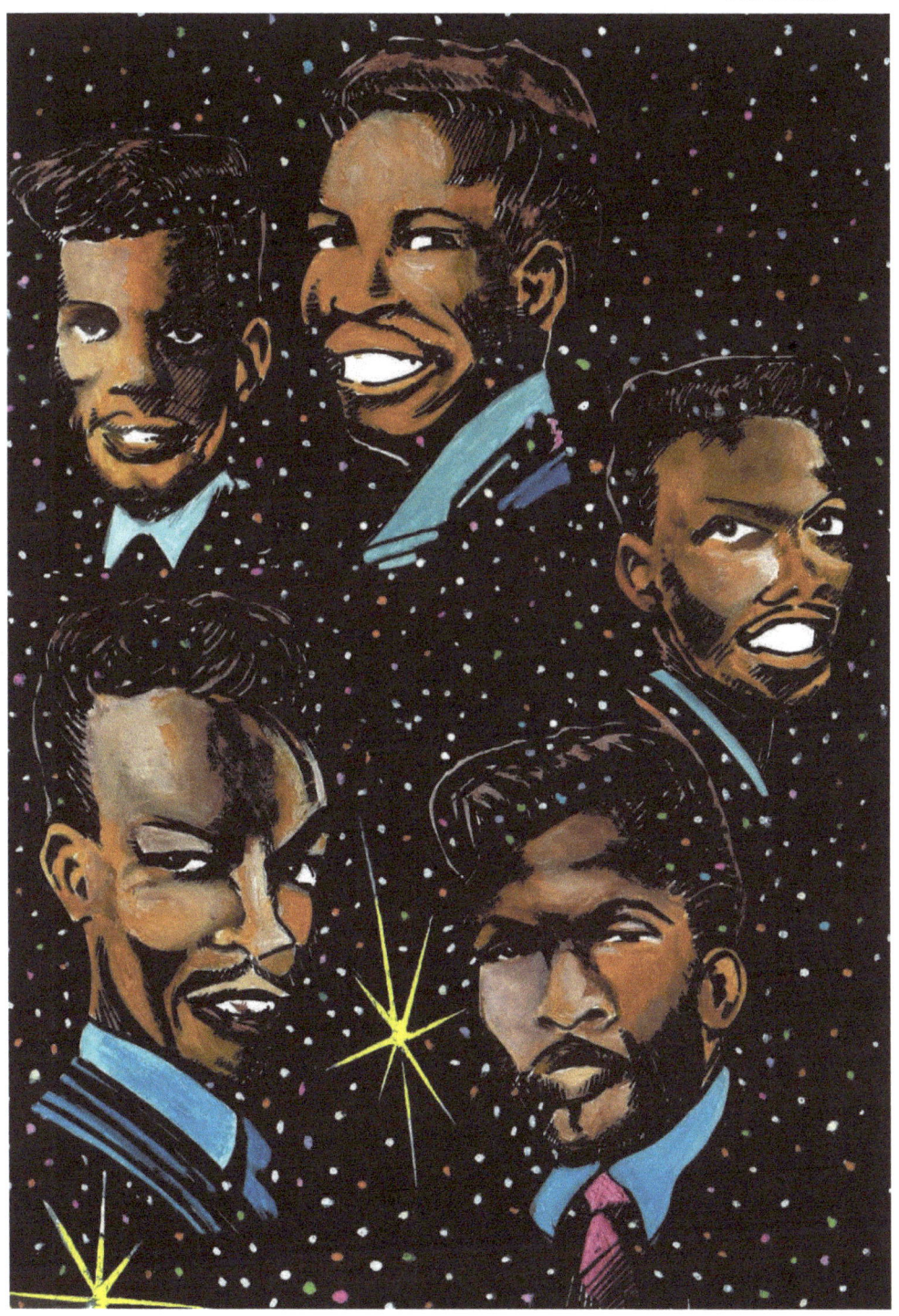

The Drifters

Having left Billy Ward & The Dominos, in May 1953, Clyde McPhatter was approached by Ahmet Ertegun of Atlantic Records and signed him to the new Atlantic label, to form a new group, The Drifters. McPhatter was drafted into the Army in May 1954 and arguably started an ongoing trend for The Drifters that would, up to date see 65 members come and go and sometimes come back again into the line-up. One such person was Johnny Moore who stepped up to the mike for, amongst other hits, "Ruby Baby". By the mid-50s, they had begun working with legendary songwriters Jerry Leiber and Mike Stoller, who eventually became the group's producers as well. What made them different as well was that the group's name was a brand, owned by their manager George Treadwell, that would lead to much confusion throughout the group's history with past members touring under a Drifters related name. Johnny Moore was drafted in November 1957 and replaced by Bobby Hendricks on "Drip Drop". Having done his Army service, Clyde McPhatter returned to Atlantic but not to The Drifters, instead he tried to make it as a solo artist, a move that would prove to be a mistake. Manager George Treadwell eventually fired the entire Drifters' singing personnel and hired most of the group previously known as The Five Crowns, including lead singer Ben E. King, promoting them under the name of The Drifters. This is the group whose sound is now generally associated with the name. The group had several successive hits, including "There Goes My Baby", "This Magic Moment", "I Count the Tears" and the most famous of all, "Save the Last Dance for Me". Ben E. King continued to record with The Drifters for about a year before beginning a successful solo career. His "Spanish Harlem" was written by Jerry Leiber and a rising songwriter/producer Phil Spector while The Drifters' "Please Stay" was co-written by another aspiring songwriter, Burt Bacharach. More creative teams housed within the famous New York Brill Building had begun to contribute to the songs, sometimes collaborating with Leiber and Stoller or going it alone. For example, "Up on the Roof" written by more future song writing legends, this time Gerry Goffin and Carole King. In 1963 Leiber and Stoller pulled away from writing and producing the group but one of their finest moments in that final year was "On Broadway". Clyde McPhatter moved to England, where he still had something of a following but returned to America in 1970, making a few appearances in rock-and-roll revival tours but lived mostly as a recluse. On June 13, 1972, he died in his sleep at the age of 39, of complications brought on by alcohol abuse.

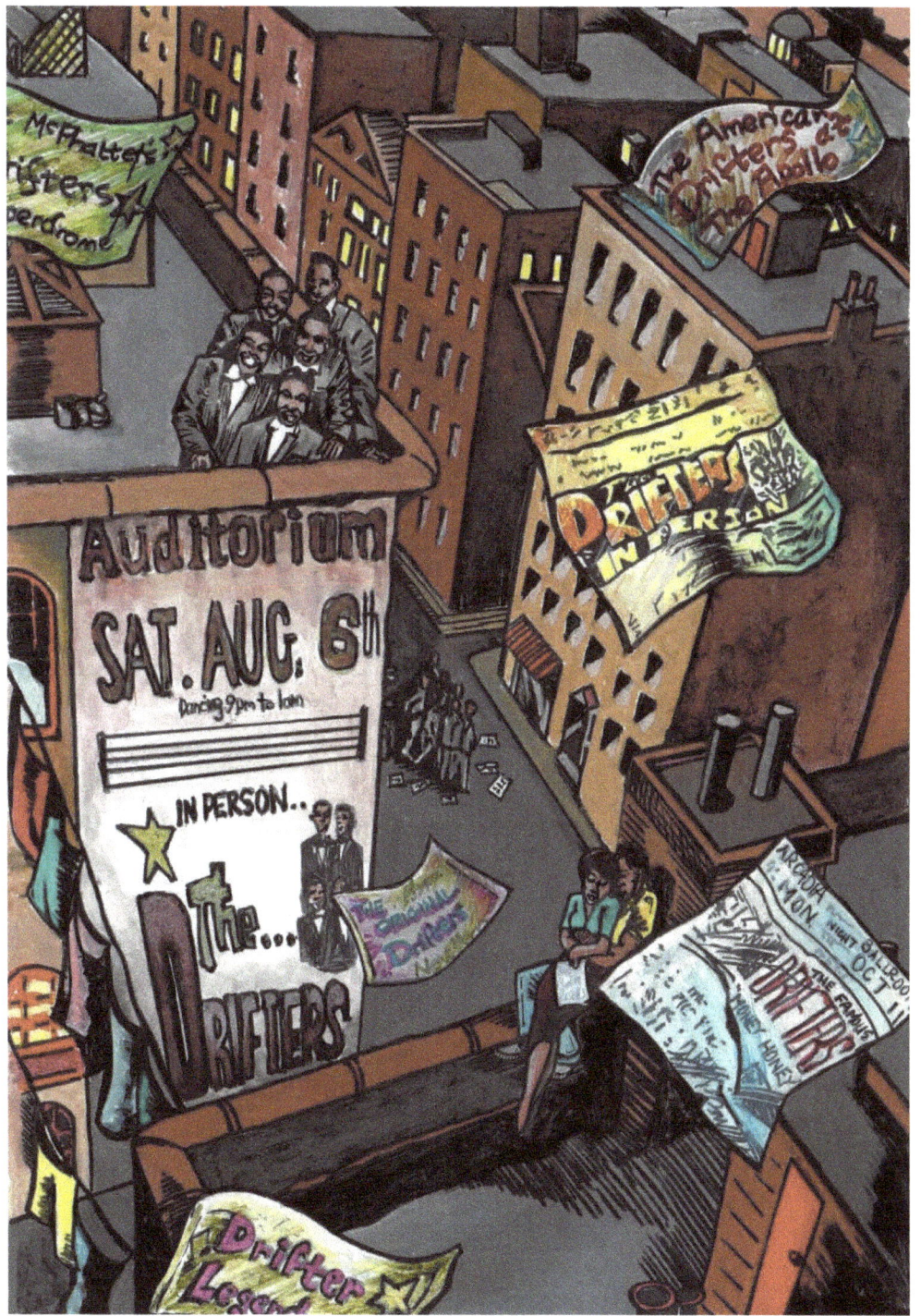

Sylvia Robinson

On the 13th day of July 1950 one Sylvia Vanderpool went into a New York recording studio and cut "Chocolate Candy Blues" with the Nelson Clark Orchestra. Five years on and the still youthful Sylvia met one Mickey Baker her guitar teacher who persuaded her mother that they should record as Mickey and Sylvia. Mom agreed and the Mickey and Sylvia partnership continued for eight years. It was in 1963 that the recording duo split up; Baker moving to France after becoming disillusioned with the New York scene. This left his recording partner, the newly married Sylvia Robinson to take a step in another creative direction by opening up the Blue Morocco night club with her husband Joe. Despite this move Sylvia still cut the occasional side with Joe's blessing. A year later and the Platinum label was launched only to be changed to All Platinum to avoid confusion with a Miami based company. Joe also decided that he wanted to add something beginning with "A" because distributors paid in alphabetical order. At first the label was run from a basement on West Palisades Avenue before success afforded a move to the more salubrious trappings of West Street. All Platinum, quite rightly, started with Sylvia and "I Can't Help It" although Sylvia had decided already that the other side of the recording industry was more for her. Turbo powered on with Brother To Brother's handling of Gil Scott-Heron's classic "The Bottle". So tight were the people who made All Platinum a force to be reckoned with in those dizzy Disco days. Changes were about to see All Platinum slowly wind down as the enormity of rap began to be understood, with Sylvia pioneering the new musical movement with her Sugarhill Record label and the Sugarhill Gang's "Rappers Delight" released in 1979. The story goes that Blondie's Debbie Harry invited Nile Rodgers from Chic to a hip-hop event in New York. In September the following year, the two groups shared a concert and whilst playing "Good Times" members of the Sugarhill Gang jumped on stage and started 'freestyling'. Moving on a few weeks and Nile Rodgers was at the Leviticus Club in New York when he heard the bass line from "Good Times". Rodgers questioned the disc jockey about the track which turned out to be a rough cut of "Rappers Delight". Nile Rogers and Bernard Edwards initially threatened legal action but settled out of court with their names being added as co-composers. When Nile Rogers and Bernard Edwards went into the studio to cut this rhythm, little did they know that they had given future generations invaluable DNA to keep the dancefloors full for years to come with over 150 tracks sampling it.

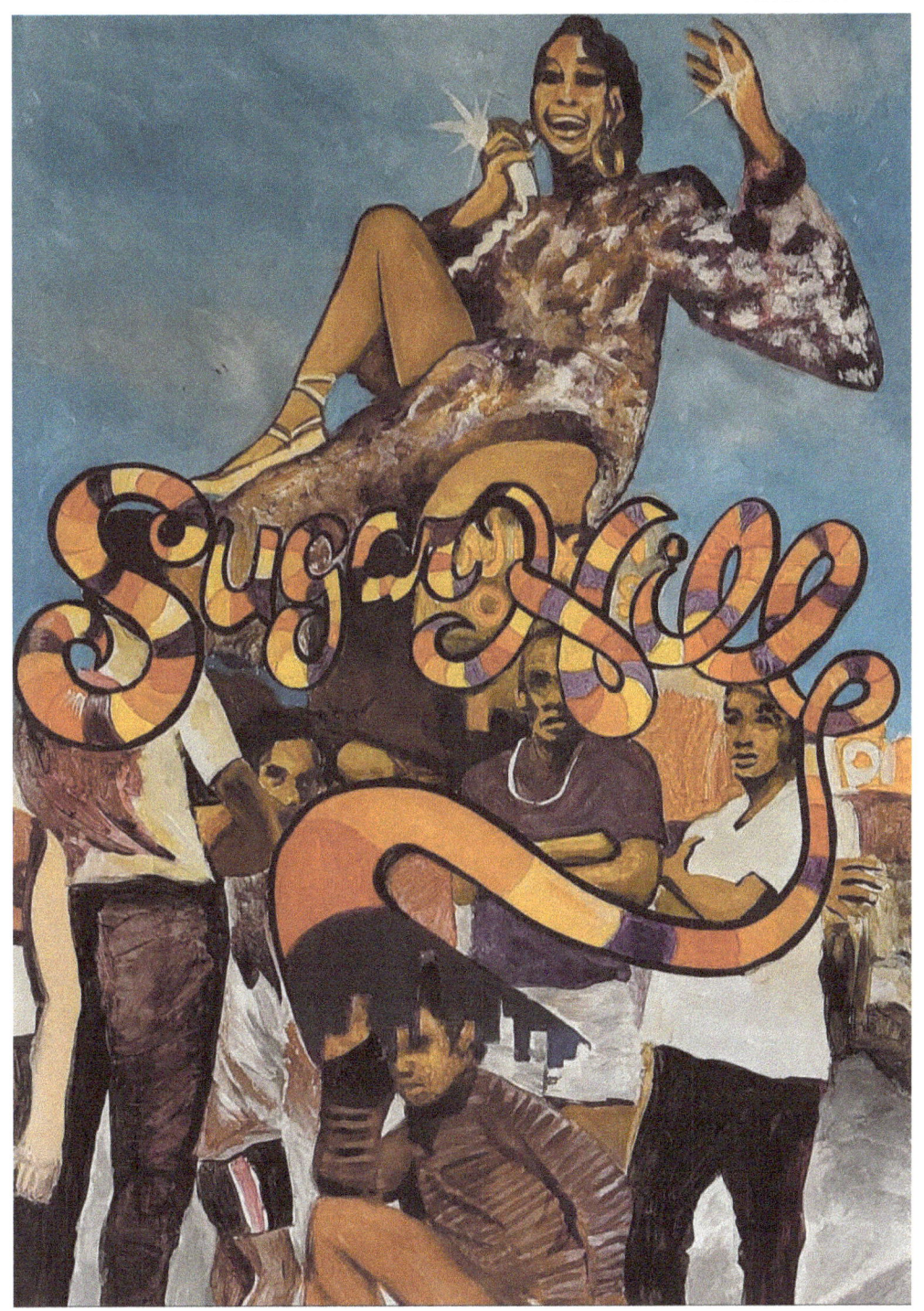

Roberta Flack

For every Laura Lee there was a Millie Jackson, just like for every Minnie Riperton there was a Deniece Williams and for every Aretha Franklin there was a Shirley Brown. We should remember that Soul music was part of a business and like any business, money mattered so if Hot Wax were selling millions from Detroit, Spring in New York would like a piece of the pie. When Donny Hathaway died the market was flooded with sound-a-likes; so for every Roberta Flack there was, well actually, there wasn't. What she had was unique and if critics found it hard to equate her uniqueness with Soul that was their problem. Artists often push boundaries, whether in their choice of songs, lyrics or instrumentation which was what Roberta Flack did. Listen to "Business Goes on as Usual", a protest song about the Vietnam conflict and I dare you not to be moved. Born Roberta Cleopatra Flack on February the 10th 1937 in Black Mountain, North Carolina she played piano for the Lomax African Methodist Episcopal Zion Church, often going to a nearby Baptist church to hear more contemporary Gospel as supplied by Sam Cooke and Mahalia Jackson. By fifteen she became the youngest student to enrol at the renowned Howard University and was awarded a full music scholarship and began to drift towards singing as well as keyboard. At nineteen she graduated but her father's sudden death saw a move to Farmville, North Carolina where she taught English and music. In Washington, D.C. she continued teaching but at night she was beginning to perform at local clubs. At the Tivoli club she would accompany opera singers but during intermission she'd sing blues, folk and pop standards in a back room, just her and the piano. This progressed to a professional gig at Mr Henry's Restaurant on Capitol Hill, Washington where Jazz artist Les McCann saw her and arranged an audition at Atlantic Records. In November 1968 Roberta recorded thirty-nine song demos in less than ten hours and in June 1969 her debut album "First Take" was issued. The response wasn't good but her luck changed when Clint Eastwood asked for her version of Ewan McColl's "The First Time Ever I Saw Your Face" to be used in his directorial debut, "Play Misty for Me". In 1972 the song stayed at number one on the pop chart for six weeks and became a gold record selling over a million copies. The following year saw it receiving the Grammy Award for Record of the Year. 1972 was also the year that she began recording with Donny Hathaway winning another Grammy for "Where is the Love" Roberta Flack became the first artist to win two consecutive Grammies, following "The First Time Ever I Saw Your Face" with "Killing Me Softly" in 1974. After an incredible career it was announced that Roberta was diagnosed with amyotrophic lateral sclerosis which made it impossible for her to sing.

Art & Soul

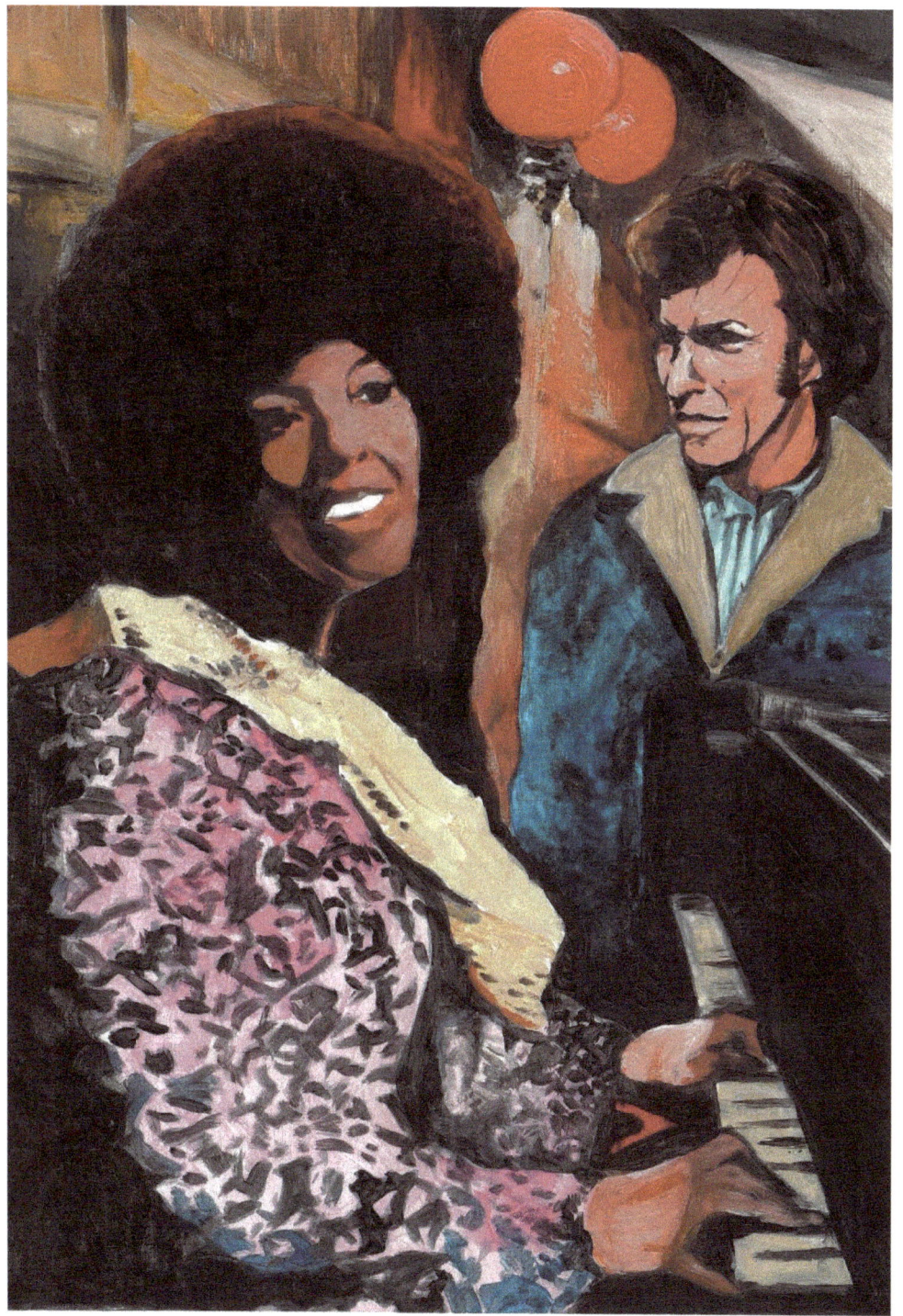

Esther Phillips

Esther Mae Jones was born on December the 23rd 1935 in Galveston, Texas. By the time she was in her teens her parents divorced so her time was divided between her father in Houston and her mother in Watts, Los Angeles. I first became aware of her through her New York based Kudu material starting in 1972 with her rendition of Gil Scott-Heron's song about a junkie's life, "Home is where the Hatred is". The song was nominated for a Grammy, but the award went to Aretha Franklin who selflessly handed the trophy to Esther Phillips who she felt deserved it more. The song could have been her own story as she became a heroin addict at the same time as her career was taking off. Like others Esther sang in the church and reluctantly entered a talent competition at the Barrelhouse Blues club in 1949 aged fourteen. The club was owned by performer Johnny Otis who signed her to the Modern label and also put her in his California Rhythm & Blues Caravan touring team. She was given the name Little Esther, later taking the name Philips from a sign in a Gas Station. Her first hit was on the Savoy label in 1950, "Double Crossing Blues" a number 9 hit on the R&B chart but by 1954 her hits began to slow down but not her heroin addiction so she returned to Houston to her father and began her first recuperation. Over the next few years, she would work nightclubs to pay her bills and feed her ongoing addiction. It would take country singer Kenny Rogers to help her out after seeing her singing in Houston. This was now 1962 and he got her contracted to his brother's Lenox label where she adopted the Esther Philips moniker on her records and cut a version of "Release Me", later a British number one for Engelbert Humperdinck in 1967. After Lenox she signed to Atlantic where, in 1965 she cut a version of The Beatles "And I Love Him" which led to them flying her over to the UK for live performances. Her new popularity wasn't enough to keep the heroin at bay and in 1969, even though she was having treatment, she still found time to record, this time for the Roulette label and then Atlantic before re-uniting with Johnny Otis for the Monterey Jazz Festival in 1970. This was her brightest period with the new decade taking her to the Kudu label, part of Creed Taylor's CTI set-up, where she recorded seven highly commended albums and her most successful single, her disco-flavoured take on Dinah Washington's "What a Difference a Day Makes". At the age of forty-eight she was dead because of liver and kidney failure due to her drug abuse and to add insult to her self-inflicted injury she was initially buried in an unmarked pauper's grave. She pre-dated Soul but certainly suffered with the Blues.

Art & Soul

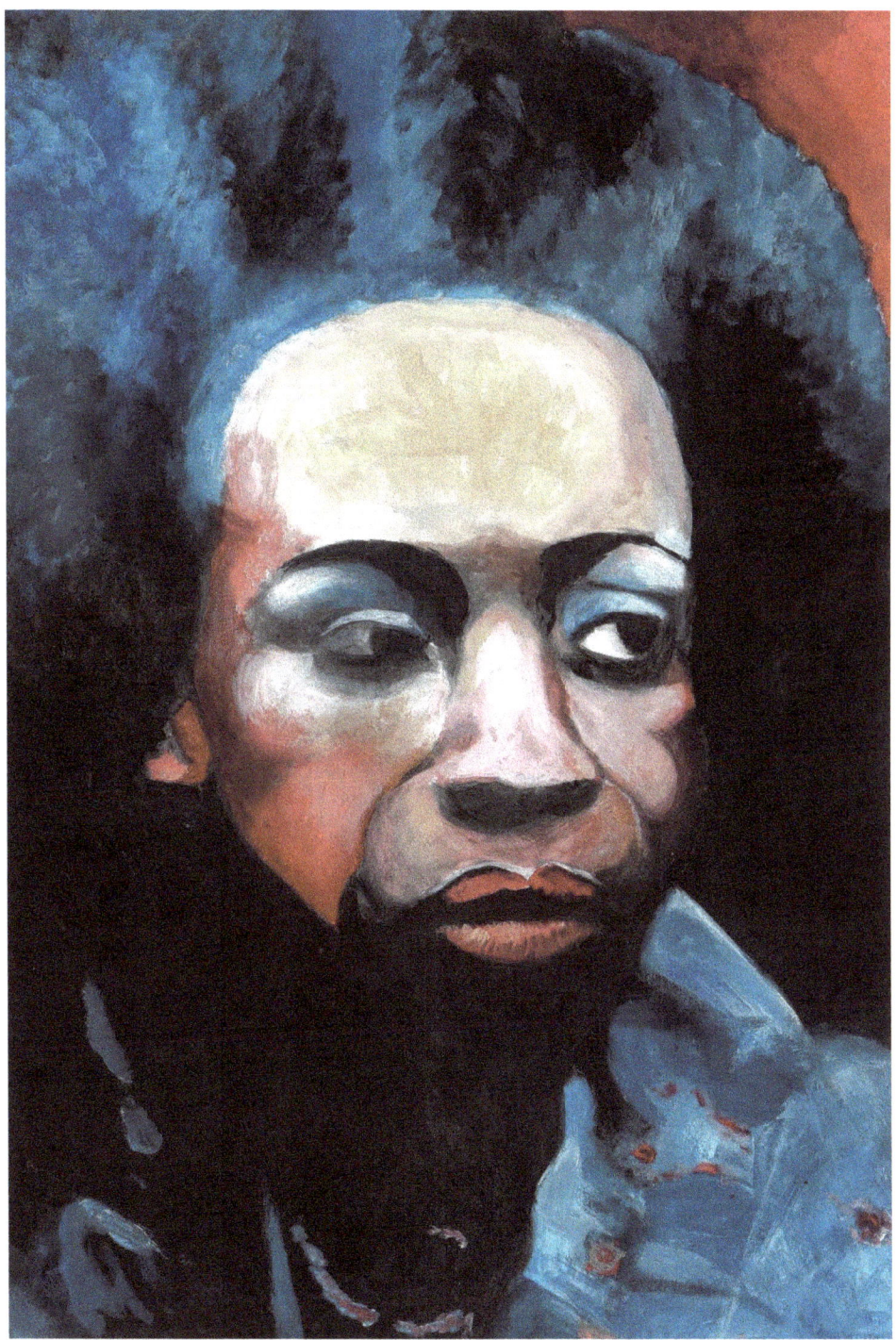

Melba Moore

Melba Moore is her stage name. She was born either Beatrice Melba Hill or Smith on October the 29th 1945 in Harlem, New York. That much is clear but when your career has shifted in as many directions as Melba's you can understand and forgive an element of confusion. Her mother was Gertrude Melba Smith who sang under the name of Bonnie Davis while her father Teddy Hill was a big band leader. At the age of nine her mother remarried Jazz pianist Clement Leroy Moorman and they moved across to Newark, New Jersey. Melba graduated High School in 1958 and began her recording career in 1967 cutting "Magic Touch" which didn't see a release until 1986 but also started her performing career in the musical 'Hair'. Three years later she graduated from Montclair State College with a BA in music and won a Tony Award for Best Performance by a Female Actress in a Musical for her part as Lutiebelle in "Purlie". Following this she got two movie roles in 1970 and a television series in 1972. Despite this continuing success, her accountants and managers left her in 1973, so she returned to Newark performing in benefit concerts but after a performance at Harlem's Apollo Theatre in '74 she met record manager and business promoter Charles Huggins who secured a deal for her with Buddha Records in 1975 where her critically acclaimed album "Peach Melba" was released. In 1976 she began to move within her recording career with the worldwide hit "This is It" written and produced by Van McCoy. The same year saw the song "Lean on Me" receive a Grammy nomination. The song was previously cut by Melba's idol Aretha Franklin. In 1978 Melba returned to Broadway appearing in "Timbuktu!" alongside Eartha Kitt while her recording career took a step backwards. Then in May 1979 the Philadelphia duo McFadden & Whitehead produced "Pick Me Up, I'll Dance" and a cover of The Bee Gees' "You Stepped into my Life" on the Epic label which returned her to the charts. A new decade brought a new label, Capitol and with it a new hope for success which started with 1982's "Love's Comin' at Ya" and continued with "Mind Up Tonight". In 1983 she re-recorded "This Is It" as a tribute to Van McCoy who had passed away in 1979. In 1985 "Read My Lips" got Melba another Grammy nomination but this time for Best Female Rock Performance. This made her only the third black artist, behind Donna Summer and Michael Jackson to be nominated in the rock category. She continued with her musical successes in 1986 with two number one R&B hits including the duet with Freddie Jackson "A Little Bit More". As the decade drew to an end the musical side went to the back burner again but the acting side was heating up once more for Moore.

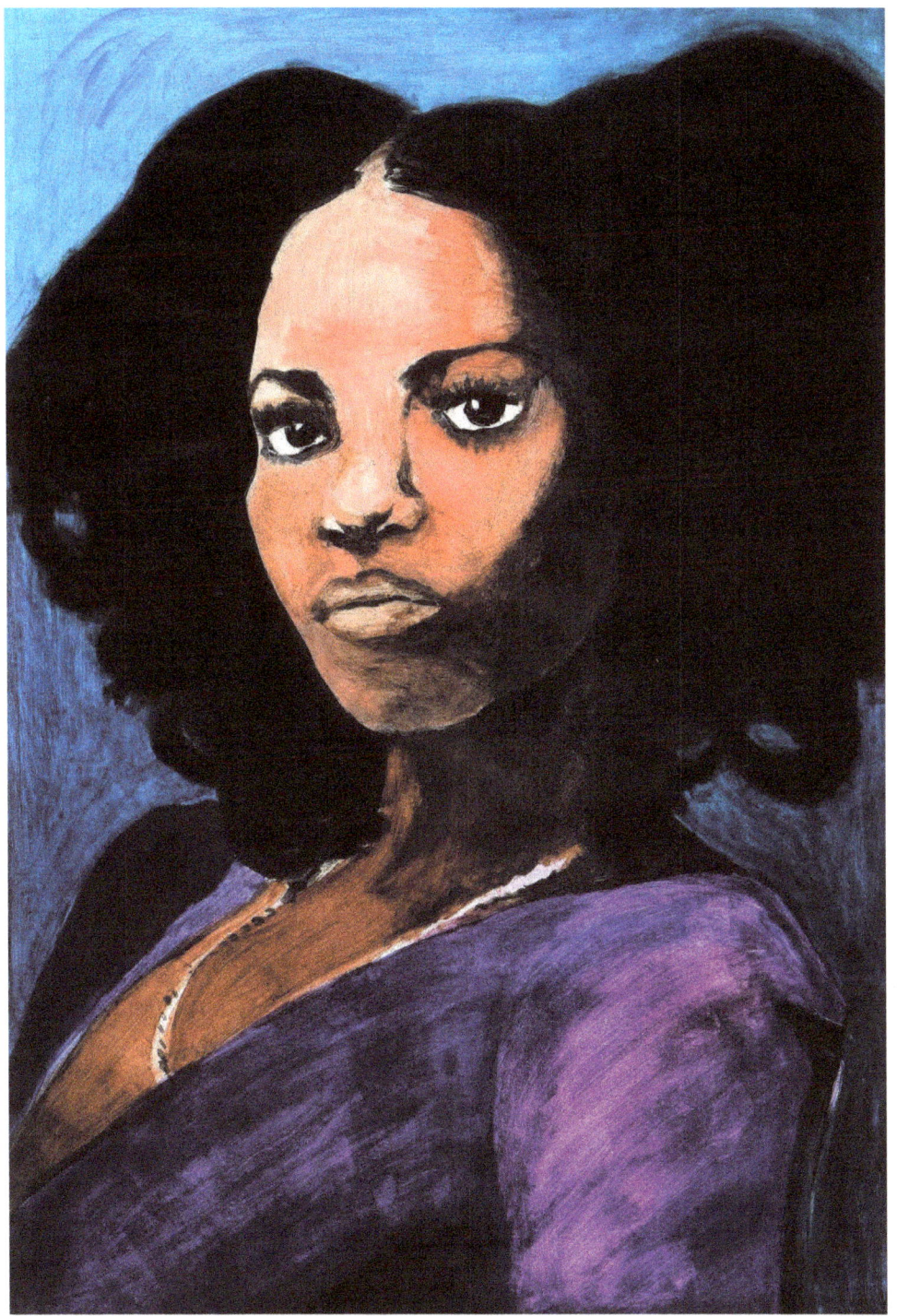

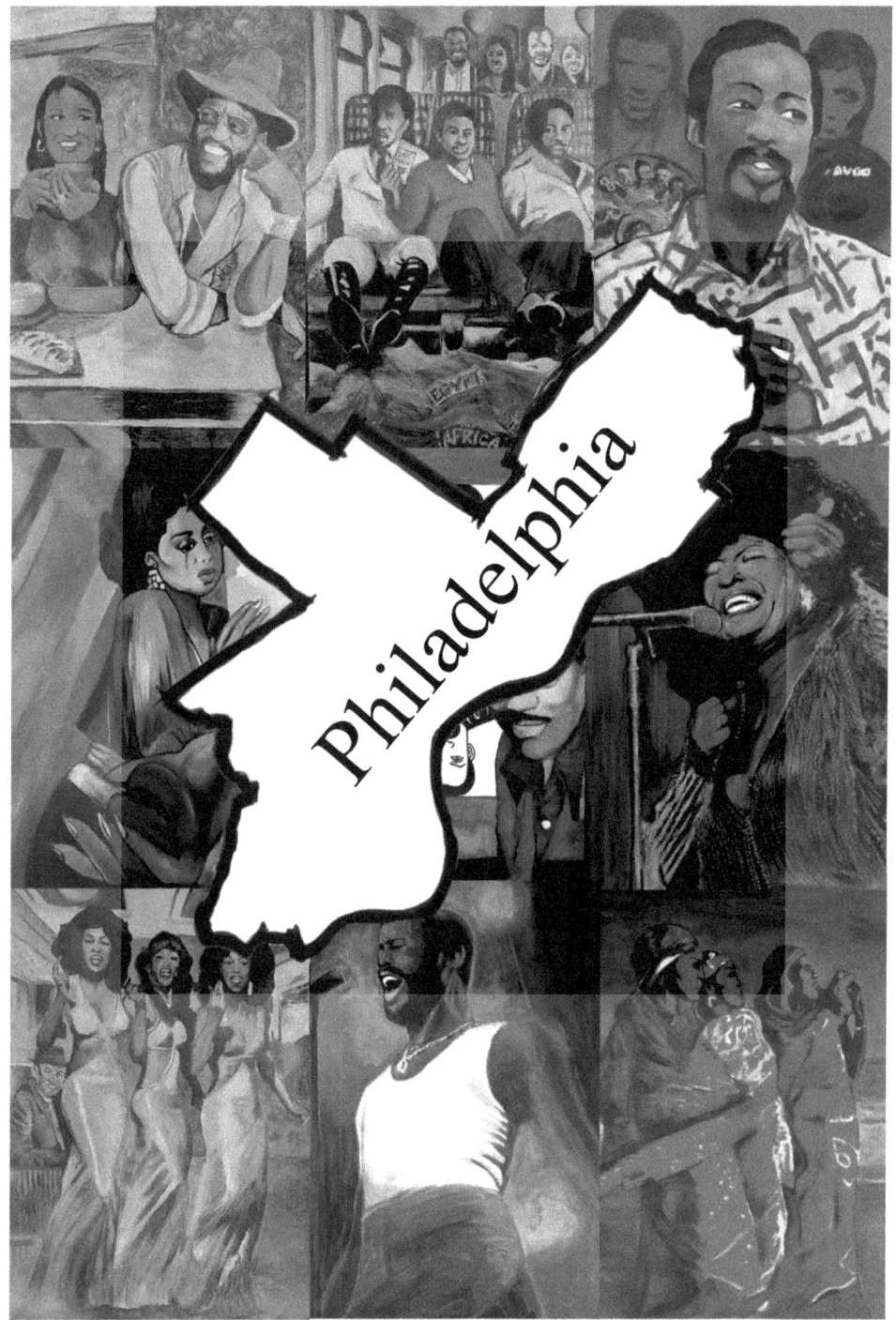

Art & Soul

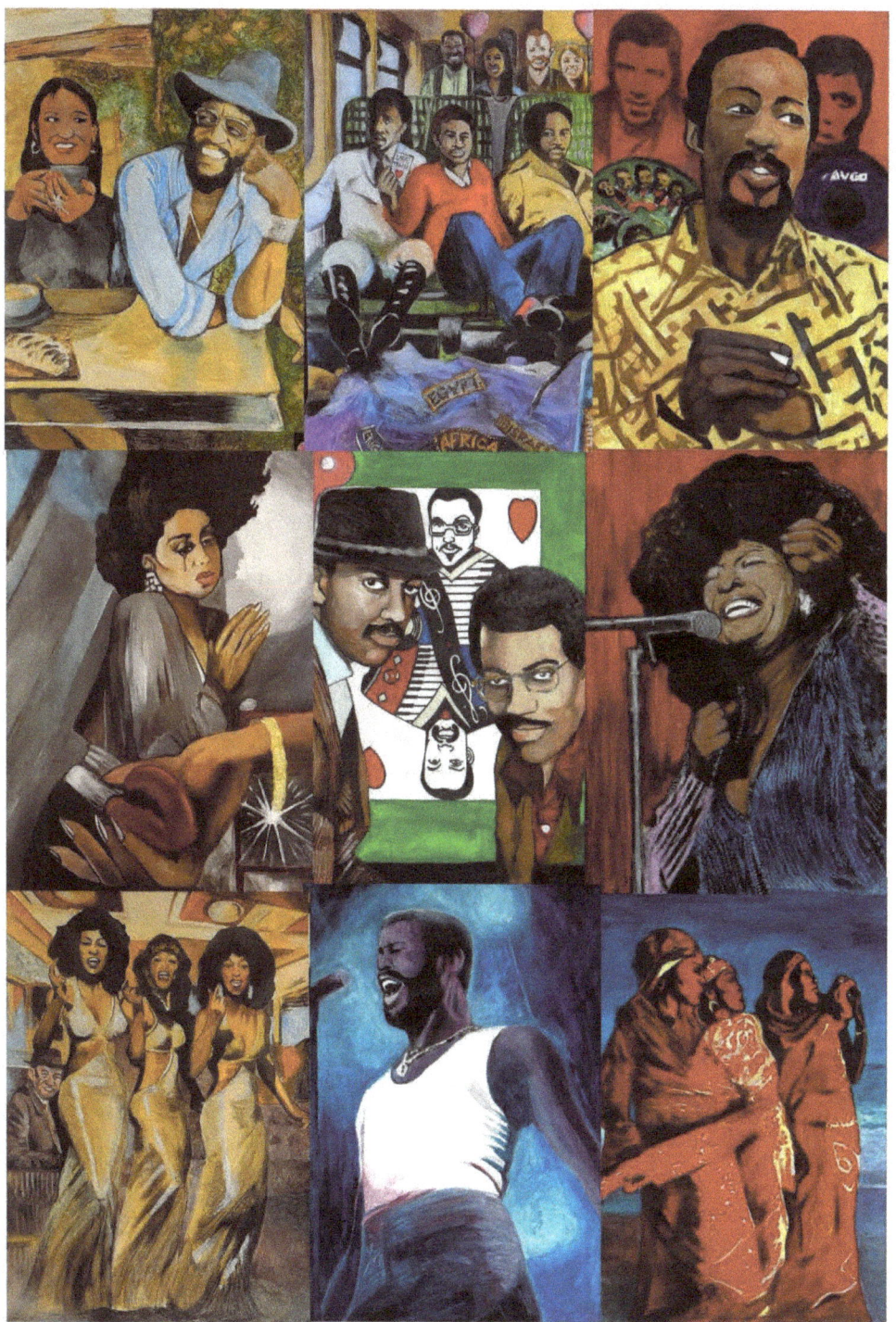

Gamble & Huff

What is unique about Gamble & Huff is that they epitomize what became known as The Sound of Philadelphia in a much greater way than say Holland-Dozier-Holland represented Detroit or Willie Mitchell Memphis. The Philly Sound seemed to be forged by Gamble & Huff whereas the others were extensions of their Cities heritage. This isn't to say that the two conquered Philadelphia single-handedly, again their strength was to recognize gifted creators and allow them their own projects whilst retaining the Philly sound. As with Detroit and Memphis much of the sound relied on a nucleus of session men whose individuality added to the sound and made it easy to pinpoint where a record had come from. Gamble & Huff had climbed slowly, becoming respected writers and producers before turning their hand to label owning. A move that would make them soul survivors of the 70s and 80s and continue into the 90s and beyond.

In 1965 Leon Huff first worked with Kenny Gamble. Both had begun working in Philadelphia as songwriters, Leon also as a session pianist. After working on Candy & The Kisses 'The 81' the two started to talk and soon realized that they shared a common belief that, although they hadn't been treated badly, their potential could be better realised. By 1966 the duo decided that it was time to form their own label, Excel and released The Intruders, "Gonna Be Strong". Excel soon became the Gamble label with The Intruders supplying the label's first release, "United". They were on their way. The following year Bunny Sigler and Billy Paul joined the label and by 1968 Gamble & Huff were creating more interest and Chicago's Chess Records distributed their new label, Neptune. During its short life Neptune brought in The Three Degrees, The O'Jays and The Vibrations then Gamble & Huff became a trio, with respected Philly arranger / producer Thom Bell joining the team. After more outside productions on other artists, most notably Wilson Pickett with his classic 'In Philadelphia' set and Joe Simon's Gold 'Drowning in the Sea of Love', the team made perhaps the biggest decision of their professional lives, proudly announcing the birth of their new baby, the Philadelphia International label, in 1971. The next two years would show Gamble & Huff's faith in themselves and in their growing roster of stars and supporting musicians. Trouble, when it did come, wasn't as drastic as at first thought and Gamble & Huff were able to weather the storm due mainly to love and respect for each other and their artists. Their set up seemed to thrive off such a philosophy, acts were reluctant to leave when the problems began and many returned when they could. Love can bring you home.

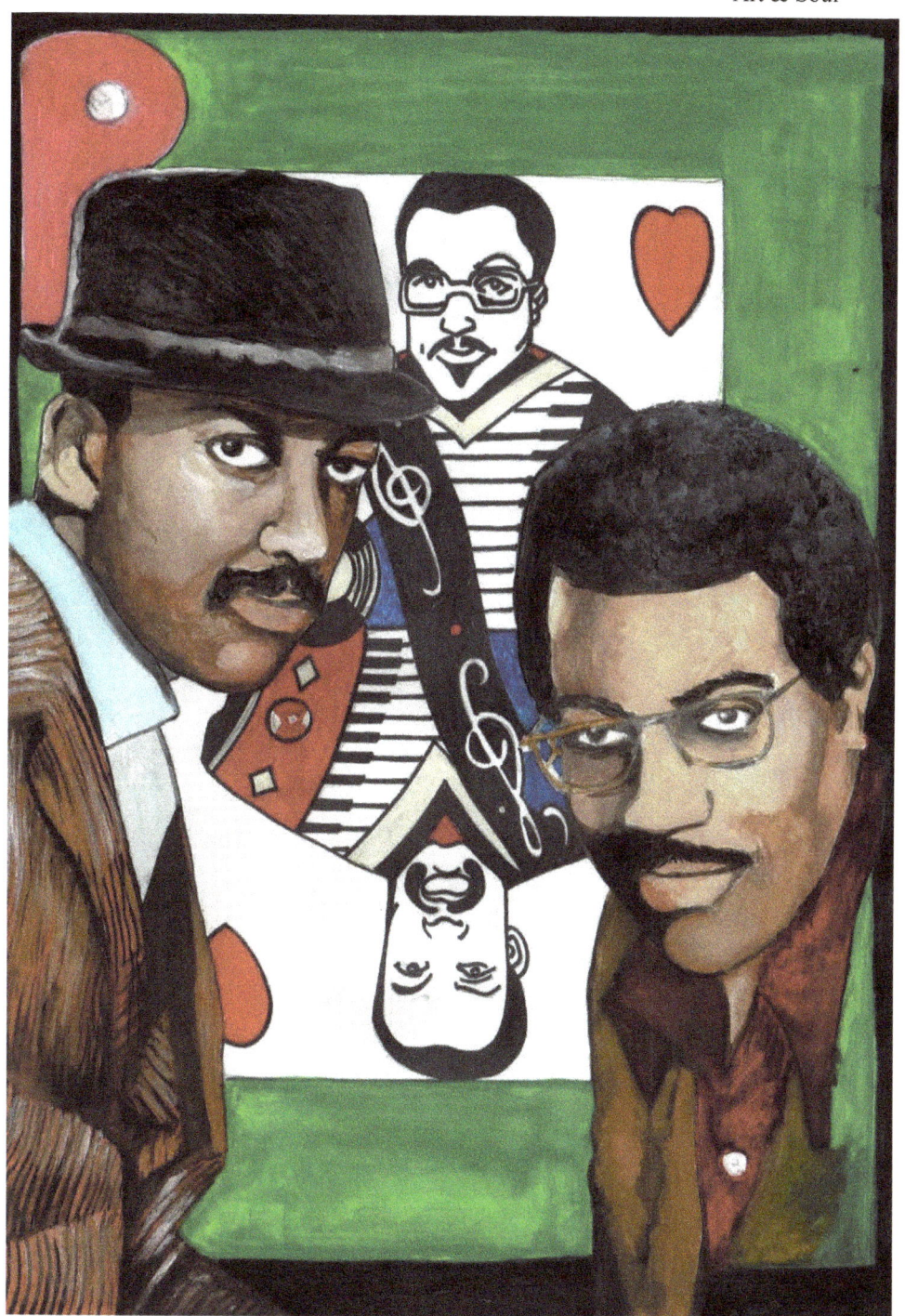

Thom Bell

Here's a mystery. Thomas Randolph Bell was born in Philadelphia or Kingston, Jamaica, on January the 26th 1943, the son of Leroy Randolph and Anna L. Burke. His father was from Portsmouth, Virginia and his mother from Baltimore. Thomas Bedward Burke, his maternal grandfather, was born in Kingston, Jamaica. However, Thom Bell stated in a National Public Radio interview that he was born in Jamaica and migrated to the US as a child, with his parents who were both Jamaicans and discussed their lives as immigrants during this interview. That aside, what we do know for a fact is that Bell was classically trained and as a teenager sang with Kenny Gamble, Leon Huff and Daryll Hall of the group Hall & Oates. His first break came with Philadelphia's Cameo label where he became a session musician and arranger. 1966 saw him introduced to The Delfonics and he produced "He Don't Really Love You" for them on the Moon Shot label. This was the beginning of a great period not only for The Delfonics but also for Philadelphia Soul. The group left to join the Philly Groove label run by their manager Stan Watson and Bell brought along new classically inspired arrangements that introduced instruments rarely heard before in Soul. "Didn't I (Blow Your Mind This Time)" was a perfect example of this and was nominated for a Grammy in 1970. Bell was a perfectionist and demanded that the musicians played his compositions by the note with no improvisation allowed. Thom also joined up with his friends Gamble and Huff arranging Jerry Butler, Dusty Springfield, The O'Jays and Archie Bell & The Drells to name but a few. The trio also formed the Mighty Three Music publishing company. When Gamble & Huff created the Philadelphia International label in 1971 Thom Bell continued arranging for them. In that same year Bell was working on a new group for the Avco label, The Stylistics. He also teamed up with another writer, lyricist Linda Creed and between them they created some of the most popular ballads of the 1970s including "You Are Everything", "Betcha by Golly Wow", "Stop, Look, Listen to your Heart" and "You Make me Feel Brand New". In 1972 Bell was offered to work with The Spinners who had just left Motown. With Bell in control they managed five gold albums with a slew of memorable singles, "Mighty Love", "I'll Be Around", "Could it be I'm Falling in Love" and "Rubberband Man". In 1974 Bell received the Grammy for Best Producer Of The Year and having teamed The Spinners with Dionne Warwick for "Then Came You" produced her "Track of the Cat" album in 1975. In the 1980s his success continued with Deniece Williams' top R&B hit "It's Gonna Take a Miracle" and then in 1990 "I Don't Have a Heart" for James Ingram. After a lengthy illness Thom Bell passed away at the age of 79 on December the 22nd 2022.

Art & Soul

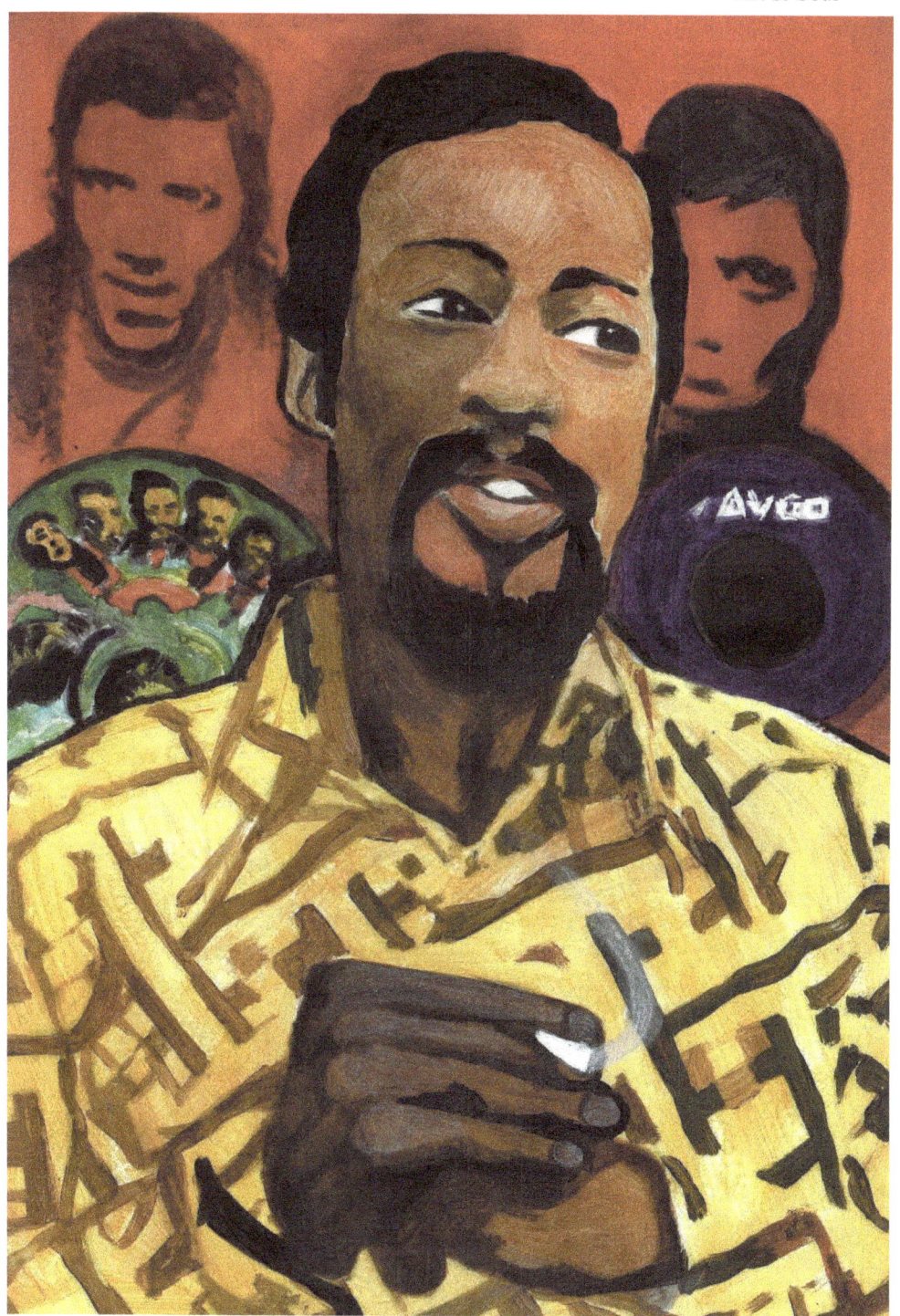

Barbara Mason

Barbara Mason was born in Philadelphia on the 9th of August 1947 and on record appears to be the other woman who most women resent or fear. This wasn't always the case though, not to say she didn't have an edge to her material from a relatively young age. At twelve her journey began with practicing on her grandmother's piano leading to her forming a procession of vocal groups and being both lead singer and accompanist. She was fortunate to have a neighbour, Weldon McDougal III, belong to a popular Doo Wop group, The Larks were interested in her musical talent and invited her to be part of their local shows. Further introductions got her to the Philly based Crusader label where she cut her first single "Trouble Child". From there she moved to the more successful Arctic label where her own compositions "Come to Me" backed by "Girls Have Feelings Too" received more interest if not commercial success in 1964. Things got better in 1965 when Arctic released another of her compositions "Yes I'm Ready" which has since been cited as one of Philadelphia's first Soul classics and on the session had Kenny Gamble, Bobby Eli, Roland Chambers and Earl Young who would go on to help form the Philly Sound. My earliest memory was it being on Gladys Knight & The Pips' Motown debut album of 1967 "Everybody Needs Love" and even then, the lyrics seemed 'interesting' with its tale of a girl becoming a woman. Barbara recorded two albums at Arctic before moving to National General in 1971 and then settling at Buddha where her debut set was "Give Me Your Love", a Curtis Mayfield song that had first appeared on the "Superfly" soundtrack. "Bed and Board" skipped from this to her next album "Lady Love" in 1973. The new "Bed and Board" was extended over eight minutes and added a 'rap' predating the popularity that Millie Jackson would gain from "Caught Up" in 1974. Another trend was to write responses to other Soul hits, starting with "Me and Mr Jones" but most famously came "From his Woman to You" from the 1975 album "Love's the Thing". The track starts with a phone call and you hear Shirley pick it up, then Barbara tells her what's what from her side. Shirley was Shirley Brown whose hit "Woman to Woman" had started with a phone call to Barbara. A nice twist that kept Barbara in the public eye. In 1977 Barbara signed to Curtom for one ambiguously titled duet album with Bunny Sigler, "Locked in This Position" and returned to the charts in 1978 with "I Am Your Woman, She Is Your Wife". She continued the theme with 1981's "She's Got the Papers (But I Got the Man)" and in 1984 found yet another angle with "Another Man" telling the tale of how her man fell for another man from the album "Tied Up", think we've heard enough now.

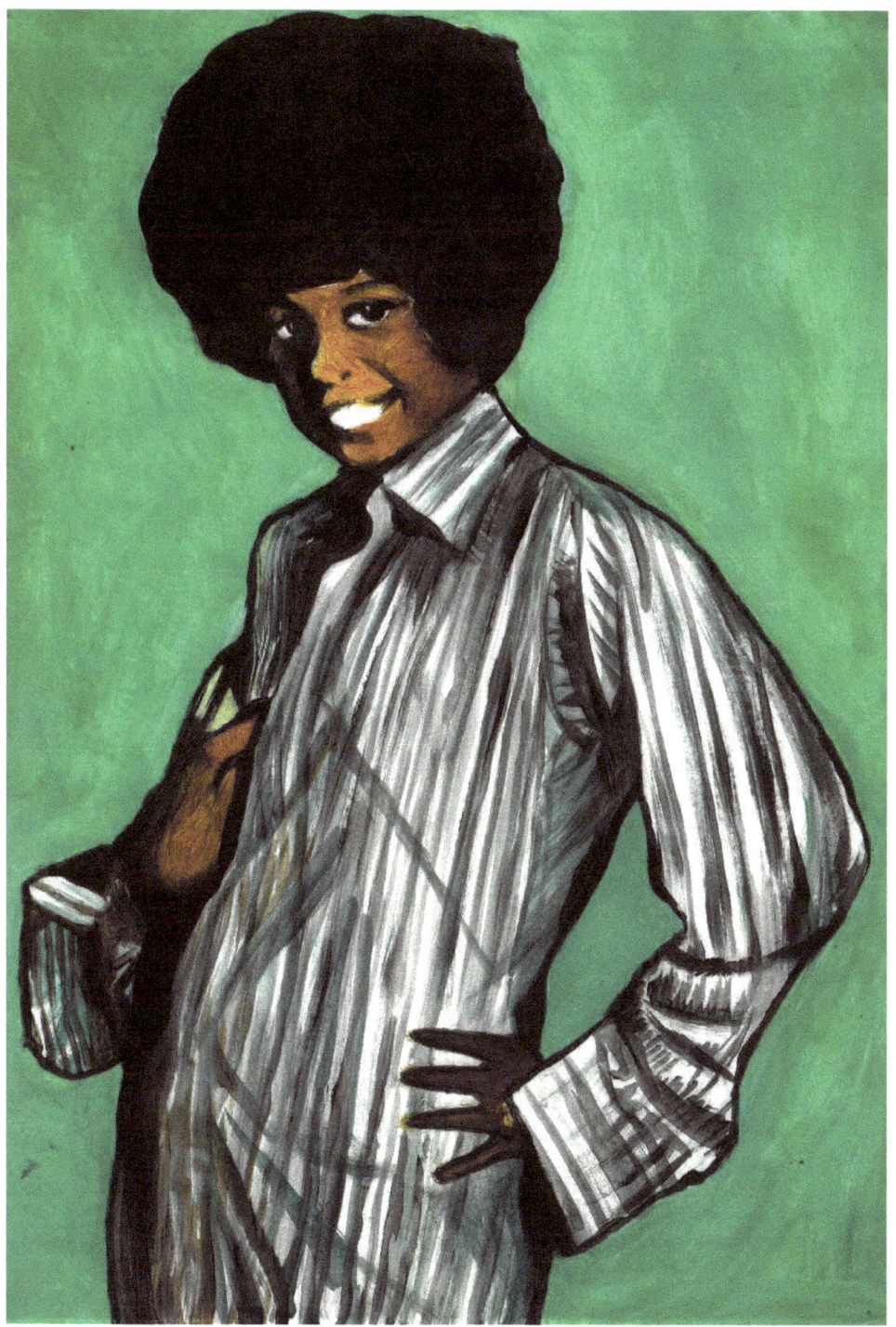

Billy Paul

Billy Paul was born Paul Williams in Philadelphia on the 1st of December 1934. His earliest musical influence was jazz played in the house by his mother. Nat King Cole was a major inspiration but surprisingly, due to their higher vocal range, he admired the female jazz performers such as Ella Fitzgerald, Billie Holiday, Sarah Vaughn and Carmen McCrae. For good measure Johnny Mathis and Sam Cooke were in there. At the age of 16 he was performing at Club Harlem in Philly for a week and shared the bill with Charlie Parker. In April 1952 at the age of 17 he was able to have two singles released on the Jubilee label before being drafted into the army where he was sent to Germany alongside Elvis Presley. Billy Paul and other draftees aimed to start a band to get them away from heavier duties. All Elvis wanted to do was drive a jeep, so the Jazz Blues Symphony Band had to go on without him. After his service two more releases followed, one on Finch in 1960 and another on New Dawn in 1966. Along the way he briefly joined Harold Melvin's Blue Notes but because of his reluctance to dance, Melvin fired him. By 1967 Billy Paul had joined the Gamble record label and 1968 saw his first album, a live set of jazz covers called "Feelin' Good at the Cadillac Club". This was followed by 1970s "Ebony Woman" and "Going East" a year later. My first knowledge of Billy came the next year with the release of "Me and Mrs Jones", taken from his album "360 Degrees of Billy Paul". During this period the Gamble label was absorbed into the Philadelphia International label and "Me and Mrs Jones" became the label's first Number 1 and also gained the Grammy Award for Best Male R&B Performance in 1973. Things looked good for everyone until what some may consider a major marketing fault happened. As a follow up single the label chose "Am I Black Enough for You?" Now bear in mind that this had been a popular phrase in 1970 spurred on by the success of the movie "Cotton Comes to Harlem", when the words were constantly paraphrased. Gamble and Huff may have thought that this was a great marketing ploy but it only reached Number 79 on the Pop chart. Billy Paul himself had opposed the release, preferring "Brown Baby" or the equally controversial "I'm Just a Prisoner" with its lyrics about the incarceration of black Americans in the penal system. Call me old fashioned but why was everyone more comfortable with a song about infidelity?

In 1976 Billy Paul was once again condemned for the controversial "Let's Make a Baby".

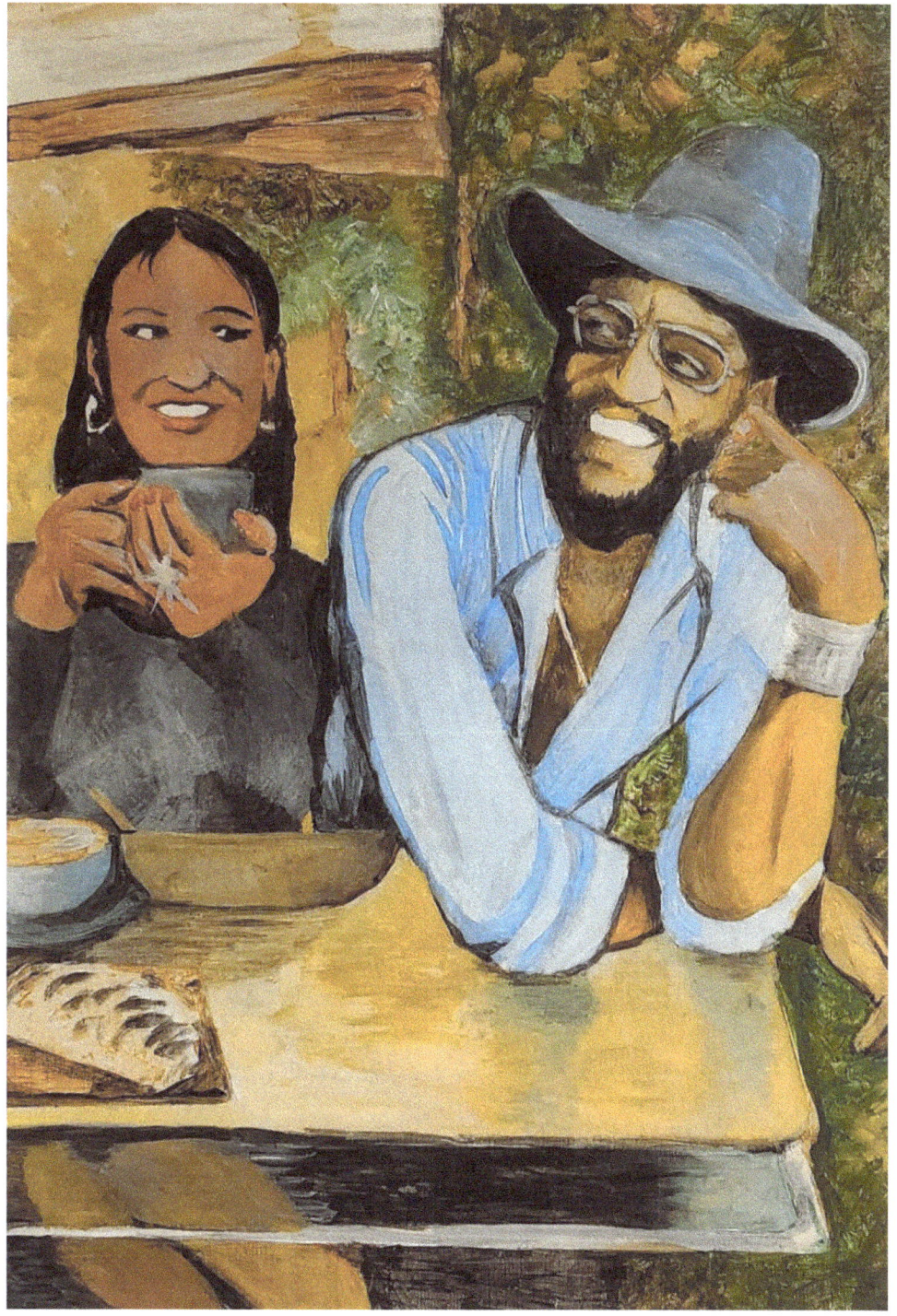

The Jones Girls

The Jones Girls, Shirley, Brenda and Valerie, released their first recording, "Learning How to Love" in 1970 on the local Detroit label GM Records before doing backgrounds for another local label Fortune. When Fortune fell upon misfortune. The sisters then moved to Holland-Dozier-Holland's the Music Merchant plus continuing their tradition of backing others such as Freda Payne and Holland-Dozier themselves, on the "Why Can't We Be Lovers" session. The Jones Girls came across as Music Merchant's Honey Cone with their catchy performances and they were arguably one of the most successful groups ever to emerge from Holland-Dozier-Holland's company, albeit long after the trio's interests in them had gone. Instead of grooming the young, talented sisters to be another Freda Payne or Honey Cone through their singles they were left to falter but although there were no more releases, they did continue to provide background vocals for Holland-Dozier-Holland whilst releasing their own product on Curtis Mayfield's Curtom label out of neighbouring Chicago in 1975 before touring with Diana Ross in 1976. This led them to the doors of Philadelphia International and worldwide prominence three years later. They had felt that Eddie Holland was unapproachable unlike Kenny Gamble with whom they would strike up a mutual respect in 1979 when they launched their career in Philadelphia and interestingly their vocal style changed too and sadly so did their internal relationship. Shirley Jones had become the lead vocalist much to the dismay of Denise and Brenda although this was more to do with the label than Shirley's own choice. On record though they were in perfect harmony and announced their arrival with 1979's "You're Gonna Make Me Love Somebody Else" written and produced by the golden Philly team of Gamble and Huff. The single turned platinum and was followed with other perfect productions on the 1980 album "At Peace with Woman" under the guidance of Gamble and Huff and a relatively new master mind of Philly Soul, Dexter Wansell. Their third album "Get as Much Love as You Can" followed in 1981 and included the stunning "Nights Over Egypt" written by Cynthia Bigg and Dexter Wansell but behind the scenes things were changing. They left the label to try their luck at RCA but their own conflicts led to the group quitting. In 1986 Gamble and Huff coaxed Shirley Jones back to be a solo artist and her album "Always in the Mood" was yet another success. Sadly, this led to more bitterness from which the girls never fully recovered and in 2001 Denise died at the age of 45 partly through her continued dependence on alcohol. Then in 2007 Brenda died after crossing a road and being hit by several vehicles, she was 63.

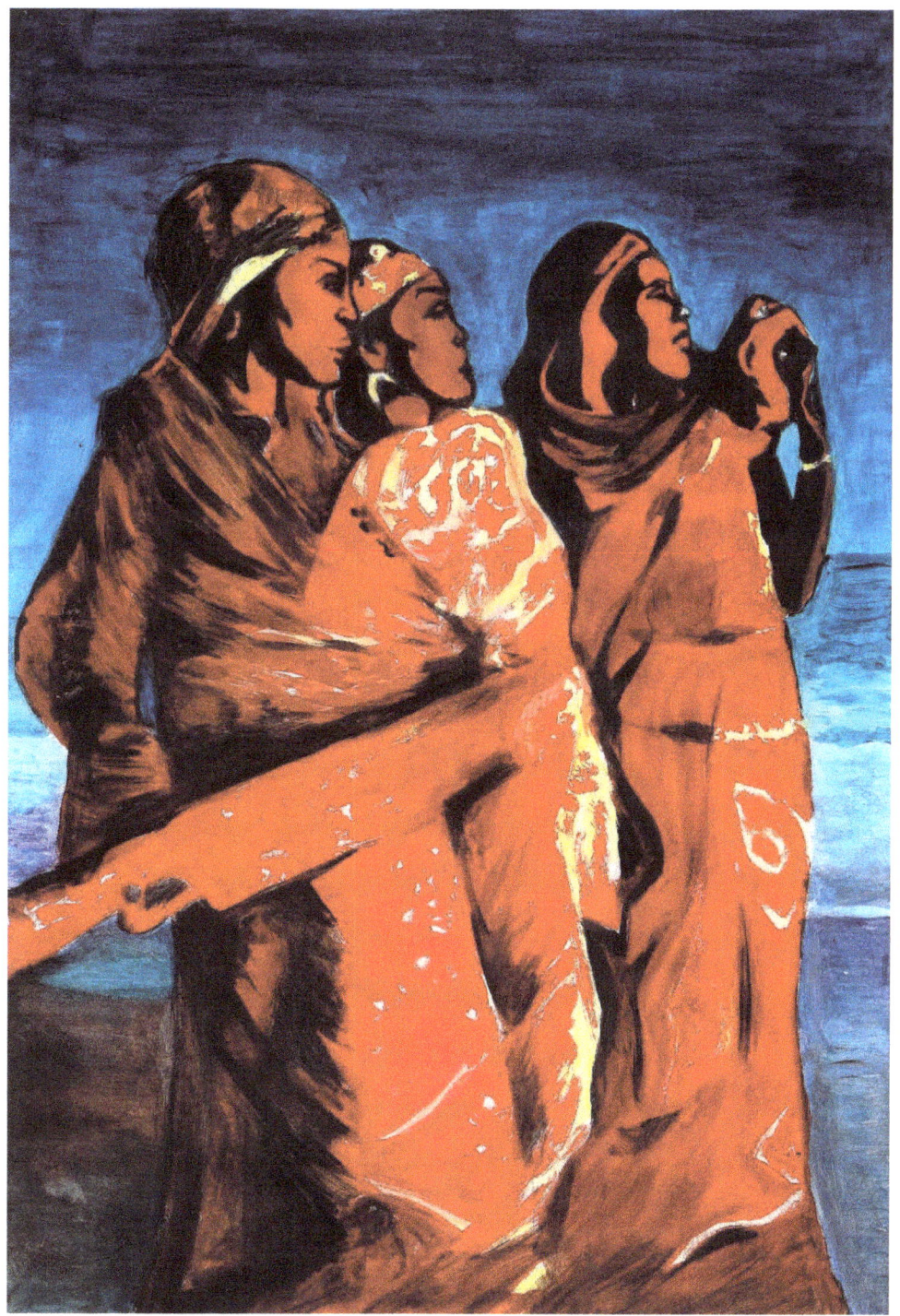

Phyliss Hyman

The death or destruction of beauty is one of life's tragedies. When that beauty snuffs itself out, the tragedy seems all the more avoidable and leaves people asking the question, why? Phyllis Hyman chose to end her life in July 1995 at the age of 45 thus denying the world of one of the most easily recognisable female soul vocalists. A statuesque woman of devastating beauty who saw the faults within. The faults that we the observer chose to overlook for the love of the music and the performer that was presented to an always appreciative audience. It seems to be par for the course that beauty is often flawed, maybe a cruel game played by whoever put us here to create a balance in us, one that many find hard to live with. Phyllis Hyman's career had progressed from her early start with the 1971 group, The New Direction through to her multiple success twenty years later taking the Best Female Vocalist Award as well as 3rd Best Album, 4th Best Live Show and 3rd Outstanding Personality at the annual Blues & Soul Magazine Awards. A feat made even more incredible by the fact that the album that caused all of this fresh interest, "Prime of my Life" was never released in the UK. What was equally remarkable was that she performed to a sell-out audience at the Hammersmith Odeon on the strength of it. Yet despite success there is something inside that often fails to acknowledge achievements to the one person that should always matter - yourself. Phyllis had often spoken about her inner feelings and how she had acted her way through a career, the acting came to a tragic halt spurred on by what was speculated as continued disappointment at not having made it in the recording business. Phyllis Hyman started her life in Pittsburgh where she quickly realised that success could not be found there. After the usual too and froing she was able to sign to Buddha and made way for her debut album simply entitled 'Phyllis Hyman'. Towards the end of 1979 her third album, "You Know How to Love Me" saw her really take off under the guidance of writers/producers Mtume & Lucas. Her confidence was also growing and Phyllis began to write songs. As she was spending more time in the city of Brotherly Love it was only a matter of time before she touched base with the City's musical maestros Kenny Gamble and Leon Huff of Philadelphia International. Phyllis signed to Philadelphia International for her outstanding "Living All Alone" set in 1987. She was personally happier with this set than with any since her Buddha debut back in '77. It would be five years before Phyllis Hyman released what would prove to be her final album in her lifetime, ironically entitled "Prime of my Life".

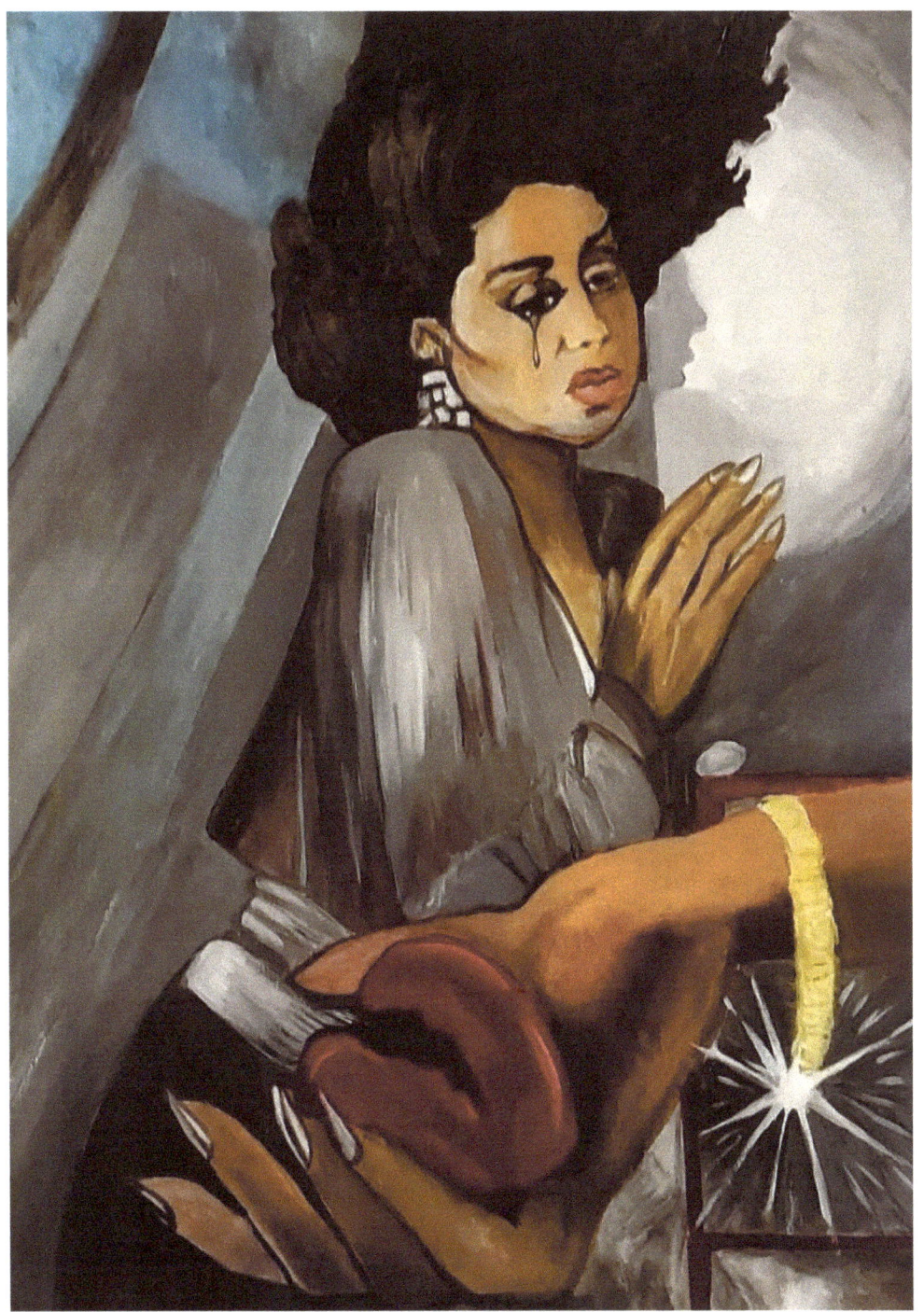

The O'Jays

Canton, Ohio was where it all started in 1958 when five students attending Canton McKinley High School got together to form The Mascots, later becoming The Triumphs who recorded "Miracles" in 1961 for the Apollo label. Then in 1963 in tribute to Cleveland radio deejay Eddie O'Jay they changed the name and also had their first national hit, "Lonely Drifter" on Imperial. 1964 brought "The Jerk" while "Pretty Words" were spoken in '66. The group managed to have minor success throughout the 1960s such as "Lipstick Traces" but things would soon get better. By 1968 Gamble & Huff were creating interest throughout the Soul world and The O'Jays signed to Neptune in May of 1969. They began their long association with Gamble & Huff with the classic 'One Night Affair' as their debut single. An album followed with arrangements by Philly legends Thom Bell and Bobby Martin. Surprisingly the group was considering quitting in 1972 despite being a successful live act and Bobby Massey and Bill Isles did go, leaving the trio of Eddie Levert, Walter Lee Williams and William Powell. The O'Jays would have an astounding run of hits beginning in 1972 with 'Backstabbers' culminating with 3 gold singles, 5 gold albums, 2 platinum singles and 4 platinum albums. The O'Jays struck gold with 'Backstabbers' and 'Love Train'. They, again, took top writing and producing honours for 1973 with The O'Jays receiving 5th and 8th top album awards. As 1974 became 1975 The O'Jays prepared to hit the dizzy heights again with a number1. US gold album, 'Survival' and single, "Give The People what they Want". A year later Gamble & Huff appeared to have gone independent once again with the O'Jays continuing their longstanding relationship and Gamble and Huff helping the then Presidential candidate Jesse Jackson with a record, "Run, Jesse, Run" in the Philadelphia All-Stars mold. A year after announcing that they would stay with Gamble & Huff through their new changes, The O'Jays finally left the team to sign for EMI with the "Serious" album. It was a move that did them no harm. In 1988 they reached the number1 single position, again, with "Have you had your Love Today?" The group had grown within the Gamble & Huff nursery and was now ready to break into the 90s, even if they would be overshadowed by the success of the junior strain of The O'Jays, Levert. Their legacy lingered on though. The O'Jays have remained at the top and Eddie Levert duetted with his son Gerald to produce another number 1 Soul single "Baby Hold on to Me". The O'Jays were inducted into the Rock & Roll Hall of Fame in 2000, the Vocal Group Hall of Fame in 2005 and honoured with BET's Lifetime Achievement Award in 2009. In 2013, they were inducted into The Official R&B Music Hall of Fame.

Art & Soul

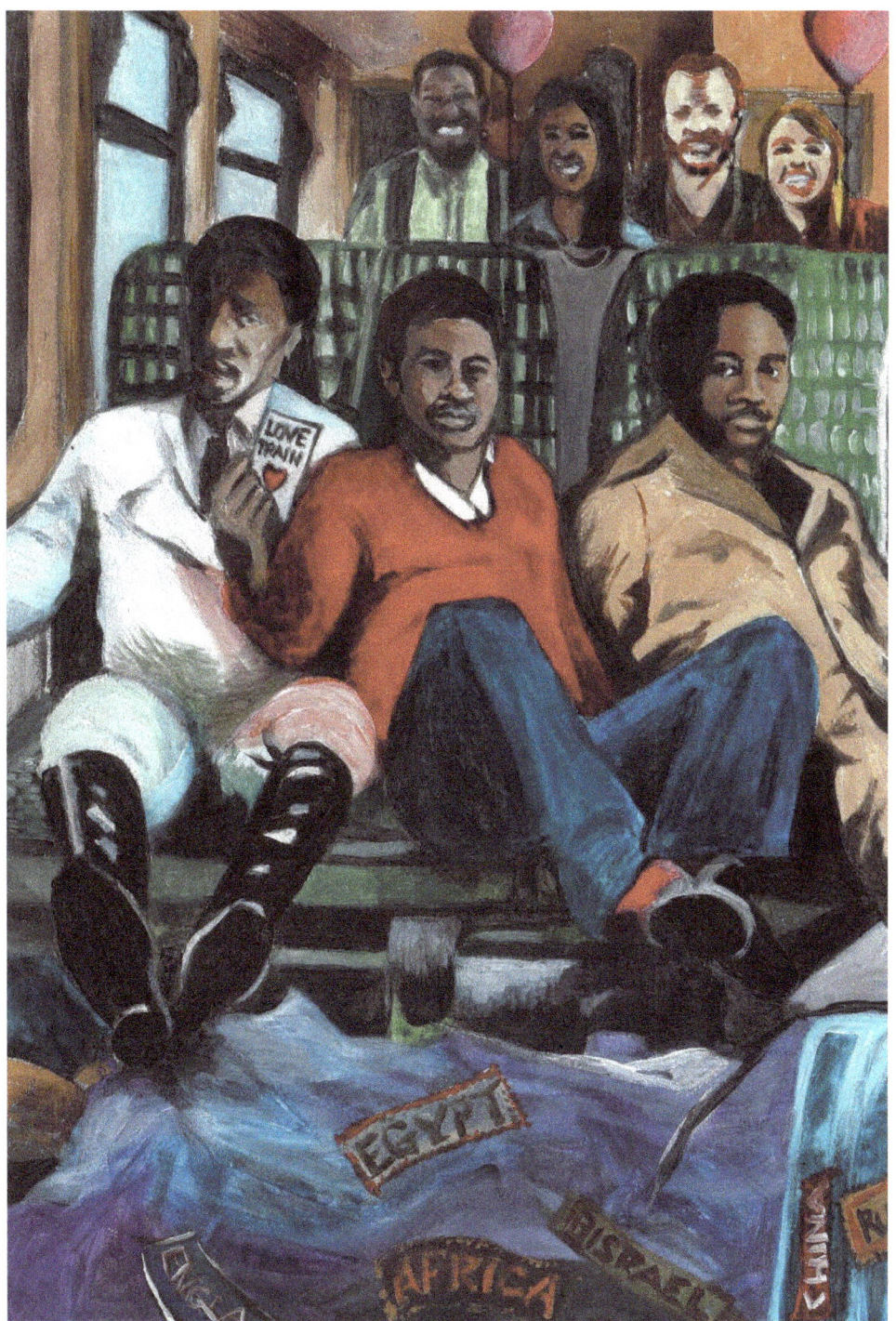

Patti Labelle

Patricia Holt was born on May the 26th 1944 in Philadelphia and cut her teeth at the Beulah Baptist Church but as a young girl growing up in the 1950s there was the lure of secular music and a dream of stardom. By 1961 Patti and her friend Cindy Birdsong formed The Ordettes which quickly led to a foursome with Sarah Dash and Nona Hendryx from The Del Capris becoming The Bluebells. The group was building a reputation for its live act around New York, Chicago, Washington D.C., Atlanta, Detroit, Baltimore and their hometown of Philly and it wasn't long before the group name changed to Patti & The Blue Belles. The group signed to the Parkway record label before joining Atlantic in 1965 where they stayed for three relatively unsuccessful years. Things were changing and 1968 saw the group becoming a trio having lost Birdsong to Motown. The 1960s were soon to change to the '70s and with that came a new opportunity. Vicki Wickham, a British television producer became their manager and immediately changed the group name to LaBelle. They signed to Warner Brothers and instead of being put on the Soul circuit began touring with rock bands like The Who. This change meant that their image had to go with the new flow and so they replaced their sequinned dresses to more science fiction attire that felt more at home in this cosmic age. In 1975 they arrived again, when Allen Toussaint produced their acclaimed 1975 album "Nightbirds", which contained the number one hit "Lady Marmalade" but her solo career took off when she signed with Philadelphia International Records in 1981. Patti Labelle released a single at year's end, "I'll Never, Never Give Up" produced by Leon Huff and the ever-faithful O'Jays were artistically rewarded with new production by Gamble & Huff. More Patti Labelle material appeared in 1984 resulting in a number 1 soul single, "If Only You Knew". The Gamble & Huff team were spreading their wings around the company. Patti followed the single with an equally stunning album, "I'm in Love Again" that also included input from Womack & Womack who had also formed a Philly affiliation at the beginning of the decade. By April,1984, P.I.R. seemed to be picking itself up. On the strength of Patti Labelle's success, a new energy was being felt and the company seemed to be going back to its original format of a writing and producing unit, leasing product to Epic. Bobby Womack's "The Poet II" released in 1981 on the Beverly Glen label featured a heart stopping duet between Womack and Patti Labelle, "Takes a Lot of Strength to Say Goodbye" as well as "Love Has Finally Come". In 1986 her greatest success as a solo performer was actually a duet, "On My Own" which she sang with former Doobie Brother, Michael McDonald.

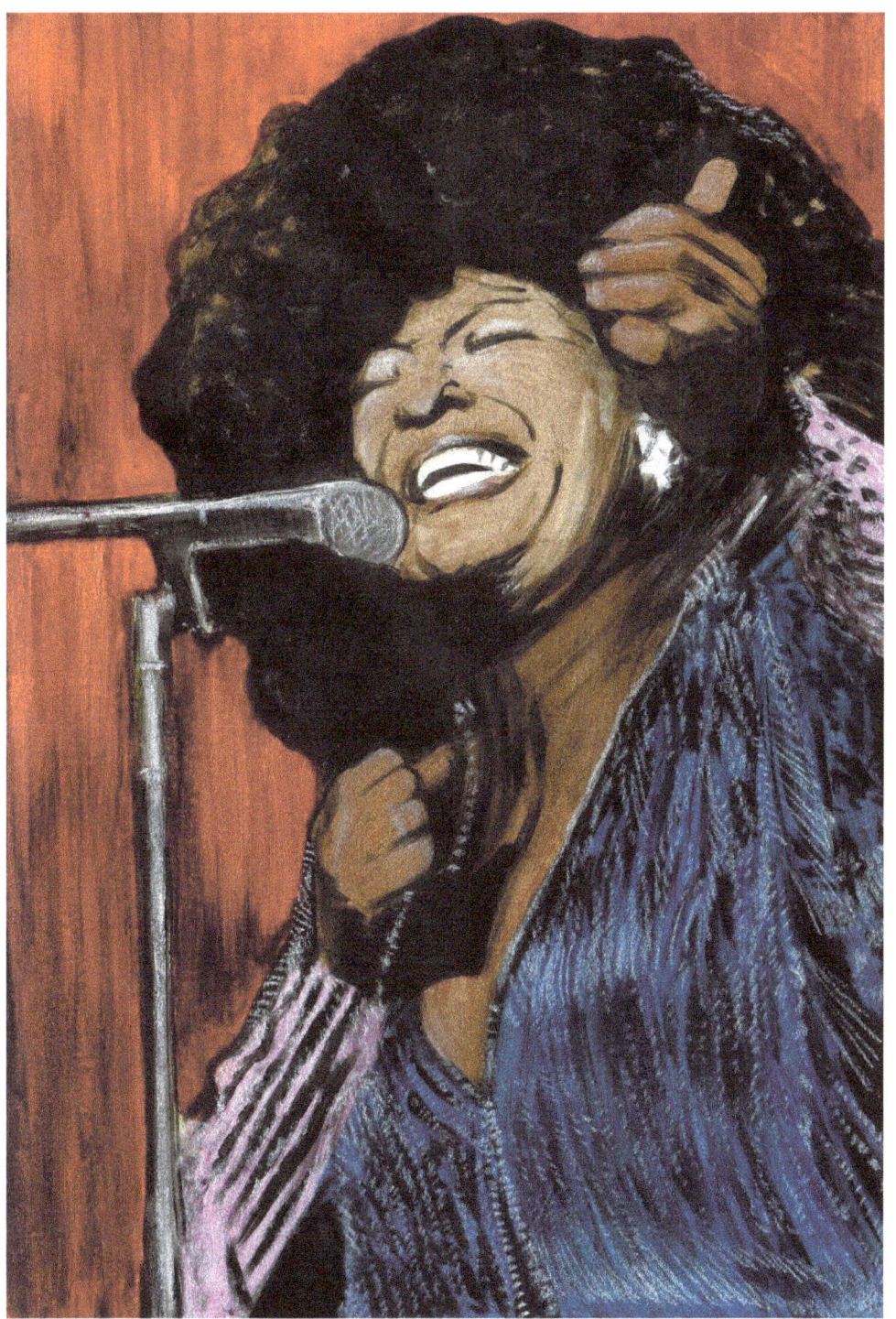

Teddy Pendegrass

When "I Miss You" by Harold Melvin & The Bluenotes came out in 1972, shockwaves moved through the Soul world. This was a Philadelphia ballad and Philly wasn't known for 'deep soul'. What was also a bit strange was that Harold Melvin wasn't the lead vocalist even though his name was above the group's. As people became more accustomed to this earth-shaking sound the singer's identity was revealed as belonging to Teddy Pendergrass. Teddy was born on March 26th 1950 and began as many other did by singing Gospel in Philadelphia churches, even become an ordained minister at the age of ten and was also a self-taught drummer. By his late teens he was a drummer for local group The Cadillacs and in 1970, The Blue Notes broke up. Gamble and Leon Huff, owners of Philadelphia International Records, had wanted Marvin Junior of The Dells for their roster but the group was unavailable, so Pendegrass still only 20 years of age filled the gap. Beginning with "I Miss You," the group could do no wrong and followed the debut single with another ballad "If You Don't Know Me by Now". Pendegrass was more than a balladeer though as shown on more hits like "The Love I Lost", "Bad Luck" and "Wake Up Everybody" which reached the top R&B spot in 1976. Internal disagreements led Pendergrass to sign a solo deal with Philadelphia International Records in late 1976 and he burst back on the scene with "I Don't Love You Anymore," "You Can't Hide from Yourself," and "The More I Get the More I Want." He received several Grammy nominations during 1977 and 1978 as well as Billboard's 1977 Pop Album New Artist Award, an American Music Award for best R&B performer of 1978 and awards from Ebony magazine and the NAACP. In 1977 Taazmayia Lang was Pendergrass' girlfriend and manager and in April she was shot dead on her doorstep, a murder that remains unsolved although Philadelphia's Black Mafia were suspected. Things got even worse for him and on March 18th 1982 a car accident left Pendergrass a tetraplegic with a severed spinal cord. There was a suggestion that the car's brakes had been tampered with, but the facts were that he was paralyzed from the waist down and wheelchair bound. After almost a year of physical therapy and counselling he returned to the recording scene, signing a contract with Elektra/Asylum in 1983. In 1987 he married one of his former dancers Karen Still but the couple amicably divorced in 2002 although Karen stayed as his carer. In 1988 probably his biggest post-Philly success was the album "Joy" whose title track went to number one R&B for two weeks. In 2009, Pendergrass underwent surgery for colon cancer and had difficulty recovering from that disease from which he eventually died on January the 13th 2010, at age 59.

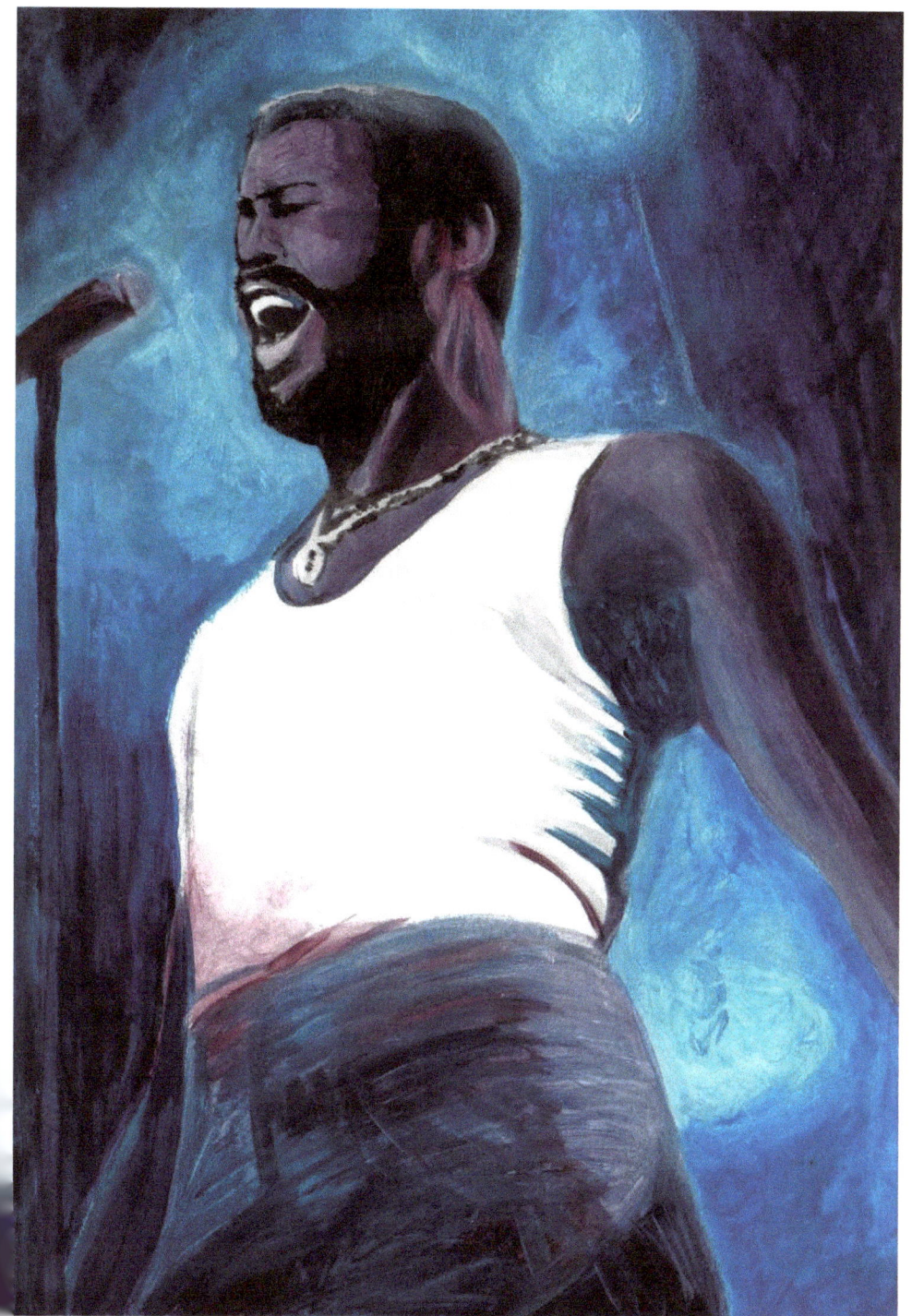

The Delfonics

Before The Stylistics and Blue Magic came The Delfonics who, under the teamwork of group leader William Hart and the quickly emerging behind the scenes master Thom Bell, would create the sound that would be revisited, re-worked but never re-invented. Philly Soul was always too smooth for me back when I started collecting my records but "Didn't I Blow Your Mind" from late 1969 was the key to unlock the rest when I ready. Cue yet another hit, "Ready or Not (Here I Come)" released earlier the same year and brought to a new generation by The Fugees in 1996. In 1997 Director Quintin Tarantino used "La-La (Means I Love You)" as well as "Didn't I Blow Your Mind " in his movie "Jackie Brown" that starred Blaxploitation Queen Pam Grier and Robert DeNiro, whilst "Ready or Not (Here I Come)" and "Funny Feeling" found their way onto the Grand Theft Auto V video game. The foundations for this continued popularity started back in 1965 when William Hart was working as a barber. A customer called Stan Watson, who had been a member of The Del-Vikings, came in one day when William hadn't a customer and would spend his time strumming his guitar and singing songs he'd been writing. Watson told him that he knew a young producer/arranger and was happy to introduce him. Hart went along and met the guy who just happened to be Thom Bell and the very first song he pitched. "He Don't Really Love You" was good enough for Bell to take on board and arrange it. Hart, his brother Wilbert and Randy Cain had formed a group around 1964 called The Orphonics who became The Del Fonics and it was they who recorded "He Don't Really Love You" released in August, 1966 on the Cameo Parkway subsidiary Moon Shot label. Now changed to The Delfonics their second single was "You've Been Untrue" this time released in April 1967 on the main Cameo Parkway label, again produced by Thom Bell. By year's end Cameo Parkway was on its way out and a quick move to a new Stan Watson label, Philly Groove, not only kept the momentum going with "La-La (Means I Love You)" a 1968 gold seller but also paved the way for what would internationally be known as the Philly sound. On the horizon though were The Stylistics who had formed in Philadelphia in 1968 and in 1971 Randy Cain left The Delfonics, helping to form Blue Magic in 1973. Major Harris joined for a couple of years deciding to go solo in 1974 and Thom Bell had started to create the phenomena that The Stylistics were to become. The remaining Delfonics were quick to release a new album in 1974 with a title that suggested a call to the doubters, "Alive and Kicking". This was produced by Stan Watson, but he failed to follow Thom Bell's footsteps. That said, it wasn't that the material was lacking but the timing perhaps was and by 1975 they'd become history, albeit it a significant part.

Art & Soul

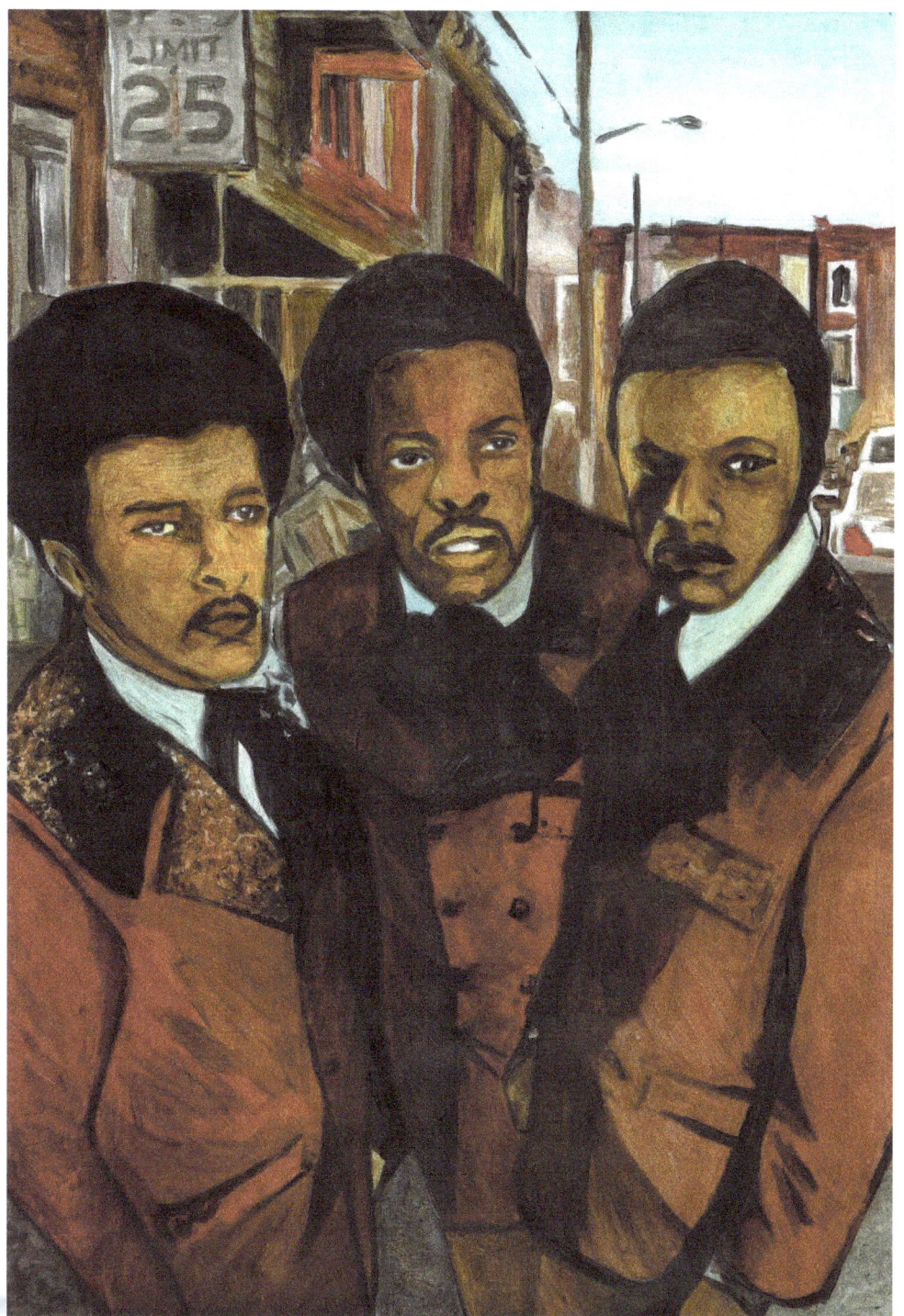

Three Degrees

Three Degrees had started back in Philadelphia around 1963. Record producer Richard Barrett got them their first single "Gee Baby (I'm Sorry)" two years later on the Swan label. Barrett also managed Sheila Ferguson and signed her to Swan. As the group line-up changed it wasn't long before Ferguson became the most famous member of The Three Degrees. The first time I came across them was in the Gene Hackman movie "The French Connection" back in 1971. Apparently because of success on the Roulette label, they were offered a cameo appearance filmed at New York's Copacabana Nightclub performing "Everybody Gets to go to the Moon". Roulette released their first album, "Maybe" with the title track, an update of the Chantel's 1958 hit taking them up to Number 4 in the R&B Chart. This was followed by "I Do Take You" and "You're the Fool". Their second album, "So Much Love" nailed the movie role for them. By 1973 their Roulette contract came to an end and after a short stint at Neptune they were snapped up by Kenny Gamble and Leon Huff to be part of their growing Philadelphia International label. Their first success was unusual in that they appeared as backing singers on MFSB's hit TSOP (The Sound of Philadelphia). Despite speculations MFSB stood for Mother Father Sister Brother not Mother F*ckin' Sonofabitch! This was also the theme song for the Soul Train Television Show. In the television series 'Sanford & Son' they made a guest appearance singing "I Didn't Know". The groups self-titled debut album included "Dirty Ol' Man", "Year Of Decision" and the monumental "When Will I See You Again?" which I have to admit to feeling was borrowed from The Sweet Inspirations' "Am I Ever Going To See My Baby Again?" released on Atlantic in 1968 but that was about Vietnam, this was about missing memories not a missing person. In the UK the song reached the top of the pop charts, the first time in nearly ten years since the Supremes in '64. Again, that was Motown then, now it was Philly's turn to shine. Their second album didn't have the hat trick of hits but still supplied a winner in "Take Good Care of Yourself". What made it more interesting was its marketing. The album was named The Three Degrees International and was given different names and languages. Despite these successes 1976 saw them departing from Gamble and Huff and a move to Sony/Epic where the album "A Toast of Love" was marketed for the Far East. A year later after releasing "Standing Up for Love" they themselves were released and in 1978 signed to Ariola where they joined forces with Giorgio Moroder the Disco producer who created Donna Summer's finest moments. The singles "Givin' Up, Givin' In", "Woman In Love", "The Runner" and "My Simple Heart" kept them in the charts.

Art & Soul

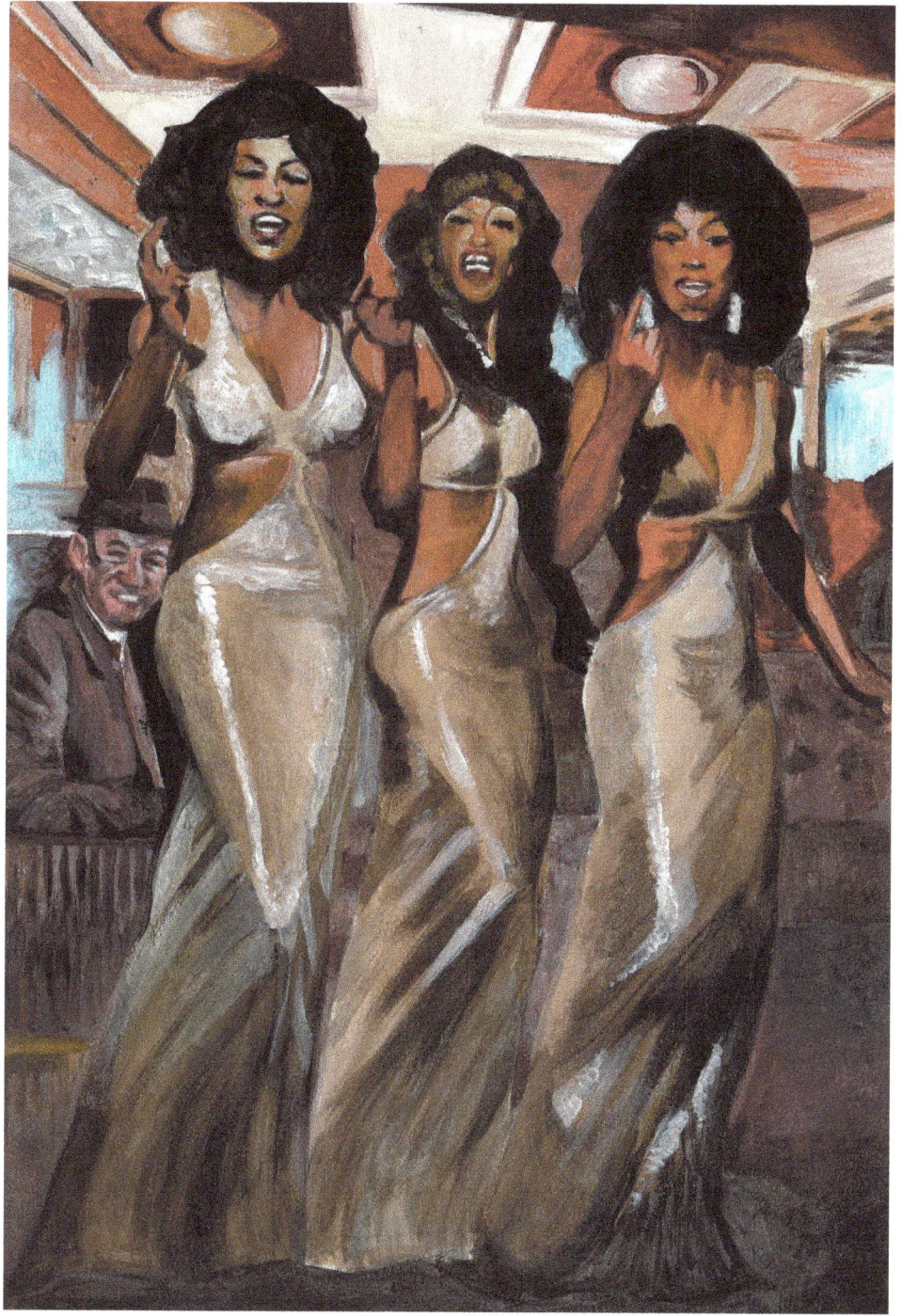

Van McCoy

In 1975 the Avco label released an album called "Disco Baby" by Van McCoy with limited success. Then a single was pulled off it which reached the top of both the pop and R&B charts in the States as well as number three on the UK pop chart, winning a Grammy Award along the way to disco history. The thing is, depending on when you come in you can read the room wrongly. I did. I was already passionate about Soul and had my favourites, "Giving Up" by Donny Hathaway, "When You're Young and In Love" by The Marvelettes, "Baby I'm Yours" by Barbara Lewis and "I Get The Sweetest Feeling" by Jackie Wilson being four examples all written by Van McCoy. So, where do we begin? Washington D.C. on the 6th of January 1940 when the second child of Norman and Lillian was born. By the age of twelve Van had done his piano playing and Gospel singing with the Metropolitan Baptist Church and was writing his own songs and entering local amateur shows with his older brother Norman. Bringing on board two friends they became The Starlighters while still attending Theodore Roosevelt High school. In 1956 they recorded "The Birdland".

The record was good enough to secure them a tour and three releases on the End label which was the end for the group, due to marital commitments and other diversions. His own marital commitments were scuppered when he put off marrying Kendra Spotswood because of a contract he had to fulfil for Columbia Records. In 1958 Van McCoy moved to Philadelphia where he set up his own label, Rockin' Records and issued "Hey Mr DJ" that caught the attention of Scepter Records; he was hired as both a staff writer and AR representative. His first success was "Stop the Music" by The Shirelles in 1962. The work for Scepter didn't stop McCoy expanding his own industry and he co-owned Vando Records, Maxx and fully-owned the Share label. These brought him to Gladys Knight & The Pips and The Ad-Libs, both who cut "Giving Up" and Ruby & The Romantics who did the original version of "When You're Young and in Love". He wrote Betty Everett's stomper "Getting Mighty Crowded" and "You're Gonna Make Me Love You" for Sandra Shelton formerly Kendra Spotswood. Van McCoy also brought together the duo Peaches & Herb. When the 70s rolled around McCoy's reputation was pretty faultless and he had successfully taken up the challenge of following Thom Bell's time with The Stylistics and in 1975 he brought David Ruffin back to the front with Motown after leaving The Temptations. The single "Walk Away from Love" and the album "Who I Am" was the beginning of a beautiful friendship. He re-united with Gladys Knight & The Pips on Buddha and with Melba Moore with the hit "This Is It". Then it was. On July the 6th 1979 Van McCoy suffered a heart attack and died at 39.

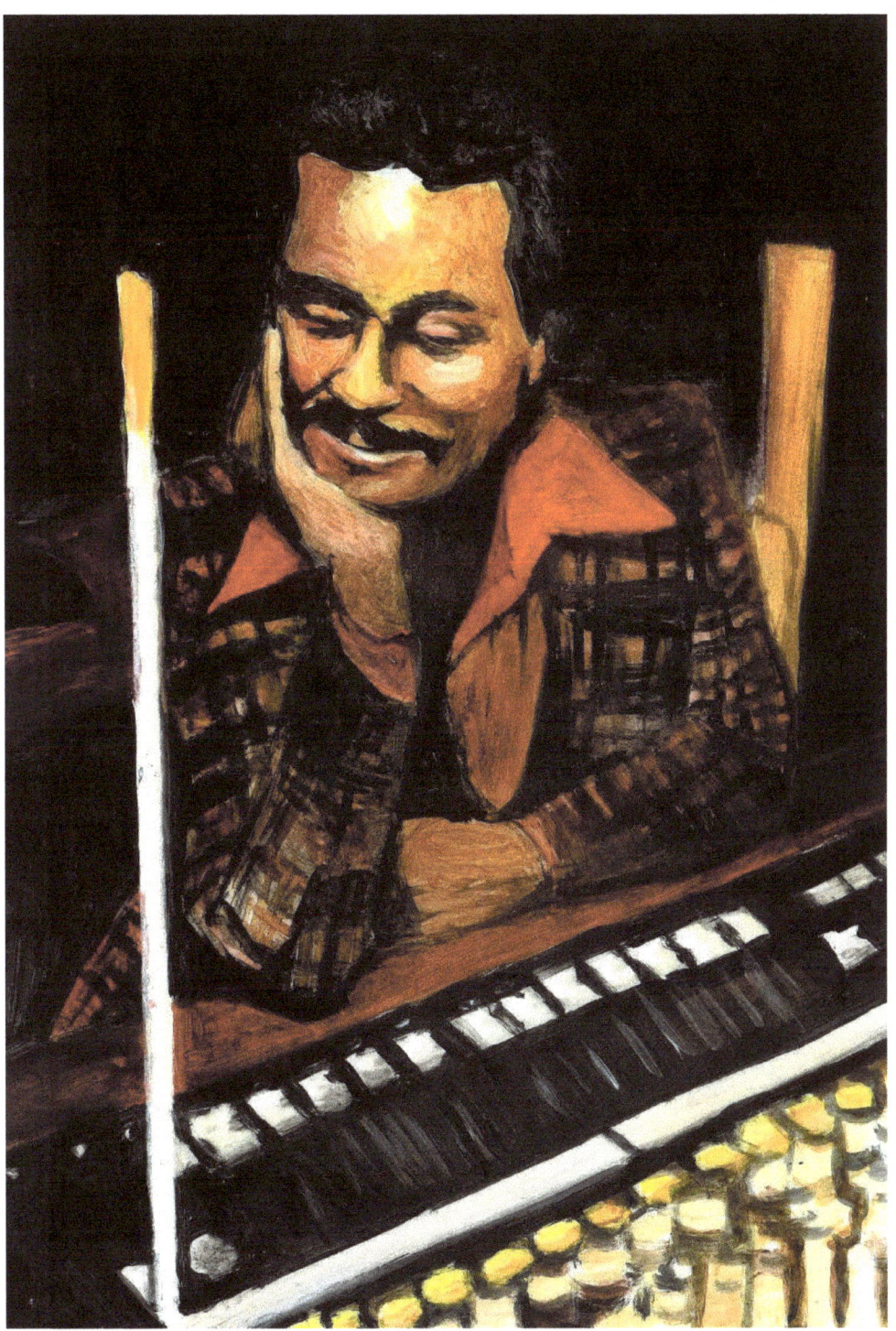

Art & Soul

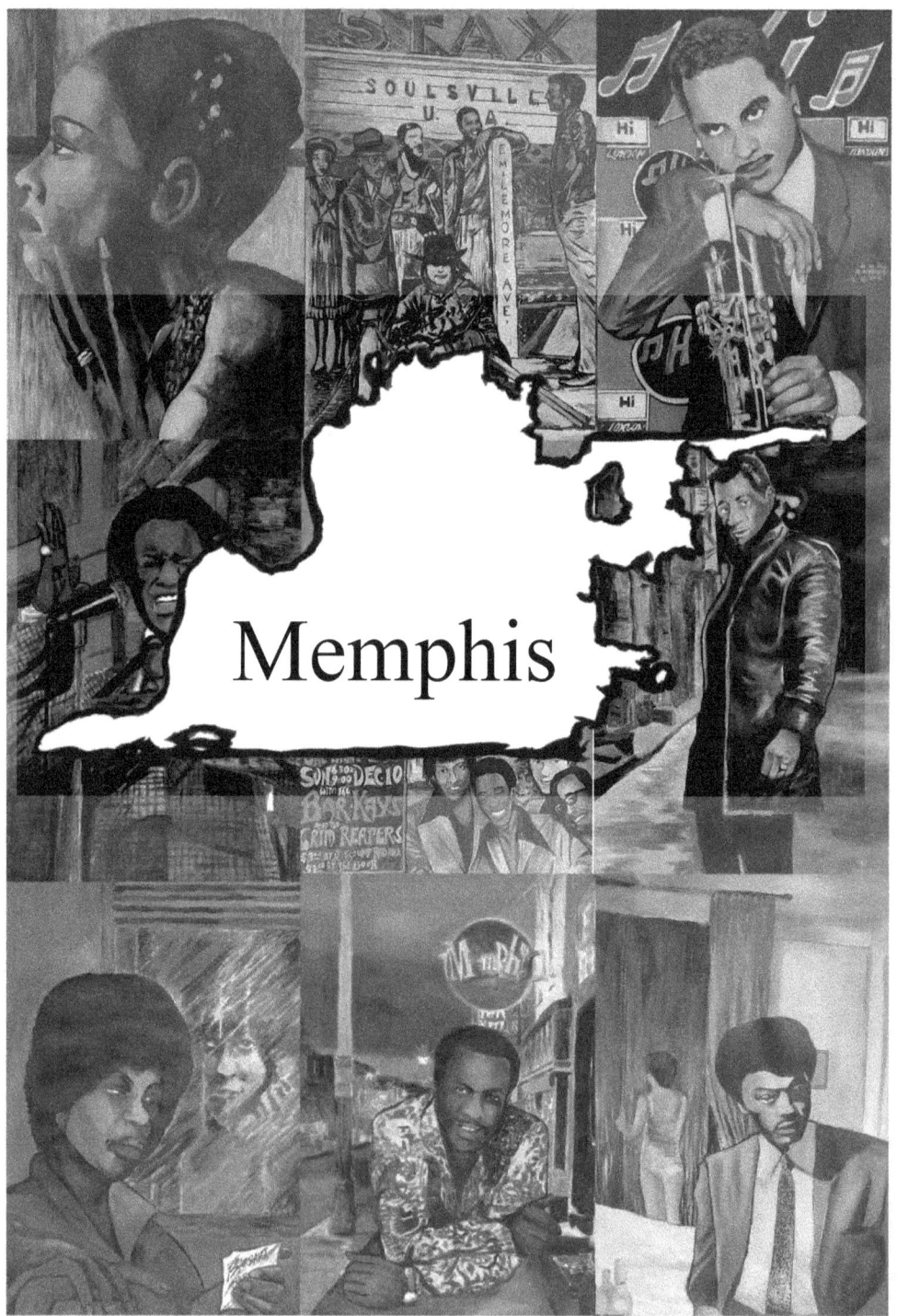

Art & Soul

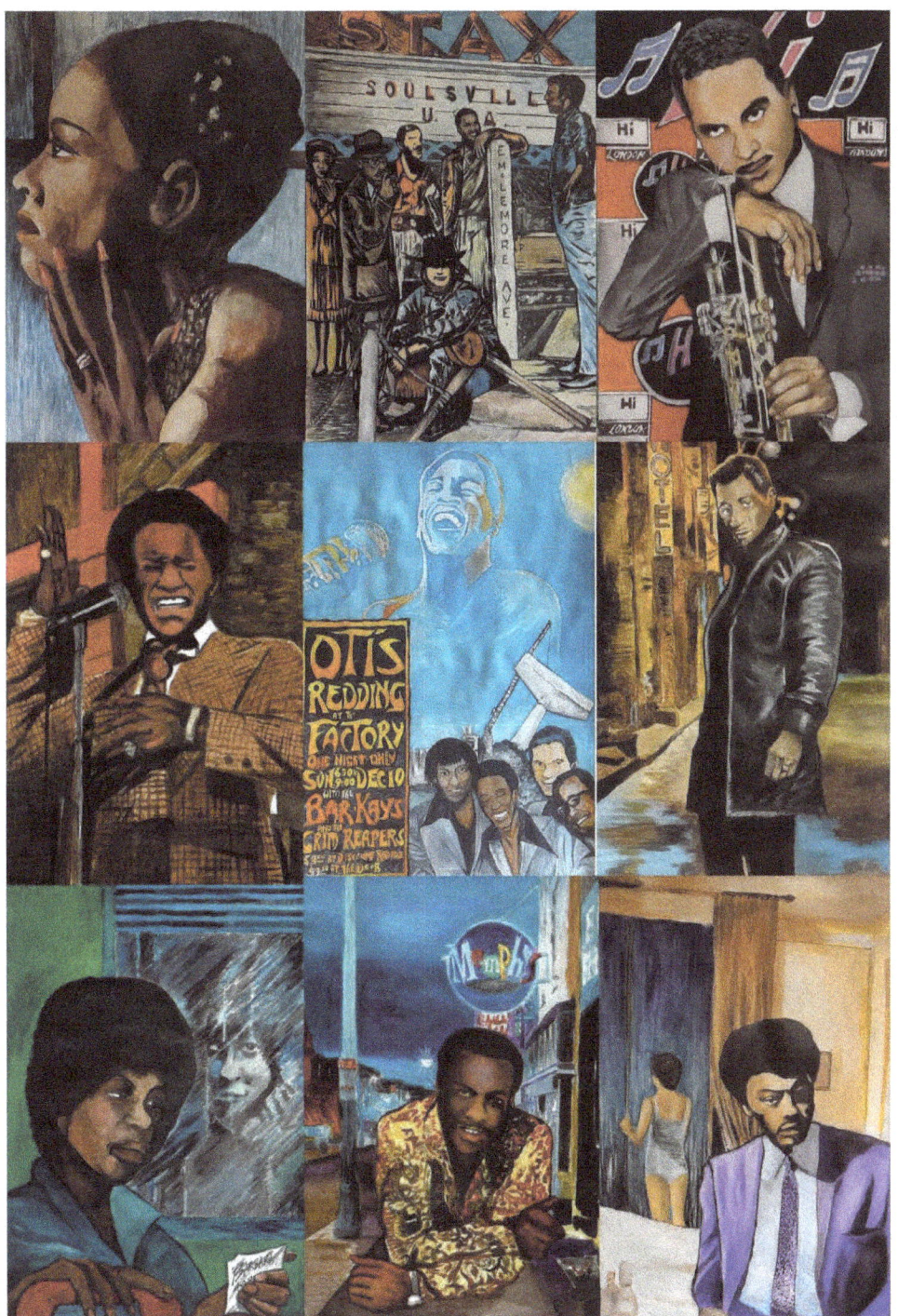

Al Green

Albert Greene was born on April the 13th in 1946 in Forrest City, Arkansas but in 1964 the family moved to Michigan where he formed his first group The Creations. At the time it probably didn't sound significant, just a new group name but as his career grew, the 'creator' himself would play a major role in his life and near death. Al Green's inspiration was Sam Cooke who had left Gospel for secular pastures and found himself ostracised by the church. Green, on the other hand would come to bring the two together. Before that though his group would tour the 'chitlin' circuit down in the South and rename themselves Al Green & The Soul Mates. Forming their own label, they released the "Back Up Train" album in 1968, the title track beginning to show indications of where Green's voice was heading. That year, while in Texas he met Willie Mitchell, now the chief producer and vice president of Hi Records in Memphis with what was about to become life-changing. In 1969 Green, now a solo artist, cut The Beatles "I Want to Hold Your Hand" where the unique Green voice was in full flow. 1971 brought a blues-inspired take on The Temptations "I Can't Get Next to You" which reached the top spot on the National Soul Chart but it was the next track, written by Green that saw him arrive, "Tired Of Being Alone" which had some critics suggesting that he was the new Otis Redding. I never saw that myself, to me they both stood uniquely alone. This million-seller paved the way for the even more popular "Let's Stay Together" which reached the top of both the pop chart and the rhythm & blues chart whilst turning gold. The track was composed by Green alongside Mitchell and Al Jackson, the drummer with Booker T. & The MGs over at the Stax label. More Soul classics followed from "I'm Still in Love with You" in 1972, "Call Me" "Love and Happiness" and "Here I Am (Come and Take Me)" all from 1973. Then it hit the fan. On October the 18th, 1974 a female acquaintance Mary Woodson poured hot grits over him as he was laying in his bath. She then took Green's gun and killed herself. Green had second-degree burns to his back, stomach and arms. To him this was a wake-up call, although he would continue to be accused on more than one occasion of violent attacks on his wife, even his secretary who he was alleged to have pushed through a glass door. Green avoided some of the criminal charges and found God, not surprising, for in my humble opinion, it can be a crutch. 1976 saw his full emersion into Christianity establishing the Full Gospel Tabernacle church in Memphis and by 1980 he was fully devoted to the ministry and became the Reverend Al Green. Mark Cohn's "Walking in Memphis" name checked him in 1991.

Art & Soul

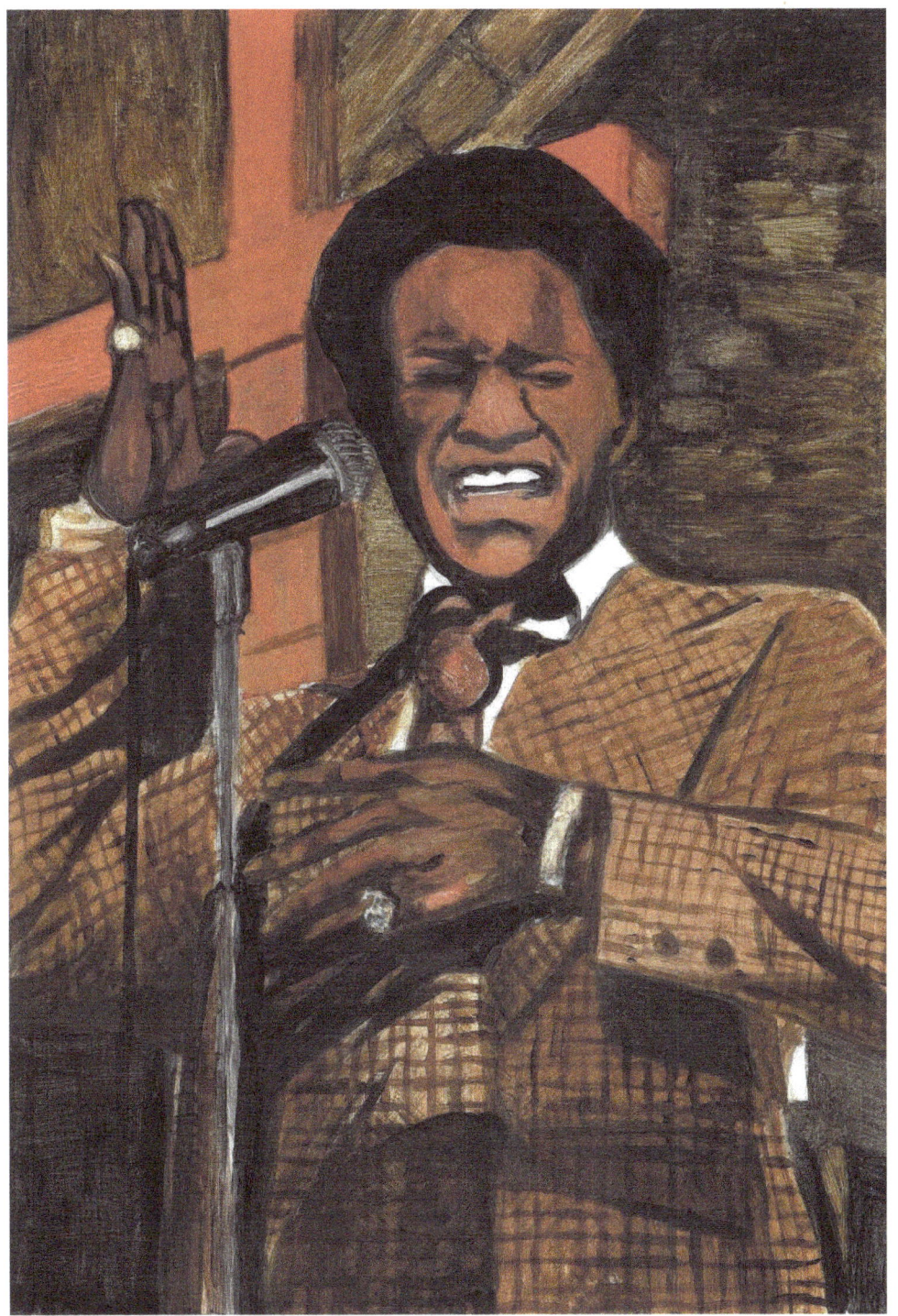

Ann Peebles

Ann Peebles was born in Kinloch, Missouri, the seventh child of eleven on April the 27th, 1947 and began her singing career in her father's church as well as with the Peebles Choir who were known for opening shows for Mahalia Jackson and Sam Cooke's Soul Stirrers. She was however, also beginning to enjoy the music of Muddy Waters and Aretha Franklin and began to sing in St Louis clubs and joined a revue led by bandleader Oliver Sain. When I heard "I Can't Stand the Rain" by Ann in 1973 I was mesmerised by the sound. Stepping into Soul through Stax and Motown's doors didn't prepare me for this slab of solid, pounding intensity. The Memphis horns and most importantly Howard Grimes' faultless precision on drums supplemented Ann's incredible voice perfectly. Ann got to be on the Hi label after a 1968 trip with her brother to Memphis where she had the chance to sing with Gene 'Bowlegs' Miller who introduced her to the people at Hi. Even though the label had been going since 1957 there was a new feel to it and with Willie Mitchell rising up the ranks it wasn't going to be long before the label was heard worldwide. The roster though was predominantly male with artists such as O.V. Wright, Otis Clay, Syl Johnson and Al Green dominating everything. That would change as Ann Peebles made her mark beginning in 1969 with "Walk Away" written by Oliver Sain. This and the follow up single "Give Me Some Credit" both dinted the R&B chart which led to her debut album, "This Is Ann Peebles". In 1970 the breaks started with her version of Little Johnny Taylor's "Part Time Love" reaching Number 7 on the R&B chart but more significantly making the pop top 50 chart. She started to work with Hi staff writer Don Bryant who married her in 1974. Before that he was helping to form her relationship with the general public with songs like 1971's "99 Pounds". This was included in her next album, "Straight from the Heart" released in 1972 which also included "I Pity The Fool". She continued to have R&B hits in the early 1970s, including "Slipped, Tripped and Fell in Love" originally cut by "Clarence Carter and the classic "Breaking Up Somebody's Home". From the title alone you knew you were in for a rough ride. The lyrics clearly placed a pacing Peebles in her home on a rainy night, waiting to drop the bomb on the other woman. Then on another rainy night Ann and Don Bryant who by now were courting were getting ready to go to a concert. Ann said that she couldn't stand the rain and they never got to the concert. Even though it only reached Number 38 on the pop chart John Lennon called it the best song ever. That alone guaranteed both the song and Ann's place in history.

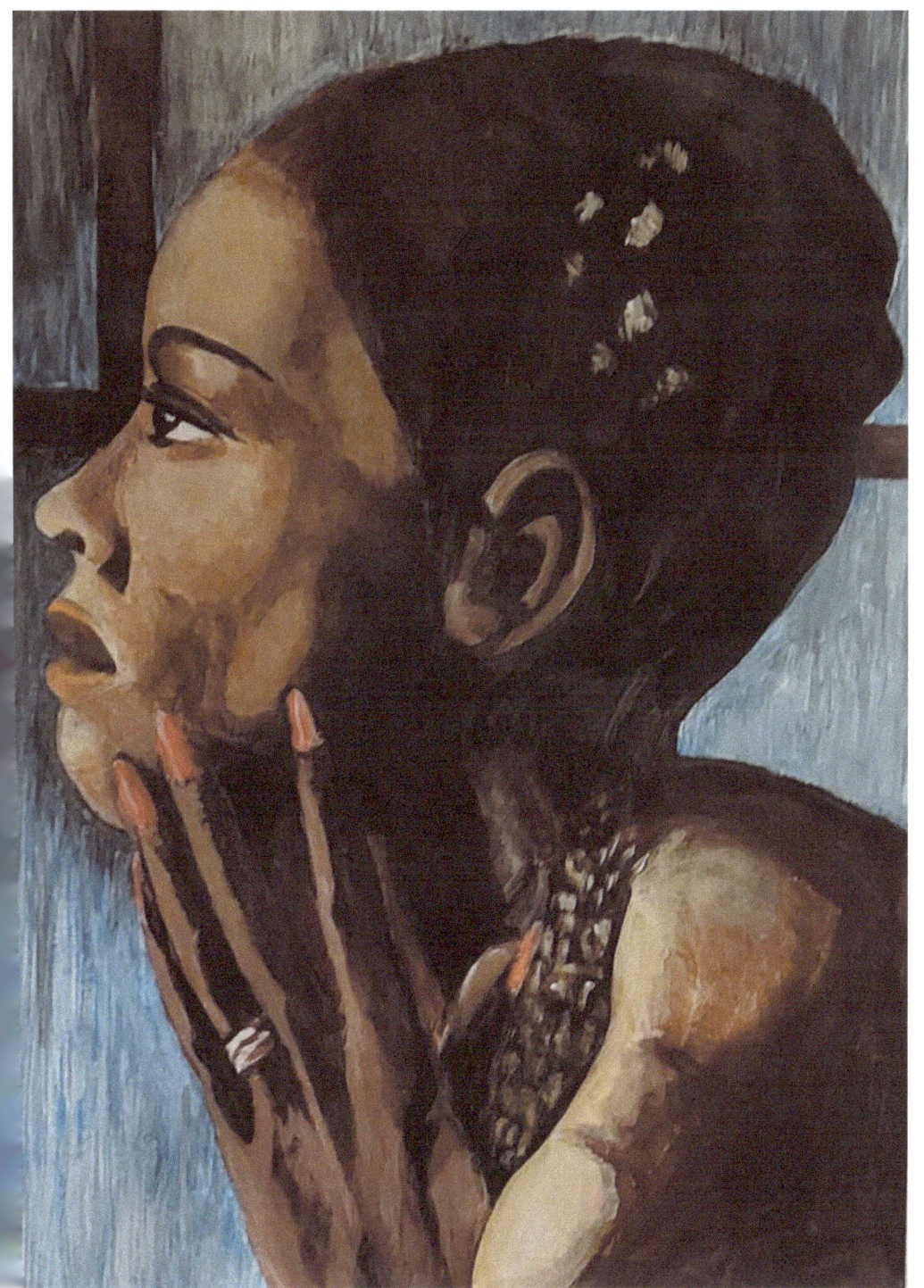

Booker T. & The MGs

Donald 'Duck' Dunn grew up with guitarist Steve Cropper and realising that there were enough guitarists around chose to try his hand at the electric bass. That friendship and that decision would help to form the beat that made Memphis one of the most important cities in the history of Soul. The two friends formed their first band, The Royal Spades which evolved into the Mar-Keys and had a hit with "Last Night" earning the label a gold disc. The group's line-up also included Booker T Jones and Al Jackson who along with Dunn and Cropper would break away to become Booker T & The MGs, becoming key players on some of the most celebrated Soul to come out of Memphis. Stax released many sides through the Atlantic label but also non-Stax artists who were signed to Atlantic and who travelled to Memphis to be supported by the musicians, these included Don Covay and Wilson Pickett. Freshly signed to Stax was Johnnie Taylor, his debut album for the label "Wanted One Soul Singer" featured the musicianship of Booker T and The MGs and a year later the group backed bluesman Albert King on some classic Memphis Blues that included "The Hunter" written by the group. With Redding's death at the end of 1967 and the assassination in Memphis some five months later of Martin Luther King, the musicians were rocked, Dunn felt the tension when he was approached by Police officers outside Stax days after King's assassination to see if he was okay. He was a white man standing with Isaac Hayes and David Porter. 1968 saw a new direction for Stax Records but the new product still relied heavily on the input of Booker T and his MGs but the rawness was now balanced with a smoothness not heard previously, a new sophistication. One of the most successful marriages of this new style came with 1969's outstanding ballad from William Bell, "I Forgot to be your Lover". With the production came an intricate interplay between the instrumentalists and orchestra and within it Donald 'Duck' Dunn's bass line moved faultlessly between the other outstanding performances; Soul perfection. One of the most interesting collaborations from 1971 is that Booker T. and The MGs were the key musicians on Bill Wither's debut album "Just as I Am". An album incidentally produced by Booker T. Jones. In 1971 Booker T. quit the band and moved to Los Angeles. In September 1975 the four decided that it was time to get back together but a week later Al Jackson Jr was shot dead by an intruder in his house. Donald "Duck" Dunn died in his sleep on May 13th at the age of 70, after performing two shows at The Blue Note Club in Tokyo with his lifelong friend Steve Cropper. Booker T. said that God was calling names in the music world and that he had given us treasures but now was taking them back.

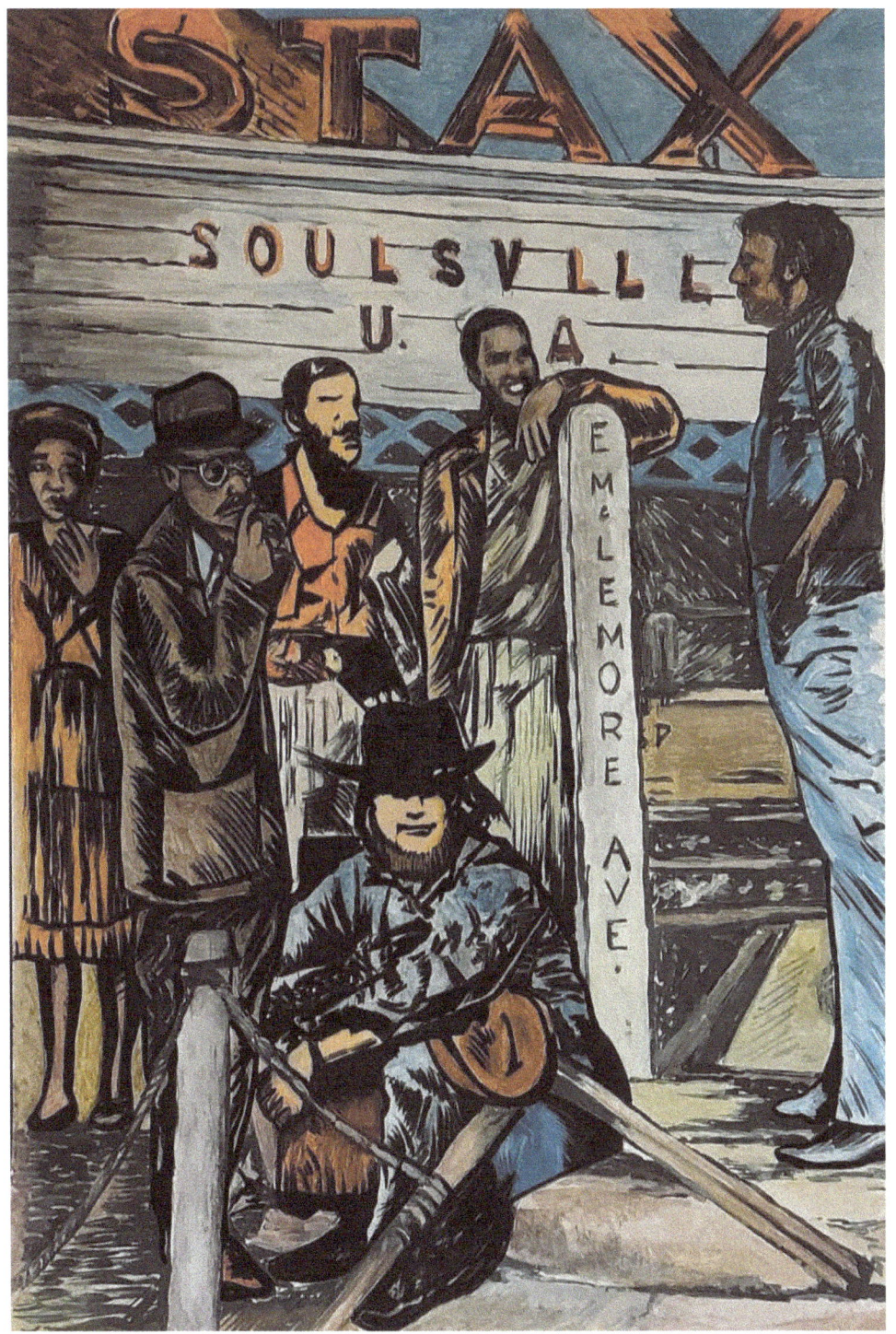

Carla Thomas

Carla Venita Thomas was born in Memphis on December the 21st 1942, the daughter of Rufus Thomas. If Rufus happily bore the nickname 'The Clown Prince of Dance' Carla was known as the Queen of Memphis Soul. When she was 10 years old, she joined the WDIA Radio's Teen Town singers. Fourteen was the minimum age requirement but, somehow, she was able to blag her way in, the fact that Dad was a local radio personality on the station may have helped. Historically Carla and Rufus were the very first artists to record in the 926 E. McLemore studio that would be the headquarters of Stax Records. Carla was still at High School and only seventeen. The regional success of "Cause I Love You" which sold more than 30,000 copies started Jim Stewart and Estelle Axton thinking about changing the label's name to Stax incorporating the beginning of their surnames. At the time they were still deliberating which way their Satellite label should go, having already dabbled with country and rockabilly. In 1961 Carla started her ascendency with her own composition "Gee Whiz (Look at His Eyes)" and also found time to gain an undergraduate Degree from Tennessee State University. The song reached the US R&B top 5 and number 14 on the US Hot 100 chart. Her album of the same name was released that year and its success cemented the decision to change the label's name. Her second album, "Comfort Me" was released in 1965 and, though solid, contained too many covers but then in July of 1966 she released "B-A-B-Y" written by Isaac Hayes and David Porter, reaching number 3 on the R&B chart and number 14 on the US pop chart. The end of the year saw her third album "Carla" issued and another Hayes and Porter song "Let Me Be Good to You" got to Number 11 on the US R&B chart. The album also highlighted Carla's songwriting skills. In 1967 she recorded the LP "King & Queen" with Otis Redding and as before the album was littered with covers like Aaron Neville's "Tell it Like it Is", The Clovers "Lovey Dovey" and most famously their take on Lowell Fulsom's "Tramp". In the same year she was one of the stars of the famous European Stax/Volt Revue alongside William Bell, Booker T. & The MGs and Otis Redding. By the end of the year the King was dead and her next album was entitled "The Queen Alone" released in 1969. In between times Carla moved to New York where she would continue to record but where she studied at Howard University with classmates Roberta Flack and Donnie Hathaway. After the Watts riots in Los Angeles, Carla performed at the Wattstax concert in 1972 and continued at Stax until 1973 when she quietly faded from the spotlight but didn't stay gone. Valerie June's horn driven, Stax sounding single "Only A Fool" released in 2021 starts with dialogue by Queen Carla.

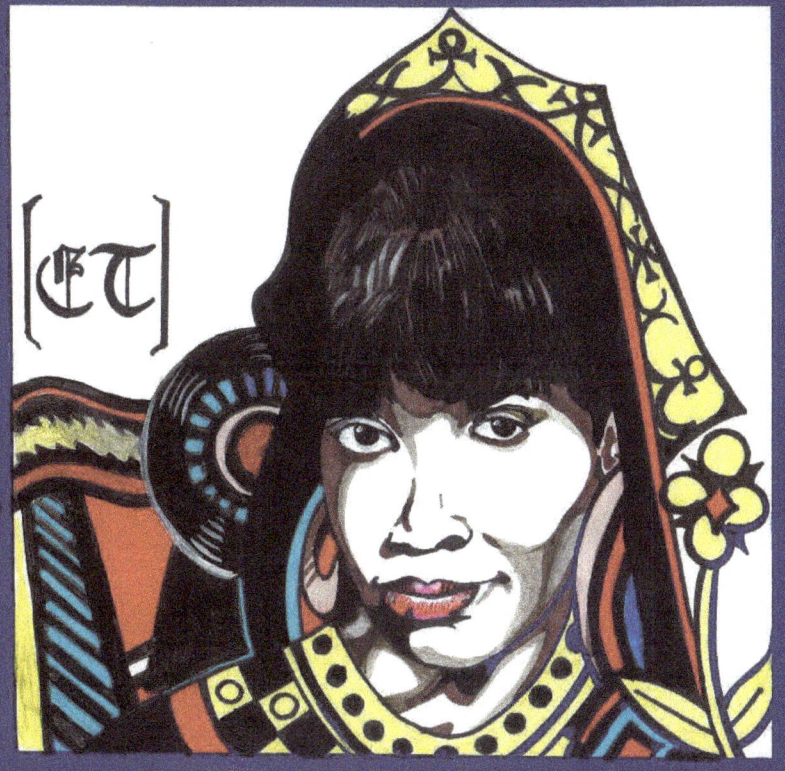

James Carr

Lost in a dream, way out on a voyage are words James Carr once used to describe himself. If you can make a record that everybody knows the world over then you yourself should be remembered. True? Sadly, no. Making music may be wonderful but surviving life can be a different thing. James Carr was born on June the 13th, 1942 in Mississippi, moved to Memphis at the age of three and worked his way through various Gospel groups finishing with the Jubilee Hummingbirds but Carr wanted to make it in the secular world. Goldwax was formed in 1964 in the wake of Stax' success in Memphis and like Stax was created by a white businessman, Quinton Claunch, putting a finger up to the segregated South. One night around midnight there was a banging on the door. He opened it and Roosevelt Jamison, James Carr and O.V. Wright stood there and then presented him with a tape recorder. He let them in and after listening to their demos signed them with Jamison managing Carr. Wright and Carr had sung together in the Redemption Harmonizers whereas Jamison had been approached by them to get them across the line into Soul music. As a songwriter he wrote a Soul standard, "That's How Strong My Love Is" originally recorded by O.V. as well as Otis Redding, Laura Lee and The Rolling Stones. In 1966 his first single "You've Got My Mind Messed Up" did well in the R&B chart but mental health issues were starting to show. Carr played at New York's Apollo Theatre that year as part of a tour with Otis Redding, Wilson Pickett and James Brown. He announced to Jamison that he was going to sign a contract with Phil Walden and Larry Utal, Redding's managers. An agreement was made and Jamison went back to Memphis, still remaining friends. A couple of months passed and he hadn't heard from Carr, his Bi-Polar was taking hold and he had no one to support him. Jamison started to get phone calls out of desperation and despair. He would call from an airport or a street where he'd lost his way. One snowy night there was a knock on his door and there sat James Carr, who said he'd been looking for him for a long time and asked him where he'd been. This behaviour dogged his career and the year Otis Redding died, Carr released his greatest song "The Dark End of the Street" making some critics suggest that he was Redding's successor and even dubbed him the world's greatest Soul singer. Bi-Polar, drugs and alcohol were all reasons why his career never got to where it should have and in the late '90s he was diagnosed with lung cancer and died aged 58 on January the 7th, 2001 in a nursing home. The dark end of the street was sadly where Carr seemed to exist.

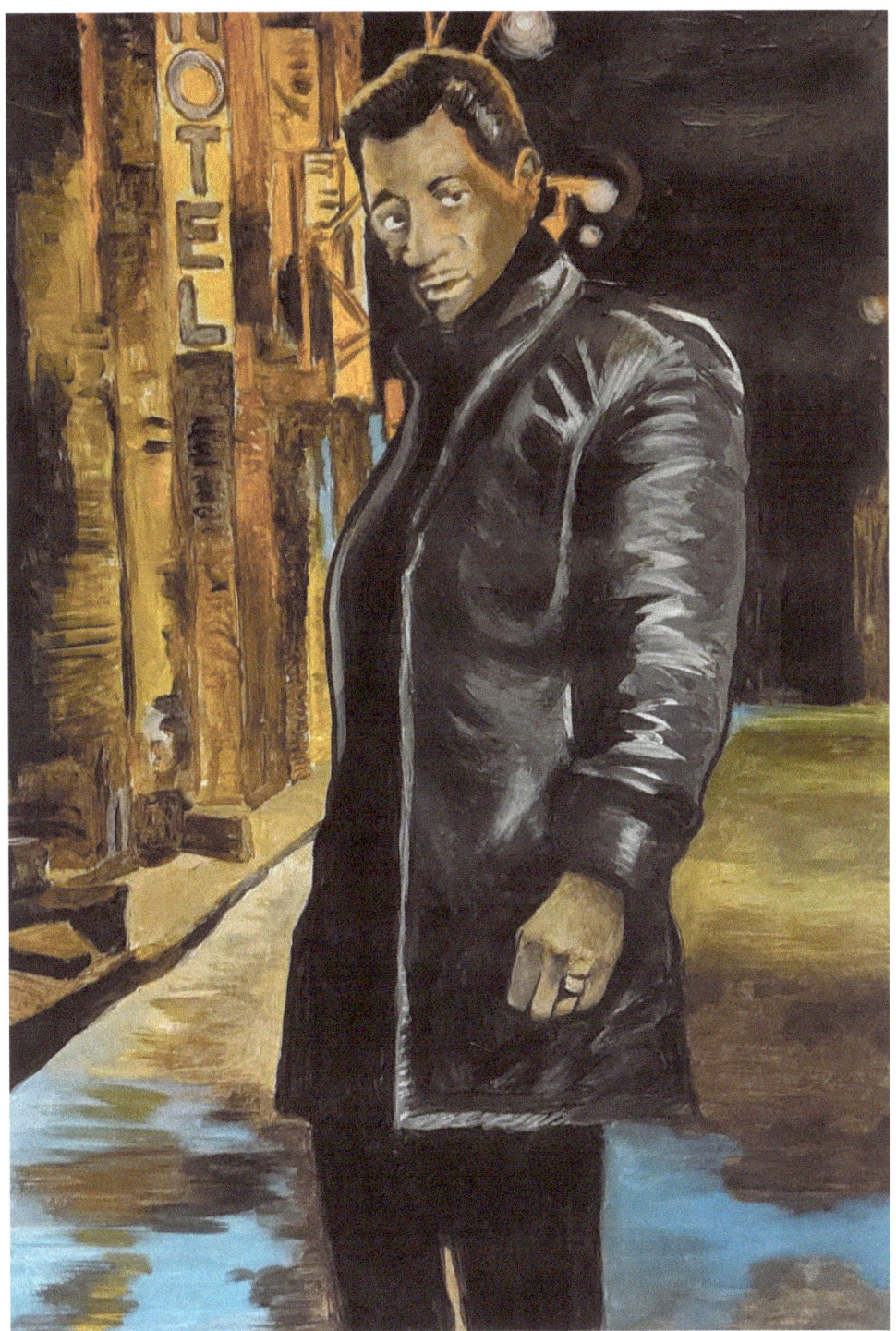

Johnnie Taylor

Taylor's popularity during his stay at Stax has never fully been recognised and yet vocally he ranks alongside Sam Cooke and Otis Redding. The thread that weaves the three together is also more than a tenuous one. Johnnie Taylor started life in Crawfordsville, Arkansas on May the 5th 1938 moving shortly thereafter to West Memphis where he studied at the local College before moving to Kansas City Missouri. His early musical training saw the teenage Taylor joining The Five Echoes and releasing one single on the Chance label before moving on to join the Highway Q.C.'s (a group that had once boasted Sam Cooke amongst its numbers), in 1957 and recording "Somewhere To Lay My Head", on the VeeJay label out of Chicago. After this Taylor sang with a Kansas City gospel group The Melody Masters and it was at this point that his career would take an upward direction albeit still within the Gospel field. After it had been noted that Taylor and Sam Cooke bore a striking similarity Cooke suggested Taylor as his replacement in The Soul Stirrers. In 1963 after a spell away from singing and brief careers as a preacher and a pimp, Taylor followed Sam Cooke as a solo artist turning away from Gospel but without the backlash felt by Cooke. It took a trip to Memphis visiting relatives to finally set Taylor's career off in the right direction. 1966 was the year and Stax was the place to be in Memphis. Initial product was created by the aspiring team of Isaac Hayes and David Porter who succeeded first time around for Taylor with his initial release "I Had a Dream". Following the success of this single and further success with "I've Got to Love Somebody's Baby" Taylor's first Album, "Wanted One Soul Singer" was released. The name derived from the fact that, unbeknown to him, label co-owner Jim Stewart and Al Bell had been looking for Taylor. The work with Hayes and Porter kept Johnnie in a bluesier mood whereas his later work moved him around the dance floor as well as scoring with the tenderest of ballads and Taylor would have nine happy and successful years at Stax right up to the company's collapse in 1975. Just as he had replaced Sam Cooke in The Soul Stirrers, in 1967 Stax records began to groom him as Otis Redding's successor to the Memphis throne after the tragic death of Redding. It was in the winter of 1968 when he struck gold for the first time with the single "Who's Making Love". The record became a number one R&B hit exceeding sales of three million. It was the label's biggest seller to date and even though he may occasionally have walked the path between good and evil one thing was for sure, whatever he was weaving, this Taylor was no dummy.

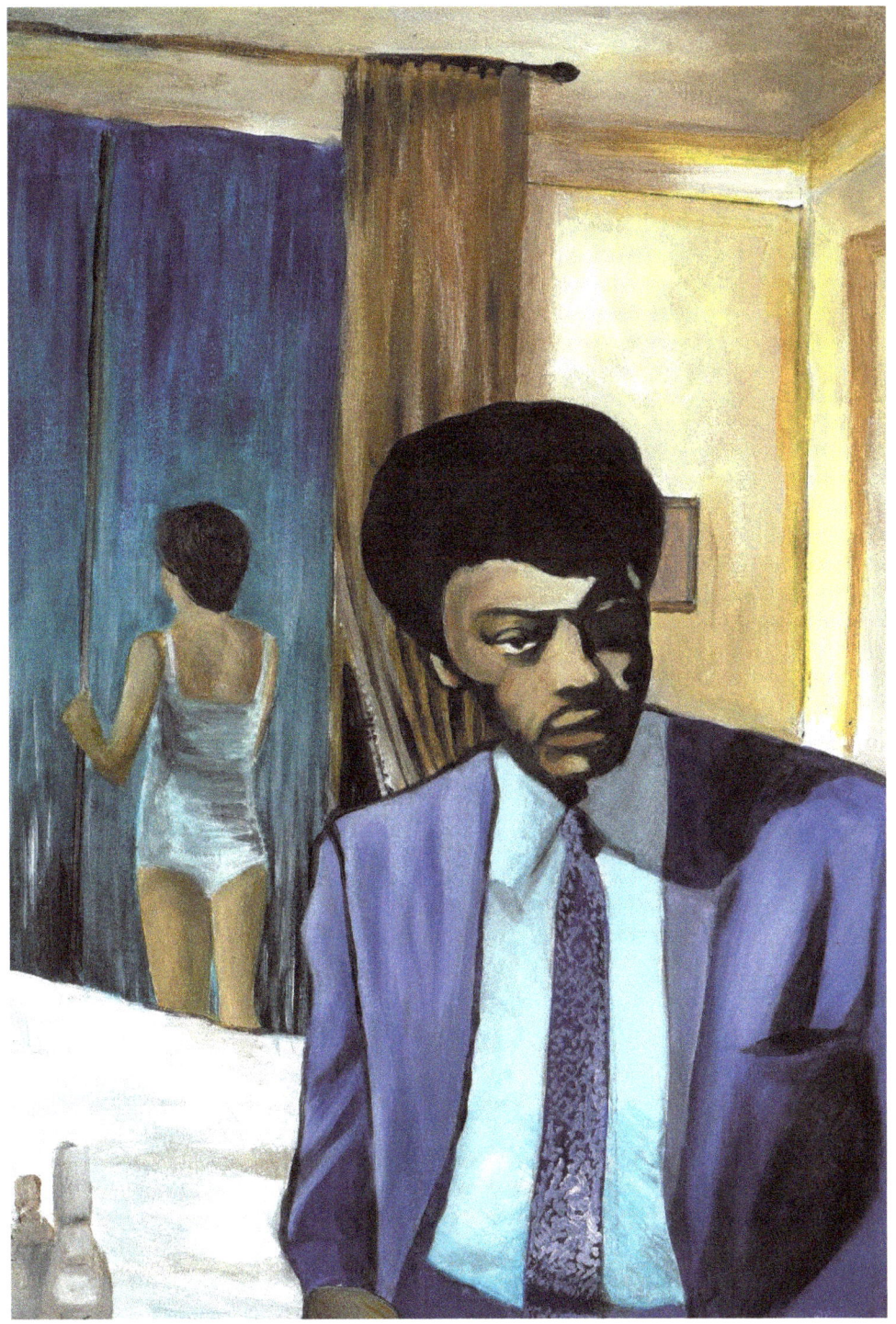

Otis Redding Part 1

Otis Redding was 26 when he died. Old enough to be recognised and respected for his craft and young enough to be the stuff of legends like James Dean and Marylin Monroe and black America would raise Otis to the dizzy heights of immortality. Redding's father was a farmer and part time preacher and Otis, one of 6 children, was born on the 9th September 1941. His early musical influences took the same tried and tested route as the best, the church. When he was eight Otis joined the choir at the Mount Ivy Baptist Church and like Sam Cooke, was beginning to sneak a look out of the window at what was going on outside the church's restrictions. Standing outside was Little Richard, a fellow Maconite, who was to be as great an influence as the church, the opposite attractions that make up Soul. Redding began singing in local talent contests becoming featured vocalist with Little Willie and the Mighty Partners and in December 1959, met Zelma, marrying her in August 1961. The role of husband was supplemented by the role of father and with these two responsibilities came the realisation that singing wasn't going to feed the family and so Otis had to take on another job which leads us nicely to the legend. By now Redding was chauffeuring as well as working with Johnny Jenkins and the Pinetoppers. With studio time left Otis took to the microphone to sing one of his own compositions, "These Arms of Mine". At this time Stax was being distributed through Atlantic and whilst not yet signed to Stax he found "These Arms of Mine" released on its subsidiary Volt in 1963 thanks to the producer and co-founder of Stax Jim Stewart. "These Arms of Mine" also introduced Booker T. Jones and Steve Cropper to Otis and although Atlantic weren't particularly happy at having a potential like Otis Redding snapped up, having financed the Jenkins sessions in the first place, they didn't make too much of it. Atlantic allowed the wavering of what was essentially an agreement by handshake rather than a written contract and so Otis went on to record his debut Stax album, "Pain in my Heart" in 1964. Otis respected those he worked with and would always find time for friends and family. Zelma saw in Otis a supportive partner, the opposite of many men, the type that most women seemed to find who might be poor but as they grew richer would go. Otis seemed to grow closer with the rise in his popularity. Redding's friendship with Steve Cropper grew and Cropper became co-writer and producer for many of Redding's greatest recordings, "Mr Pitiful" and "Dock of the Bay" to name just two. To many his was the epitome of the new Soul movement, the antitheses of what was going on up country at Motown. He had become increasingly aware of Sam Cooke's style and was able to move away from the church without the backlash that his predecessor felt from the purists.

Art & Soul

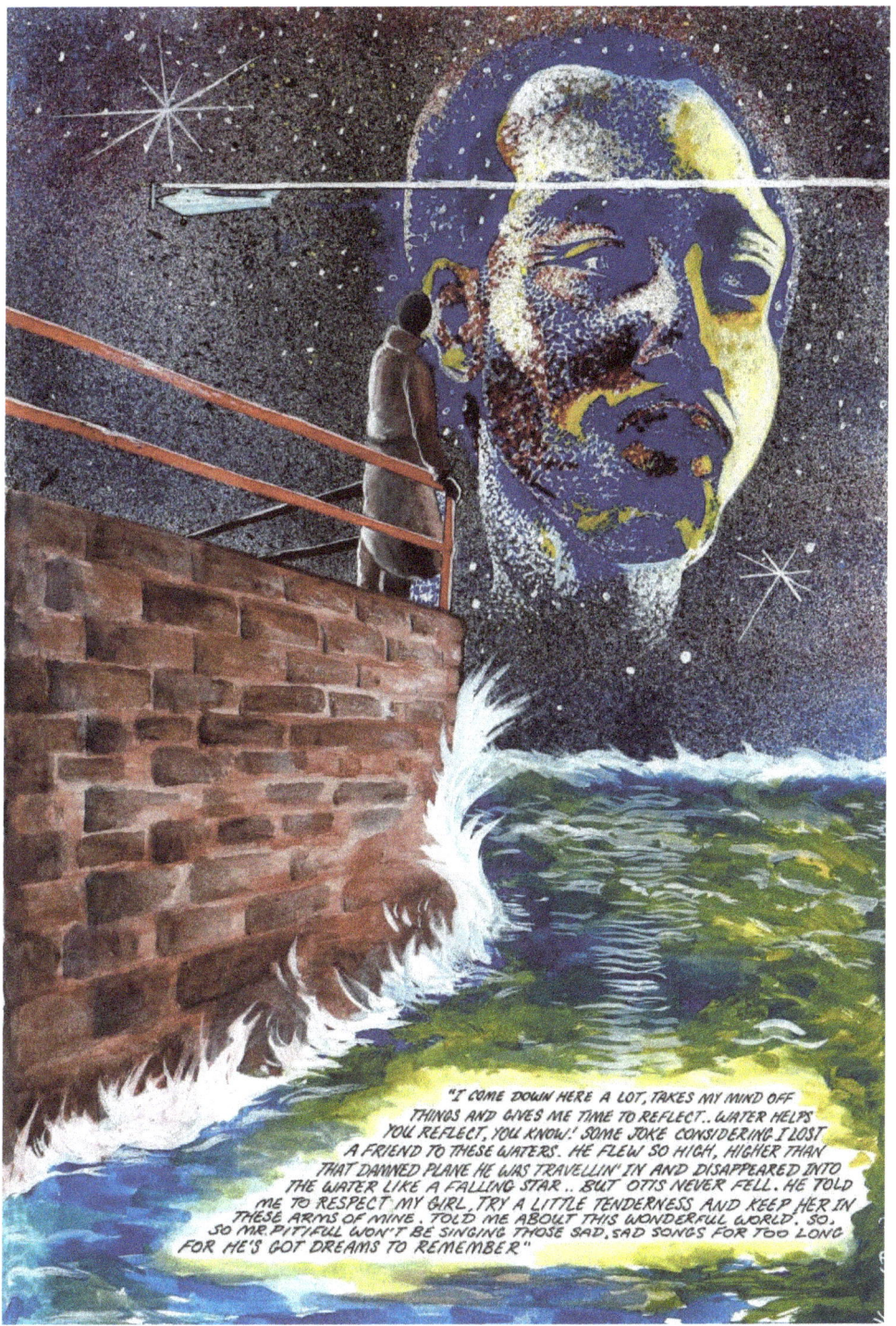

Otis Redding and The Bar Kays

Otis Redding had to go on the road to meet his ever-growing army of fans, particularly abroad where he stunned the British beat generation on the Stax/Volt tour in March of '67. The same year he had his finest moment at the Monterey Pop Festival when he wowed the Peace Generation and found a home-grown following which he had previously struggled to obtain. In his own way, he had broken through the race barrier to become an ambassador not only for Soul music but for integration in general. Otis had been doing it for some time now in the South and because he chose to remain there, he helped the Civil Rights Movement by appealing to a mixed audience. Although he never recorded any, one of Redding's musical favourites, Bob Dylan, was due to be given the Otis treatment. He did record the Rolling Stones' "Satisfaction" and The Beatles "Day Tripper" and whatever he chose he had a knack of making a song his own, in particular, standards like "Try A Little Tenderness". "My Girl", however remained the property of The Temptations but was responsible for Otis's recognition abroad when it was lifted from the 1965 "Otis Blue" album. Earlier in February of 1967 he had also taken the path trodden by many earlier artists and recorded a duet album. This particular one was Stax Royalty, Carla Thomas and the album was titled "The King and Queen" which raised Redding to Royal stature. The album included their hit single "Tramp". On December 10th, 1967, Otis Redding, along with members of The Bar-Kays, set off for a gig in Madison, Wisconsin. At 8.30am he had phoned Zelma from Cleveland sounding concerned about something: no explanation was ever given but it was clear that something was troubling him. He had started doing weekend gigs having rested after a routine operation to remove polyps from his throat, a common complaint of growths brought on by stress. Yet the weeks leading up to that fatal plane journey were just as unusual, as if Otis was planning to take that one-way trip and leave behind as much of himself as was humanly possible. He reworked old material adding new vocals to fourteen tracks in two weeks. At 3.38pm that Sunday the plane he was in began to hit a heavy bank of fog and the pilot made the tragic decision to make a premature landing and in so doing ended the life of Otis Redding. The plane crashed into the icy waters of Lake Monona drowning Otis and all but one of The Bar-Kays on board. Sepia Magazine would later callously print a photograph of Otis's body still strapped into his seat but erase that now. We didn't see Marylin Monroe's body as she lay on her bed or Jimmy Dean's body in the car. What we do see is Marylin still liking it hot or James Dean still revelling in being the first teenager so we should see Otis Redding loving us too long to stop now.

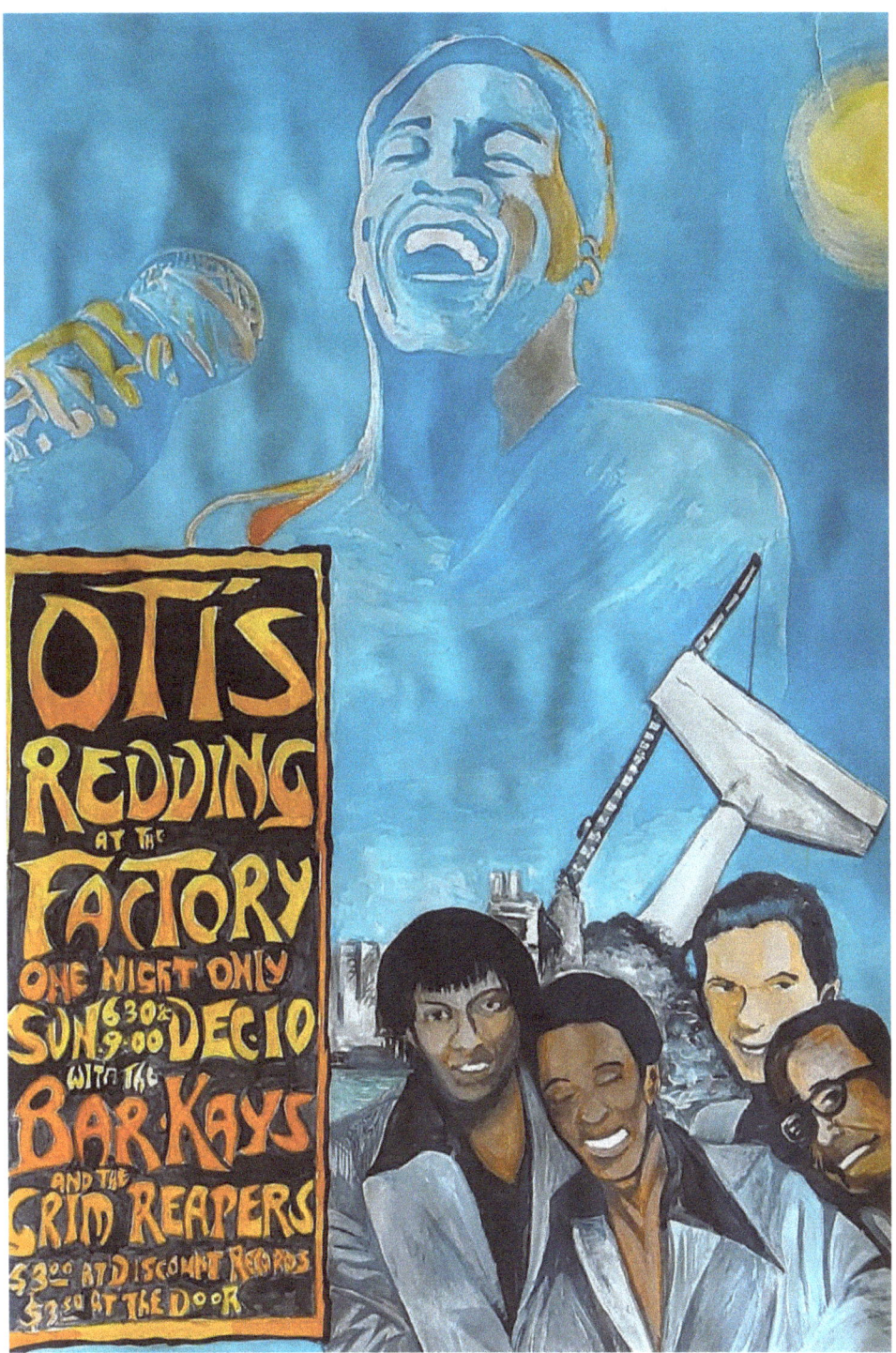

Sam & Dave

Sam Moore and Dave Prater had several nicknames, "Double Dynamite", "The Sultans of Sweat" and "The Dynamic Duo" and according to the Rock And Roll Hall Of Fame were the most successful soul duo and are acknowledged for bringing the word 'soul' into the music dictionary even though the genre was already established. Their song "Soul Man" came about after the 1967 race riots where many black owned businesses would paint the word 'Soul' on their shop fronts to detract looters. The song won them their first gold disc and Grammy Award for Best Performance by a Rhythm & Blues group and helped raise peoples' consciousness. Something Berry Gordy Jr may have contested, having created the Soul label as a Motown subsidiary back in 1964. Between them their musical starting points crossed over from Gospel through to doo-wop and R&B. Around 1961 they were on both the Gospel circuit as well as local clubs in Miami where, at the King of Hearts club, they sang together and became the duo immediately afterward. They began opening for other better-known acts such as Little Willie John who introduced Sam to heroin. Between 1962 and 1964 they had two singles released on Henry Stone's Marlin label and Roulette label in New York after Stone got them signed. Later he helped the guys out again by introducing them to Jerry Wexler from Atlantic. At the time Atlantic were distributing Stax Records out of Memphis and Wexler asked Jim Stewart, co-owner, to take them 'on loan'. It was when they were teamed with another 'dynamic duo' Isaac Hayes and David Porter, that everything started to come together. "You Don't Know Like I Know" reached number one on the R&B chart in 1966 and was the first of ten consecutive top twenty R&B chart hits. It was later named the number One R&B song of the year. "Hold On, I'm Comin'" was apparently created when Porter was in the bathroom and Hayes was calling for him to hurry up to which Porter responded "Hold On, I'm Coming" although the title would later cause controversy and need a light re-spelling and singing to allow for more radio play. Their popularity continued over the next few years but things changed dramatically between them in 1968 when Dave Prater shot and almost killed his wife leading to Sam Moore losing respect for him. They continued to perform but off stage there was hate and anger. Despite this personal disagreement the two performed at a tribute to Reverend Martin Luther King in June of that year and became the first black soul act to headline the Filmore East in December. In 2019, "Soul Man" was selected by the Library of Congress for preservation in the National Recording Registry for being "culturally, historically, or aesthetically significant" so to quote one of their songs, I thank you.

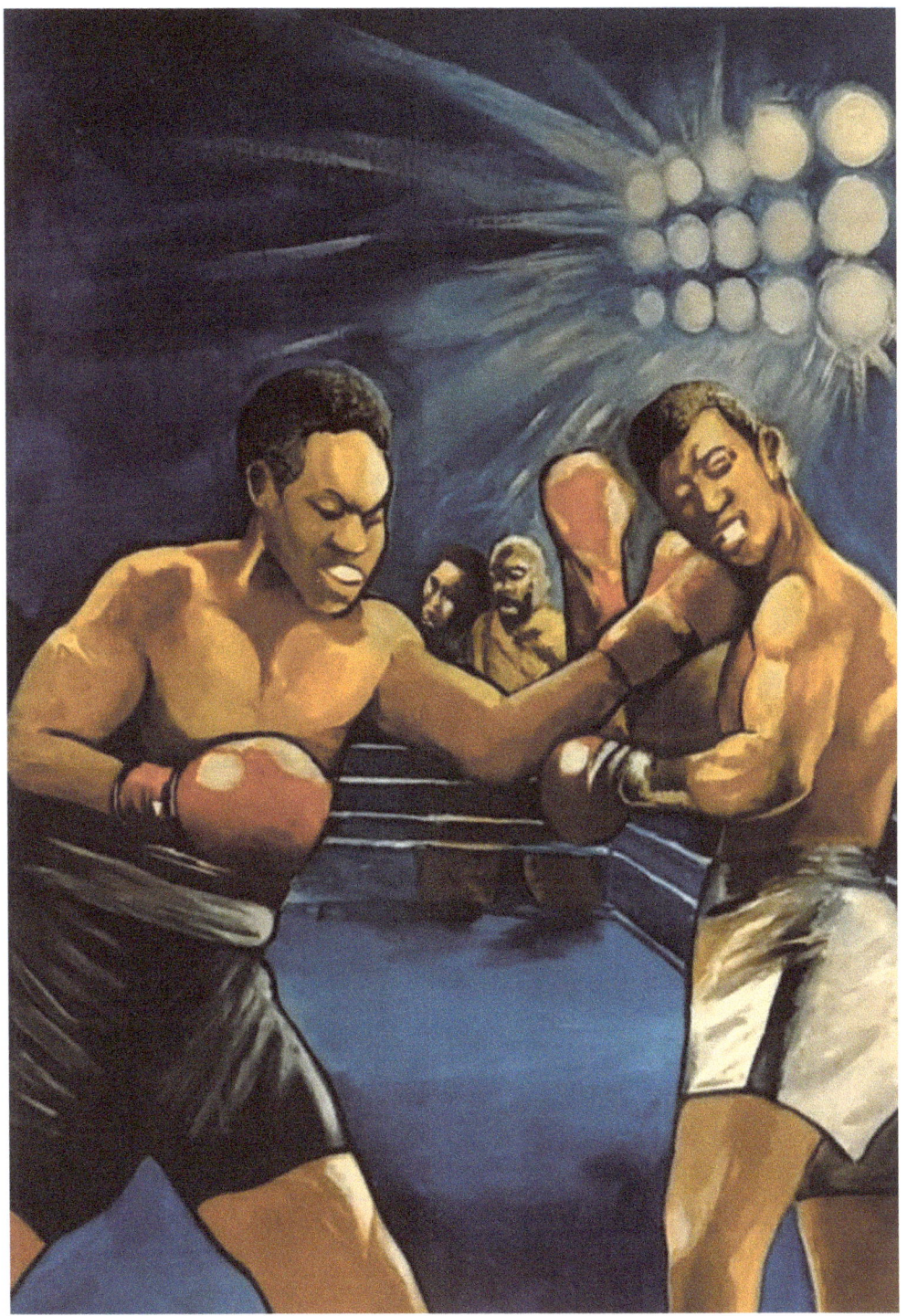

Shirley Brown

When Stax released "Woman to Woman" in 1974 the company was sadly going through major financial problems that would sadly see the label's collapse but for one glorious moment before disco emerged, Shirley Brown epitomized all that was great about a Memphis sound that some critics felt had stagnated since the death of Otis Redding. I would argue the opposite. Otis's presence could still be felt in many Memphis recordings but other producers and writers were working to develop the sound and lyrically the songs here were dealing with aspects of love seldom dealt with by Otis; after all anybody familiar with the Gary Larson 'Far Side' cartoon... "Same planet different worlds" knows that even if we are of the same race a woman's perspective is different than a man's and vice versa. Shirley Brown spelled it out in the title cut of this, her debut album. The single, 'Woman to Woman' sold one million copies in eight weeks and imitations or answer records sprung up. It appeared as though Shirley had opened up the proverbial can of worms. The title track actually opens up side two on vinyl, so appears halfway through the proceedings. The set starts powerfully with 'It Ain't No Fun', a Frederick Knight composition that helped to shake off his novelty tag after 'I've Been Lonely for So Long'. It's as deep as you want to go without suffering cramps and what always appealed about the track was the build up from early acceptance of an unacceptable situation to a penetrating climax of sheer emotion. The second track, 'As Long as You Love Me' calms the feelings down but only until track 3 when Shirley gives her interpretation of Lorraine Ellison's greatest moment 'Stay With Me'. This track was actually the demo that was sent to Stax by Shirley's manager, the late Bluesman Albert King and led to her signing. An adequate cover of William Bell's "I've Got to go on Without You" follows, calming the storm before the pressure builds again to the stunner that 'Woman to Woman' remains. The story of how Shirley found the other woman's name and number in her husband's pocket and decided to tell her woman to woman how things were, remains a classic. The rest of the album showcases Shirley Brown's voice, a voice that has gone on to win the respect of Soul collectors and who, despite record label changes and constant references to her Aretha type vocals, has remained consistent in her quality of output. The remaining tracks fluctuate from mid-paced movers to ballads that leave you with the same feelings that come from life, allowing you to experience and appreciate the quieter moments in order to survive the more turbulent times.

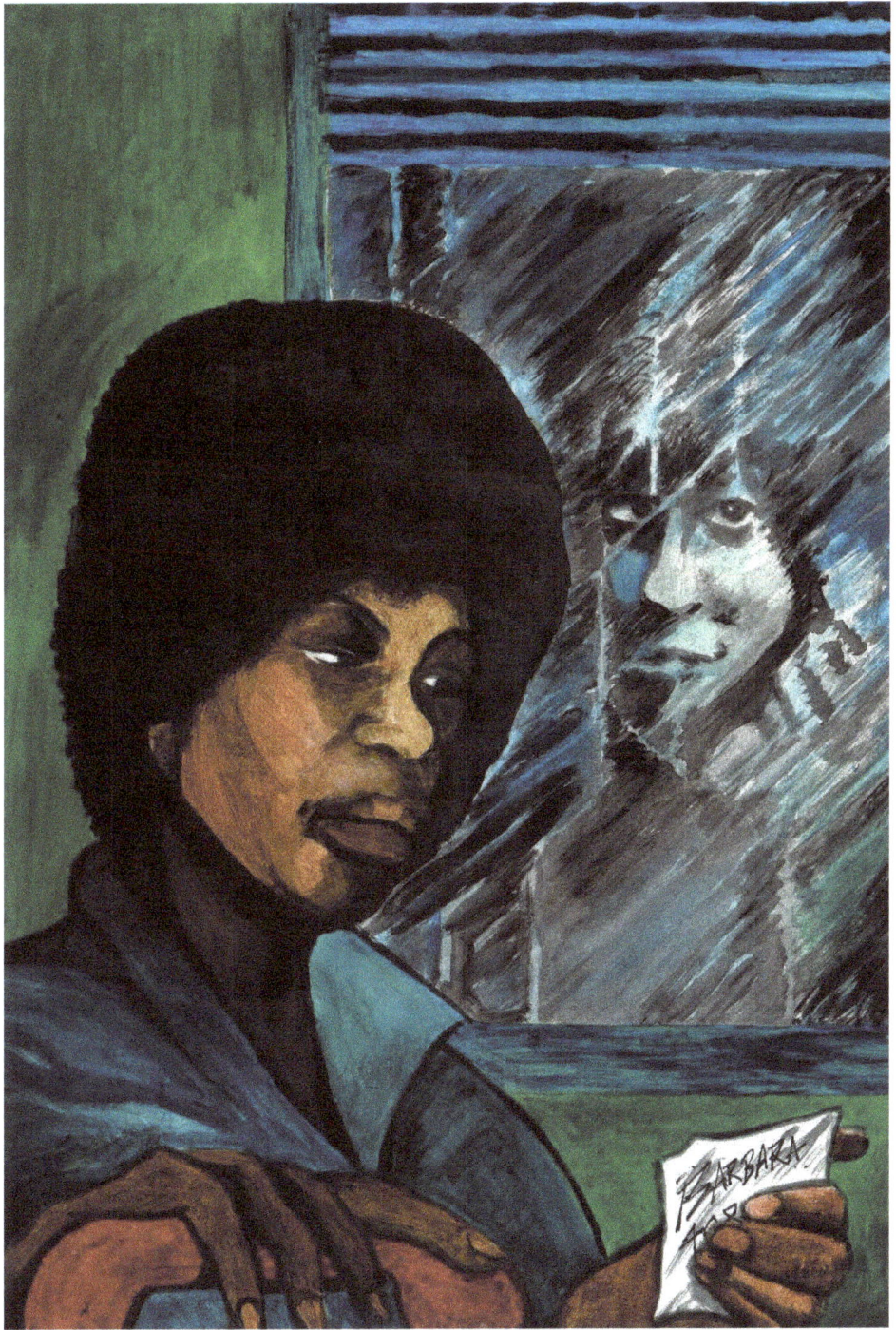

William Bell

Bell was born William Yarbrough in Memphis on July 16th, 1939. He had joined the local group The Del Rios whose members included Louis Williams who would later join The Ovations and Norman West who like Bell would join Stax records as a member of The Soul Children.

His very first song he wrote was as a member of The Del Rios when he was still only 14. In 1955 he had his first solo single released on the Meteor label, "Alone on a Rainy Night". After finishing High School, Bell took more formal musical training as well as piano lessons then his big break came when he signed to the Stax label in 1962 but after creating a splash with "You Don't Miss Your Water (Til Your Well Runs Dry)" he was drafted into the army. After serving his three years Bell returned to Stax in 1965 and as well as going back to the label he also opened a nightclub and used the fledgling Bar Kays as his band, even though they were still in middle school. On weekends he would take them on the road as his backing musicians and it was during this period that the young musicians were seen by such Soul luminaries as Wilson Pickett, Isaac Hayes and most significantly Otis Redding who would frequent the club. Times had changed since Bell's first period of recording for Stax and Otis Redding had become the label's number one male artist but Bell was a grafter and cut enough tracks in the first two weeks to give the label a slew of singles as well as picking up previous material from his first time around to issue his debut album," The Soul of a Bell". In 1967 Bluesman Albert King recorded Bell's composition "Born Under a Bad Sign" but it was also the year that the world lost Otis Redding. A man who had contributed to putting Stax on the international stage perhaps more than any other Stax artist. At the height of his career and only 26 years of age Redding was dead, drowned along with most of the original Bar Kays. This was a turbulent time for Black America. A year later Martin Luther King would be assassinated, and America would erupt in a second wave of race riots of the 1960s. Troubled times lay ahead for the country. As a tribute to Redding William Bell cut "A Tribute to a King" in 1968. Within the lyrics Bell told the story of Otis Redding. Written within days of Redding's death Bell recorded it for Otis's widow Zelma but it was her who later requested Stax to release it. In 1968 Bell was also responsible for one of Soul's best-known anthems "Private Number" a duet with Judy Clay. In 1976 Stax folded but a year later, despite feeling that the label's closure was like a divorce for him, he had his biggest success, now signed to Mercury with "Trying to Love Two".

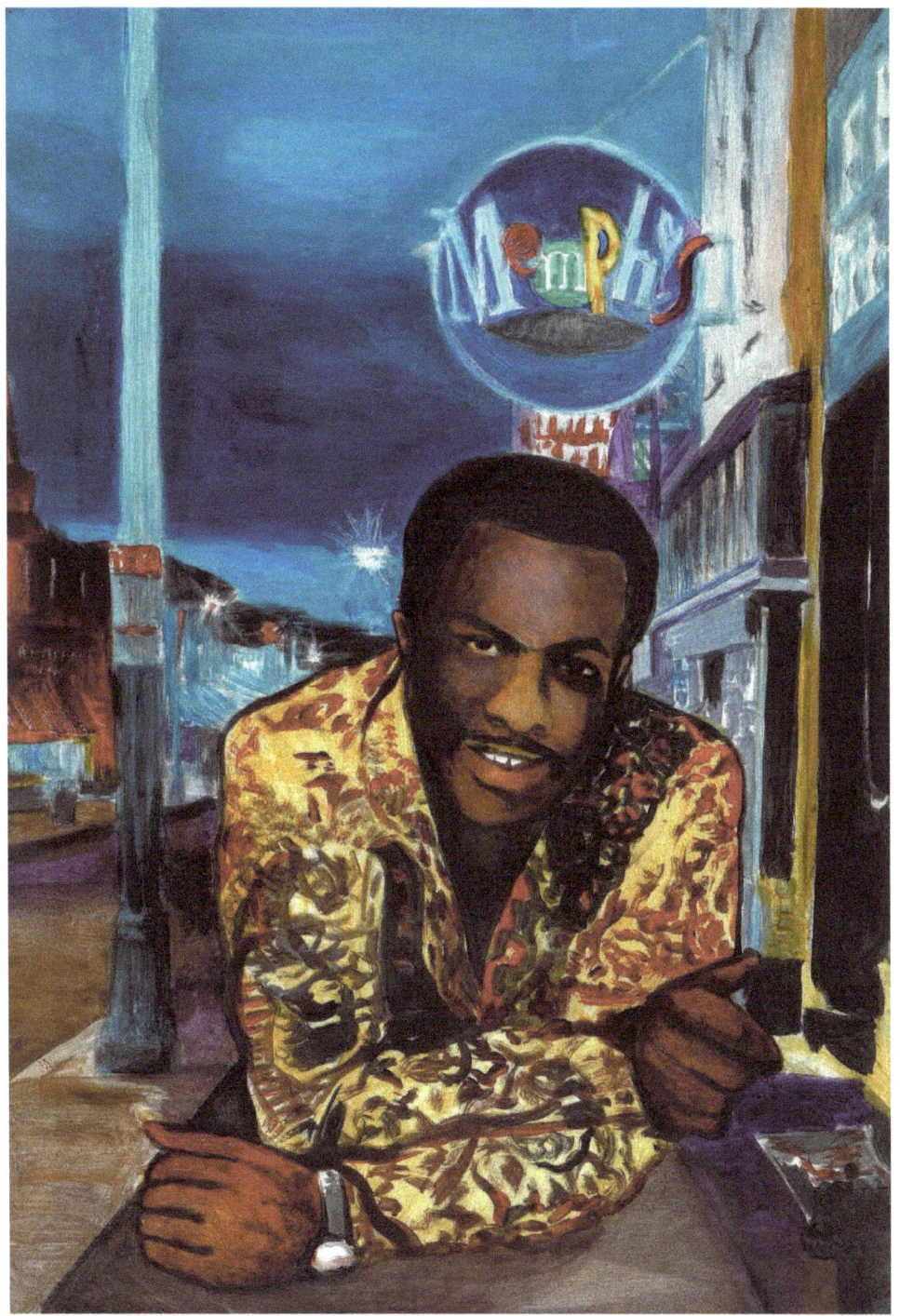

Willie Mitchell

Willie Mitchell was born on March 23rd, 1928, and raised in Ashland, Mississippi before moving to Memphis when he was in high school. At the age of eight, he began to play the trumpet and while still in high school was a featured player in popular local big bands. In 1950 he was drafted into the army and four years later returned to Memphis. Here he formed a band and played in the local clubs until, in 1960 he delved into the recording industry as a producer, session musician and artist for the Home of the Blues label. Here he was able to develop what would later become his signature horn arrangements for the Hi label based at the Royal Recording Studio and where he also orchestrated the Hi Rhythm section which mirrored the integrated black and white musicians who had created the Memphis sound over at Stax records. At Hi Mitchell was able to release a series of instrumental singles starting with "The Crawl" but his talent lay beyond this and he was able to nurture vocal talent, most notably Ann Peebles and Al Green. Ann Peebles had joined the label in 1968 and as well as being a vocalist had started composing songs with another staff writer Don Bryant. The Detroit Emeralds were touring and whilst in Memphis cut some tracks with Mitchell which found their release on Detroit's Westbound label, "You Want It, You Got It", "Baby Let Me Take You (In My Arms)" and "Do Me Right". Vocals and strings were added back in Detroit but this soulful hybrid gave them their hits. In 1971 this collaboration worked again with Denise LaSalle's "Trapped by this Thing Called Love" giving Westbound its first number 1.

Despite these successes the greatest achievement for him was with the arrival of Albert Leornes Greene from Forrest City, Arkansas in 1969. Albert Greene, or Al Green, was originally hired as a vocalist to perform with Mitchell's band but he soon signed him as an artist for Hi. Mitchell became Green's vocal coach and his first album released in '69 "Green Is Blues" was a slow start but laid the way for 1971's more successful "Al Green Gets Next to You". Although the Blues were there, so too was the sound that Green would be more known for and the track which housed all of this was "Tired of Being Alone", the first of eight gold records, Green would collect during his time with Willie Mitchell.

At the end of 2009 Willie Mitchell was still working when he had a heart attack. On the 5th of January the eighty-one-year-old Mitchell passed away from a cardiac arrest. Mitchell not only had his own family but formed a family of talented writers, musicians and above all vocalists who loved him not only for giving them their careers but because of the genuine love he gave to them.

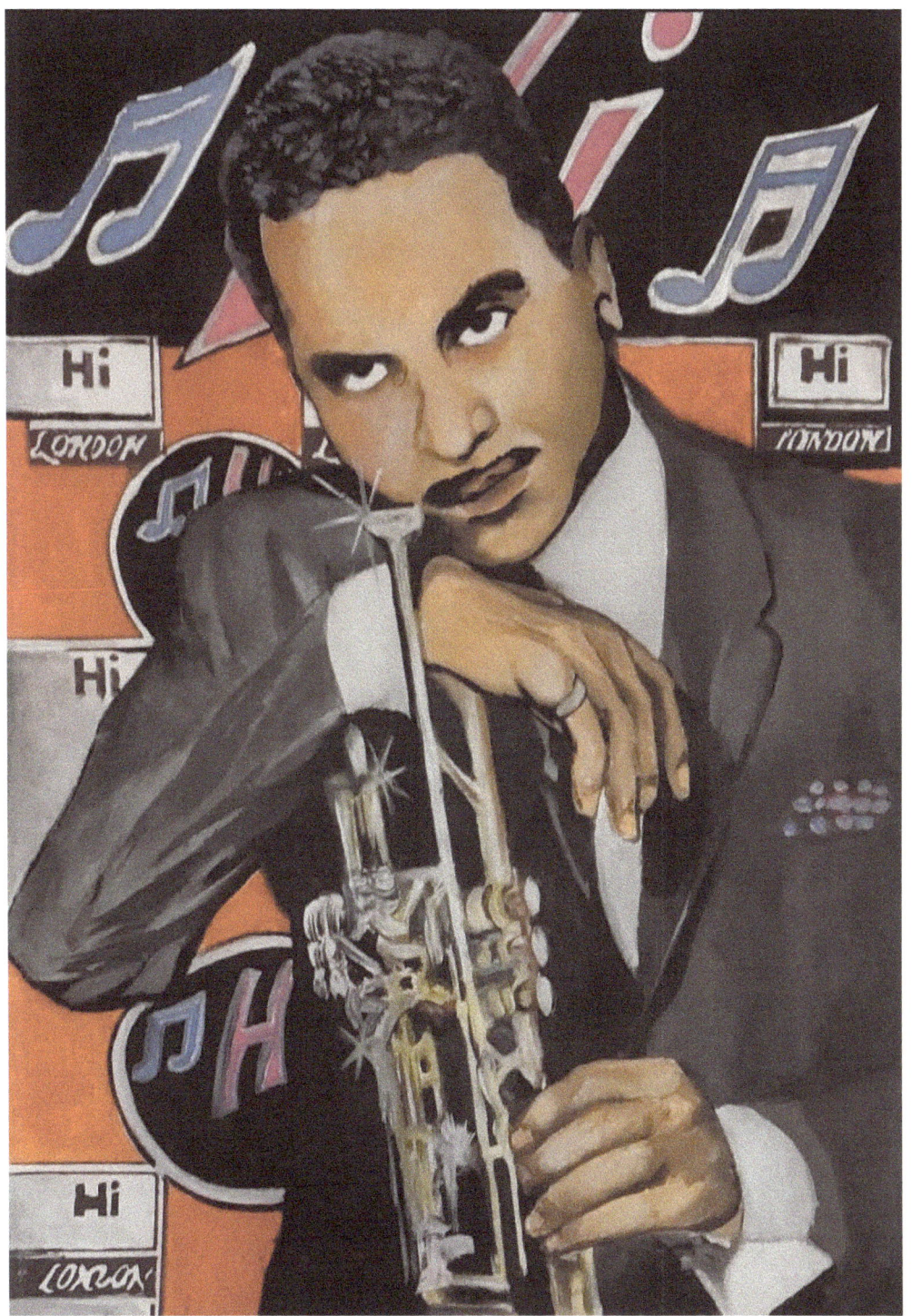

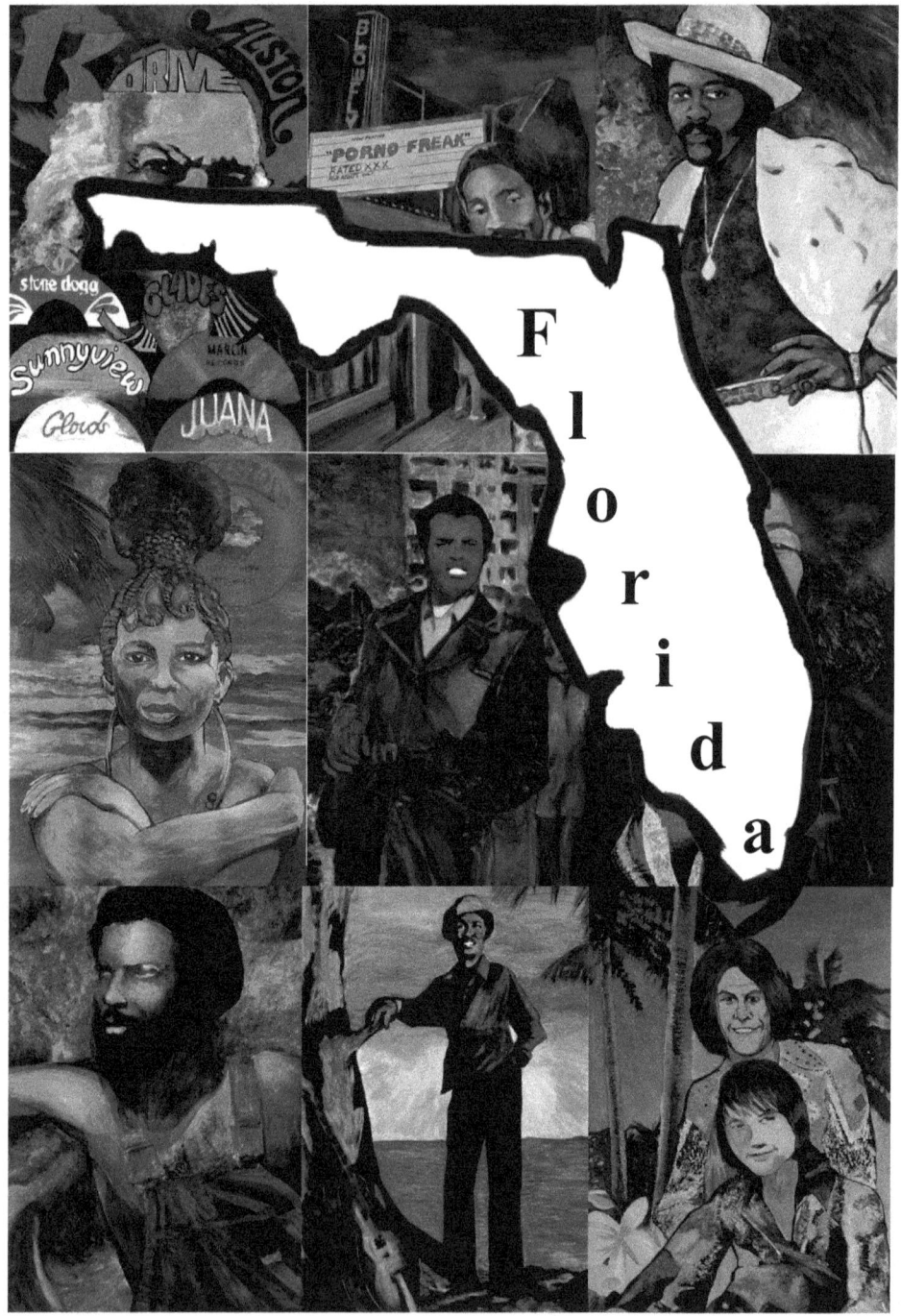

Art & Soul

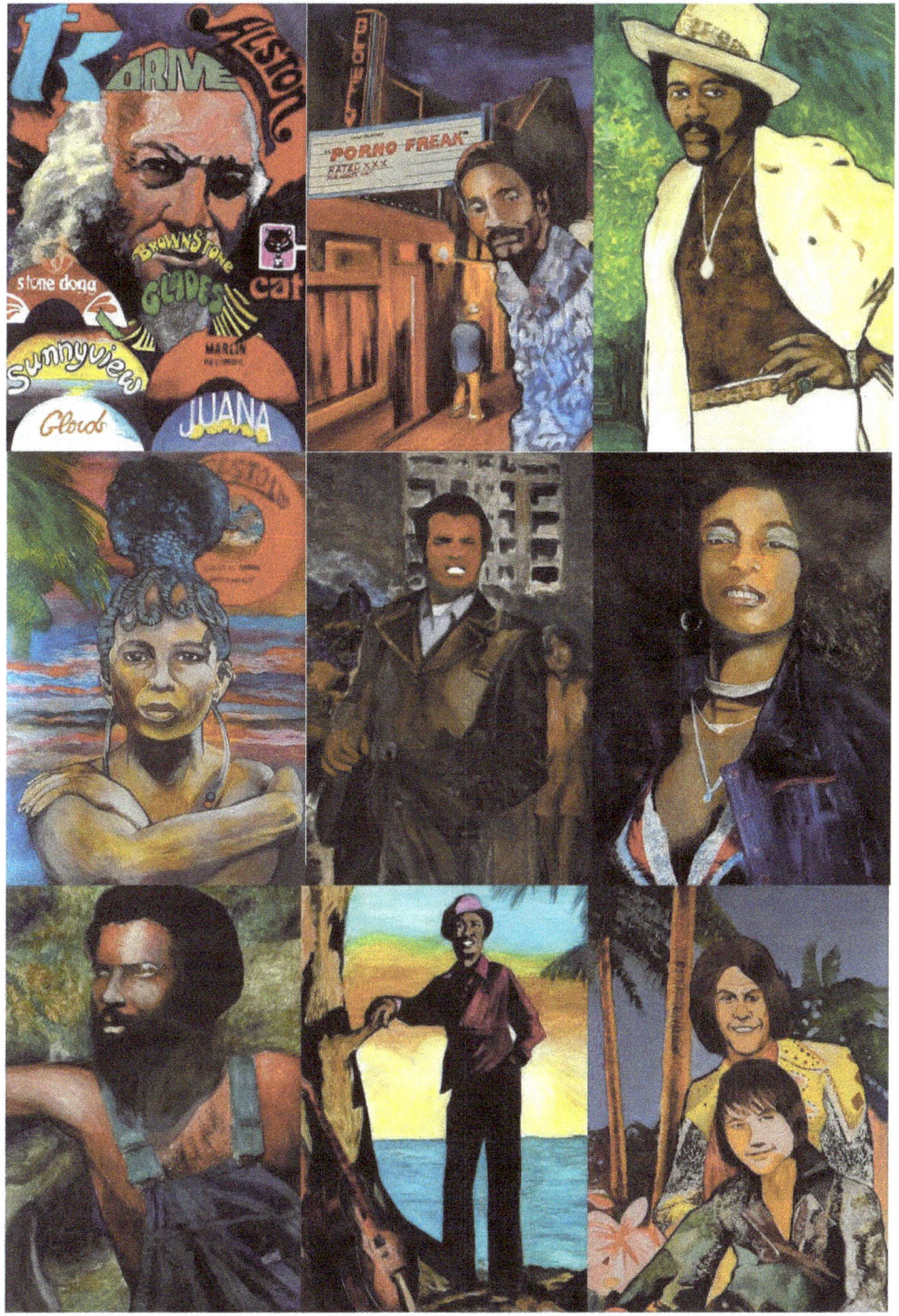

Betty Wright

Betty Wright was born Bessie Regina Norris in Miami, Florida on December the 21st 1953. She began her professional career at the age of two when her siblings formed the Gospel group, the Echoes of Joy. Betty contributed to vocals on the group's first album, released in 1956. They performed together until 1965, when she was 11 years old. Betty moved away from Gospel music and began singing in local talent shows where she was spotted by a local Miami record label owner, who signed her to his label, Deep City Records in 1966 when she was still only twelve. She released the singles, "Thank You Baby" and "Paralyzed", which were big on the local scene in Miami. In 1967, still only 13, she was responsible for discovering other local talents such as George and Gwen McCrae and her first album "My First Time Around", was released when she was still aged 14. At the age of 16, while still in high school, she released "Pure Love" in 1970 and a year later, released "Clean Up Woman". The record reached number 2 on the R&B charts, where it stayed for 8 weeks. It crossed over to the pop charts, peaking at number 6 and staying on the Billboard Hot 100 for 14 weeks. It eventually sold over a million copies and was certified gold on December 30, 1971, nine days after the singer turned 18.

By 1974 there was already far more to Betty Wright than her just wanting to make it as a successful singer. One of Wright's most popular albums, "Danger! High Voltage!" was released that year. The track rewarded Betty Wright with her first Grammy Award, this was for Best R&B Song for 1975. Towards the end of the 1970s Betty Wright's albums became less successful and in 1985 she formed her own label, Miss B Records making history as the first black female artist to score a gold album on her own label, with her 1987 album, "Mother Wit". The album was notable for the hit "No Pain, No Gain," which returned her to the top 20 on the R&B Chart for the first time in a decade and giving birth to a new phrase. In 1989 Betty released the album "4U2NJOY" which displayed her incredible vocal range on "Valley of the Lonely". Betty Wright would go on to arrange the backing vocals on Jennifer Lopez's 1999 debut album, "On the 6." Then another career highlight came along when she became involved in the debut album for British singer Joss Stone. Betty Wright passed away at the age of 66 from cancer. Her energy and support for others through her music spanned 64 out of 66 of her mortal years but what she has left behind isn't just her music, no. With all its love, its loss, the pain and the pleasure, with its softness and strength Betty Wright left us her Soul.

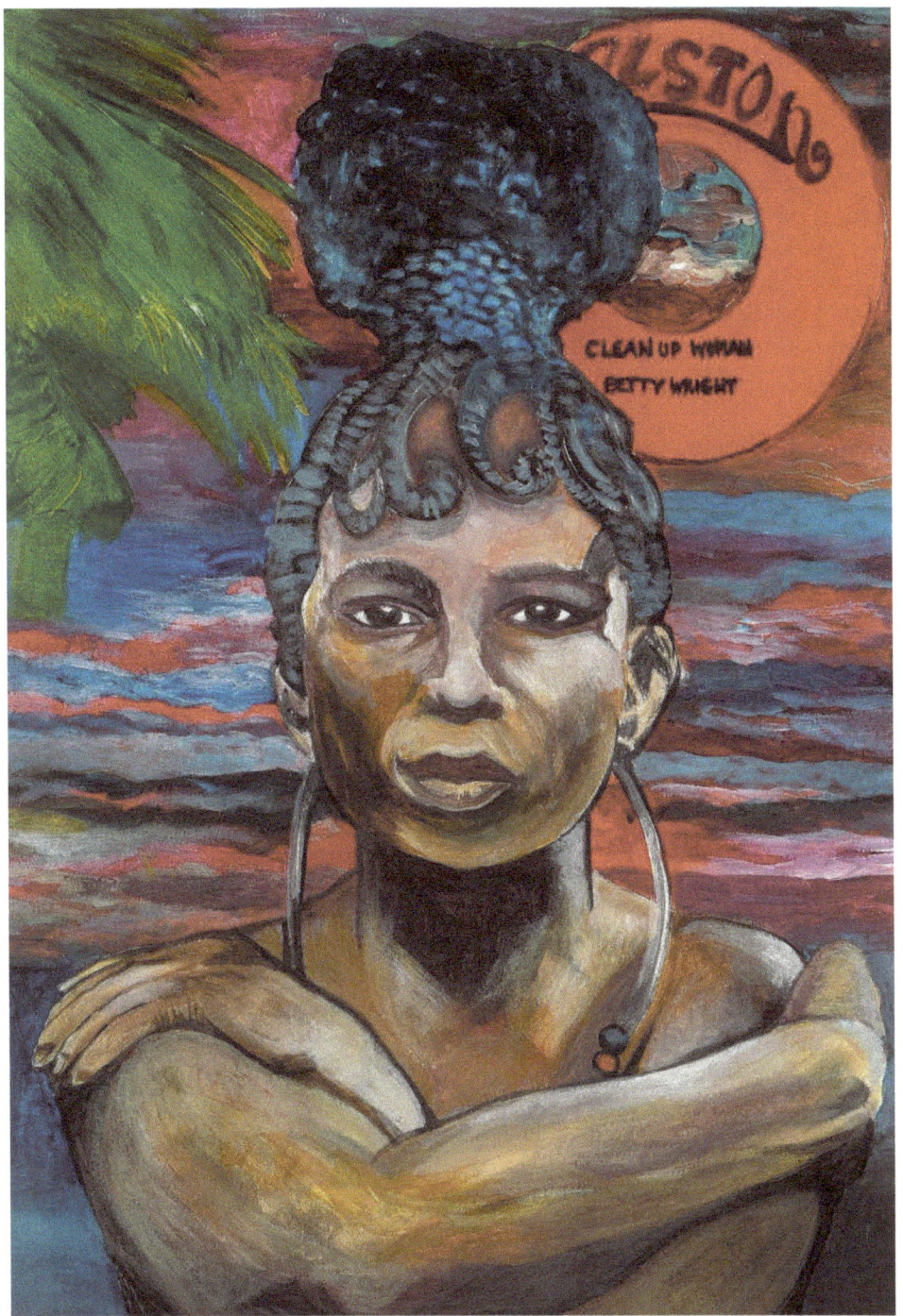

Casey & Finch

If you can't change anything, then just dance. That seemed to be the message coming out of Florida and signified by one particular group, or two individuals, H.W. Casey and Richard Finch. H.W. Casey was called the "Founder of the Dance Revolution". He is Harry Wayne Casey. Who, you may ask is Harry Wayne Casey? Well, abbreviating Casey he became KC, better known as the founder and leader of KC & The Sunshine Band. In 1972 H.W. Casey who was born in Opa-locka Florida on the 31st of January 1951 grew up in a multi-ethnic area that gave him access to a range of music from reggae, pop to Latin. He was sweeping floors and packing records for Henry Stone when he met Richard Finch a young bassist and part time recording engineer. The two would talk about music and songs and started writing together. Stone gave the two youngsters time to mess around in the studio and the two teens formed a creative partnership. Stone let the young men work and experiment in the recording studio when it wasn't booked and during after-midnight hours. The two cut numerous demos on themselves and in January 1973 Casey attended Clarence Reid's wedding reception where Reid introduced him to a music form called Junkanoo that had started in the Bahamas. It wasn't long before Casey took the abbreviation 'KC' and formed his own Sunshine Junkanoo Band which was very quickly changed to the Sunshine Band. People seemed eager to get away from the negativity that seemed to be circling The States and so alongside Richard Finch the Sunshine Sound was started. During his formative years Casey became both personal assistant and booking agent for fellow artist Timmy Thomas and on a trip to perform in Washington D.C. and after hearing the Pavlovian-like audience react to the whistles being blown he was inspired to write the tune "Blow Your Whistle", Casey and Finch's first leap into professional recording and the song reached number 27 on the R&B chart in September '73. February 1974 saw the release of KC & The Sunshine Band's second single, seeing them moving away from whistles they were now on horns with "Sound Your Funky Horn" which did slightly better than its predecessor but better things were on the horizon. The band proved that it was more than just a singles group and the album went multi-platinum winning five Grammys in 1976. Their chart success was slowing down, the other was that people were slowing down and the discos were dying off and it wasn't all from natural causes. It was being helped by a Chicago based anti-disco movement that reached national proportions assisted by a CBS news programme "60 Minutes" which named TK Records. Whatever your views on disco are, you can't help but admire the Miami effort which was probably of its time and yet you can still fill a dance floor with their music to this day.

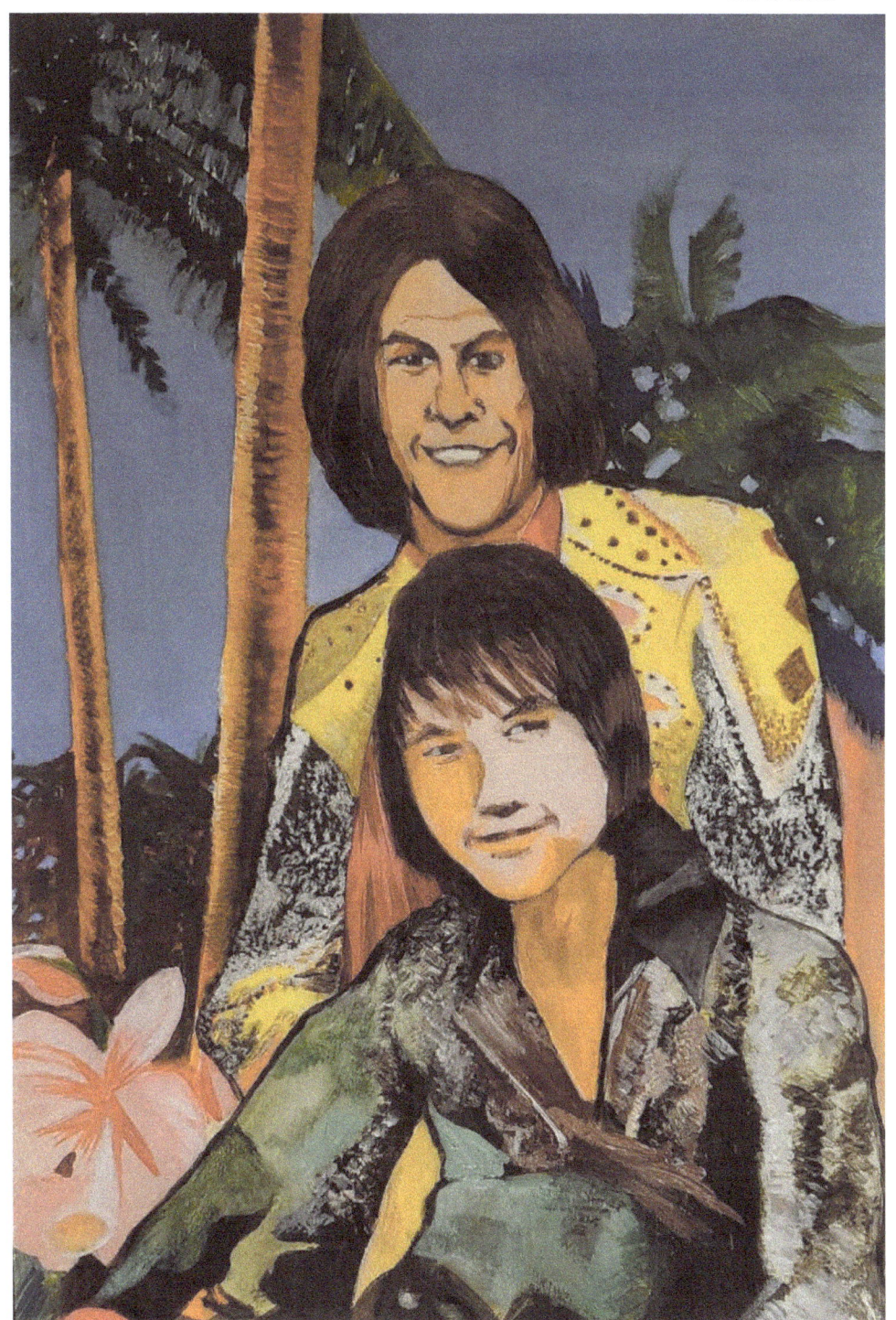

Clarence Reid

Clarence Reid was born in Cochran, Georgia on Valentine's Day 1945 and as a boy worked in the cotton fields. What the young Clarence didn't realize was that his throwaway childish word play would become a full 'blown' musical genre decades later that would lyrically follow his lead and musically sample the funky rhythms he was creating in Miami. As far back as 1965 Reid recorded what was arguably the first acknowledged rap song, "Rap Dirty" in which our hero was a truck driver on a coast-to-coast journey where he fought the Ku Klux Klan. The song didn't get a release in the States until 1976 which meant that it had been overtaken by other contenders for the tile and although Reid himself questioned whether or not he should be acknowledged as the founder of Rap he is the first rapper to be banned after an Alabama record store was raided for selling "Porno Freak." He was also sued by the President of ASCAP for recording "What a Difference a Lay Makes." When he was 13 Clarence Reid hitchhiked to Miami to follow his dream of a career in music. By 1963 he was part of a vocal group in Miami called The Delmiras. Clarence began singing at local venues where he met many of the people he would work with throughout his career and in 1964 he found a job stacking records in the TK Records warehouse run by Henry Stone. It wasn't long before Reid joined the Deep City label as well as starting up his own label, Reid. His material also began to be released on Buddy Killen's Dial imprint. His early original material contained elements of other influences as in "I Refuse to Give Up" released on Dial in 1964 that echoed The Impressions with a falsetto lead by Reid and a bass vocal behind him. "Somebody Will" from the same period was pure Joe Tex and included a Tex like Rap. "Tired Blood" released on Deep City in 1967 was more Joe Tex style music. Reid was finding his feet in the rising Miami scene and went to the Deep City subsidiary, Tay-Ster which released his first Album, "Nobody but You Babe" but when nothing happened on the sales front Reid and his collaborator Willie Clarke decided to turn to Henry Stone. By the late 60s he was beginning to settle into more commitment with Henry Stone and in August 1968 Betty Wright released her debut Alston single "Girls Can't Do What the Guys Do" which reached number 15 on the R&B Chart as well as a healthy number 33 on the National Pop Chart. An album by Betty Wright, "My First Time Around" followed in September 1968 on the Atco label. Part of his longevity was surprisingly down to clean living! For even if Blowfly was just plain nasty, Clarence Reid was a devout Christian.

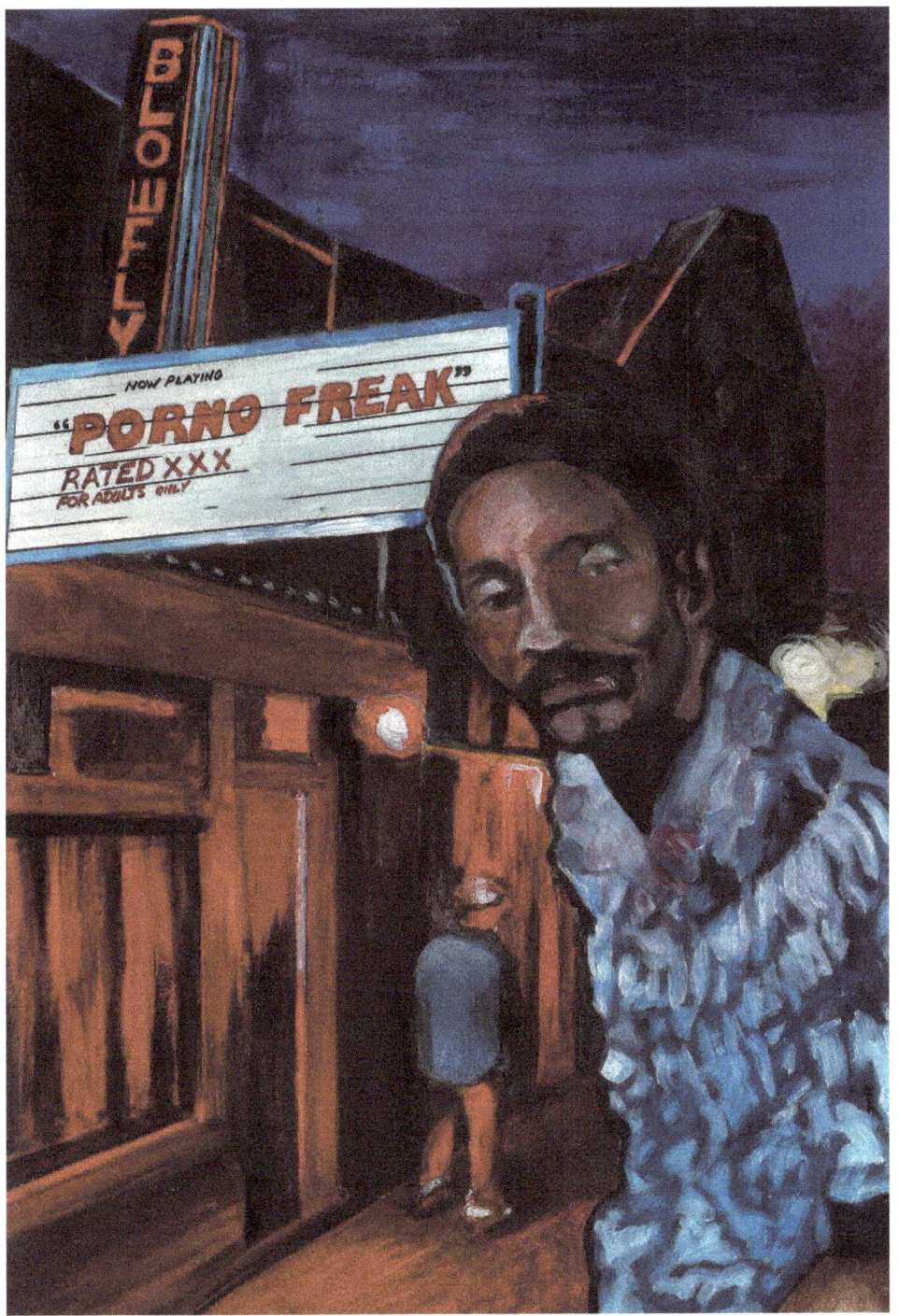

Cornelius Brothers & Sister Rose

The family that prays together doesn't always stay together. Take Cornelius Brothers & Sister Rose for example. Possibly one of the first Florida based successes in Soul the family heralded from Dania Beach and were formed in 1970. The group was made of brothers Carter and Eddie as well as sister Rose with the other sister, bizarrely unnamed in the group title, Billie Jo joining them in 1972. Prior to this the two brothers had signed to producer Bob Archibald's Platinum label as the Cornelius Brothers. Sister Rose had made a television debut in 1967 in the Ed Sullivan Show as well as performing in Las Vegas and around the world in 1970 with the Gospel Jazz Singers but at her mother's request went back to Florida to help form the new group. Still under the guidance of Bob Archibald and Platinum his product, recorded at the Music Factory in Miami, found its way to the more major outlet of United Artists. From the very start they struck gold with Eddie Cornelius' written "Treat Her Like A Lady" reaching a number 3 on the pop chart. The following year another Eddie C track, "Too Late to Turn Back Now" reached number 2 on the pop chart, higher than in the R&B chart suggesting maybe that their product was more pop oriented than Soul. In August it was given a gold award and in 1997 appeared on the soundtrack of the movie "The Ice Storm" as well as Spike Lee's 2018 film "The Black Kkklansman". Although Eddie's voice wasn't comparable to anyone else, his writing leaned towards the song structures of Sam Cooke but this didn't mean they would emulate Cooke and despite them being top quality, "Don't Ever Be Lonely" and "I'm Never Gonna Be Alone Anymore" reached the Top 40 but didn't reach the gold standard. They were also able to release three albums and their last chart hit came from their final one, "Since I Found My Baby" in 1974. Two years later and it was over when Carter Cornelius joined a black Hebrew sect in Miami and changed his name to Prince Gideon Israel. Although he had left secular music he continued writing and recording music and videos for this faith for fifteen years, building his own studio, Hangar 18 and releasing two albums, "Love Train" in 1988 and "Smooth Sailing" in 1990. He passed away on November the 7th 1991.

Eddie Cornelius struggled with alcoholism which sometimes turned to bitterness within the group and became a born-again Christian leading to him being an ordained pastor. As with Carter, he continued to perform, produce and write music but not for Bob Archibald. In June 2020 his memoirs were published called "It's Not Too Late to Turn Back Now (Back to the Arms of God). Rosie continued performing in Port Saint Lucie, Florida and God only knows where Billy Jo went.

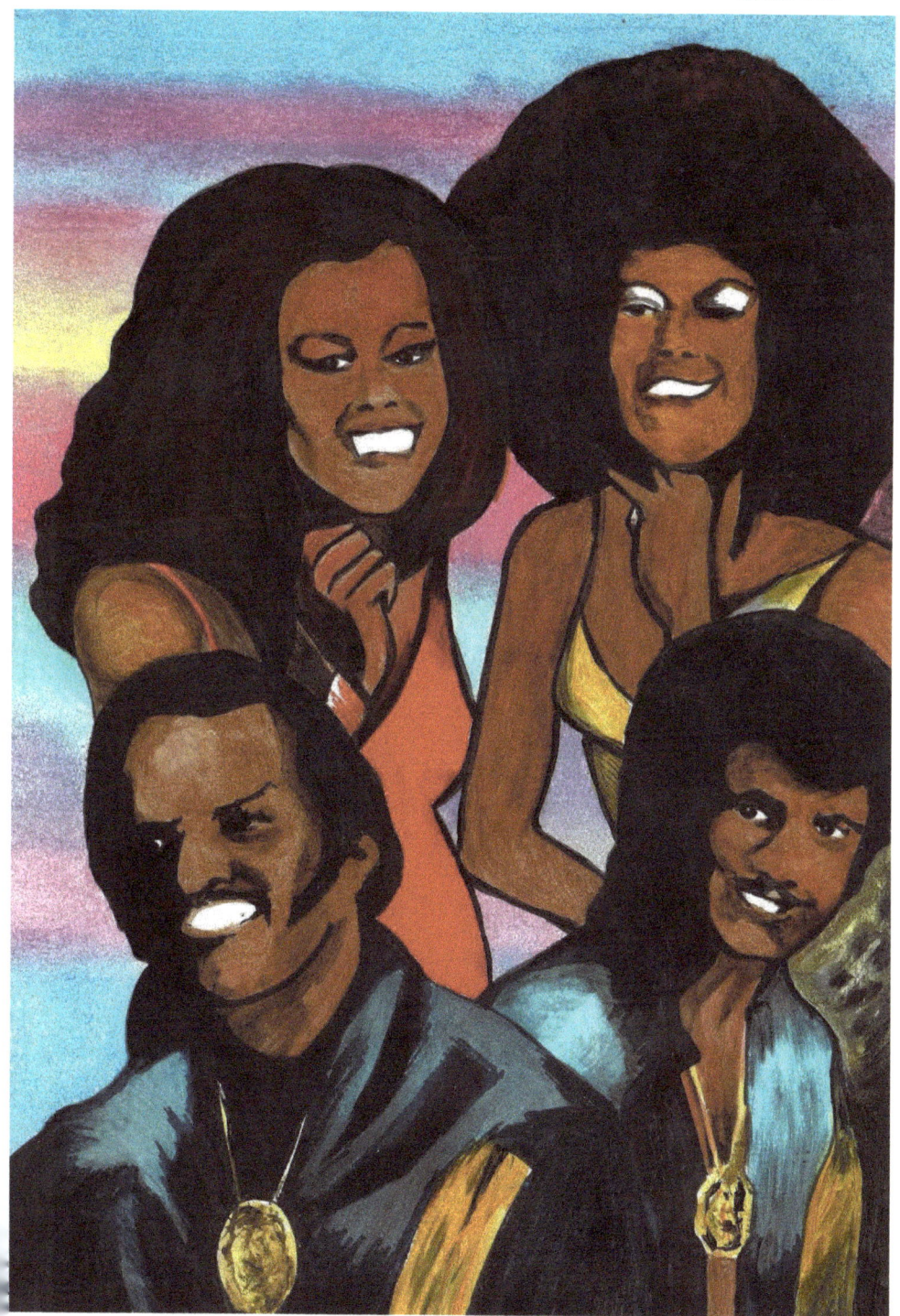

George McCrae

George Warren McCrae Jr was born on October the 19th 1944 the second of nine children in West Palm Beach, Florida. Because he came in at the time disco was muscling in on music you forget that there were some amazing singers being drowned by dross. In 1962 he formed the short-lived group The Jivin' Jets; what lasted slightly longer was his marriage to Gwen Mosley the following year, who, as Gwen McCrae, would make her own way onto the Florida scene. They worked as a duo, simply called George and Gwen recording for the Alston label; starting with 1969's "Like Yesterday Our Love Is Gone" written by Clarence Reid and Willie Clarke, followed by a play on "Three Coins in a Fountain" named "Three Hearts in a Tangle". 1970 saw one final release for them, "No One Left to Come Home To" before George went solo, moved to the Glades label and released "Back Dues". They carried on working the local clubs but things weren't moving fast enough for George and he was planning on going back to college to study law enforcement. Then the break happened. He'd already added his voice to KC & The Sunshine Band's hit "Queen of Clubs" but after H.W. Casey and Richard Finch of KC & The Sunshine Band fame were looking back at some of their unrecorded demos, one in particular stood out but was in a high key which they felt was beyond their own range. Henry Stone and his A&R man Steve Alaimo suggested offering it to George McCrae. "Rock Your Baby" was a phenomenon, reaching number 1 on both the pop and R&B charts in The States in June 1974 and smashing the chart globally. Rumour had it that the "Rock Your Baby" album only took two takes, such was their combined youthful daring and once dormant skills. Elsewhere George's wife Gwen McCrea was an emerging star but "Rock Your Baby" had turned her husband into an international star and helped to put the Miami sound on the world map selling over 16 million singles. At the time I was seeing my first girlfriend, a staunch Christian and I remember taking her to a disco and her refusing to dance to a record with such profane sexually charged words. That was a long, quiet walk home. In 1975, the track "I Get Lifted" which had originally been cut by KC & The Sunshine was re-worked by George McCrae reaching Number 8 on the R&B Chart in January 1975. That year Cat released the album "Together" by George and Gwen McCrae but the following year proved that to be wrong as they divorced in 1976. The same year George released the album "Diamond Touch" written and produced by Greg Diamond. At the time I thought the title was just referring to the quality of the material not the producer, no arrogance there.

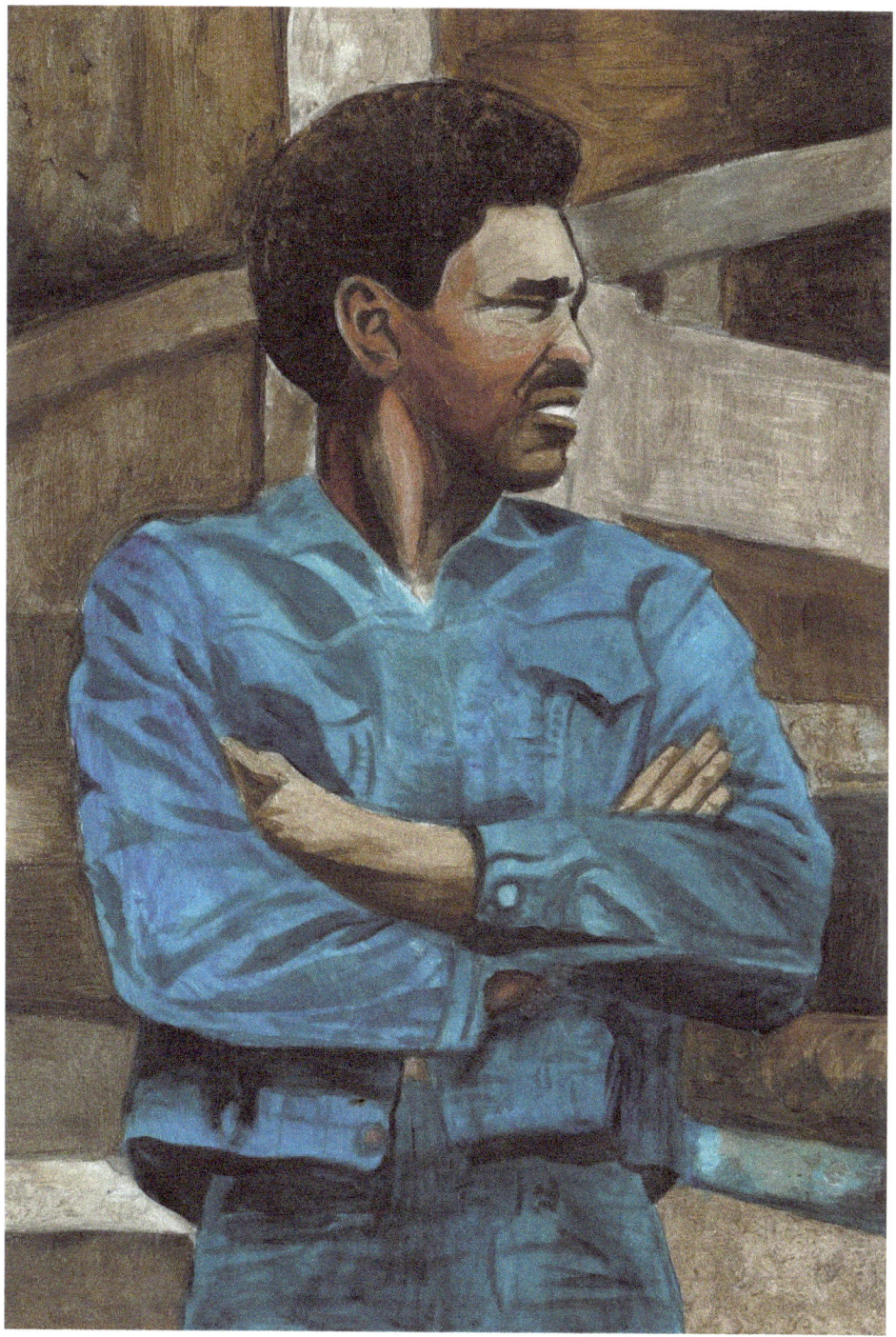

Gwen McCrae

Gwen Mosley was born on December the 21st 1943, the youngest of five children and as a teenager she started performing in local clubs and briefly joined a local group The Lafayettes and The Independents before a short stint with The Jivin' Jets which brought her into contact with future husband George McCrae. By 1967 Gwen and George were seen by Betty Wright and Willie Clarke singing in a local club which led to an introduction to Henry Stone who was now busy putting together his operation. Gwen's solo material was released through Columbia but in 1973 when her contract with Columbia wasn't renewed she signed to the Cat label, this time as a solo artist where Clarence Reid co-wrote her debut single "He Keeps Something Groovy Goin' On". She also had a hit in the R&B chart with her adaptation of Bobby 'Blue' Bland's "Lead Me On" in 1970. This was followed by her remake of a 1958 hit for Ed Townsend, "For Your Love" in 1973 reaching number 17 in the R&B chart. Gwen was also the first person to release "You Were Always on my Mind", later cut by Elvis Presley, Willie Nelson and The Pet Shop Boys. 1973 saw the original version of "90% of Me is You" by Vanessa Kendrick issued on Glades, later re-cut on Gwen McCrae. In April 1974 a Clarence Reid co-composition, "It's Worth the Hurt" reached number 66 on the R&B chart for Gwen McCrae and as Henry Stone continued to expand his roster of labels and brought in the Cat label signing Gwen McCrea. Clarence Reid had originally intended to have Della Humphrey record "Rockin' Chair" but it was the material he cut on Gwen that pushed his song writing further forward and the following year she reached number 1 on the R&B chart with her Grammy nominated version, also reaching number 9 on the pop chart. Gwen McCrae followed "Rockin' Chair" with "Love Insurance" in September 1975 and "Cradle of Love" released in March, 1976; both written and produced by Reid. Her Album "Something So Right" was released towards the end of 1976 and included more Clarence Reid delights including the single "Damn Right It's Good" backed with "Love Without Sex". After TK Records crashed Gwen moved to New Jersey and signed to Atlantic where her single, "Funky Sensation" kept her in the charts. She continued recording and some of her earlier material became popular on the British Northern Soul scene. In 1982 she cut "Keep the Fire Burning" written by former Motown artist Willie Hutch and she also became a regular visitor to Europe. Moving back to Florida she released "Do You Know What I Mean" on the local Black Jack label and then temporarily retired from the music business. After a visit to the UK in 2012 Gwen had a stroke leaving her unable to walk and with paralysis in her left side.

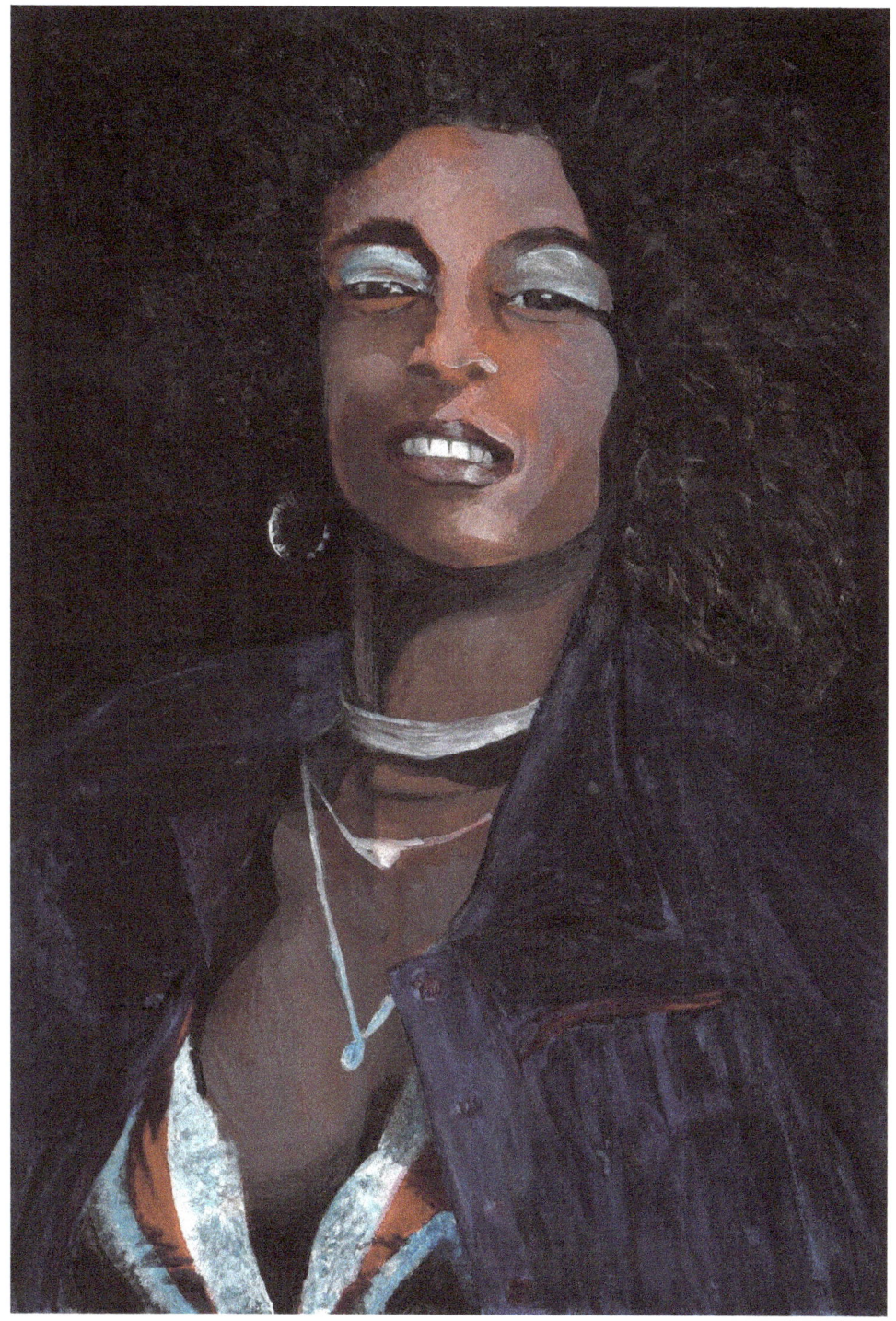

Henry Stone

Henry Stone was born on the 3rd of June, 1921 in the Bronx and in his formative years he was a trumpeter but then had to join the army during World War II. After returning he moved to Los Angeles where he made a living selling records to jukebox owners from the trunk of his car. By 1948 he relocated to Miami where he would stay and build his own Soulful empire. He began recording and also distributing his own Chart, Rockin' and Glory labels and most importantly DeLuxe Records that was distributed by King that introduced him to James Brown. In 1954 he had his first big success with "Hearts of Stone" by The Charms and was there to help Brown with his first hit "Please, Please, Please." Over the years Stone launched many Miami based labels such as Dade in 1955 and Glades in '59. In 1960 he had success with "(Do the) Mashed Potatoes" by Nat Kendrick & The Swans, in reality James Brown's backing band that had Brown on piano and backing vocals. 1970 saw the launch of the Brownstone label which he formed with James Brown as an outlet for his group members. As the 60s progressed, his main label was Alston which benefitted from a distribution deal with Atlantic then in 1972 Atlantic decided to do their own distribution but Stone adapted and moved forward quickly. Alston had had a major success with Betty Wright's "Clean Up Woman" in 1971 and this epitomized the new Miami sound as practiced by a band of musicians and writers that included Little Beaver, Willie Clarke and Clarence Reid. The Glades label was revived with a million selling single called "Why Can't We Live Together" by Timmy Thomas which was also the first single to be nationally distributed by the TK Corporation, Stone's latest venture. This led to his greatest achievement when he launched the TK record label out of a group of warehouses in Hialeah, Florida which brought all his independent labels to a worldwide stage. His first hits came from two young white kids who worked in these warehouses, Harry Wayne Casey and Richard Finch who was a student recording engineer. Casey became KC and with his Sunshine band scored fifteen hit singles. Henry Stone continued expanding his labels and included a new one, Cat which became home to Gwen McCrae who launched a successful career as did her husband George whose "Rock Your Baby, courtesy of Casey and Finch, became a worldwide success in 1974. Steered by seventies disco Stone caught the fever and his output began to mirror (ball) this. Marlin Records released the Ritchie Family's "The Best Disco In Town" whilst Jimmy 'Bo' Horne asked you to "Dance Across The Floor" and of course Anita Ward said "Ring My Bell". By 1980 disco fatigue had set in and a year later Stone filed for bankruptcy for his TK empire.

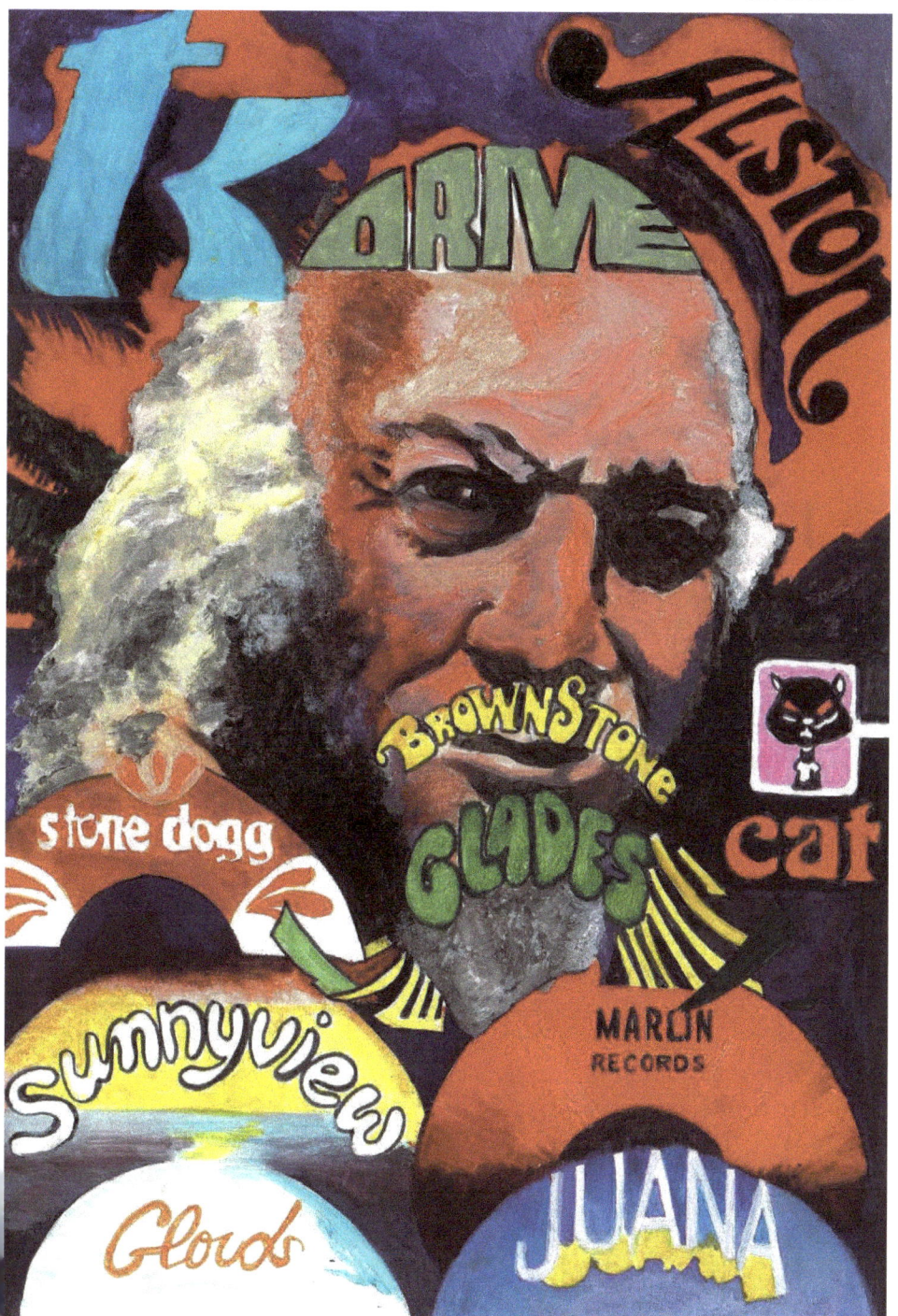

Jimmy 'Bo' Horne

Jimmy Horace Horne was born in West Palm Beach, Florida on September the 28th, 1949. He was an only child with parents who were both teachers. In 1971 Horne did a Sociology Degree at Bethune-Cookman University in Daytona Beach before moving to Miami to forget all the above and become a recording artist as part of the fledgling Florida sound. As with most Florida wannabees Horne found his way to Henry Stone who had him added to the Dade label before its temporary closure. In 1969 he had his first single released, "Street Corners" written by Clarence Reid and Brad Shapiro but didn't see any chart action. The same applied to his 1970 release, this time on the DIG label, "Don't Throw Your Love Away" written by Reid and Willie Clarke. 1971's "Sweet Love Power", again courtesy of Reid and Clarke followed suit. The key Miami players were all there but nothing much was giving them that break. The Cornelius Brothers & Sister Rose had been independent of Stone's developing empire whose first major success came with Betty Wright's "Clean Up Woman" released in November 1971, so it may well have made sense to cash in on its success and give Horne the chance to record an answer record which DIG released in January of '72. As before it failed to make any impact on the charts and it would be September before he issued his next single, "If You Want My Love" on Alston and again courtesy of Reid and Clarke. If nothing they were consistent as proved with the 1973 release "If We Were Still Together". Then in 1974 Reid teamed up with H.W. Casey (KC) for "Don't Worry 'Bout It" released on Drive. The sound was closer to the George McCrae hits and should have done far better than it did, even a re-issue on Alston failed to score but they weren't finished and in July 1975 "Gimme Some" written by the golden boys H. W. Casey and R. Finch made it into the R&B chart, reaching number 47 but on the dance chart it got as high as number 8. "Gimme Some" was also covered by a British group, Brendon in 1977, reaching the Top Twenty pop chart. The follow up "Get Happy" from the same creative team had similar success in both charts; then in March 1978 and on a new label, Sunshine Sound "Dance Across the Floor" courtesy again of H. W. Casey and R. Finch went Double Gold finally breaking into the National Pop chart at number 38. It would be two 1979 releases "Spank" and "You Make Me Hot" that would be Horne's last R&B and dance chart hits. In 1976 Horne founded his own company Joy Productions working in events management but many of those near misses and of course successes weren't lost and found their way into popular culture by being sampled, used on TV Shows or even onto a fictional radio show as part of the Grand Theft Auto video game.

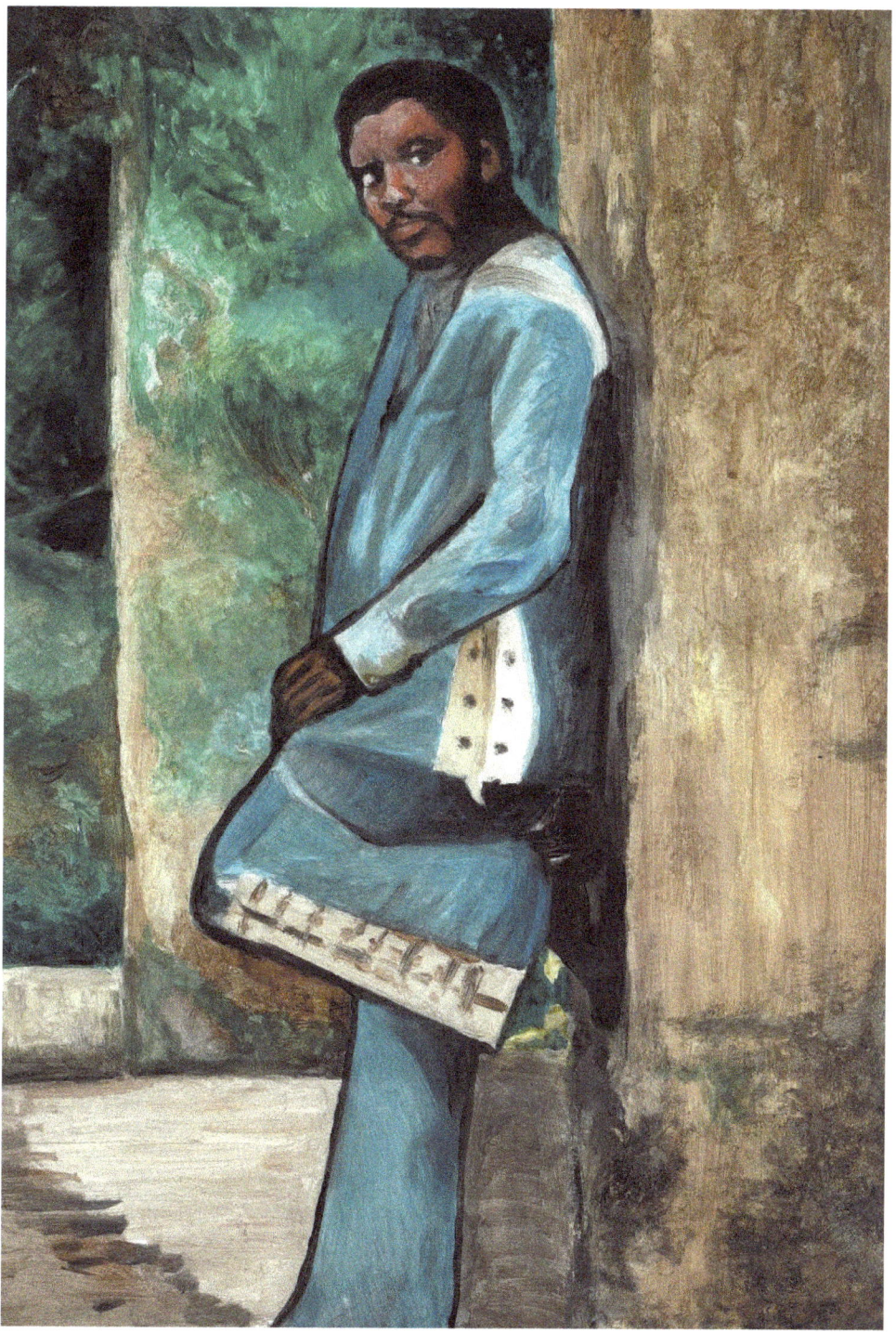

King Sporty

Reggae never really made it in America, well, as far as making an impact on the music scene. Bob Marley managed it in 1976 but the beat rarely made it, except perhaps in William Bell's "Lonely for Your Love" and The Staple Singers simply lifting the opening chords of Harry J All Stars 1969 "Liquidator" and placing it at the beginning of "I'll Take You There"; both on Stax in 1972. Miami was only five hundred and sixty miles from Jamaica so it made more sense if there was going to be a Reggae influence it would most likely be in the sunshine state; which was where Noel Williams, born on the 19th of September 1943 in Portland Parish, Jamaica ended up under the name of King Sporty. He had already made a name for himself in Jamaica at the famous Studio One studio as well as being a top deejay and this didn't slow down once he landed in Miami in 1968 where he created his own Tashamba and Konduko labels. When he arrived he was very knowledgeable about the music business and how to make it advantageous. He wrote his own music, had all of it copyrighted to his own publishing company through BMI and also bought the rights to others material which he could then release on his own labels, re-record himself or even sell on. It wouldn't be long before he met Henry Stone and got involved in the establishing TK organisation. What was interesting was the fact that he was able to offer Stone access to his catalogue of material, most famously 1972's "Why Can't We Live Together" by Timmy Thomas which cost Stone $75,000 to gain. KC & The Sunshine Band worked as his session musicians in 1975 and the same year he issued the album "Mr Rhythm" on his Konduko label. In 1978 Bob Marley came to the TK Studios in Hialeah to work with King Sporty on "Buffalo Soldier", the famous song about the Civil war African American soldiers so called by the native Americans because of their hair. King Sporty continued well into the '80', creating 1983's "Do You Wanna Dance" and "Meet Me at The Disco" even though disco was dying. In 1985 the King married the Queen of Miami Soul, Betty Wright, who would also tour with Bob Marley and The Wailers. Another decade rolled on and King Sporty set up Sporty's Studio in Miami which welcomed many Reggae performers even though his own music was channelling more towards Electro-funk such as 1996's "Computer Age" under the name of Sporty & The Laptop. In 2010 the International Reggae and World Music Awards presented King Sporty with their Lifetime Achievement award and in 2013 Justin Timberlake sampled his track "Self-Destruct". He died on the 5th January 2015 in Miami, Florida, aged 71 but everything he planted continues to grow throughout the music industry. Long Live the King.

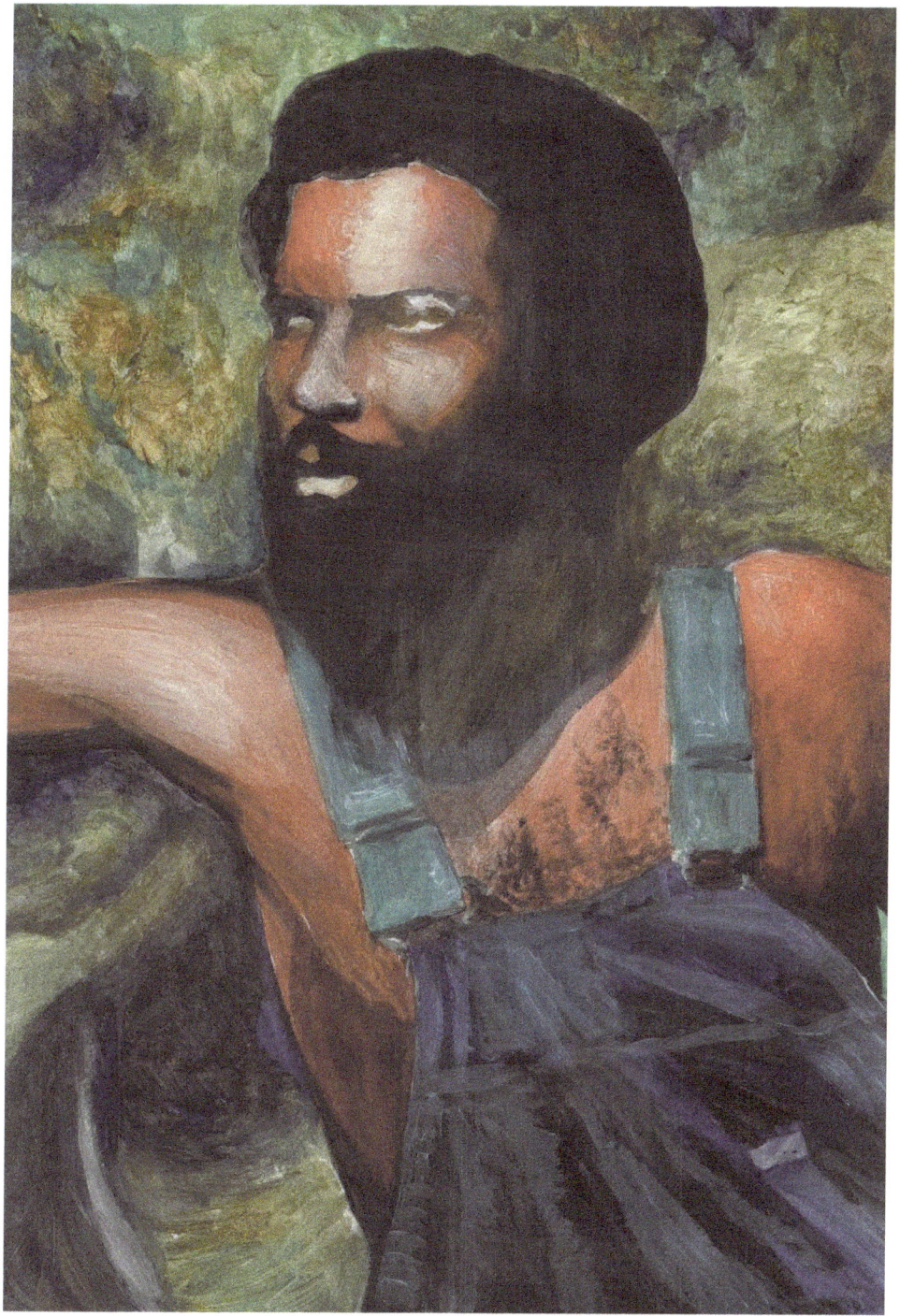

Latimore

Have you ever gone to a party and been the first there? In some ways I feel that's what happened to Benny Latimore when he went to Florida but as is usually the case before long the party is in full swing. Latimore was born in Charleston, Tennessee on the 7th of September 1939 where he found a variety of influences that ranged from the blues, country and the Baptist choir where he started his journey. In Florida his first professional work wasn't as a vocalist but as a pianist for many Florida artists including Steve Alaimo, later vice president of TK Records. Before that though his first recording was on the Nashville based HIT label with "Snap Your Fingers" originally cut by Joe Henderson that reached number 2 in the R&B chart and number 8 on the pop chart. Henderson sounded like Brook Benton but two years later was dead at 27, leaving Benny Latimore to try his hand at the BB style which he did in 1967 with Benton's 1959 hit "It's Just a Matter of Time". Benny signed to Henry Stone's Blade label in 1966 and released the funereal "I Can't Go on Anymore" which he co-wrote. The same year saw another beat ballad with "Have a Little Faith" which found him on the Dade label and 1968's rendering of "Power and the Glory" was another strong ballad but the upbeat flipside "Love Don't Love Me" written by Steve Alaimo and Clarence Reid was closer to what would evolve into the Florida sound. "Girl, I Got News" offered both sides of Benny Latimore, not quite a beat ballad, more a ballad and a beat. The self-composed flipside "Ain't Gonna Cry No More" was upbeat blues as was his handling of "I Pity The Fool" released in 1969. 1970 saw him teamed with Clarence Reid and Willie Clarke on a track which got ever closer to the Miami sound. Latimore's sound came to fruition though with his 1971 handling of "If I Were Your Woman" originally cut by Gladys Knight & The Pips the year before, while T-Bone Walker's standard "Stormy Monday" did even better on the R&B chart, originally appearing on his self-titled debut album that included backing singers Betty Wright, Gwen and George McCrea. In November 1974 he finally made the number one Soul spot as well as number thirty-one on the pop chart with "Let's Straighten It Out". "Latimore III" released in 1975 included the number five R&B hit "Keep the Home Fire Burnin'" and 1976 continued his success with the single "Somethin' 'Bout 'Cha" from the album "It Ain't Where You Been" that housed his composition "All The Way Lover" including a rap that was re-worked and re-rapped by Millie Jackson on her 1977 "Feelin' Bitchy" set. Soon the party was over in Miami but in 1982 Latimore found a new one at Malaco Records, based in Jackson, Mississippi releasing seven more Soul albums and distributed by Florida's TK Records, so arguably there was an afterparty to enjoy.

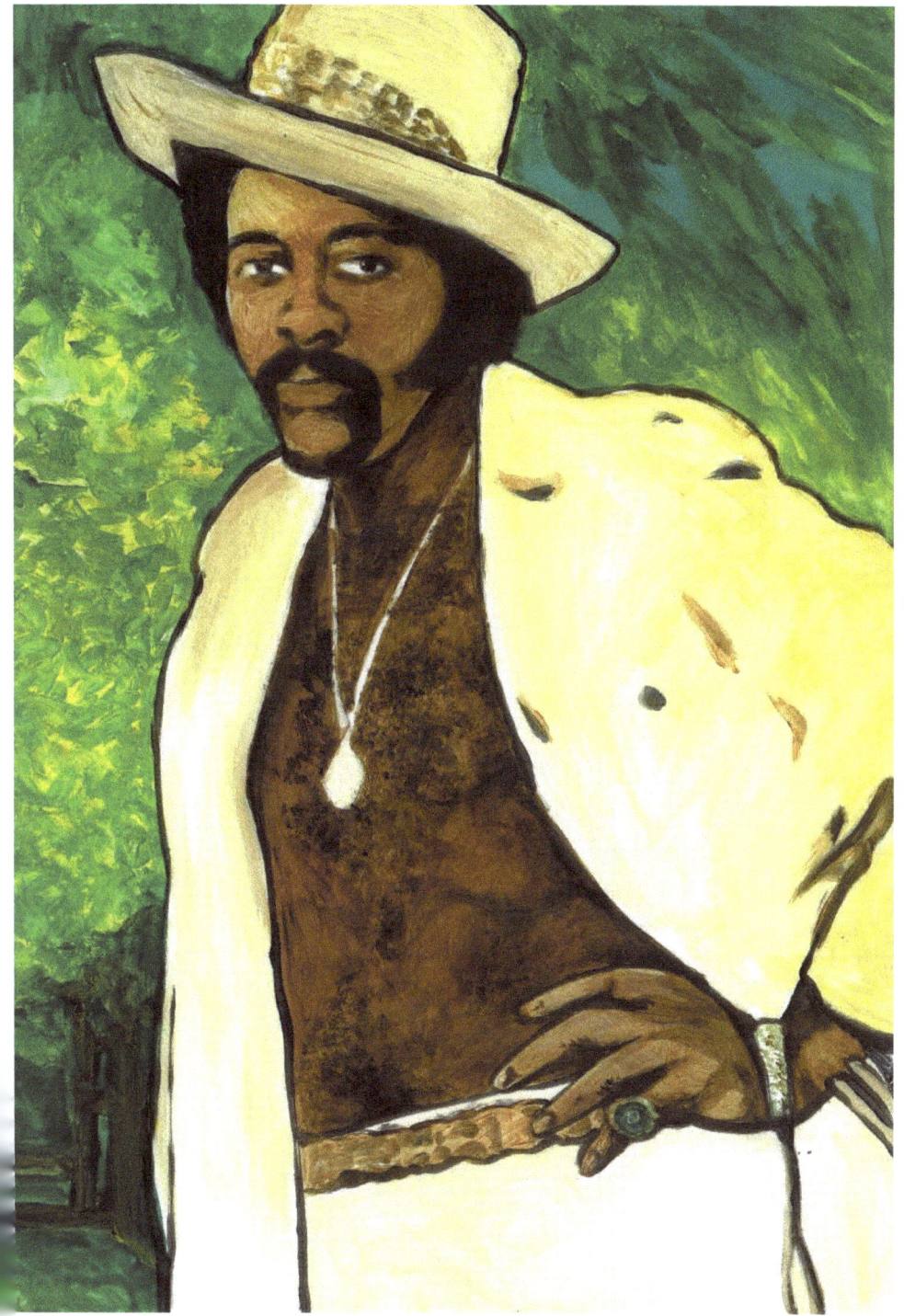

Little Beaver

Willie Hale was born on the 15th of August 1945 in Forrest City, Arkansas and was nicknamed Little Beaver because of his front teeth being prominent. He showed his guitar skills at an early age and moved to Florida at the beginning of the 1960s. He initially worked with Frank Williams a saxophonist, producer, arranger, songwriter and label owner. On the Phil L.A. of Soul label out of Philadelphia, "You Got To Be a Man" by Frank William's Rocketeers with Willie Hale as featured vocalist and "Soul Stuff" as Little Beaver and Frank Williams' Rocketeers were issued in 1967 then Williams' Saadia label issued "Do It To Me One More Time" by Little Beaver & The F.W. Rocketeers in 1968 and later "I Feel My Love Coming Down" under the name of Little Beaver and The Rocketeers on Octavia. When he first arrived in Miami, he played at James Club on NW 2nd Avenue and 36th Street in Overtown and walked to the gigs. Often the police would pull up and give him a lift but after 1968 and the assassination of Reverend Martin Luther King both Overtown and Liberty City were hit by riots and the entertainment was gone from there. 1969 saw Willie Clarke sign Hale to Henry Stone's new Cat label but as a session musician his unique style was all across the Miami sound most significantly at this time on Betty Wright's 1971 hit "Clean Up Woman". 1972 saw Little Beaver's debut single "Joey" issued with the flipside giving a nod to George Clinton's group with "The Funkadelic Sound" but his biggest success came in 1974 with "Party Down" that reached number two on the US Billboard R&B chart. Benny Latimore was on keys but the whole feel was inspired by Hale's time in Miami where the Latin vibe merged with African rhythms. On the album the track "I Can Dig It Baby" featured Nelson "Jocko" Padron on bass. In reality this was Jaco Pastorius considered by many to be the greatest electric bass player in the world who was part of the jazz group Weather Report but who had spent hours in the TK studio to simply observe the guitar skills of Willie Hale. In 1975 this was released as a single. By 1980 it looked like Little Beaver's career was winding down and his last album, "Beaver Fever" appeared then disappeared as the TK company filed for bankruptcy the following year. Then in 2003 a sixteen-year-old white girl from Devon in England was about to become a new Soul singer, Joss Stone. Betty Wright organised the old gang as musicians for her "Soul Sessions" debut and on "Super Duper Love" she introduces Little Beaver by name before he gives his incomparable guitar solo. In 2007 Jay-Z paid him $60,000 to be able to sample "Party Life" for the movie "American Gangster" and the following year Henry Stone Music label released a new album that included re-workings of his Cat classics. Beavering away pays dividends.

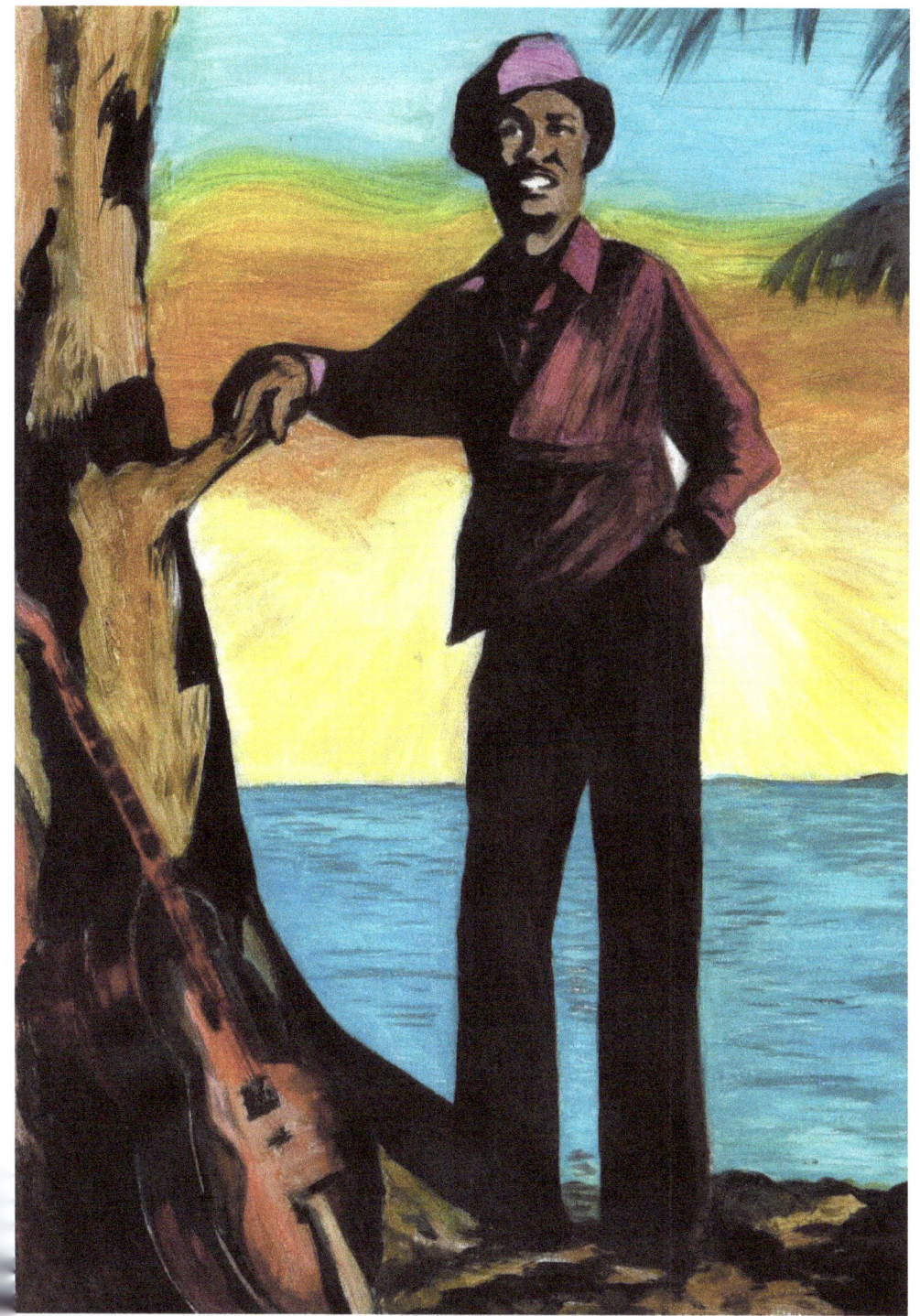

Art & Soul

Timmy Thomas

Timmy Thomas was born the son of a minister in Evansville, Indiana on the 13th of November 1944 and even before his teens he was emersed in music, playing in the school band and by ten he was playing organ for the choirs at this father's church. In 1962 he was awarded a scholarship to go to the Stan Kenton Jazz Clinic based at Indiana University and was taught by such greats as Cannonball Adderley, Woody Herman and Donald Byrd: after graduating he was offered a scholarship at Lane College Tennessee. He began earning his keep as a jazz performer with Donald Byrd before working as a session musician for Goldwax records in Memphis where he had his own couple of releases, the best being "Have Some Boogaloo" an organ led, Latin and Soul hybrid. In 1966 he went back to college to study for a B.A. in Music Education. From there he taught music whilst completing a further and higher musical degree at the University of Tennessee. Music wasn't far away though and he would play in local bands at the weekend. He was chosen to head the development programme at Florida Memorial College, so his next stop was Miami. America was still embroiled with the overseas conflict in Vietnam and Thomas happened to be watching a television broadcast and heard stories about children dying. He uttered the words "Why can't we live together?" that spurred him on to record the sentiments, giving us one of the least remembered anti-war songs of the seventies. He played all the instruments and added a lesser heard instrument to the track, his voice. Henry Stone re-launched his Glades label and issued it as the first single. It reached number one on the R&B chart and number three on the pop chart in the States but became a global hit in 1972 and was sampled by Rapper Drake for his 2015 song "Hotline Bling". Timmy Thomas never reached those heights again but "People Are Changin'" released in 1973 may have felt like the achievements people adopted after his hit. The biggest surprise was the work he did with Clarence Reid's alter-ego Blowfly. His debut set, "The Weird World of Blowfly" was sold in porno stores and truck stops because of its promiscuous lyrics. Thomas played on such tracks as "Spermy Night in Georgia" and "Baby Let Me Do it to You". He also began to do session work for fellow artists like Little Beaver whose "Party Down" released in 1974 bares his sound and the same year saw the release of his album "You're the Song I Always Wanted to Sing" which included the duet "Sweet Brown Sugar" with Betty Wright. In 1986 "New York Eyes" recorded with Nicole showed his vocal skills once again. In total contrast to his Blowfly work Thomas was made head of TK's Gospel Roots label in 1978. Timmy Thomas passed away on March the 11th 2022.

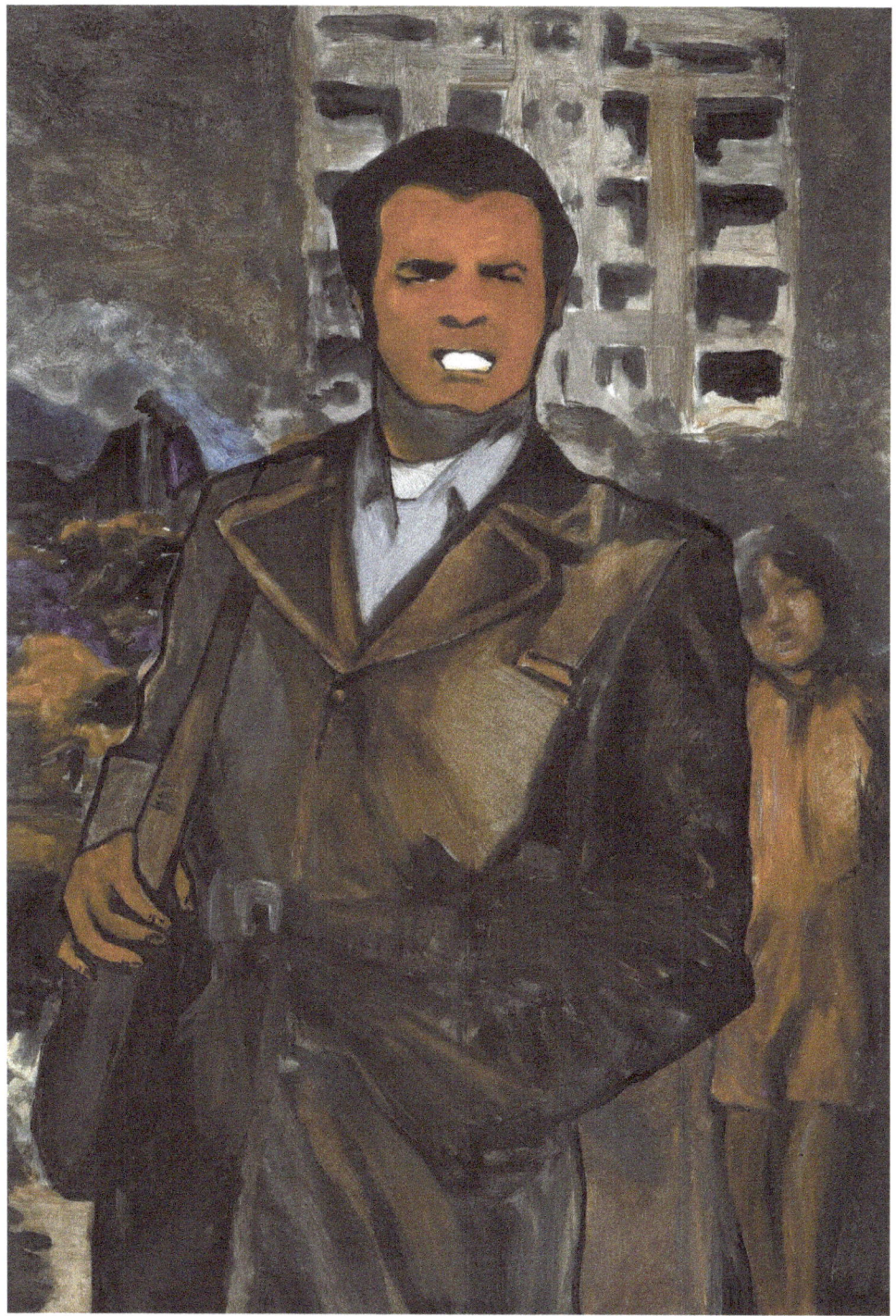

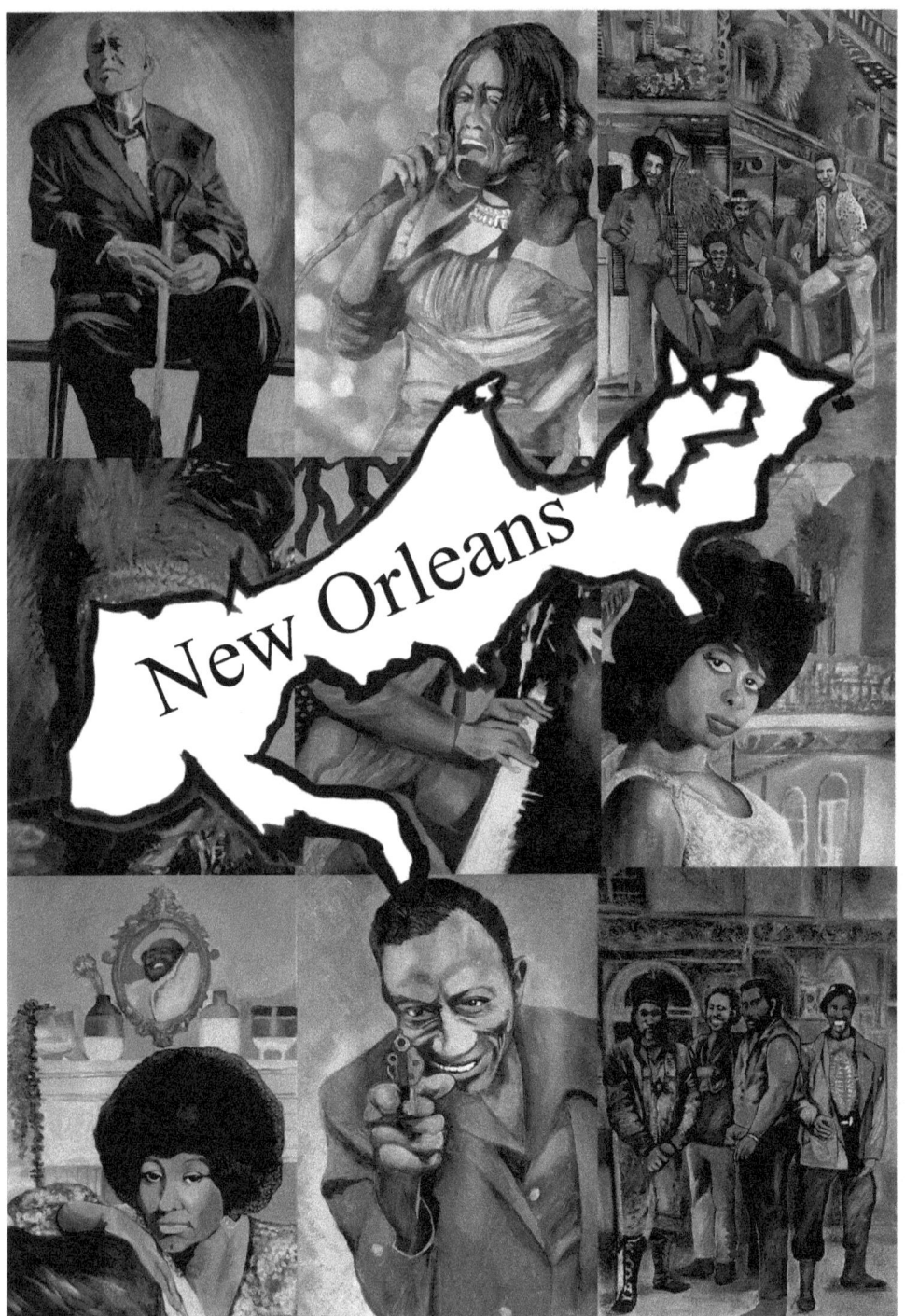

Art & Soul

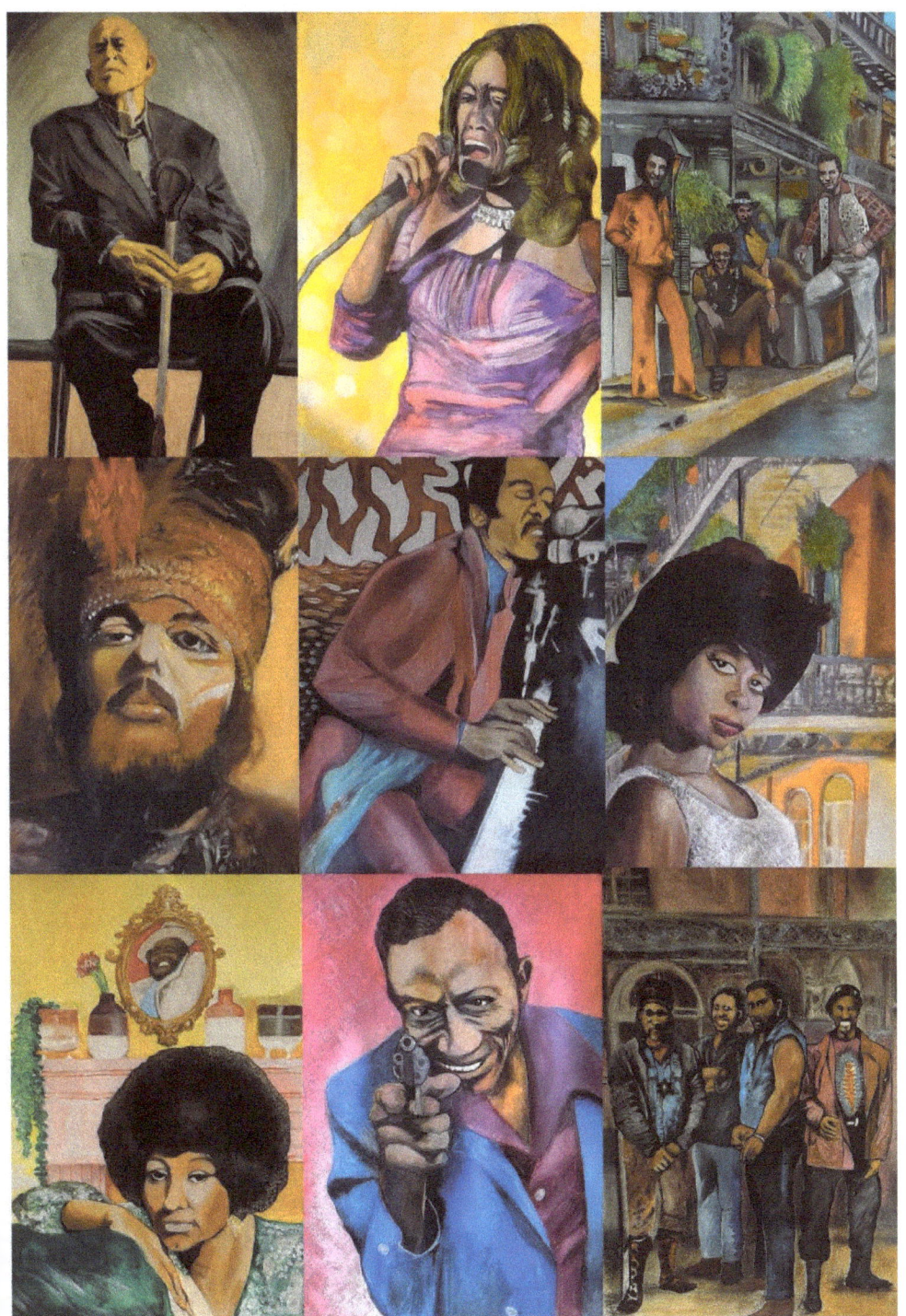

Allen Toussaint

Allen Richard Toussaint was born on New Year's Day in 1938 in New Orleans. An early influence on Toussaint was the piano style of Professor Longhair. At seventeen he stood in for Huey "Piano" Smith and was introduced to a group of local musicians who regularly performed at the Dew Drop Inn. His first recording was in 1957 as a stand-in for Fats Domino on "I Want You to Know" and in early 1958 he recorded an album of instrumentals, "The Wild Sound of New Orleans" for RCA which included Toussaint and Alvin Tyler's composition "Java" which first charted for Floyd Cramer in 1962 and became a number 4 pop hit for trumpeter Al Hurt in 1964. He was hired by Minit then Instant Records as an A& R man and producer although he continued as a freelancer for other labels where he played piano, wrote, arranged and produced hit after hit during what was considered his first creative period. "Mother-In-Law" by Ernie K-Doe, "I Like it Like That" for Chris Kenner and a two-sided 1962 hit by Benny Spellman, "Lipstick Traces", covered by The O'Jays and "Fortune Teller" are but a few examples of Toussaint's work. "Ruler of My Heart" released in 1963 by Irma Thomas written under the pseudonym Naomi Neville, his mother's name, was adapted by Otis Redding under the title "Pain in My Heart" later that year, prompting Toussaint to file a lawsuit against Redding and his record company, Stax. The claim was settled out of court, with Stax agreeing to credit Naomi Neville as the songwriter. Toussaint was drafted into the army in 1963 but continued to record when on leave. After his discharge in 1965 he joined forces with Marshall Sehorn to form Sansu Enterprises and recorded Lee Dorsey, Chris Kenner, Betty Harris and the musicians on many of the Sansu recordings would later become The Meters. In 1973 Toussaint and Sehorn created the Sea-Saint recording studio and he began recording under his own name, contributing vocals as well as piano. His solo career peaked in the mid-1970s with the albums "From a Whisper to a Scream" whose title track was cut by Esther Phillips and "Southern Nights" again, the title track become a hit single for country singer Glen Campbell. Both songs showed the range of material Toussaint was continually creating and with 1973's "Yes We Can" cut by Lee Dorsey future president, Barack Obama used it for his 2008 presidential campaign. Most of Toussaint's possessions were lost during Hurricane Katrina in 2005 and following this he left New Orleans for several years settling in New York where he would regularly perform at Joe's Pub. He eventually returned to New Orleans and lived there for the rest of his life. After a concert in Spain, he had a heart attack at his hotel and was pronounced dead on his arrival at hospital. He was 77.

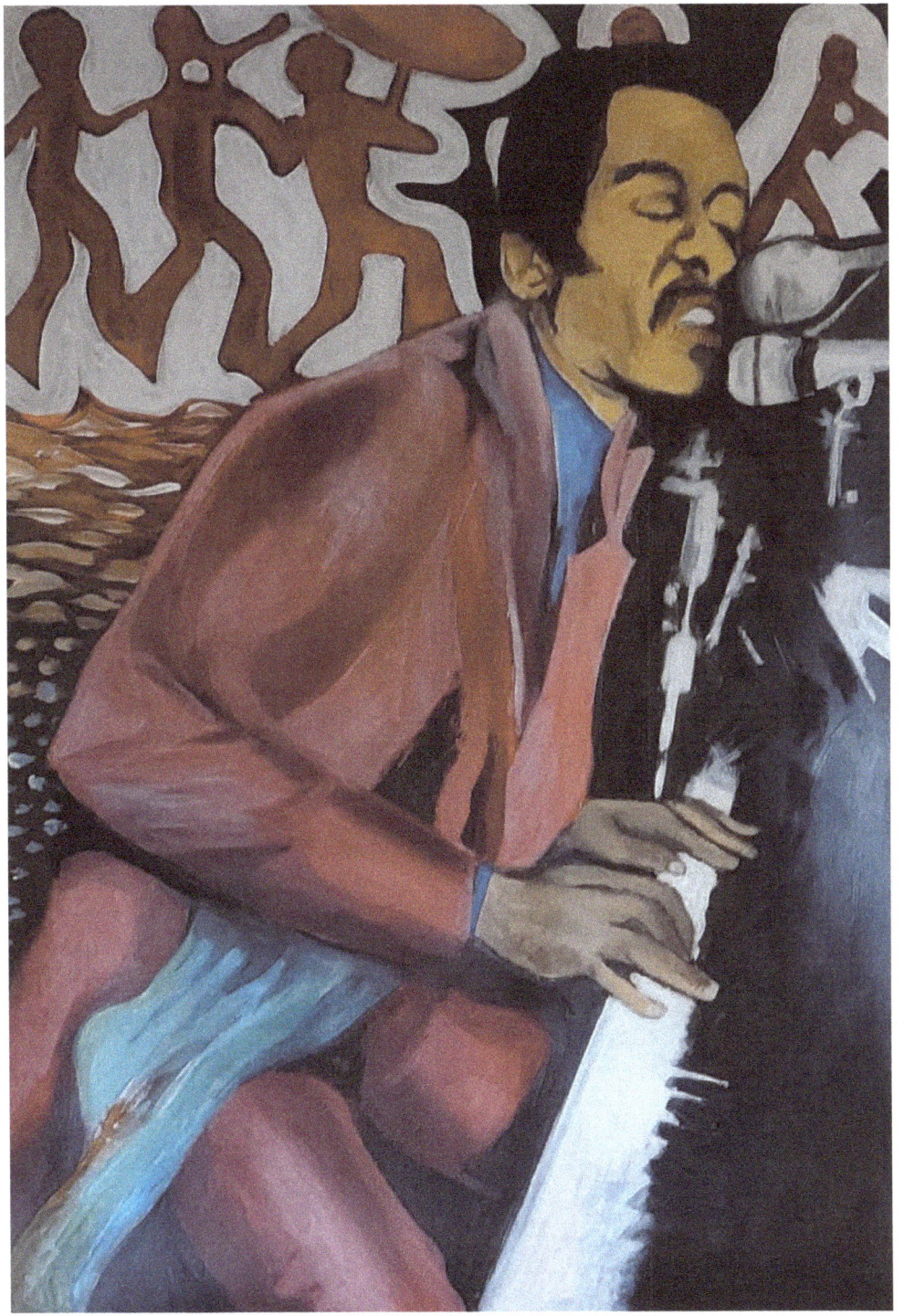

Betty Harris

Betty Harris was born on September the 9th, 1939 in Orlando, Florida but before she turned four the family moved to Alabama. As well as being a minister her father had a strange role as a booking agent for Gospel singers like Sam Cooke, Sister Rosetta Tharpe and The Blind Boys of Alabama. Being surrounded by music through the church, on the radio and by meeting musicians inspired her to become a singer in her own right. To make the dream a reality she knew that she would have to leave Alabama and at seventeen saw an advert for a job in New Jersey and was off. The breaks began and while performing in a nightclub she was seen by producer Zelma Sanders so in 1958 she recorded "Like Later Baby" as lead singer with the group The Hearts on the J&S label. Two years later the R&B singer Big Maybelle took her on and mentored her, while including her on a cross country tour. In 1962 she released "Taking Care of Business" on the Douglas label and on the DRA label "Love is to Blame" as Betty and Jay, Jay being Jay Lewis. Then a year later she met songwriter and producer Bert Berns who she persuaded to cut her own version of Solomon Burkes recent hit "Cry To Me". "Cry To Me" was directed by Berns but produced by Leiber & Stoller and released on the Jubilee label. The single was a pop and R&B hit and in 1964 she issued two more singles on Jubilee, "It's Dark Outside" and "Mojo Hannah. In the same year it was time for another change which saw Betty relocate to New Orleans and to legendary music maestro Allen Toussaint. This was Betty's most prolific period. Her first release on the Sansu label was "What A Sad Feeling" written by Allen Toussaint under the pseudonym of Naomi Neville but arranged under his real name. This was released in September 1965. The 'B' "I'm Evil Tonight" was a beat ballad that proved popular on the British Northern Soul scene. "I Don't Want to Hear It" ended the year with the same writing and arranging set up but it would be the following May before her next single "12 Red Roses" arrived. Because of this regular output Betty Harris became an adopted daughter of New Orleans and began to be recognised as the uncrowned Queen of Crescent City. In November 1967 she duetted with Lee Dorsey on "Love Lots of Loving" and as before the Southern sounding arrangements of Toussaint's compositions epitomised all that was unique about the City's sounds. In 1968 Betty even recorded Dorsey's "Ride Your Pony" before SSS International took over the distribution of Toussaint and Sehorn's material with arguably Betty Harris's anthemic track "There's A Break in the Road" in 1969, then in 1970 Betty Harris took a break to raise her family.

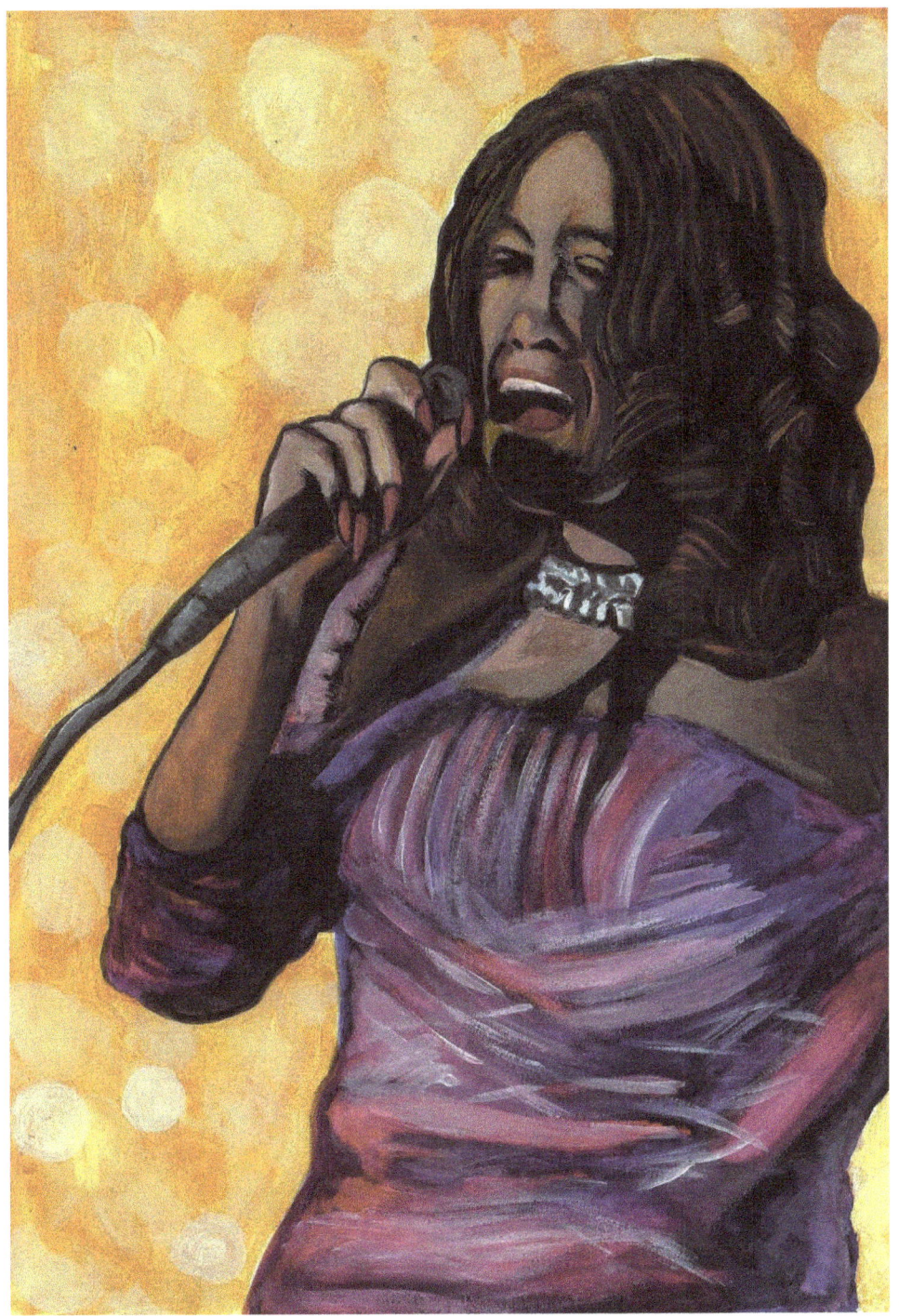

Art & Soul

Dr John

As our journey has progressed, I hope you have seen the uniqueness displayed at each stop we've made. New Orleans has been home to more than the rest put together. Mac Rebennack was born in the Crescent City on November the 20th 1941 and had an astounding career that only stopped when he stopped. The son of Dorothy Cronin and Malcolm John Rebennack he had a mix of German, Irish, Spanish, English and French running thorough his veins. His father ran an appliance shop that combined the fixing of radios and televisions plus selling records. His Gospel roots ended when he was tossed out of the choir, but he was beginning to take an interest in Jazz musicians Louis Armstrong and King Oliver. Father's work got him access to recording studios where Rebennack junior met Little Richard and Guitar Slim but it was as a young teenager that he met and became inspired by another New Orleans legend Professor Longhair. That was when his professional career started, first as a guitarist but almost ended at the beginning of the sixties when his ring finger was injured in a shooting incident. Undeterred by this he took to playing the bass before choosing the piano as his main instrument. The trouble with him was trouble, particularly the using and selling of drugs and running a brother. The drugs got him arrested and he had to serve a two years' sentence in Fort Worth's Federal Correctional Institution. After his release in 1965 he moved to Los Angeles where he became a member of the legendary Wrecking Crew, a conglomerate of renowned session musicians and appeared on recordings by Canned Heat, Sonny & Cher and Frank Zappa. Rebennack had started to look deeper into another interest that stemmed from his formative teenage years, voodoo. Hence was born Dr John, based on a Haitian prince who kept a lovely collection of snakes, lizards, embalmed scorpions, animal and human skulls and sold people 'gris', voodoo amulets intended to protect the wearer from harm, or possibly any of the aforementioned. Rebennack decided that this was to be his identity on stage and on record, a New Orleans statement made in California. In January 1968 his debut album, "Gris" was released and was a mesmerising mix of his 'voodoo medicine' that included the much-covered classic, "Walk on Guilded Splinters. Over his lifetime Rebennack recorded thirty studio albums and nine live ones and in 1973 reached another plateau by collaborating with Allen Toussaint for "Right Place, Wrong Time" featuring The Meters. Dr John also wrote over a hundred songs with Brill Building's master songwriter Doc Pomus and on March the 17th performed "My Buddy" at his funeral. On July the 20th 2016 he performed at the Hollywood Bowl as a tribute to another fallen friend Allen Toussaint: then on June the 19th 2019 at the break of day, a heart attack took him.

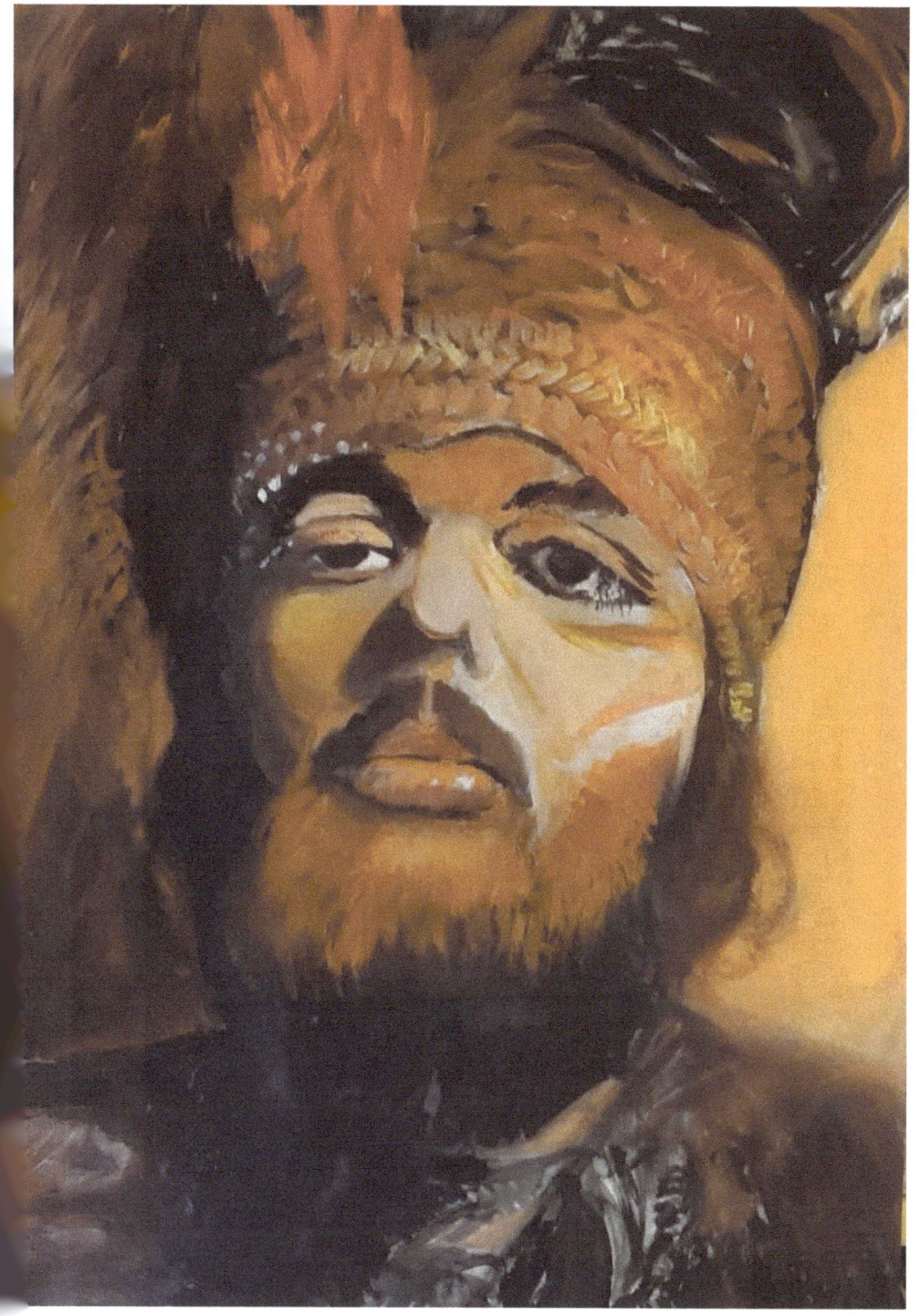

Ernie K-Doe

There are some artists who only really belong in one place as was the case of Ernie K-Doe who was born in New Orleans on the 22nd of February 1933 but when he died, well the jury's still out on that one. In 2006, his wife Antoinette K-Doe campaigned for him to become the mayor of New Orleans even though he had been dead for five years. It was partly done as a stunt as his name didn't appear on the ballot, but she did make a tidy sum of money on the campaign's t-shirts and car stickers all of which went towards the re-building of the Mother-In-Law Lounge as well as the New Orleans Musicians' Clinic, two buildings that were also damaged by Hurricane Katrina. So, what's his Mother-In-Law got to do with it? Well at the beginning he was in the group The Blue Diamonds in 1954 but it was only a year later that he recorded "Mother-In-Law", written by Allen Toussaint. This was his first hit and reached the top position in both the Billboard pop chart and R&B chart. Two more successes followed although neither reached the same heights. "Te-Ta-Te-Ta-Ta" in 1961 and "Later for Tomorrow" in 1967 both reached the R&B top 40. It was a 1970s song, "Here Come The Girls" that made him internationally recognised even though it failed to chart. It was re-issued in 2007 as a result of being used in a Boots Pharmacy stores television advertisement and then a year later the British group The Sugababes re-cut it and saw it rise to Number 3 in the UK pop chart. As well as his career in music he was also an alcoholic which may have explained much of his erratic behaviour.

In between times Ernie did shows on the local community radio stations WWOZ and WTUL in the 1980s but caused issues with his constant self-promotion in between his over-the-top exuberant energy. The promotions caused a non-for-profit station worries and for a while he promoted himself as Mister Naugahyde, Naugahyde being an artificial leather. He had to stop after complaints from the Naugahyde company. His defence was that it was a name he'd made up and was spelt M-Nauga-Ma-Hyde, unfortunately spelling doesn't sit well on radio. If Ernie K-Doe's eccentricity wasn't already apparent during the 1990s he claimed that he was the Emperor of the Universe and began wearing a cape and crown. He continued performing and occasionally recording up until his death in 2001 with "White Boy, Black Boy" being released that year. Ernie K-Doe died from liver and kidney failure brought on from years of alcoholism. His widow, Antoinette K-Doe, continued to operate his music club and bar, Ernie K-Doe's Mother-In-Law Lounge, which housed a life-size statue of him possibly using Naugahyde to cover his skin? The lounge re-opened in 2006 and Ernie K-Doe was buried in Saint Louis cemetery, New Orleans alongside his Mother-In-Law.

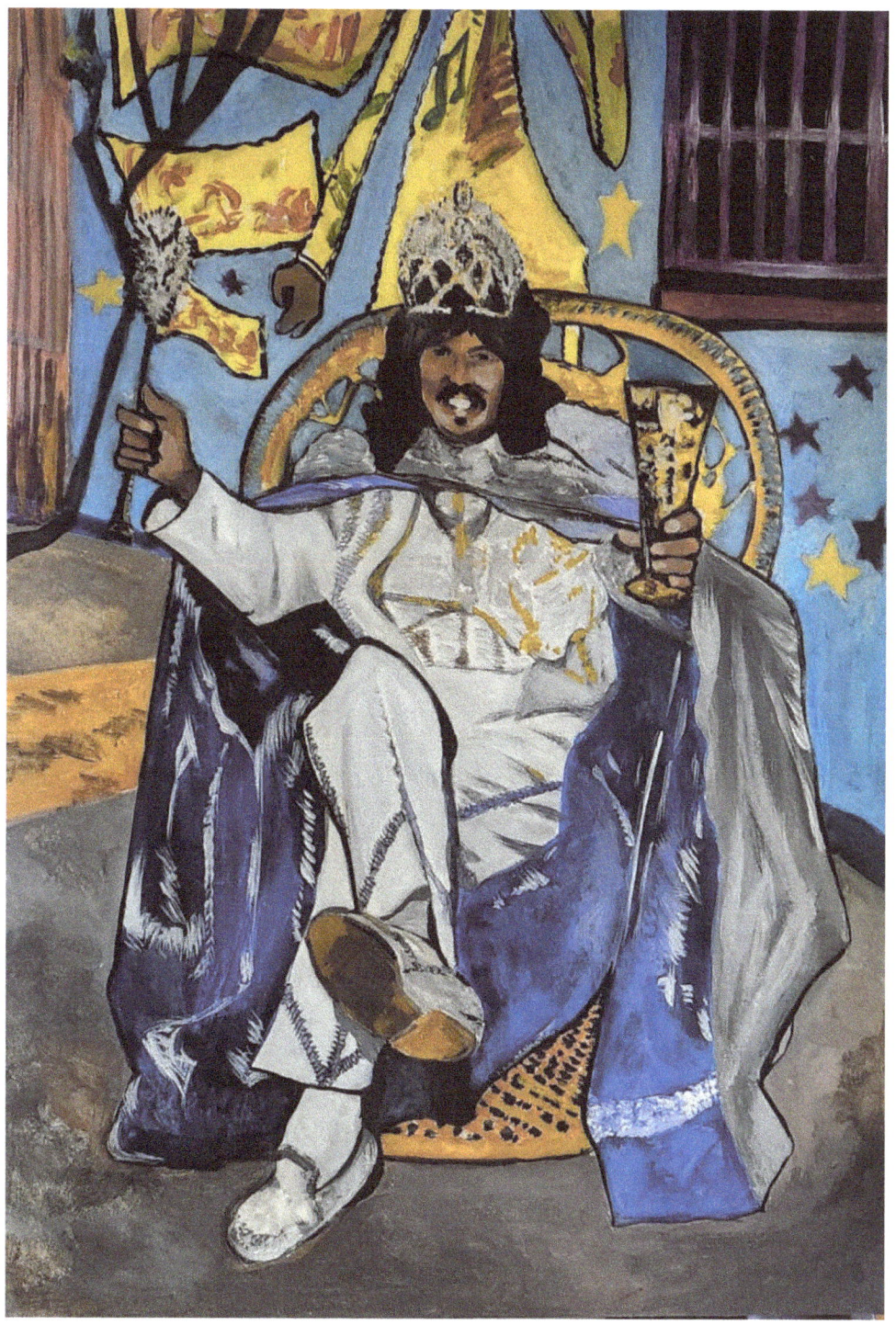

Irma Thomas

Irma Lee was born on February the 18th, 1941 in Ponchatoula, Louisiana but was raised in New Orleans. Beginning through the channel of the church Thomas started in a choir but also as part of a Gospel quartet at the Home Mission Baptist Church. Her first recording and recognition was at the age of eleven. The song was recorded at Cosmo's Studio and done with school friends, but she also won the Ritz Theatre talent night and by the age of thirteen was auditioning for Specialty Records. While she was working as a waitress at New Orleans' Pimlico Club, she caught the attention of band leader Tommy Ridgley who invited her to be his vocalist much to the displeasure of her boss who fired her. Ridgley got her a contract with Ron Records and in May of 1960 she reached number 22 on the Billboard R&B chart with "You Can Have My Husband But Please Don't Take My Man". Thomas decided that she wasn't getting the royalties she deserved from Ron and although it might have been a risk left and joined Minit. This though introduced her to Allen Toussaint who wrote and produced for her, "Ruler of My Heart" was written under his pseudonym Naomi Neville and later adapted by Otis Redding. The same year Minit was bought out by Imperial and her first single became her biggest seller reaching number seventeen in the pop chart in 1964. Thomas stayed for three years at Imperial and during that time released nine singles and two albums before moving to California in 1970. Here she took a sabbatical from the recording industry and ended up working at a department store as well as selling automobile parts although she continued singing in clubs at weekend. All was not lost though and in 1970 she recorded a new album, "In Between Tears" with Jerry Williams Jr aka Swamp Dogg for Canyon but Canyon was failing and equally the album failed to be pressed. After the collapse of Canyon, she moved to Atlantic for a time before signing to Williams' latest label Fungus but frustratingly Williams never took her into the studio; preferring instead to release what he already had in "the can". The mistress was once again the theme in "These Four Walls" in which she took pride in the home that had been financed by her lover despite bad mouthing by her neighbours. The album also included a newer version of the self-penned "Wish Someone Would Care". In the mid-70s Irma found her way back to New Orleans where she re-acquainted herself on the live circuit and in 1986 produced her next album, "The New Rules" on Rounder Records. Two Grammy nominations came her way in 1991 and 1998 and her recording career and live performances continued along with a new venture, The Lion's Den Night Club in New Orleans. Hurricane Katrina brought an end to it but as with so many 'other women', Irma Thomas would survive devasting consequences.

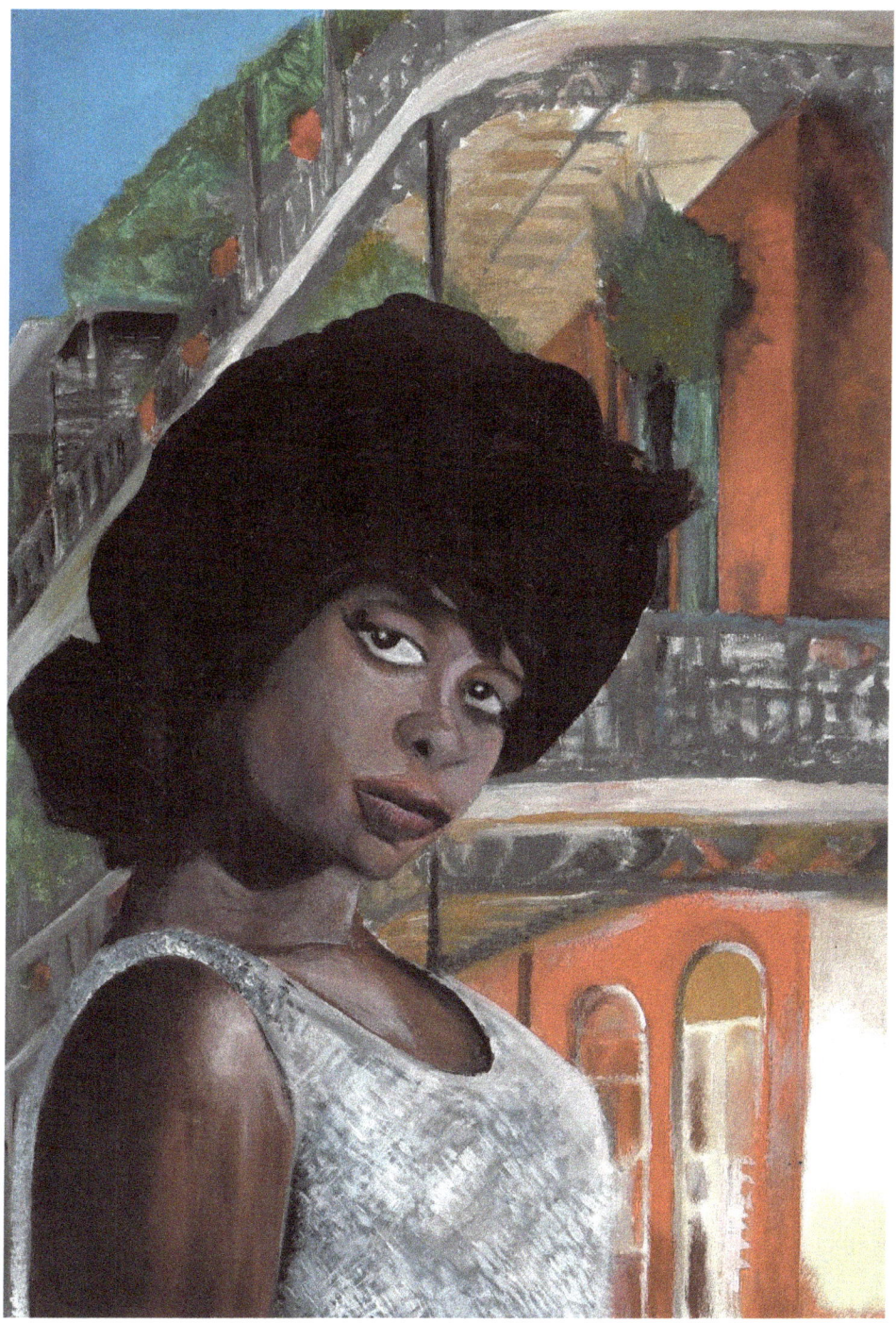

King Floyd

Floyd King was born in New Orleans on the 13th of February 1945, just a thought but I wonder if a teacher reading the register started with the surnames, ours always did. That may well account for the birth of the singer King Floyd. He started singing in his early teens and even felt back then that the best way to learn was to hang out with the people already doing it so he found his way to the Sho-Bar on Bourbon Street. Then came the draft and Floyd did two years in the army before deciding to try New York and Los Angeles. He had his first single released on the Original Sound label in 1965 and met up in L.A. with two more New Orleans escapees, producer Harold Battiste and Dr John who helped him with his first album "A Man in Love" issued on the Pulsar label in 1969. Most of the songs were penned by Floyd with help from Dr John and Bluesman Little Milton but it failed to do anything commercially. Surprisingly Motown re-issued it in 1971 under a new title of "Heart of The Matter" on their VIP label but again it sank without a trace. King Floyd returned to his wife and daughter in New Orleans where he got a job at the post office to support his family. In 1970 an unexpected meeting with Wardell Quezergue (pronounced Kuh-zair) and local entrepreneur Elijah Walker gave Floyd the chance to go to Jackson, Mississippi to record on Sunday the 17th of May. He decided to finish his post round and follow the bus in his own car which broke down. Luckily, he got to the studio just in time to record "Groove Me" in one take. A second song was cut which needed three takes and was to be the top side of a single. New Orleans DJs started to prefer the flipside and so "Groove Me" became a local hit making Atlantic jump in to distribute it nationally. Eventually the disc sold two million copies, turned gold, reached the top spot on the national R&B chart and a healthy number six on the Billboard Hot 100. King unsurprisingly left the postal service to start a U.S. tour. The follow up "Baby Let Me Kiss You" got to number 29 on the pop chart but was considered too suggestive for some of the bigger stations to play it. Differences between himself and Quezergue began to show and his next album "Think About It" released in 1973 failed commercially although it still had some highlights. The title track and "Too Hot to Handle" were Otis Redding songs and the single "Woman Don't Go Astray" deserved to do better. King Floyd travelled to Europe and Jamaica where he met Bob Marley and Peter Tosh who introduced him to Reggae. New directions and inspirations failed to get King Floyd's career back to where it was, and he blamed the disco years for terminating his writing. Angie Stone covered "Groove Me" in 2002 but King Floyd died four years later on March the 6th from a stroke and diabetes.

Art & Soul

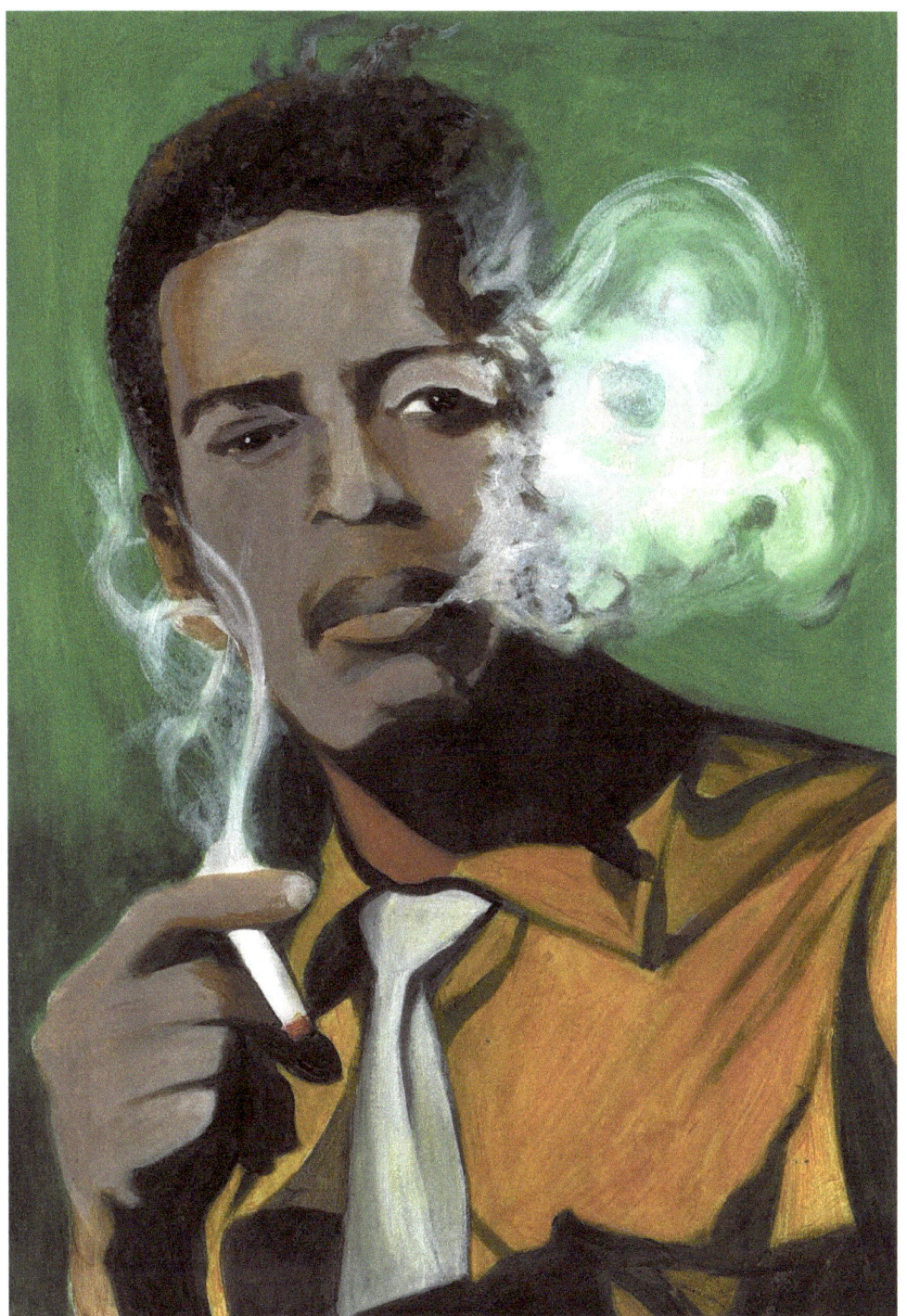

The Meters

Looking at a special sound coming out of a city the Memphis sound didn't belong to Stax just as the Detroit sound wasn't exclusively Motown's. It was the sound of a specific band of musicians, Booker T & The MGs or the Funk Brothers. In New Orleans that sound came from The Meters whose origins pre-dated Soul but once their grip tightened it would be the Soul of New Orleans. Frontman Art Neville had started a career in the mid-50s while still at high school but by 1965 the group had come together with Art on vocal and keyboard, Leo Nocentelli playing guitar with bassist George Porter Jr and drummer Joseph "Zigaboo" Modeliste being joined later by Art's brother Cyril on percussion. They became the house band for Allen Toussaint and Marshall Sehorn's Sansu label. Theirs was the powerhouse behind all the artists who entered the recording studio and often they had no idea who they were supporting. Toussaint would often get the instrumental cut and then find the right artist to fit with it. In 1967 they cut their first track "Sophisticated Cissy" which was released on the Josie label in 1968. A year later came "Cissy Strut", both were based on the way local Drag Queens strode out. Interestingly the 'B' side was the prophetic "Here Comes the Meter Man"; why Prophetic? Because in 2012 after group break ups and new line-ups Modeliste, Nocentelli and Porter would reform to become The Meter Men. These followed The Original Meters performing the year before but back in 1989 The Funky Meters were about. It seemed like The Drifters had time travelled and entered New Orleans spreading confusion under a new name. In 1970 they were named the best Rhythm & Blues Instrumental Group by Billboard and the Record World magazine. That year saw "Chicken Strut" and Look-Ka-Py-Py" bring more success but a change to the Reprise label in 1972 didn't do as well as expected and the new album "Cabbage Alley" failed to live up to expectations. All was not lost though and 1974's "Rejuvenation" was just that, beginning with the complex funk of "People Say" to the final track "Africa", covered by The Red Hot Chilli Peppers under the name "Hollywood" on their 1985 set "Freaky Styley". In between these two Reprise releases they had backed Dr John for his "In the Right Place" album as well as British artist Robert Palmer who cut Lee Dorsey's "Sneakin' Sally Through the Alley". In 1975 Mick Jagger invited The Meters to be the Rolling Stones support act on their Tour of America '75 as well as the Tour Of Europe the year after. 1976 also saw them release one of their most successful albums, "Fire on the Bayou". The final act of these guys was after they played in the Wild Tchoupitoulas alongside the Neville Brothers. Art and Cyril Neville left in 1977 but the Meters didn't run out, they just kept putting more members in the slots.

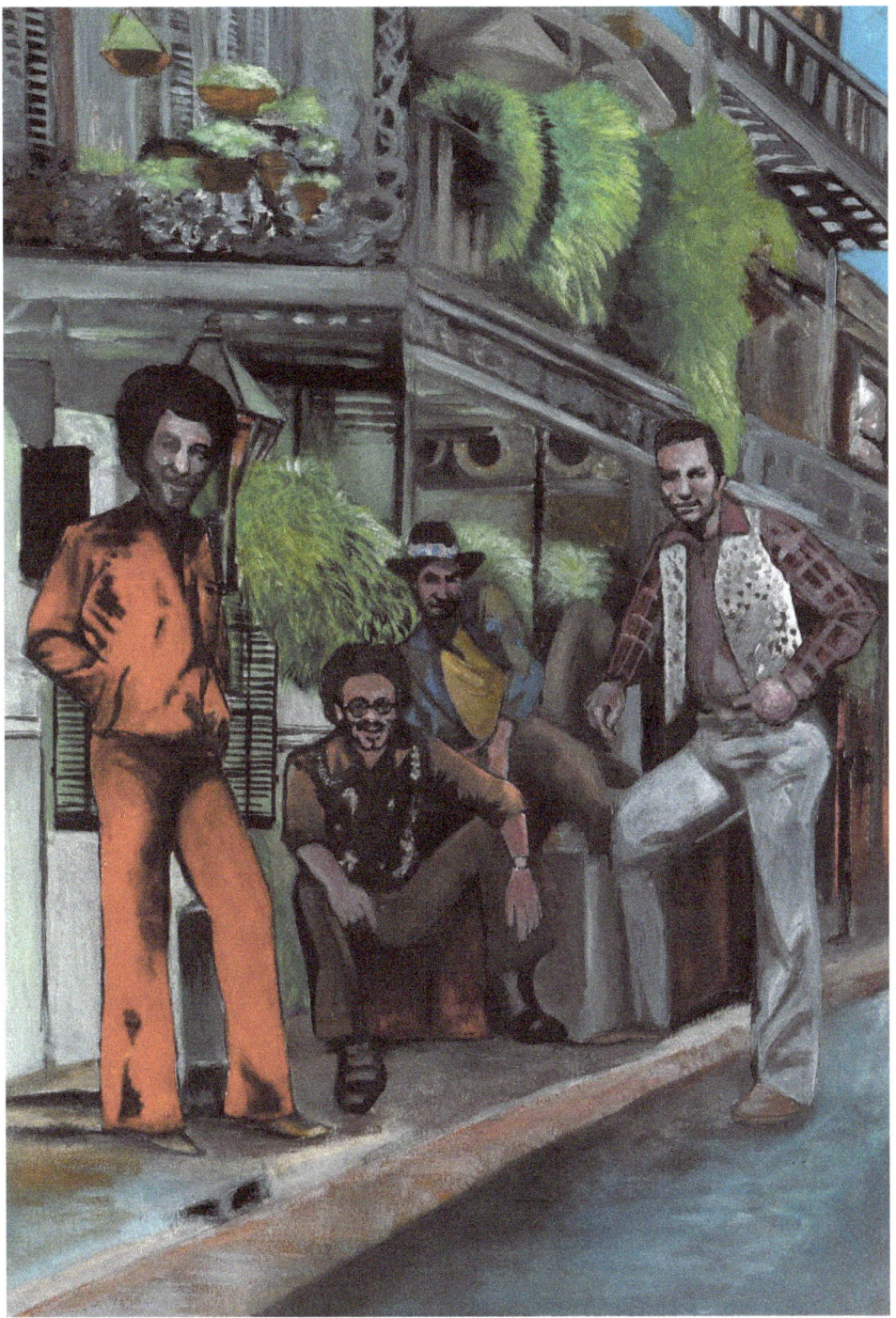

Jean Knight

Jean Caliste was born on January the 26th in New Orleans and after graduating from high school went straight to singing in her cousin's bar, Laura's Place. There she was approached by several local bands who either wanted to back her or more likely wanted her to front them. In 1965 she cut a demo of Jackie Wilson's "Stop Doggin' Me Around" which caught the attention of Houston based record producer Huey Meaux who contracted her to the Jet Star/Tribe labels. She changed her surname to Knight and released four singles but she was longing for national recognition. When that didn't happen, she took a hiatus and became a baker in the Dominican College cafeteria. A break came when she met songwriter Ralph Williams that led her to be introduced to Wardell Quezergue and in May of 1970, she took the famous coach trip to Malaco along with King Floyd and where she cut "Mr Big Stuff". After the session the song then did the rounds going to national labels but still the interest wasn't there until King Floyd's "Groove Me" hit the Pop and R&B charts the following year and a Stax producer remembered "Mr Big Stuff" which then went from forgettable to fashionable, hitting number two on the pop chart and staying at number one on the Billboard R&B chart for five weeks. It became double platinum selling over two million copies as well as a Grammy nomination for the Best R&B Vocal Performance, Female in 1972, losing out to Aretha Franklin but earning her the title of Most Promising Female Vocalist. The album of the same name was an interesting blend, "Don't Talk About Jody" continued the myths of this man that had started with Johnnie Taylor's "Jody Got Your Girl and Gone", also on Stax. Her follow-up single was a post-album track and may have seemed like "Mr Big Stuff" part two but "You Think You're Hot Stuff" was a scorching hunk of Southern Funk blended with Jean's unique Soulful voice which deserved better chart placing. Jean dinted the charts again with "Carry On" and her last recording for Stax was the direct "Do Me" which found its way into the 2007 movie "Superbad". Her contract with Stax was terminated partly due to disagreements between her, Wardell Quezergue and Stax itself which led to her recording on local labels right up until 1981 when producer Isaac Bolden signed her to his Soulin' label. Between them they created an answer record to another New Orleans Soul artist Richard 'Dimples' Fields' hit of that year "She's Got Papers on Me" called "You Got the Papers but I Got the Man". Incidentally Barbara Mason over in Philadelphia also cut an answer record called "She's Got the Papers but I Got the Man". In 2003 Jean Knight was inducted into the Stax Museum of American Soul Music and in 2007 she was honoured by the Louisiana Music Hall of Fame.

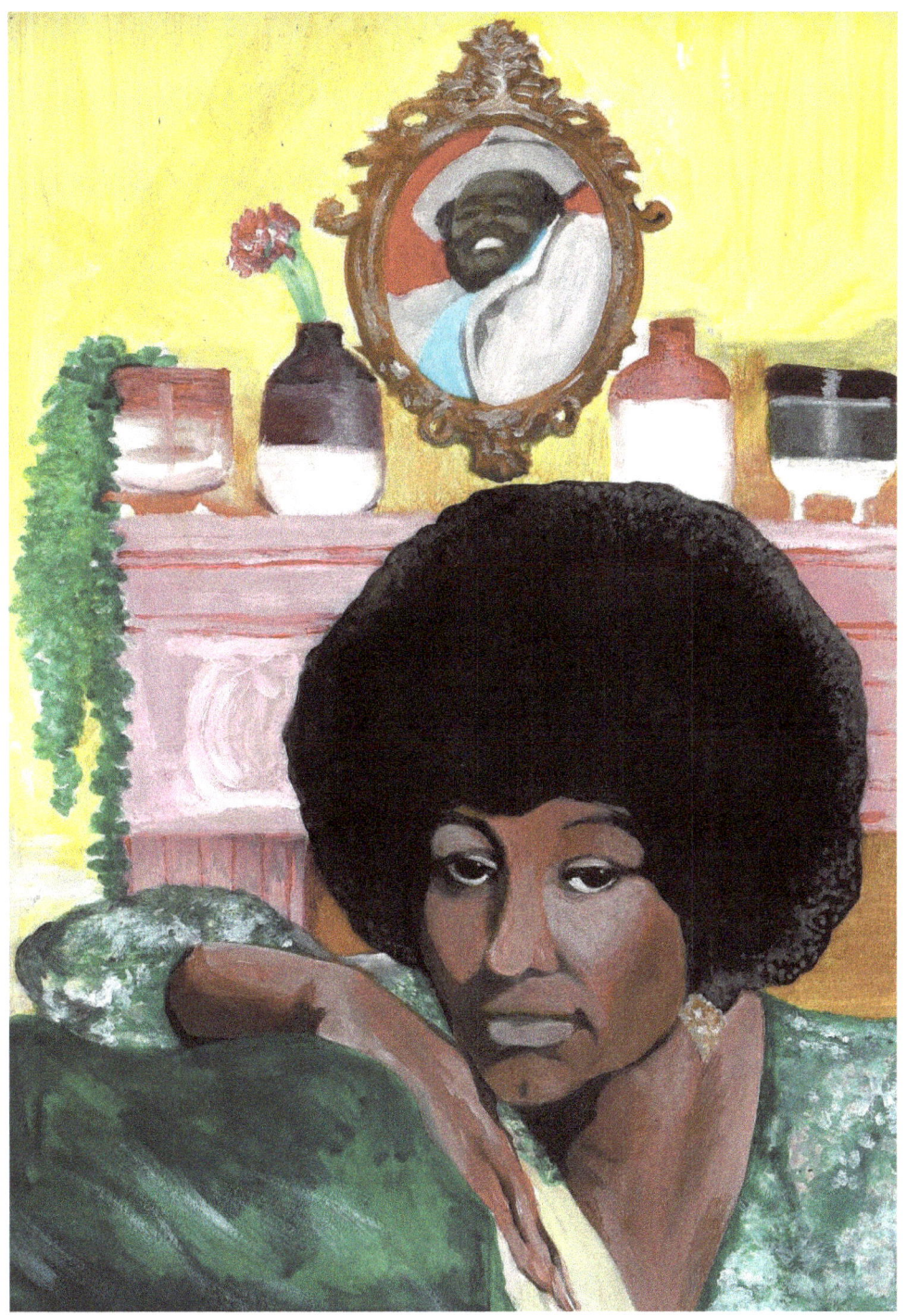

Lee Dorsey

Irving Lee Dorsey was born in New Orleans on Christmas Eve, 1924, during World War II he served in the navy and then became a featherweight boxer, Kid Chocolate, in Portland. He had one fight and was knocked out in round two so returned to New Orleans in 1955 opening an auto repair shop and singing in clubs. In 1958 his first recording was "Rock Pretty Baby" on the Rex label. Two years later his second release, on Valiant, was "Lottie Mo". Neither went anywhere but around 1960 he met Marshall Sehorn who got him signed to the Fury label. He then met Allen Toussaint at a party and under his guidance found his feet with 1961s "Ya". His follow up "Do-Re-Mi" was a hit, but nothing stuck so he went back to fixing cars. Toussaint's army stint was over and he returned to New Orleans in 1965 where both him and Sehorn launched the Sansu label. Dorsey had hits with several of Toussaint's songs, including "Ride Your Pony" in 1965 and "Working in the Coal Mine" and "Holy Cow" the following year. He wasn't the world's greatest when it came to singing but what he had was his own sound. A rich New Orleans texture that weaved in and out of the patterns provided by the Meters. His debut album's title reflected this stage in his life, "The New Lee Dorsey" and included more Crescent City classics like "Get Out My Life, Woman" and "A Little Dab A Do Ya". A personal favourite of mine was 1968's AMY release, "Wonder Woman". In 1970 Lee Dorsey and Allen Toussaint worked together for the album "Yes We Can Can", the title track ended up being Dorsey's last single to be in the US chart which didn't mean the product wasn't as good. In fact, the track was used effectively by Obama for his presidential campaign and in 1972 "Freedom for the Stallion" was issued. Before I knew about Soul music I knew about Lee Dorsey. When I was 10 years old, I heard "Working in a Coal Mine" and "Holy Cow" but in 1966 I was still at Junior School and they just seemed like funny novelty recordings. The lyrics didn't really mean much to a young child and it was "Freedom for the Stallion" that woke me up to his brilliance. In 1976 he appeared with Southside Johnny & The Asbury Jukes on their album "I Don't Want to Go Home" which led him to ABC records who released his final album "Night People". Allen Toussaint produced and wrote every track on the album and included Irma Thomas on backing vocals. So unique and diverse was Lee Dorsey that he supported the punk band The Clash on their 1980 US Tour as well as Jerry Lee Lewis and James Brown. In 1986 Lee Dorsey developed emphysema and passed away on December the 1st aged 61.

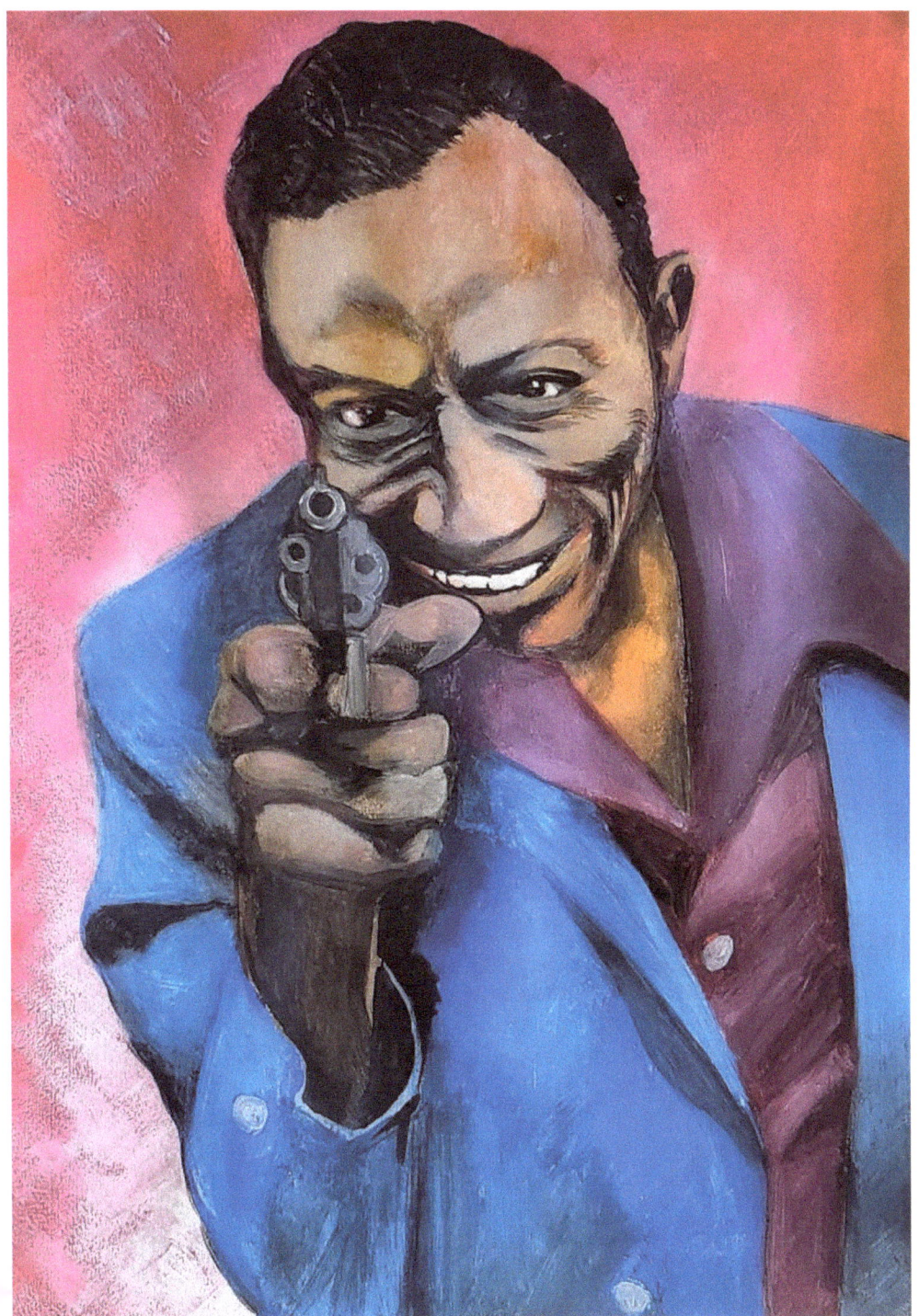

Neville Brothers

The Neville Brothers came from the Calliope Projects in New Orleans with parents who embraced French, Caribbean, Spanish and Native American culture. The four boys could be heard singing on street corners, but it was Art who showed the others the way into the recording industry with his group The Hawketts who recorded "Mardi Gras Mambo" in 1954 while still in High School. In 1965 he also founded The Meters, the most sought-after musicians in the Crescent City. Back in 1960 brother Aaron released his first single "Over You" on the Minit label. Cyril was a late arrival on the scene and Charles took a different direction altogether. He had worked with Larry Williams who had penned "Bony Moronie" and "Dizzy, Miss Lizzy" but whose life also included violence and drug addiction. Charles himself struggled with heroin addiction which saw him incarcerated at the Louisiana State Penitentiary. After his release he moved to New York to explore jazz before returning to New Orleans in 1976 when the four brothers came together to take part in the recording session of the Wild Tchoupitoulas, a Mardi Gras Indian group led by the Neville's uncle, George Landry or "Big Chief Jolly". Their self-titled debut album was released on Capitol in 1978. In 1987, the Neville Brothers released "Uptown" on EMI and featured Rolling Stones' Keith Richards, Branford Marsalis and Carlos Santana. The following year saw the release of "Yellow Moon" on yet another label, this time A&M. The track "Healing Chant" won the Grammy Award for Best Pop Instrumental Performance in 1990, Charles' alto saxophone playing an important part in its success. The album also included a stirring version of Sam Cooke's "A Change is Gonna Come" as well as "Sister Rosa", dedicated to Rosa Parks who refused to give up her seat in 1955 which sparked the Montgomery Bus Boycott and instigated the progression of the American Civil Rights movement. The same year saw the release of another album, "Brother's Keeper" and from it came their adaptation of Leonard Cohen's "Bird on a Wire" which also appeared in the movie of the same name starring Goldie Hawn and Mel Gibson. Due to the fact that Art Neville spent time with his other band, The Meters, this meant that the brothers were in hibernation in the late 90s through until 2004 when their own Neville Nation Records released the album "Walkin' in the Shadow of Life" with the lead single being their unique adaptation of the Temptations' 1970 hit "Ball of Confusion" updating the lyrics to include Outkast instead of The Beatles. Cyril and Aaron moved out of the city after Hurricane Katrina but finally returned to perform there at the New Orleans Jazz & Heritage Festival in 2008. The group formally disbanded in 2012 but reunited in 2015 for a farewell concert in New Orleans.

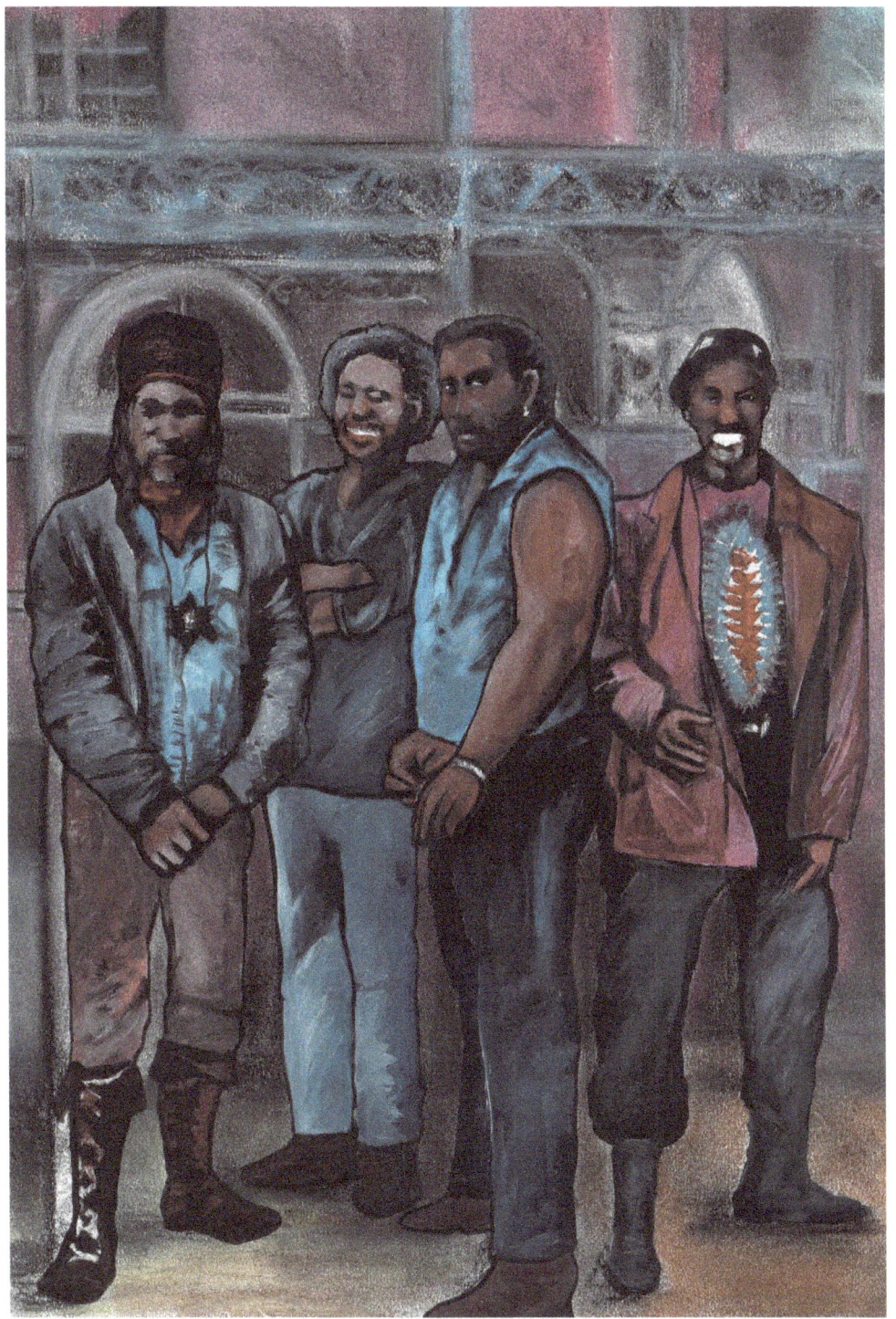

Willie Tee

Wilson Turbinton was born in New Orleans on February the 6th, 1944 and by the age of three was playing the piano which he continued to do throughout his career as well as being a songwriter, singer and producer. Possibly not as well-known as Allen Toussaint, Willie Tee was acknowledged as being one of the instigators of what was soon to be recognised as New Orleans Soul and Funk. His own influences ranged from Professor Longhair to John Coltrane and he made his early mark in 1962 courtesy of his music teacher Harold Battiste who had him join his jazz combo the AFO (All For One) Band and on the local AFO label he released the single "Always Accused" with the band backing him. Move forward three years and now on Atlantic records, he released and wrote "Thank You John" followed by "Teasin' You" which was released on the local Nola label, formed by his cousin Ulis Gaines, local journalist Clint Scott and another legend of New Orleans, producer and arranger Wardell Quezergue. "Teasin' You" was the label's first local hit that was leased to Atlantic and also recorded by The Righteous Brothers. A third Atlantic release was "Walking Up a One Way Street", another of his compositions. Atlantic cancelled his contract and he moved to Nola's subsidiary Hot-Line for "Please Don't Go" but when Nola folded in 1968, he co-founded Gatur Records, releasing "I Peeped Your Hole Card". The following year he was able to co-compose "One More Chance" for Margie Joseph over at Memphis' Volt label and from the late '60s Willie Tee & The Soul Brothers played venues that ranged from The Ivanhoe on New Orleans' famous Bourbon Street through to the equally famous Apollo Theatre in Harlem, New York. In 1970 he had his debut album, "I'm Only a Man" released on Capitol while his own Gatur label was kept alive by his single "The Man That I Am". In 1973 Tee was asked to form a backing band for the Wild Magnolias. He arranged, co-wrote and led the band on their self-titled debut album which introduced the world to the Mardi Gras native Americans brand of funk. 1976 saw another label change for his second album with United Artists issuing "Anticipation". During the 1980s Northern Soul DJs rediscovered his music and by the '90s he appeared at London's Jazz Café but in 2005, as Hurricane Katrina did its best to destroy the Big Easy, Willie Tee was offered a job as a visiting lecturer at Princeton University in New Jersey working with music students. In January 2006 he returned to Louisiana where he settled in Baton Rouge. In 2007, he passed away from colon cancer but before he left, the Louisiana Music Hall of Fame honoured him for his contribution to the music that he had been so important in developing.

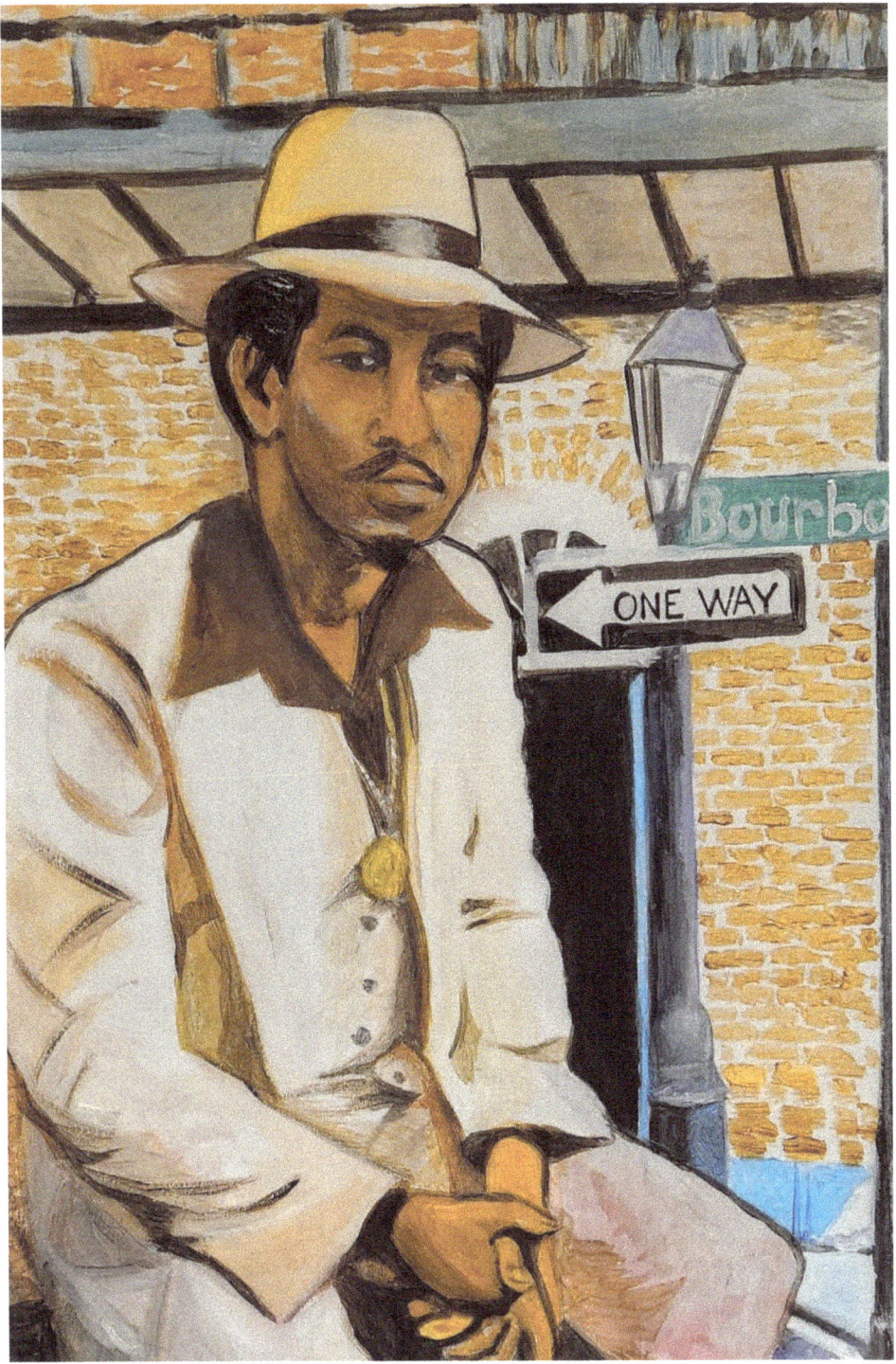

Wardell Quezergue

Wardell Quezergue was born in New Orleans on the 12th of March 1930 and was a 'Creole of colour', weaving both European and African roots into magnificent New Orleans music. Father played a guitar and mother a clarinet but Wardell chose the trumpet and composed his first piece of music for his school band. Before he even got into his teens, he was playing gigs and then in 1951 was drafted into the army and was posted to Tokyo where he conducted an army band. On returning to New Orleans, he used the GI bill to study music and started his journey around the clubs with his first band The Royal Dukes of Rhythm, later becoming Wardell & The Sultans who recorded for the Imperial label. In 1964 he helped to form the Nola label and a year later released "Teasin' You" by Willie Tee. Jerry Leiber and Mike Stoller formed the Red Bird and Blue Cat labels in New York and showed an interest in buying some of Wardell's master copies to release on their labels. These included The Dixie Cups' "Chapel Of Love" in 1964 and "Iko Iko" from 1965. A year later he wrote and produced "Barefootin'" by Robert Parker who had been the tenor saxophonist in his band. In 1970 he shipped a coach load of musicians along with singers Jean Knight and King Floyd from New Orleans across to a studio in Jackson, Mississippi and in one session created "Mr Big Stuff" for Jean and "Groove Me" for King Floyd. One was a hit for Stax in Memphis, Tennessee the other for Chimneyville in Jackson but both were born and bred in New Orleans. In 1965 Atlantic's Jerry Wexler heard Tami Lynn singing at a convention and got her to record "I'm Gonna Run Away from You" which was never released until 1971 when it stormed the UK Northern Soul clubs. It led to an album being co-produced by Wardell Quezergue alongside Blues & Soul magazine's British editor John Abbey. Had side two lived up to the genius of side one this could have been the greatest album ever pressed. The first side of "Love is Here and Now Your Gone" was classically structed in four seamlessly crafted movements. Every possible genre was either steeped in Soul traditions or showed willingness to embrace newer trends such as monologues, called rap in some places. From "Wings Upon Your Horns" originally a Country song by Loretta Lynn the monologues linked each track, next Holland-Dozier-Holland's title track slowed down almost beyond recognition and followed by Allen Toussaint's "Can't Last Much Longer" before the climactic "That's Understanding" originally cut by the Patterson singers earlier that year. In 1974 Wardell returned to Malaco studios to produce another Soul gem, Dorothy Moore's version of the country song "Misty Blue". In later life, because of diabetes, Wardell Quezergue lost his sight but never his vision. He passed away on September the 6th 2011.

Art & Soul

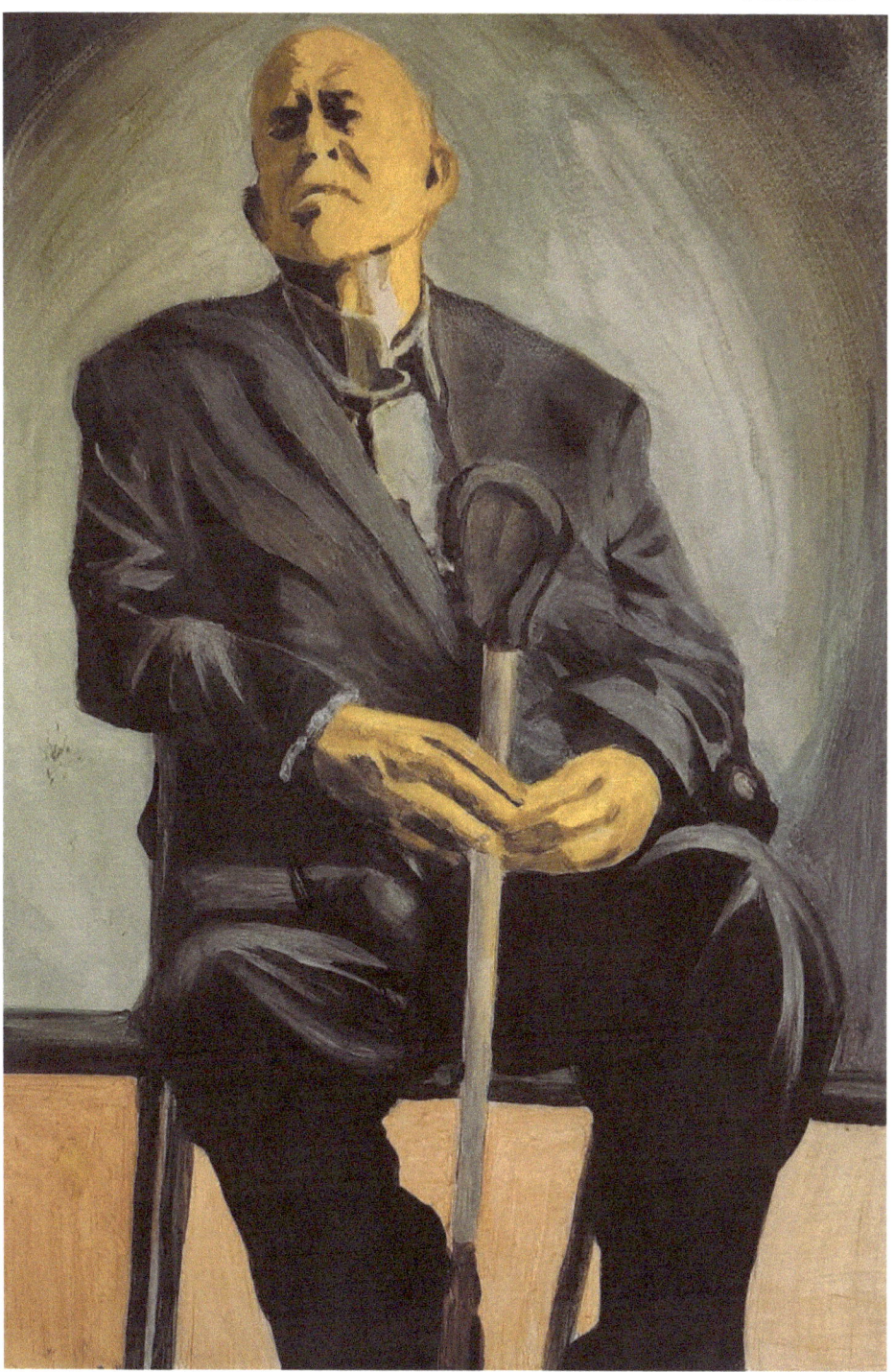

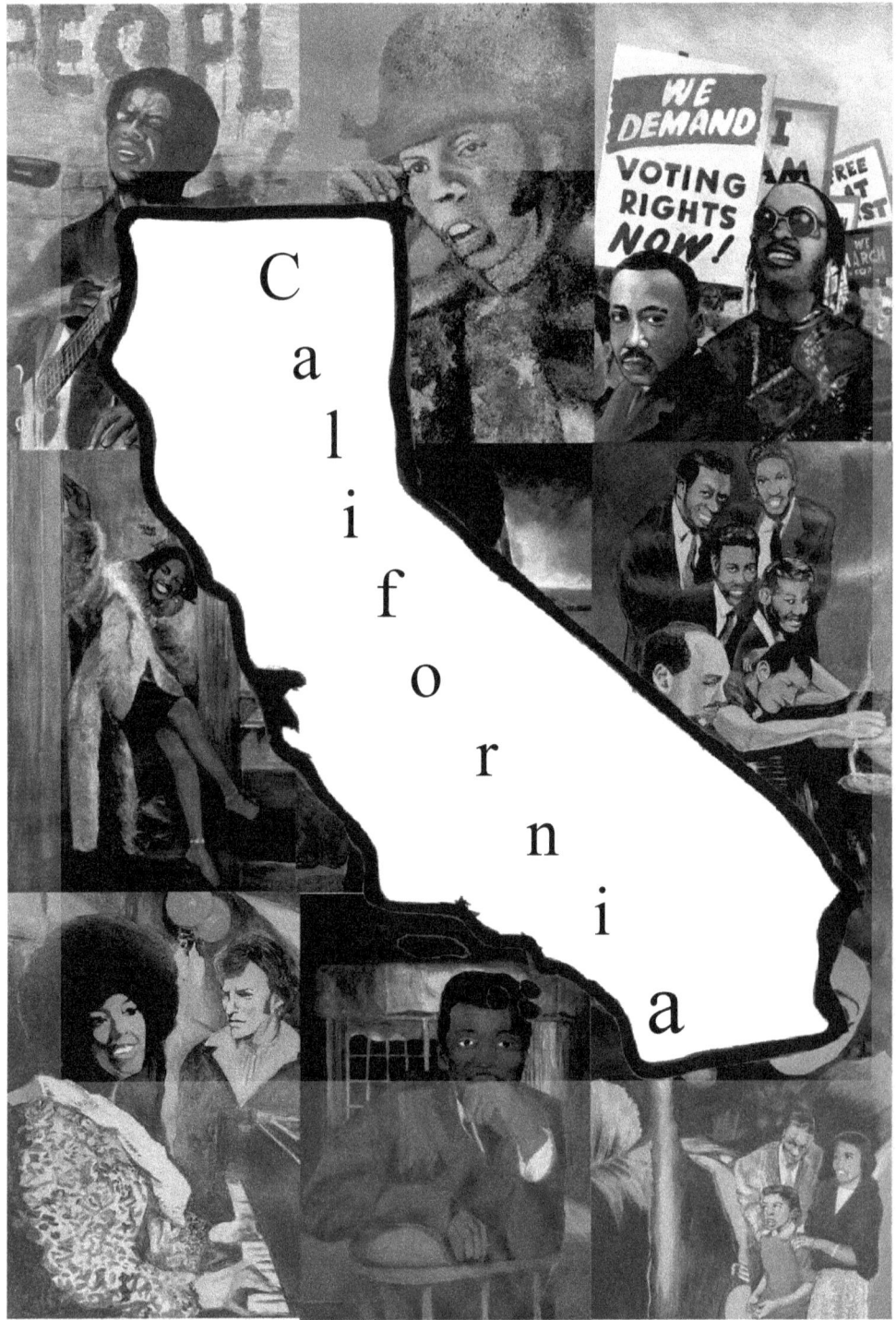

Art & Soul

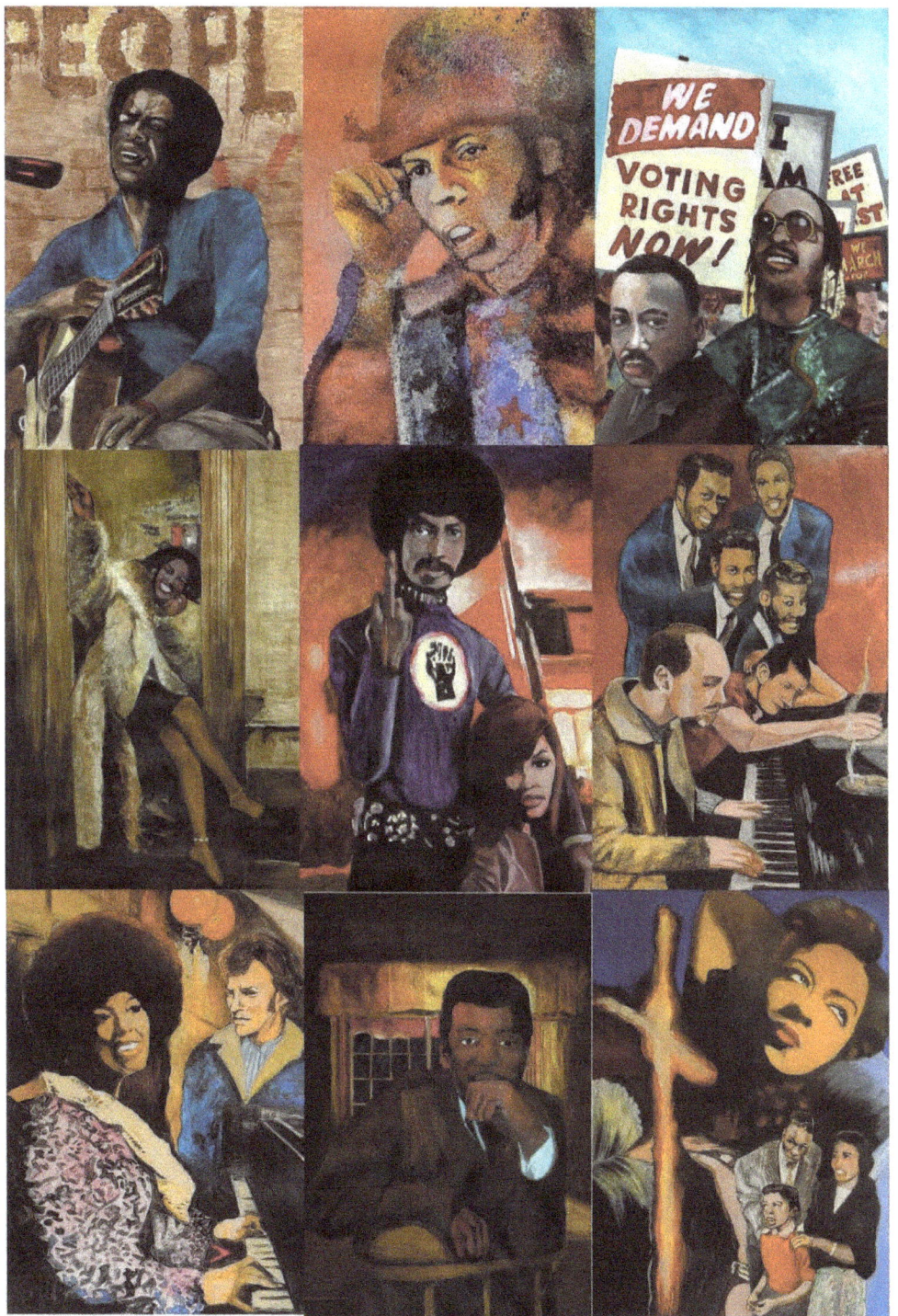

Barry White

Barry Eugene Carter was born on September the 12th, 1944 in Galveston, Texas his father, Melvin White was a stay-away Dad and at the age of six months Barry moved to Watts in South Central LA with his mother Sadie. By the time he was eight he sang in his local choir and became the organist and assistant director. This may sound far-fetched, but he was eleven when he played piano on Jesse Belvin's 1956 R&B hit "Goodnight My Love". By the time he was sixteen he'd already fathered two children, quit school, and served time for stealing tyres. As Barry Lee he sang bass on singles by The Upfronts, The Atlantics and The Majestics, none of which charted but he was showing more interest behind the scenes and acted as a writer and arranger for small obscure Californian labels. Surprisingly he then chose his father's surname. By now he had a wife and four children, and they had to survive on welfare cheques. Things changed in 1963 when he arranged Bob & Earl's "Harlem Shuffle". This led him to meet Gene Page who was making moves himself as an arranger. White wrote and produced "I Feel Love Comin' On" for Felice Taylor in 1967 then, in 1969 put together Love Unlimited, his own female trio plus the Love Unlimited Orchestra, a forty-piece ensemble that would travel with White. In 1972 we heard White's voice tucked away in the song "Walking in the Rain" by Love Unlimited. The single started atmospherically with the sound of the rain and footsteps running to escape the shower, the simple intro suddenly burst out with Gene Page's orchestral arrangement before the sound effects returned and the lead singer rang her boyfriend. The voice on the other end was Barry's. The story goes that he put it on the demo tape but didn't plan for it to be used on the finished recording. White's business partner, Larry Nunes, wanted it leaving on and that pretty much sealed White's fate. The success of Love Unlimited led to White's first album, "I've Got so Much to Give with the lead single being "I'm Gonna Love You Just a Little More, Babe" but the album started in great style with an eight minute version of the Four Tops' "Standing In The Shadows Of Love" before dipping into a most beautiful ballad that had the sound of an Italianesque waltz, "Bring Back My Yesterday". White had helped to redefine the genre but wasn't averse to parodying himself with an appearance in The Simpsons. Because of his larger-than-life appearance and the lyrical content of his songs he was also laughed at though and on Franklyn Ajaye's 1976 comedy album "Don't Smoke Dope, Fry Your Hair" he was called the Walrus of love. In 1983 Barry White gave a speech to the United Nations about South Africa's apartheid policies, no laughing matter. In May 2003 he suffered a stroke while waiting for a kidney transplant which led to his death on Independence Day 2003.

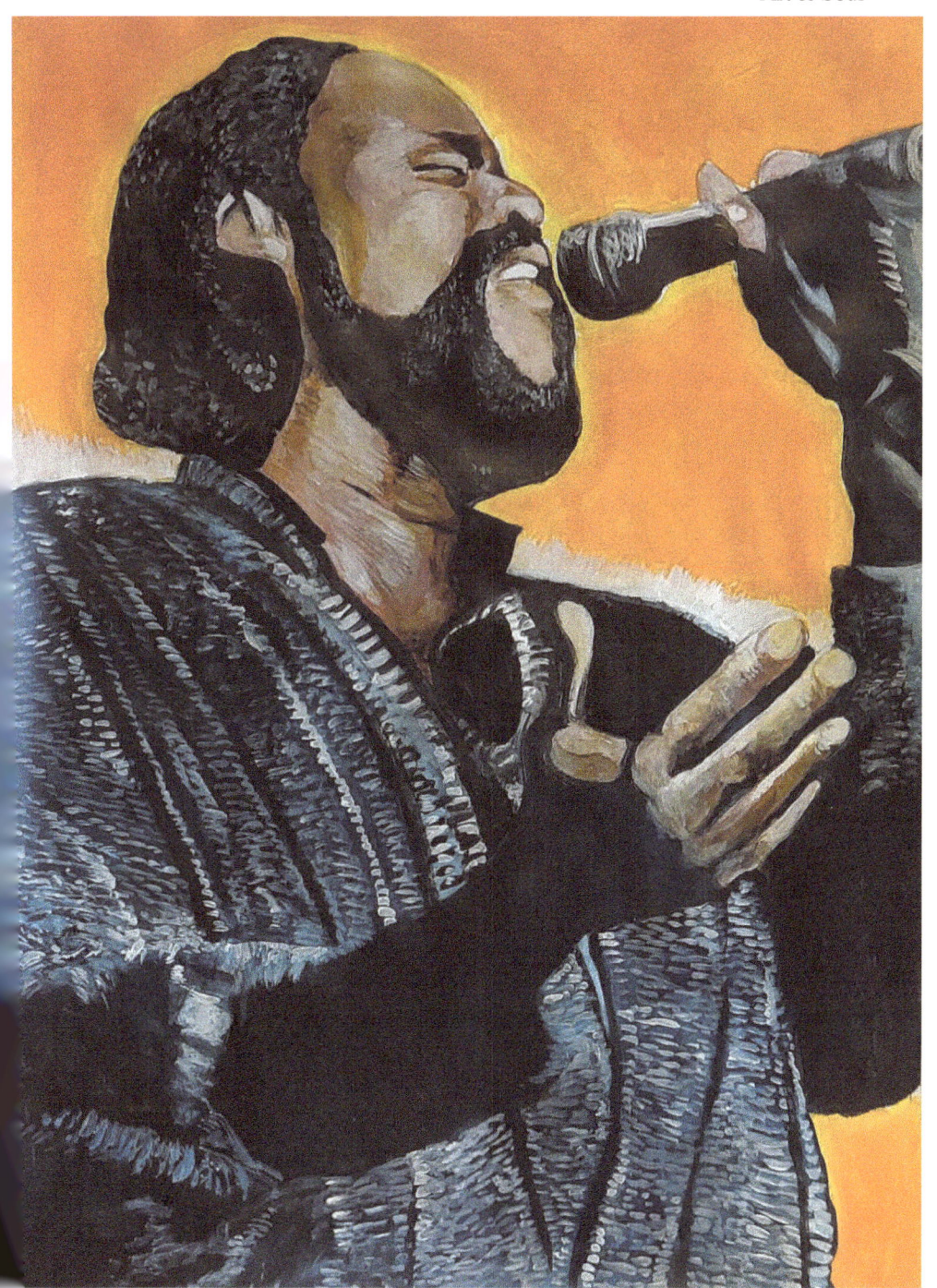

Bill Withers

When I was beginning to collect Soul music, I was too young to have experienced the feeling people must have had when they first heard the sounds of Motown and Stax records. To me Bill Withers was a contemporary artist and as such was a massive influence on the direction I was to take from then on in my personal pursuit of Soul. Bill Withers was born on the 4th of July 1938, in Slab Fork, West Virginia. In 1967, just as I was beginning 'big school', Bill Withers moved to Los Angeles to pursue a career in music after spending nine years in the navy and after three years, he got a record contract with Sussex Records. In 1971, Bill Withers released his debut album "Just as I Am", which contained the hits "Ain't No Sunshine" and "Grandma's Hands". It was produced by Booker T Jones and Withers was awarded his first Grammy Award for "Ain't No Sunshine". Right from the word "go" he marked himself as different and there were no high-profile studio shots to herald his arrival. Instead, the cover showed him standing by a hanger holding his lunch box in between putting toilet seats into airplanes. The album ended with the most chilling sound imaginable. "Better Off Dead" dealt with alcoholism, unchartered territory for Soul artists as the singer tells of his life and everything he has lost: "Better Off Dead" finishes with the sound of a gunshot. Bill released his second album, "Still Bill" in 1972, with the hit singles "Lean on Me" and "Use Me". This time the musicians were mainly from Charles Wright's 103rd Street Rhythm Band. In 1973 Bill Withers was asked to be recorded live, which produced the album, "Bill Withers Live at Carnegie Hall". This included the chilling anti-Vietnam war song "I Can't Write Left-Handed" and "Friend of Mine", tracks that never made it into the studio for album inclusion. His final album for Sussex was 1974s "+Justments", again scattered with classics such as "Who is He and What is He to You?" As is often the case, legal issues stopped him from recording for Sussex again and in 1975 he found his way to Columbia where "Making Music, Making Friends" continued his successes along with 1976's "Naked and Warm". In 1977 Withers released his timeless single "Lovely Day" off "Menagerie" but he had grown tired of the recording industry and its, sometimes, dubious games and so having released more of his own product and guested on others' such as The Crusaders' "Soul Shadows" and Grover Washington Jr's "Just The Two Of Us" both in 1980, Withers decided to call it a day and raise his family.

I for one am glad that Bill Withers, the man, his music and his honesty were there at that time and that I was able to be there from his beginning and I know that he will be with me until my turn comes.

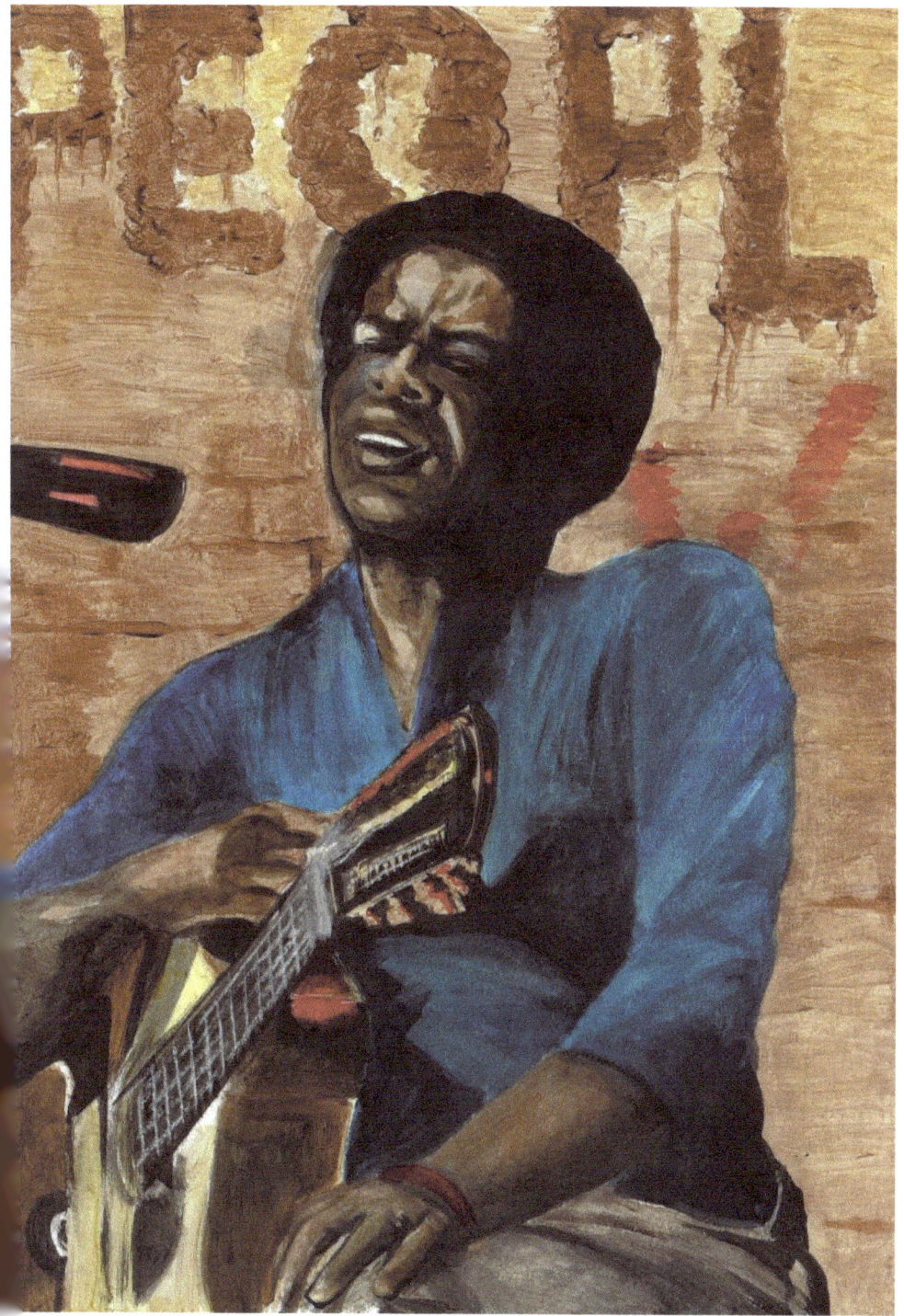

Deniece Williams

Deniece Williams was born in Gary, Indiana on the 3rd of June 1950 and trained in Baltimore as a nurse and anaesthetist before working as a ward clerk at the Chicago Mercy Hospital. She had dabbled as a singer at the Casino Royal club before finally dropping out to pursue a more musical career. Her first single "Lover's Tears" was released at the age of 16 on Chicago's Toddlin' Town label before a move to the Atlantic distributed Lock label. There were no successful outings from the Windy City so in 1972 she left for California where she replaced Lynda Lawrence in Stevie Wonder's Wonderlove group with Lawrence choosing to join The Supremes. For the next three years Deniece toured the world with Stevie developing her own artistry along the way, constantly encouraged by the Wonder to pursue her writing. She had her first major songwriting breakthrough with "Slip Away" and prior to including it on her debut album she got good mileage out of it with versions recorded by Merrie Clayton, Frankie Valli and Jean Terrell, Diana Ross's replacement in The Supremes. Most famously it was recorded by The Emotions for their "Flowers" album, produced by another former Chicago artist Maurice White. When Deniece decided to leave Wonderlove it was to continue her career as a songwriter. Deniece approached White with some songs aimed at having them performed by another signing to his new Kalimba company, The Emotions. Instead of that, Deniece was asked to perform them herself and the album "This Is Niecy" was released at the end of 1976 with her signature tune "Free" smashing the singles chart wide open and her debut album being certified gold in April. There was yet another link to The Supremes with another singer and songwriter having recently joined the trio, Susaye Greene. Greene was also another former member of Wonderlove who had a similar vocal range to Williams and co-wrote "Free". Despite her sudden success Deniece was able to continue fulfilling her musical interests and was herself 'free' to move from Soul to Gospel music. From the rousing intro track, "It's Important to Me" through to the finale "If You Don't believe", her songs, mostly co-written by her, moved with ease from upbeat dance tracks through to sensuality, self-determination and spiritual praise. Despite some critics saying on its release that the album was too highly polished and artistic for commercial punters, Will Downing revisited "Free" on his debut album in 1988, introducing the track to a new, arguably, more artistically sensitive generation. To me the album came as a breath of fresh air and her next albums continued that healthy feeling. As well, though, Deniece was constantly requested as a background singer for other artists such as Roberta Flack, Weather Report and Johnny Mathis with whom she released the album, "That's What Friends Are For" in 1978.

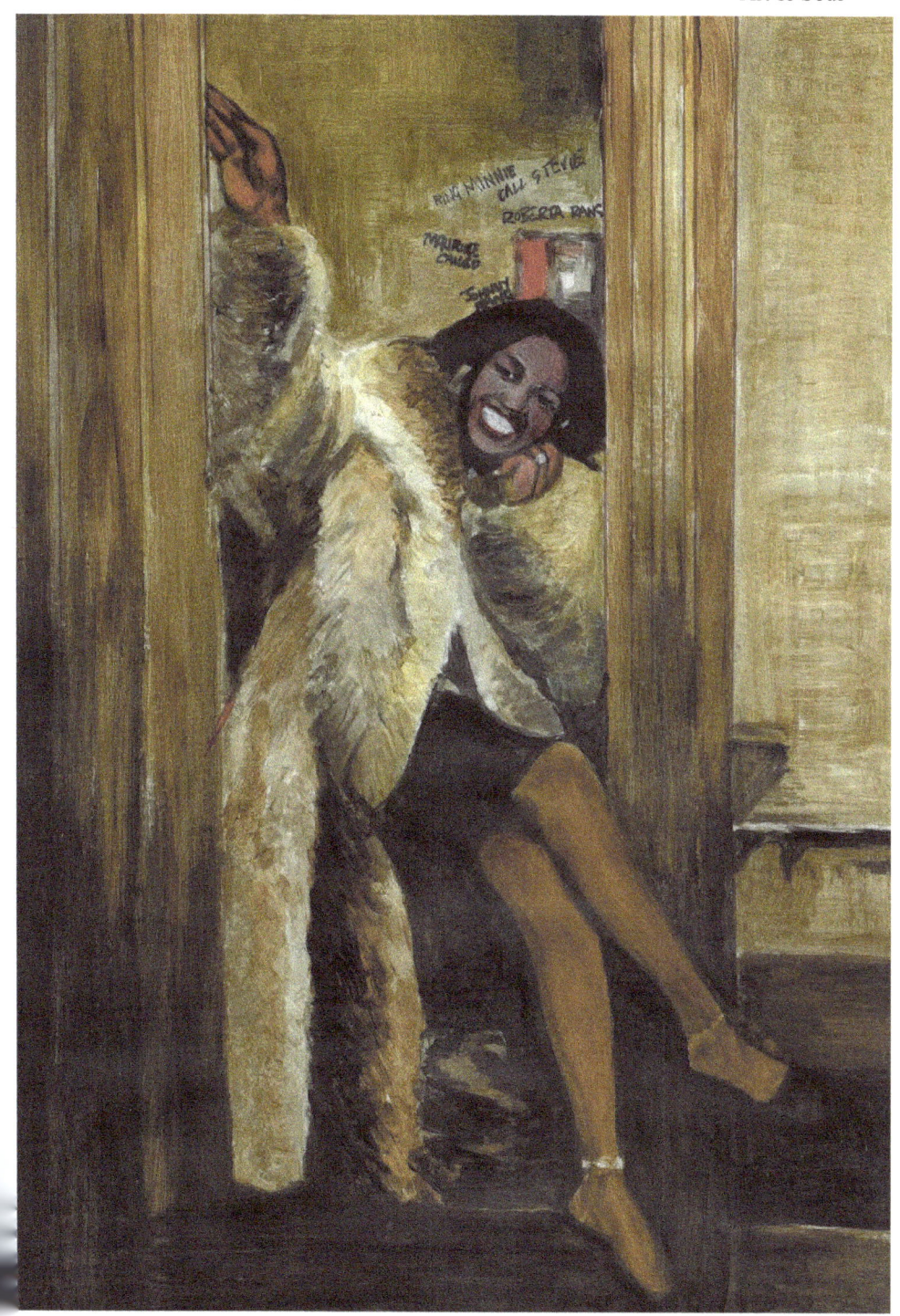

Ike & Tina Turner

Ike Wistyer Turner was born in Clarksdale, in the Mississippi delta on November 5th 1931, by the age of 8 he tried deejaying on radio station WROX. From there he took to playing the boogie woogie piano with local artist Pinetop Perkins before working with Sonny Boy Williams at the age of 11. In March of 1951, a 19-year-old Ike Turner went into Sam Phillips' Sun Recording Studio in Memphis with his Kings of Rhythm and cut "Rocket '88", acknowledged by many as the first rock and roll record. Frustratingly, the recording was credited to Jackie Brenston the vocalist and his Delta Cats. Soon after Turner changed from piano to guitar and became a session musician at Sun backing Elmore James, Howlin' Wolf and Buddy Guy. By the mid-50s Turner relocated his Rhythm Aces to East St Louis where they worked the local R&B circuit and also showed a strong entrepreneurial nature becoming a talent scout for the Modern label in L.A. In St Louis he created a revue bringing on new, talent, amongst them was Anna Mae Bullock whom he met in 1956. Two years later they were married but Ike asked Anna to consider a name change, which she did and so Tina Turner was created. Having had a well-publicised private life and an up and down career what was also creeping in was a hint of plagiarism with Blue Thumb releasing "Bold Soul Sister" in 1969 with its direct lift of a riff from Sly & The Family Stone's 1968 single "Sing A Simple Song". They were as funky as a mosquito's tweeter, to paraphrase the 'B' side of their 1971 version of Creedence Clearwater Revival's "Proud Mary", their first million seller and the funkiest of the duo who composed the track under the name of Aillene Bullock along with some of their funkier numbers was Tina. In 1973 the duo had their last big hit, the timeless "Nutbush City Limits" released on the UA label, again written by Tina. A year later the clavinet-heavy "Sexy Ida" emerged, written by Tina and produced by Ike at his own Bolic Studio in Los Angeles. By now though Tina was getting close to quitting and in July 1976 she'd had enough and walked. Two years later Ike decided to stop touring and concentrate on running his studio. The urge to rekindle past glories was too strong and so he put together a new band and went back on the road. In 1982 the studio burned down and Ike spiralled into a catastrophic dismal period of drug-related offences during which time he was arrested 11 times. In 1990 he was given a four year sentence for driving under the influence of cocaine and missed his 1991 Rock and Roll Hall of Fame Induction. Former record producer and future prisoner, Phil Spector, accepted the Award on their behalf.

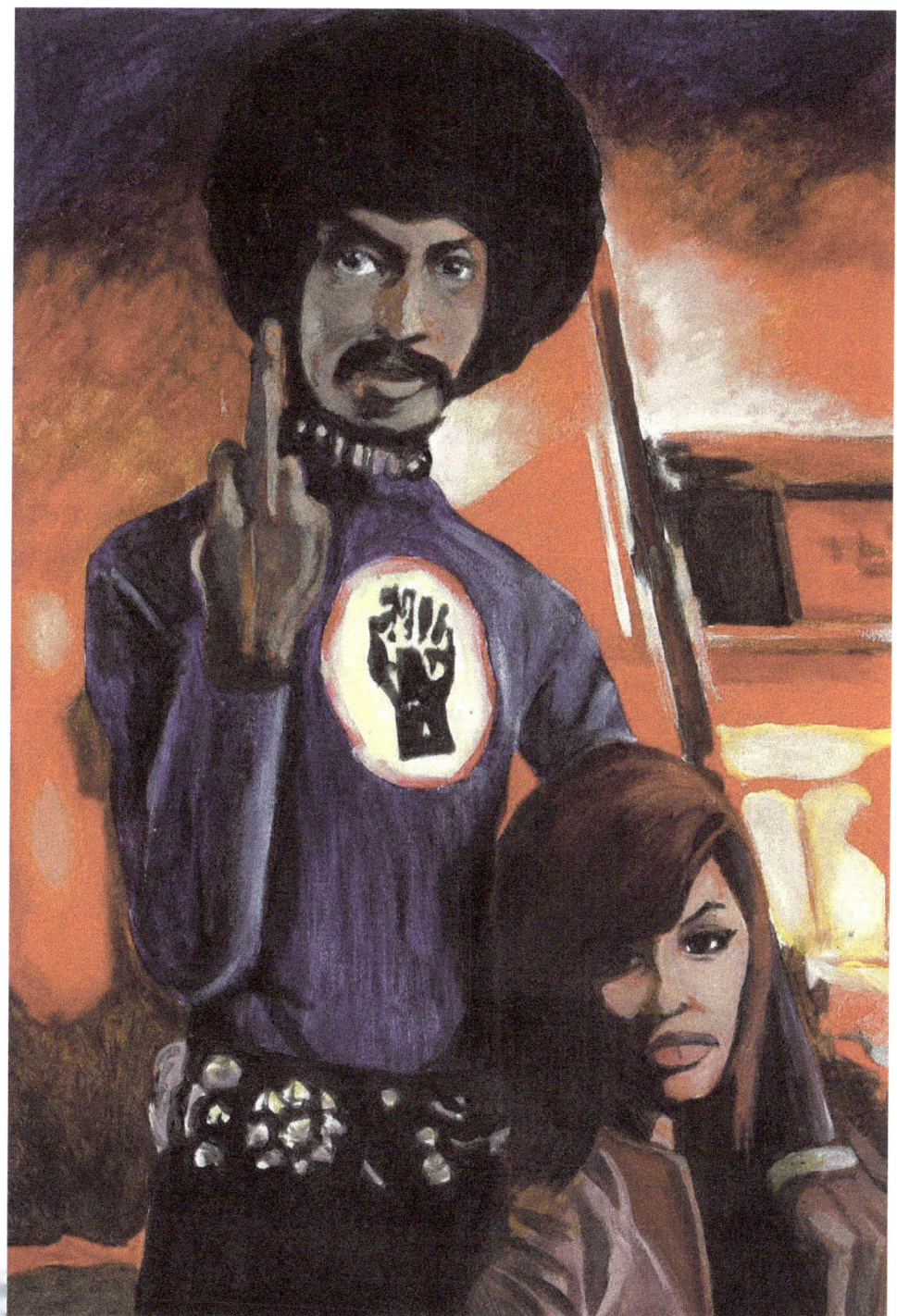

Sly Stone

Sylvester Stewart started life on March 15th 1943 in Dallas, Texas before moving to Vallejo, California with his parents KC and Alpha Stewart. Sly's father worked as a janitor and then on Sundays took the family to the local Pentecostal Church. It was well known throughout the neighbourhood that the children, by now numbering four, Sylvester (Sly), Rose, Loretta and Vietta rehearsed at the house and practised in the unholy art of rock and roll. Despite this secular interest, the children managed to arouse interest throughout the church circuit and began touring the Bay Area of California's churches. By the age of four he had already cut his first record, the Gospel song, "On the Battlefield for the Lord". By the age of nineteen Sylvester Stewart signed as A&R man and house producer for the Autumn record label and in 1964 wrote and played guitar and organ on Bobby Freeman's "C'mon and Swim" reaching number 5 on the pop chart and gaining a gold record along the way. A year later Sylvester Stewart gave spiritual birth to Sly Stone. Stone became his alter ego and after a quick course in deejaying he became regular radio deejay. His street credibility, no matter how contrived it had become to go with his cool deejay image, gave Stone another avenue down which to cruise and he became a pimp. It seemed as if Sylvester Stewart had to become Sly Stone in order to role play and slip and slide between personalities to serve a current purpose. His multi-racial band, The Stoners, embodied a nation's dream of integration but seemed alien with the emergence in the Oakland area of California of the Black Panthers in '66. The same year the group began to gain attention through their regular tours of the California scene and in 1967 signed to the Epic label. The group cut their first album, "A Whole New Thing" which sank without a trace although it met with critical approval from fellow musicians. The time was not quite right and the world was not quite ready for Sly Stone's funk. Sly Stone was about to burn brightest with the second long-playing release, "Dance to the Music" in 1968 that epitomised the late 1960s. By 1969 Sly & The Family Stone were superstars with a performance at Woodstock throwing them deeper into the international limelight and opening up their reputation to a far more cosmopolitan audience. The contradiction that was Sylvester Stone/Sly Stewart/Sylvester Stewart/Sly Stone was in the diversity of his followers. Stone remained influential and created another seemingly essential credential for some of those wishing to join the fraternity of funk. His unique Texan drawl would be echoed in the voices of The Commodores, Cameo, Slave, Earth, Wind & Fire and The Ohio Players.

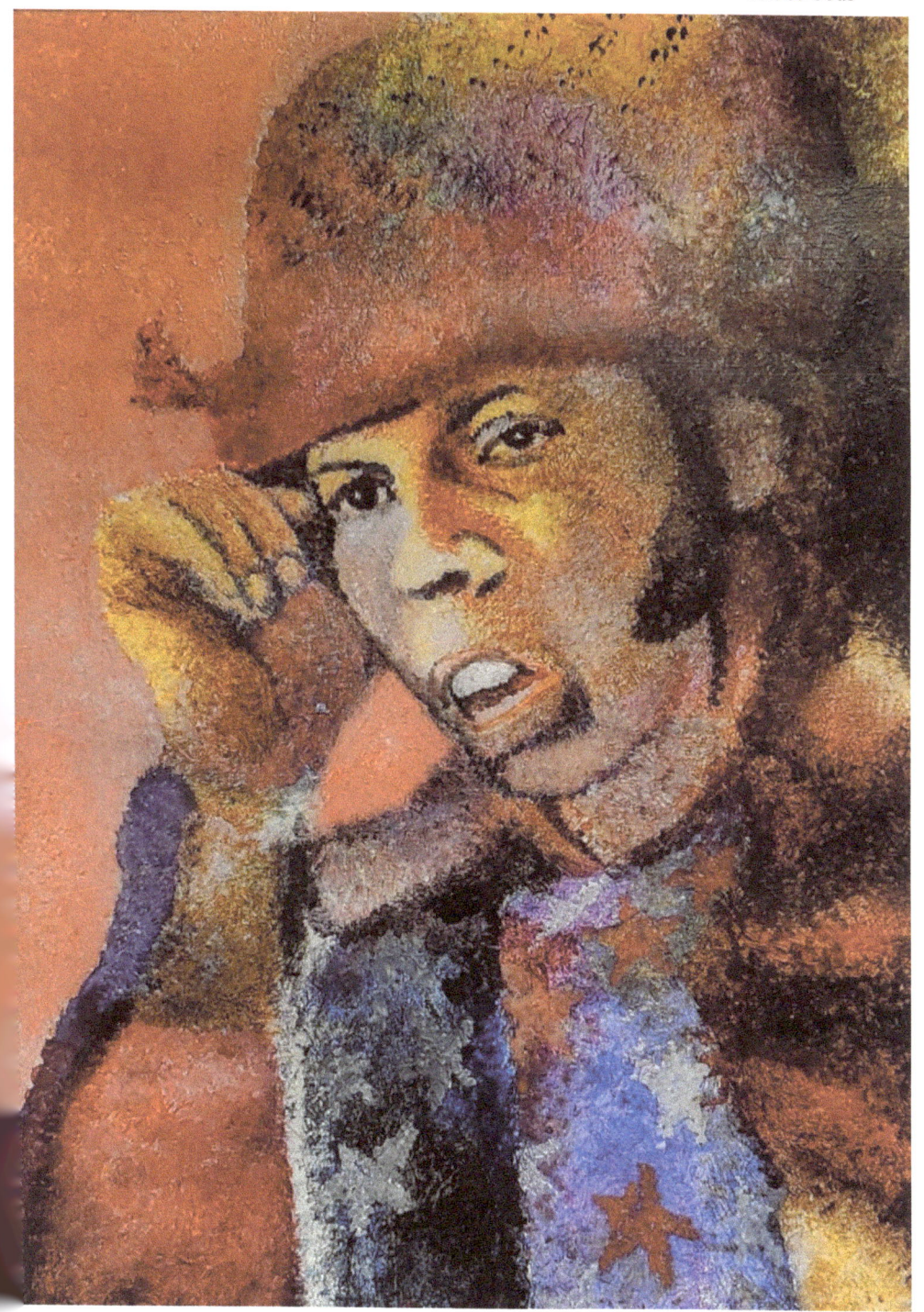

Larry Graham

Larry Graham was born in Beaumont, Texas on 14th August 1946 but by the age of two had moved with his family to Oakland, California. By the age of fifteen he was playing organ alongside his mother, Del's piano and an accompanying drummer in The Dell Graham Trio then one fateful night the organ wheezed out of action and the only instrument Larry Graham was able to find at short notice was a bass guitar. History was about to be made. This was the beginning of the Graham trademarks. After the drummer had departed the group, mother and son continued with Larry banging the bass in a fashion intended to compensate for the lack of a drummer. He became a regular feature around the Bay area of San Francisco and fate would bring more twists to the career of Larry Graham who was happily balladeering as well as making waves with his unique bass technique. One night a fan invited her friend the local deejay, Sly Stone, to hear Graham play. This was in 1966 and Sly & The Family Stone were about to be launched with Larry Graham joining from the outset. He would stay with the group until the 'Fresh' album of 1973 and was allegedly the featured vocalist on one of the groups biggest international hits "Family Affair" 1971. Before leaving, Graham had begun to look beyond the group for inspiration and had found it by working with Sly's Little Sister group; or rather with the musicians who supported the act and put them together as Hot Chocolate before they became Graham Central Station in 1974. '74 also saw the issuing of their second album 'Release Yourself' with the title track becoming the first single in October. By now there was a strong religious feel coming into the work of Larry Graham and the album stated God as the producer and Graham was coming to terms with the Jehovah's Witness form of religion. In 1976 Larry Graham became billed above the group name for the sixth album 'My Radio Sure Sounds Good to Me' but by 1980 Larry Graham's first solo effort, the stunning Sam Dees penned ballad 'One in a Million You', released in May, was at number 13 in the Soul singles with the album entering at number 42. On the single Graham sounded remarkably like Dees, unsurprising when one became aware that Sam Dees had coached Larry Graham in the style of singing required for the track. The album began to rise up the charts, whilst the single hit the top spot by the end of the month. This also marked another gold disc for Larry Graham. In October the follow-up single was ready, 'When We Get Married', a doo-wop ballad previously cut by The Dreamlovers and The Intruders that would reach the top ten by the close of the year.

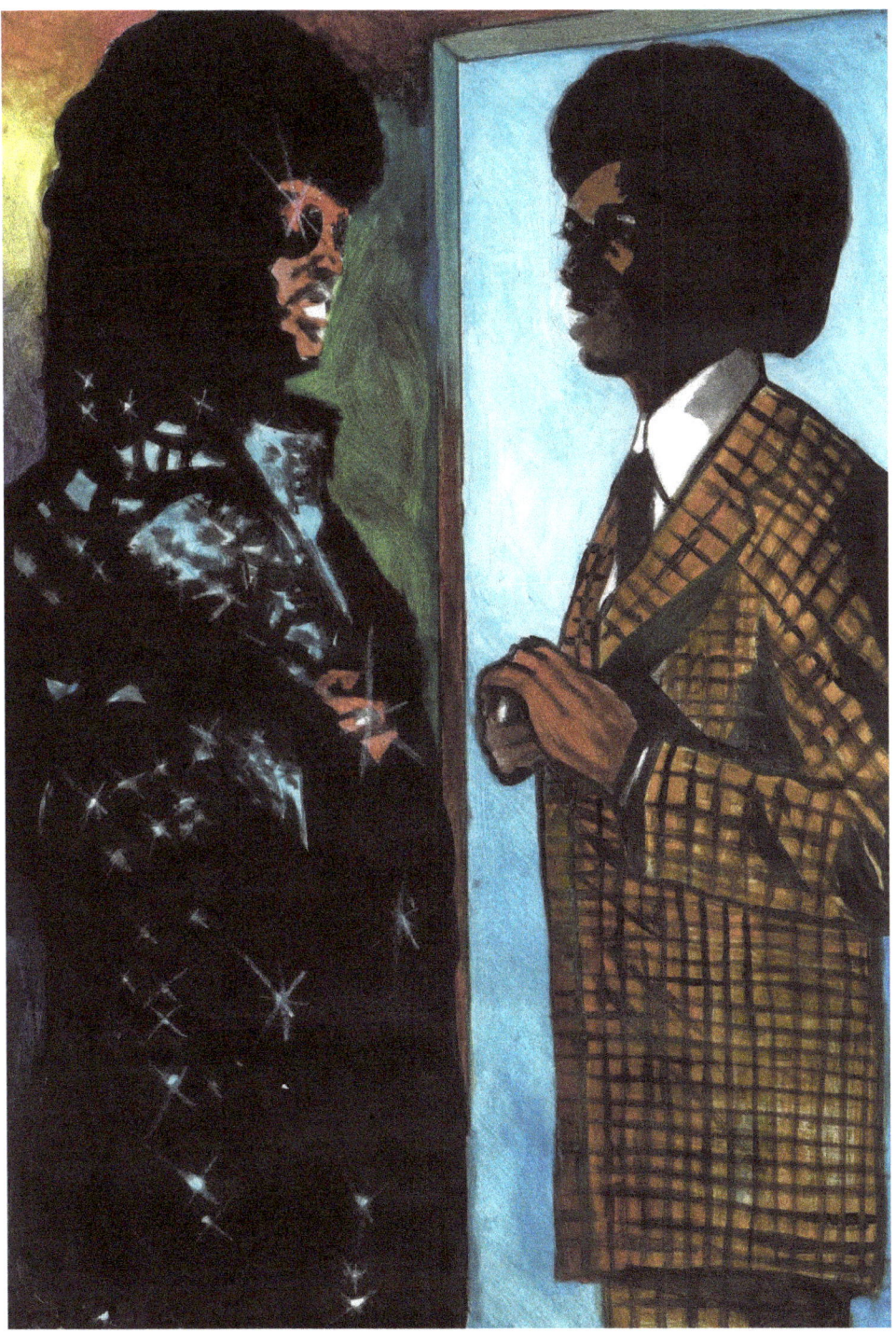

Lenny Williams

Lenny Williams was born in Little Rock, Arkansas, and moved to Oakland, California, at a young age. Learning to play the trumpet in elementary school fuelled his interest in music. His skills as a vocalist were first nurtured by singing in gospel choirs and groups around the Bay Area. Williams signed with Fantasy Records and released two singles including "Lisa's Gone" and "Feelin' Blue", written by Creedence Clearwater Revival's John Fogerty. In 1972, he was hired as the new lead singer of Tower of Power to replace Rick Stevens. A string of hits followed, including "So Very Hard to Go" with its Willie Mitchell sounding arrangement, "What is Hip", the album's opening track, "Don't Change Horses (In the Middle of the Stream)", "Clean Slate" and the Northern Soul flavoured single, "This Time it's Real". During his two years with the group, Lenny Williams sang lead vocals on three albums, the second being "Back to Oakland". "Urban Renewal" followed in 1974 and during this time Lenny Williams and Tower of Power toured throughout the United States, Europe and Asia but times were about to change again, and it was while still with Tower of Power that he recorded his first solo album "Pray for the Lion" for WB in 1974 produced by Eugene McDaniels. He had left the band to return to a full-blown solo career. Initially signing with Motown in 1975, where he released "Arise Sleeping Beauty," he later moved to ABC in 1977 where he worked with former Motown writer/producer Frank Wilson. Frank Edward Wilson was born on December the 5th, 1940 in Houston, Texas and moved to Los Angeles when he was in his teens. As far back as 1965, Berry Gordy asked the producers Hal Davis and Marc Gordon to set up an office of Motown in Los Angeles. Frank Wilson accepted an offer to join the team. Wilson left Motown in 1976, launched his own publishing firms, Traco Music and Specolite Music and began to produce material for ABC. Records' executive Otis Smith suggested to Lenny Williams that he hook up with Frank Wilson who produced "Choosing You" in early 1977 and forged a successful partnership. 1978s "Spark Of Love" included possibly the most unique Soul vocalisation you will ever hear on the ballad "Cos I Love You". Wilson's mournful strings add a quiet force that builds behind Williams' pain-filled delivery. Written by Williams and Michael Bennett the album was also a who's who of musicians and singers who could not fail to create what I feel is Soul perfection and which up to press has been viewed 56 million times on You Tube.

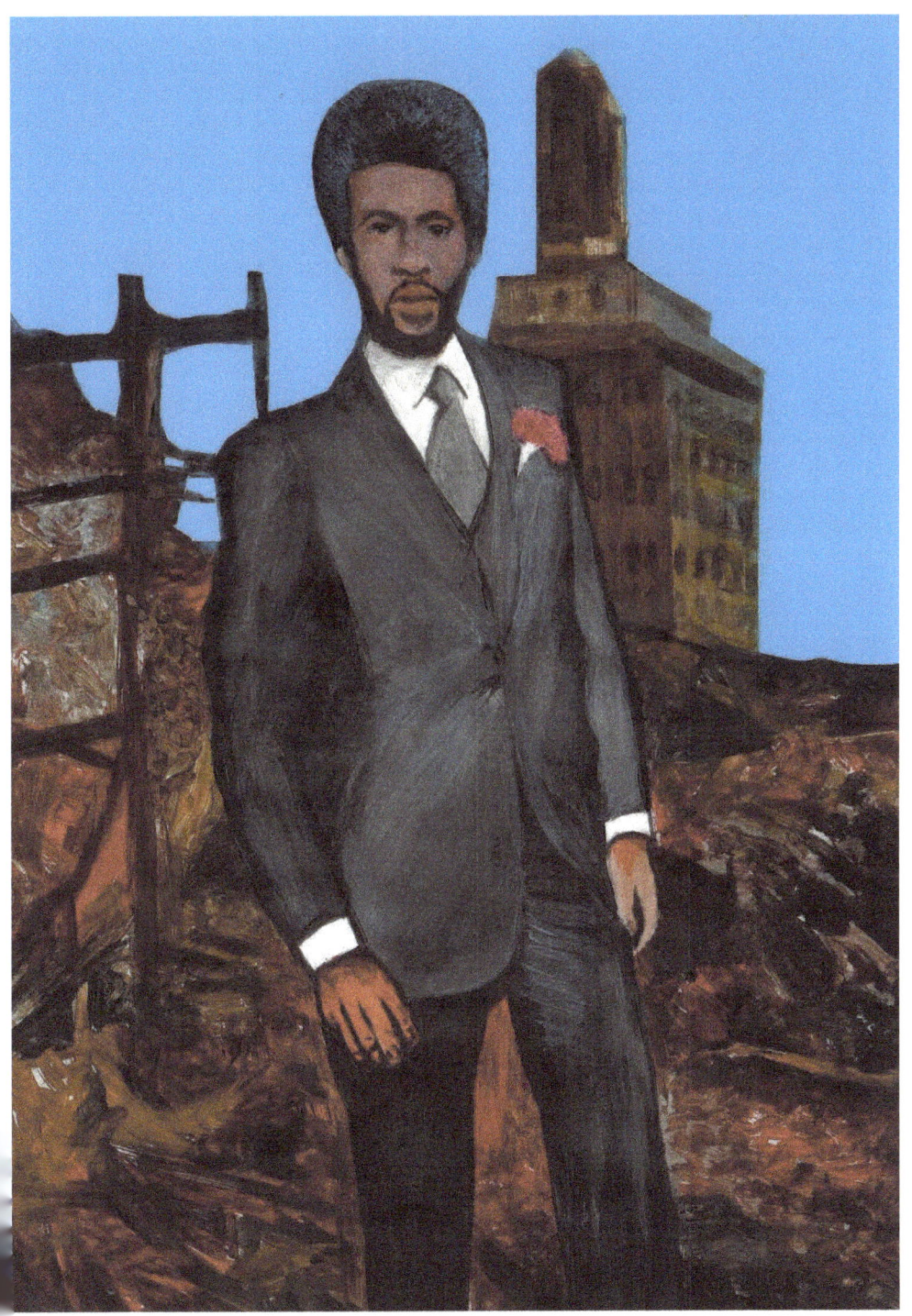

Natalie Cole

Natalie Cole was the daughter of crooner Nat King Cole and jazz singer Maria Hawkins, who worked with Duke Ellington. Natalie grew up surrounded by music in an affluent neighbourhood of Los Angeles although the family suffered from the racism of the time, including pulling the curtains back at Christmas and seeing a burning cross on their lawn. Her father died from lung cancer when she was only 15 and she struggled to come to terms with his death. Going to Chicago, Natalie met Charles Jackson and Marvin Yancy. Originally turned down by every label, Natalie finally gained the interest of her father's old label, Capitol. Jackson and Yancy wrote her first hit, "This Will Be," that reached number one R&B in 1975. It won Cole a Grammy for best female R&B performance, and she was named best new artist. After the early disappointments she was finally making it but then she was arrested for heroin possession in Toronto. The follow-up albums "Natalie" and "Unpredictable" added to her success. In 1977 she had two platinum albums and two years later received a star on the Hollywood Walk of Fame. Her greatest success came with her 1991 album, "Unforgettable... With Love", which paid tribute to her father with reworked versions of some of his best-known songs while the hit track "Unforgettable" remixed her voice with her father's 25 years after his death. The album went on to win six Grammys, including album of the year, as well as song of the year for the title track. Right from the second album through, Natalie Cole showed her passion for jazz and included her version of Billy Holiday's "Good Morning Heartache" Natalie was becoming more addicted to drugs, but this wasn't noticeable on the 1980 album "Don't Look Back" which included the track "Beautiful Dreamer". This showed a new dimension to Cole as she played piano on the self-composed song. Addiction problems in the early 1980s led to Cole spending six months in the Hazelden drug treatment facility in Connecticut. On her 1987 'comeback' album she recorded the track "Split Decision" taking a leaf from the 1986 hit for Patti LaBelle and Michael McDonald's "On My Own" and despite her personal demons constantly showing up when she least wanted them to her post-rehab period was off to an amazing start with 1987s "Everlasting", her first album on a new label, EMI-Manhattan. The album was a million-seller and included the hits, "Jump Star", "I Live for Your Love" and "Pink Cadillac", written by Bruce Springsteen. This album was followed by 1989's "Good to Be Back" which gave a her a number two pop hit, "Miss You Like Crazy" in the UK.

In 2015 Natalie cancelled a series of performances, including one on New Year's Eve. That night she passed away from heart failure at the age of 65.

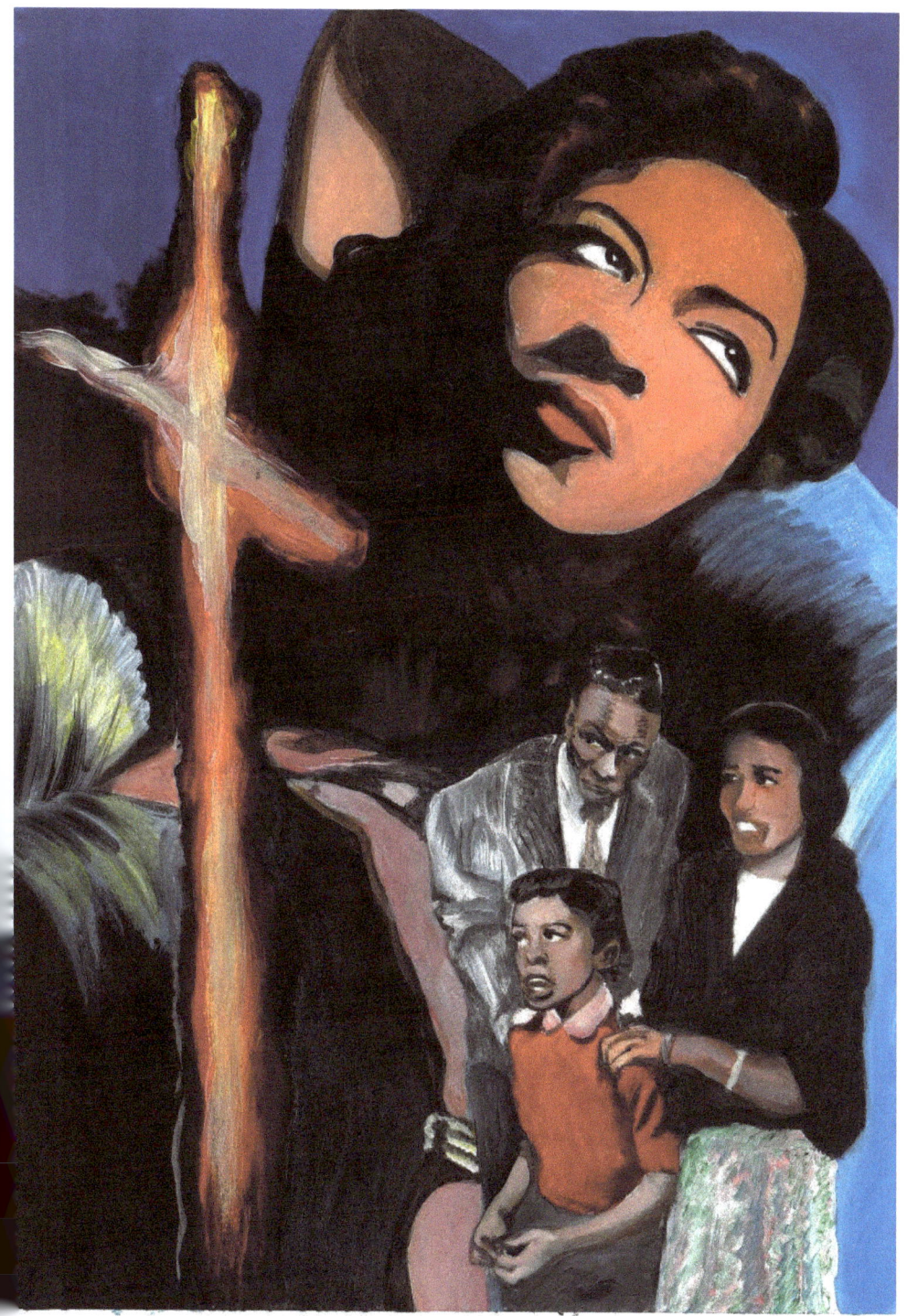

O.C. Smith

Ocie Lee Smith was born in Mansfield, Louisiana on the 21st of July 1932 and like Ray Charles gave Soul a country feeling. Smith moved with his parents to Little Rock, Arkansas before moving to Los Angeles with his mother after his parents' divorce. Then, after completing a Psychology Degree he joined the air force. After his 1955 discharge he started singing jazz to pay his bills. That said, his December 1955 debut single was a cover of Little Richard's "Tutti Frutti". Even though it wasn't a hit MGM still signed him but he had three more non-hits. He was later signed to Columbia who were also ready to let him go but that was until 1968 brought a much-needed stroke of luck with his rendition of a country song originally cut by Johnny Darrell, "Son of Hickory Holler's Tramp" which Smith recorded at Rick Hall's Fame Studios. His version reached number 2 in the UK pop chart and even got into the American Top 40. He had chosen a country song because he was always looking for a song with a story and the subject of a mother abandoned by a heavy drinking husband who ran off with someone else, leaving her to raise fourteen children alone and become a prostitute, pretty much ticked every box available. He followed this with his version of Bobby Russell's "Little Green Apples" which proved more successful reaching number 2 on the Billboard Hot 100. To many Soul collectors, me included, his music was middle of the road but now, when I listen to his material and knowing his own life, I have a different view. His is one of the greatest textured voices you could ever hear and he continued his storytelling with songs like "Long Black Limousine" with its tragic tale of how his former love came back to town, as she had promised, in a long black limousine. Sadly, she was inside a coffin. "Main Street Mission" covered homelessness whilst "Daddy's Little Man" was sung by a divorcee on a weekend meet up with his young son. In 1973 he sang Johnny Bristol's "La La Peace Song but was competing against a version by Al Wilson who won out. That year he was courted by Gamble and Huff in Philadelphia and a proposed album never materialised. In 1977 he returned to the UK pop chart again with "Together" and returned to the American national charts with the album "Dreams Come True" released in 1980. Smith was about to follow a new calling and in 1985 he became pastor and founder of The City of Angels Church in Los Angeles. Arranger H.B. Barnum held a Thanksgiving Dinner every year for the homeless and Smith always went to it. The night before he phoned Barnum saying how he may not get to it because he'd just come off a tour and wasn't feeling too good. O.C. passed away the next day on November 23rd 2001 at the age of 69.

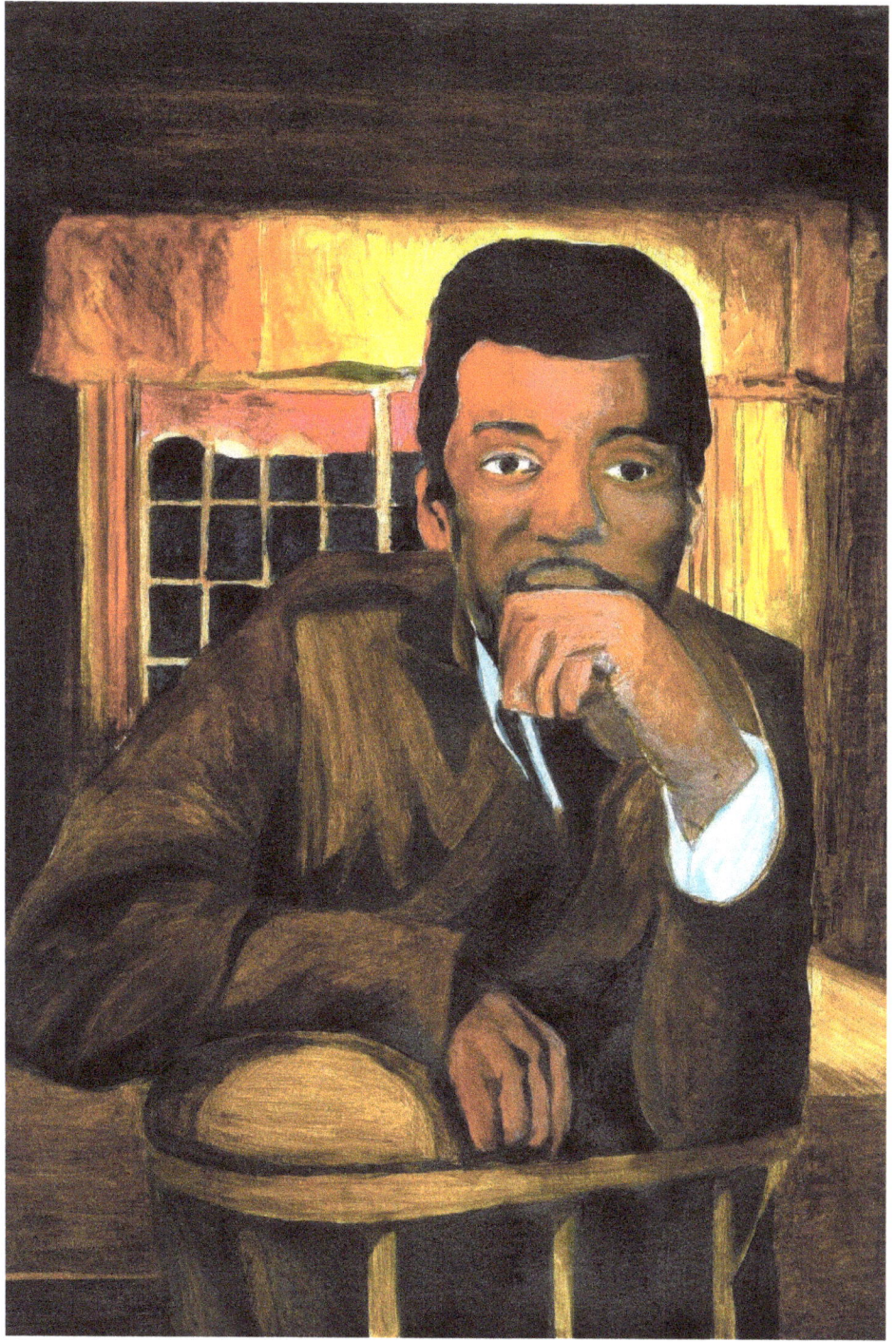

Stevie Wonder

After he had created his ground-breaking "Where I'm Coming From" set in 1971 Wonder was looking to expand his musical horizons. Over a single weekend in May he recorded seventeen songs and relocated to New York where he split his recording between New York and LA. At this point Stevie Wonder remained out of contract with Motown and was determined to enjoy his creative freedom but in March of 1972 and freshly signed to Motown "Music of My Mind" was unleashed on the world. Two singles were released, "Keep on Running" and "Superwoman" but they were only moderate successes. The album was also given a luke-warm treatment at first but Stevie Wonder could be proud of standing up for his creative rights and pushing the boundaries. Next on Wonder's own list of things to do was to build his own studio and enrol in music theory classes. With Motown he had negotiated a new recording deal including higher royalties and the establishment of his own music production company Black Bull Music. Wonder was able to retain the rights to his music as well as finally having full artistic control over his music. In November 1972 came "Talking Book". The success of "Superstition" spurred on imitators, some worked, others failed. Stevie Wonder was on a roll and in 1973 came "Innervisions" his 14th album including the tracks "Too High" and "Higher Ground" whilst the masterpiece "Living for The City" emphasised his mastery of the synthesiser in retaining his soulfulness and funkiness, seamlessly merging message with music. At the 1974 Grammy Awards "Innervisions" won Album of the Year and Best Engineered Recording. Wonder won a second Album of the Year Grammy the following year for the fourth in his self-made series, Fulfillingness' First Finale (1974). The album featured the funky "You Haven't Done Nothin". He had just signed his fourth contract with Motown, at the time the most expensive deal in history as well as escaping a near fatal road accident that had left him in a coma. This was also arguably the time that the tired phrase, "long awaited" was attached to a new Stevie Wonder project. In 1976 the waiting was over and "Songs in the Key of Life" hit the awaiting fans like a hurricane. "Village Ghetto Land" remains a statement not only of the time it was written but sadly remains as relevant today. Some say Wonder had been made aware of his own mortality after his earlier collision with death and he would often work for 48 uninterrupted hours in the studio. In 1980 Wonder released "Hotter Than July" which included the song "Happy Birthday". Many people fail to recognise that it was a tribute song to Dr Martin Luther King and through Wonder's tireless campaigning was pivotal in President Reagan passing the 15th of January, King's birthday, as a national holiday.

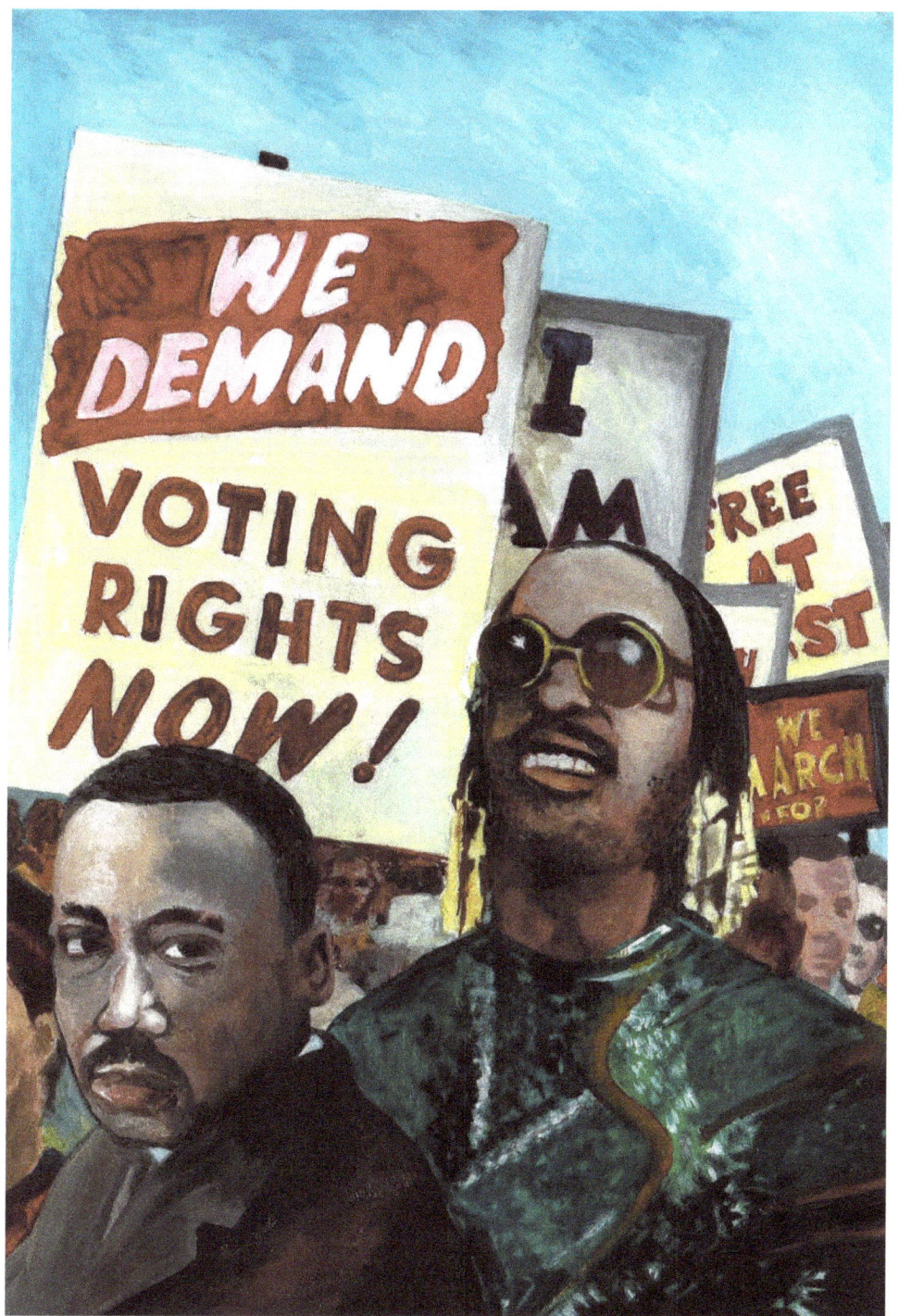

The Coasters

Joe Tex had an album out in 1972 called "From The Roots Came The Rapper", which has nothing to do with The Coasters, except that in 1960 they released the single, "Shopping for Clothes", which can arguably be a rap song. Rap has to have roots somewhere so why not from one of the greatest storytelling groups of all time. Add to that the fact that two Jewish guys had created their 3 minute masterpieces from as far back as 1951 and you have another unique tale. Jerome Leiber was the son of Polish Jewish immigrants and raised close to Baltimore's black neighbourhood where he heard jazz, blues and rhythm & blues and where he also had a go at piano lessons. In 1945 they moved to Los Angeles and at sixteen he started working in a record store but his love was word; be it in poems, books or song lyrics. In 1950 he met another young Jewish man who was a freshman at Los Angeles City College, Mike Stoller. Like Leiber, he too had emigrated from the East Coast where he embraced the be-bop jazz of Dizzy Gillespie and Charlie Parker before moving across to L.A. It was Lester Sill, Head of Sales at the Modem label who gave them their first break in 1951 with "That's What the Good Books Says" by The Robins. In 1952 bandleader Johnny Otis contacted them, needing a song for Big Mama Thornton. They obliged with "Hound Dog". In 1953 Leiber, Stoller and Still formed their own Spark label, releasing The Robins' "Riot in Cell Block Number 9" a year later. This was one of the first times sound effects would be used on a record. The same year the movie "Riot in Cell Block 11" was released and in 1971 the Beach Boys re-invented the track under the name "Student Demonstration Time" for their "Surf's Up" album. In 1955 Atlantic Records invited Leiber and Stoller to join the ATCO label which would mean a move to New York splitting The Robins up. The two Robins who flew to New York recruited two more members and became The Coasters. In 1957 they hit the Top Ten and gained a number 1 on the R&B chart with "Searchin'" and its flipside "Young Blood". The following year, on July the 15th, a Senate hearing took place because of concerns about the music industry. They were given "Yakety Yak" to listen to as a way of explaining how rock and roll music was 'cheapening American music'. This happened to be The Coasters biggest hit, reaching the top of both the pop and R&B chart. It's easy to miss the point when you're not seeking it and the committee failed to recognise the craftsmanship, the inclusivity, the commercial input, humorous output and above all the longevity that Leiber and Stoller were giving to a group who would see out the doo-wop era's tendency to have a string of one-hit wonders and leave an untouchable legacy that was both inspired.by and inspired American Popular culture.

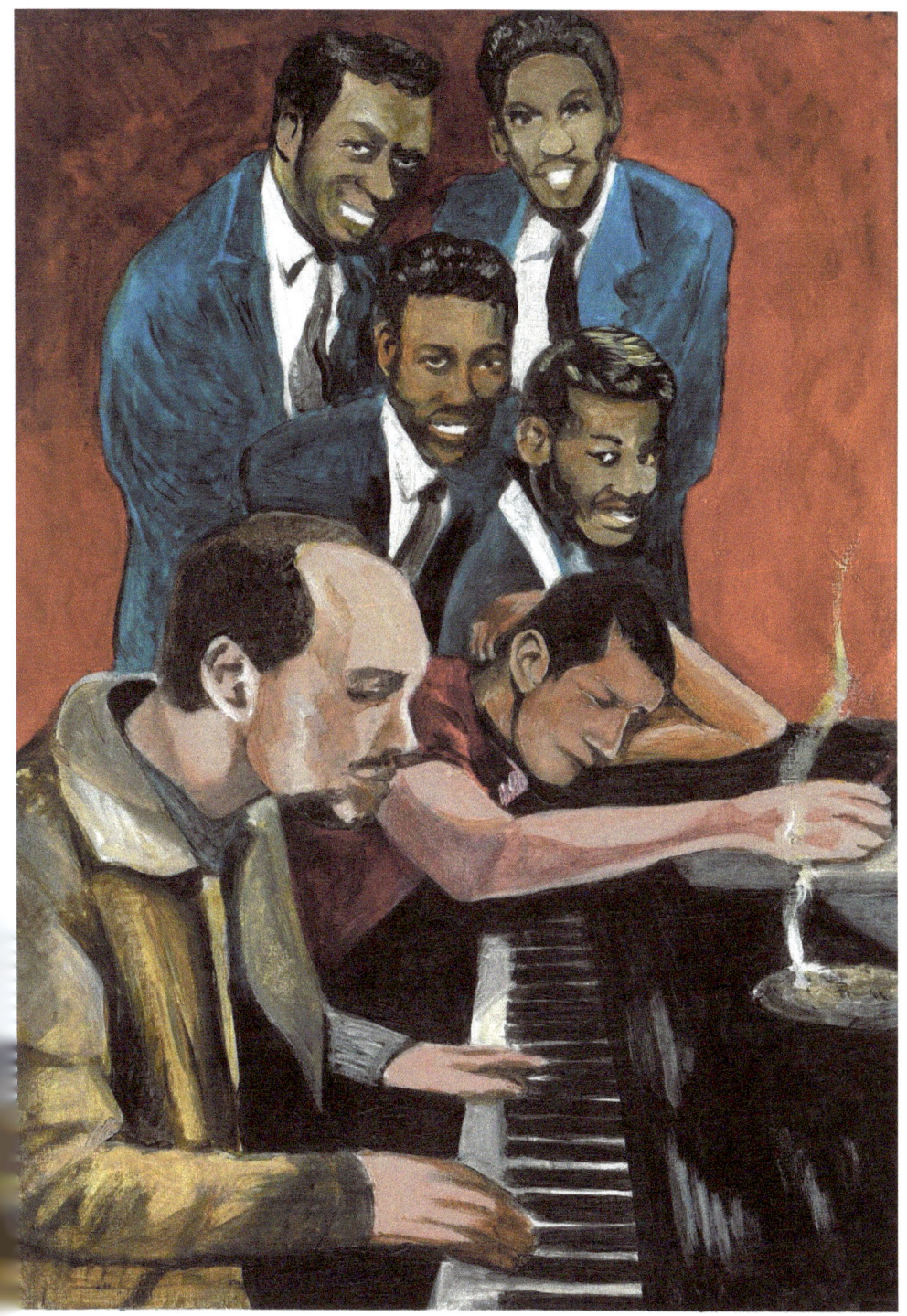

Art & Soul

For The Record – My personal best for you to discover.

Georgia On My Mind	Ray Charles
God Ain't Blessing America	Swamp Dogg
Flower Child	David Ruffin
Yesterday's Dreams	Four Tops
Reflections	Diana Ross & the Supremes
Since I Fell For You	Laura Lee
Why Can't We Be Lovers	Holland-Dozier
Skin I'm in	Chairmen Of the Board
Fever	Little Willie John
His Eye Is On The Sparrow	Marvin Gaye
Keep On Loving Me	Marvin Gaye & Tammi Terrell
Never Dreamed You'd Leave In Summer	Stevie Wonder
Wade In The Water	Ramsey Lewis Trio
Check Out Your Mind	The Impressions
New World Order	Curtis Mayfield
Giving Up	Donny Hathaway
Deep In the Night	Etta James
Rescue Me	Fontella Bass
Higher And Higher	Jackie Wilson
Got To See If I Can't Get Mommy	Jerry Butler
Alone In Brewster Bay	Minnie Riperton
The Great Pretender	Sam Cooke
The Love We Had Stays on My Mind	The Dells
My Song	Aretha Franklin
F.U.N.K.	Betty Davis
Midnight Train To Georgia	Cissy Houston
Voyage To Atlantis	Isley Brothers
Memphis Soul Stew	King Curtis
For Your Precious Love	Linda Jones
A Child Of God	Millie Jackson
That Was My Girl	The Parliaments
There Goes My Baby	The Drifters
Reverend Lee	Roberta Flack
Home Is Where the Hatred Is	Esther Phillips
You Are Everything	The Stylistics
Yes, I'm Ready	Barbara Mason
Am I Black Enough For You?	Billy Paul
Nights Over Egypt	Jones Girls

Meet Me On The Moon	Phyllis Hyman
Sunshine	The O'Jays
If Only You Knew	Patti Labelle
The Whole Town's Laughing At Me	Teddy Pendegrass
Didn't I Blow Your Mind This Time	The Delfonics
Maybe	Three Degrees
Walk Softly	Gladys Knight & The Pips
How Do You Mend A broken Heart	Al Green
I Can't Stand The Rain	Ann Peebles
B-A-B-Y	Carla Thomas
Dark End Of The Street	James Carr
Who's Making Love	Johnnie Taylor
These Arms Of Mine	Otis Redding
Soul Man	Sam & Dave
It Ain't No Fun	Shirley Brown
I Forgot To Be Your Lover	William Bell
Valley Of The Lonely	Betty Wright
Please Accept My Call	Clarence Reid
Too Late To Turn Back Now	Cornelius Bros & Sister Rose
I Get Lifted	George McCrae
Why Is It Always Raining?	Gwen McCrae
Let's Straighten It Out	Latimore
Why Can't We Live Together	Timmy Thomas
From A Whisper To A Scream	Allen Toussaint
There's A Break In The Road	Betty Harris
Walk On Gilded Splinters	Dr John
Here Come The Girls	Ernie K-Doe
Walking Up A One Way Street	Willie Tee
It's Raining	Irma Thomas
Groove Me	King Floyd
You Think You're Hot Stuff	Jean Knight
Wonder Woman	Lee Dorsey
Who Is He And What Is He To You?	Bill Withers
Free	Deniece Williams
One In A Million	Larry Graham
'Cause I Love You	Lenny Williams
I Live For Your Love	Natalie Cole
Long, Black Limousine	O.C. Smith
Frontline	Stevie Wonder
Shopping For Clothes	The Coasters

About the Author

Howard Priestley has always had an equal interest in African American culture, the world of comic books, television, movies and of course, Soul music. Almost at the same time as he began his formal Art training, he became a regular contributor to the British Comics Fan scene with stories appearing in Comics Unlimited, The Alternative Headmaster's Bulletin, Graphixus and Pssst! A Halifax based 3 issue series, Shock Therapy, was also produced. The work from this period was credited in the book, Nasty Tales – A History Of The British Underground Comic Scene, 2000.

In 1984 Harrier Comics produced a new 6-part series of Shock Therapy and during its run Howard was responsible for giving work to Stephen Baskerville and Andy Lanning, two artists who went on to work for both Marvel and DC Comics. From then on in he appeared briefly in Sideshow Comics and was pencilled in to write and illustrate a P-Funk Graphic Novel for Marvel Comics in New York that would have been a culmination of science fiction and funk mythology. Just prior to the project being started Marvel closed down its music-based section leaving him disillusioned with the comic industry. He began writing and illustrating Dog Tales for the German P-Funk fanzine, The New Funk Times. The strip was later reprinted in P-Views, another P-Funk fanzine from Germany and since that time he has remained a regular writer and illustrator for a variety of music publications from Germany, Finland and England.

He has designed CD covers and art for Bootsy Collins, Mutiny, Mallia Franklin, George Clinton, Ruth Copeland Featuring Parliament and sleeve notes for CD compilations including sleevenotes for "Sweet Taste" by former Chairman of The Board Harrison Kennedy, a 2004 Juno Nominee for Best Blues Album of the Year.

He helped to launch community radio in Calderdale and hosts a regular radio show "Soul City".